Annals

of the Association of American Geographers

Volume 82   September 1992   Number 3

The Americas before and after 1492: Current Geographical Research

Karl W. Butzer, Guest Editor

The ANNALS of the Association of American Geographers (ISSN 0004-5608) is published for the Association of American Geographers, 1710 Sixteenth St., N.W., Washington, DC 20009, tel. (202) 234-1450, fax (202) 234-2744, 4 times a year in March, June, September, and December by Blackwell Publishers, Inc., with offices at 3 Cambridge, MA 02142, USA and 108 Cowley Road, Oxford OX4 1JF, UK. Information for subscribers: New orders, renewals, sample copy requests, claims, change of address information and all other correspondence should be sent to the Subscriber Services Coordinator at the publisher's Cambridge office. Subscription rates for Volume 82, 1992 (checks should be made payable to Blackwell Publishers): Institutions, US $85.00; rest of the world $100.00; Individuals, US $85.00; rest of the world $60.00; Single Issue Rates: Institutions, US $23.50; rest of the world $27.00; Individuals, US $23.50; rest of the world $17.00.

Back issues from the current and previous three volumes are available from the publisher's Cambridge office at the current single issue rate. Microform: The journal is available on microfilm (16mm or 105mm) or 105mm microfiche from University Microfilms Inc, 300 North Zeeb Road, Ann Arbor, MI 48106, USA. Mailing: The journal is mailed second class in N. America and by International Surface Air Lift (ISAL) to the rest of the world. SECOND-CLASS POSTAGE PAID AT BOSTON, MA and additional offices. POSTMASTER: Send all address corrections to The Annals of the Association of American Geographers, Journals Dept., Blackwell Publishers, 3 Cambridge Center, Cambridge, MA 02142. Advertising: For details please contact the Journals Marketing Manager at the publisher's Cambridge office. Direct all books for review to the Book Review Editor. Copyright: All rights reserved. Reproduction or translation of any part of this work beyond that permitted by Sections 107 and 108 of the US Copyright Law without permission of the publishers is unlawful. Authorization to photocopy items for internal or personal use, or the internal or personal use of specific clients, is granted by the Association of American Geographers, provided that the base fee of US $4.50 per copy, plus $.40 per page is payable directly to Copyright Clearance Center, 27 Congress Street, Salem, MA, USA 01970. Rates for educational photocopying for classroom use are $.40 per page also payable directly to Copyright Clearance Center. For those organizations that have been granted a photocopy license by CCC, a separate system of payment has been arranged. The fee code for users of the Transactional Reporting Service is: 0004-5608/92 $4.50 + $.40. For all other permission requests or inquiries please contact the Journals Permissions Manager at the publisher. Indexing/ abstracting: The contents of this journal are indexed or abstracted in the following: Acad. Ind., Amer. Anthropol., Amer. Bibl. Slavic & E. Eur. Stud., Amer. Hist. & Life, Bibl. Cart., Biol. Abstr., Curr. Adv. Ecol. Sci., Deep Sea Res. & Oceanogr. Abstr., E.I. Field Crop Abstr., Geo. Abstr., GeoRef., Herb. Abstr., Hist. Abstr., Mar. Aff. Bibl., Mid East: Abstr. & Ind., Rural Recreat. Tour. Abstr., Soils & Fert., SSCI Soc. Sci. Ind., World Agri. Econ. & Rural Sociol. Abstr. Printed and Bound by Edwards Brothers, Ann Arbor, MI 48106.

ISSN 0004-5608
ISBN 1-55786-397-0

Library of Congress Cataloging-in-Publication Data
A CIP catalog record for this book is available from the Library of Congress.

Foreword

As the Columbian Quincentennial approached, I became increasingly aware of a number of projects, books, museum exhibits, celebrations and protests, and documentaries being planned relating to the Columbus landing, the Old World/New World exchanges, and changes in New World cultures and environments. My thinking was that it would be important for the geography community to devote its energies to this topic and related themes, in part because many in our midst have research interests in these topics and because exploration and discovery themes are an important part of our heritage. The quincentennial year would present an opportunity for a group of scholars with these interests to review what we know about selected themes and also to provide fresh evidence and accounts of the pre- and post-1492 environments, cultures, and economies.

In an April 1987 memo, I shared these ideas with a group of two dozen cultural and historical geographers. There was unanimous support for the idea of devoting one *Annals* issue during 1992 to the Columbian Encounter. Those responding offered suggestions for themes and prospective authors, many of whom are among contributors to this issue. The consensus was that the issue should focus on Old World/New World exchanges and encounters rather than on the landfall or discovery elements of the voyages. I agreed with this sentiment. I then suggested the idea to the *Annals* editorial board members and associate editors in a July 1990 memo; the support was nearly unanimous. Then I asked for support from the Publications Committee and the AAG Council, the latter giving support at its Fall 1990 meeting. My plan since its inception was to publish the issue before the International Geographical Congress meeting in Washington, DC during August 1992.

Following approval of the issue by Council, I invited Karl Butzer, Bill Denevan, Bill Turner, and Brian Harley to serve as an editorial committee. In the early planning for this issue, Karl, because of his long-standing interests in Old World and New World cultures and economies, expressed keen interest in working on the project. In December 1990, I invited him to assume the responsibilities of guest editor; his tasks included working with the editorial committee, authors, and reviewers. All papers were peer-reviewed and went through at least two drafts prior to acceptance. Karl's thinking and mine were to invite authors from the U.S., Canada, and Europe to write papers based on original research for the issue.

The title, "The Americas before and after 1492: Current Geographical Research," accurately describes the ten articles. The contents include papers on early populations, pre-Columbian environments and agricultural settlement, Mesoamerican depopulation, indigenous cartography, European mapping, and early North American settlement. While these are familiar topics for geographers, many are addressed here through the lens of how contemporary geographers look at themes such as landscape changes and perceptions, maps and mapping, and the writing of geographies. Some use archival sources, others field work, and still others a combination of methods and sources. It is possible to consider these papers within traditional geographical fields such as cultural ecology, cultural geography, settlement evolution, colonial landscapes, medical geography, and the history of cartography. But they also illustrate linkages that scholars in the humanities and social sciences are forging during the 1990s. These include transdisciplinary themes of cultural diversity; race, gender, and class; environmental change and meanings: injustices and disparities; and power and the state.

A careful reading of the articles and the research agendas presented in the introduction suggests that there remains a host of fascinating topics that await pre- and post-Encounter scholars looking at landscape changes and images, environmental settings, indigenous cartography vis-à-vis European colonial policies, gender and race issues and class formation, and the role of missions and the state in new European space. These cutting-edge topics and themes offer rich opportunities for cross-disciplinary study. I can see where our colleagues in medical history, environmental ethics, environmental history, art history, the history of science, disciplinary history, and indigenous history also would find many facets of interest.

There are a number of individuals that I wish to thank for seeing this issue emerge from its inception to completion. First, I want to thank Karl Butzer for his strong interest and commitment to this project from its inception, and especially his working with authors and my own deadlines. Much of the success of what appears in this issue is a credit to Karl's tireless energies, patience, persistence, and his high standards of scholarship. Bill Denevan was another supporter throughout; he too spent long hours and days reading and rereading manuscripts, as well as assisting Karl and other authors. Carville Earle and Bill Turner also merit special mention for their invaluable assistance in reading papers and offering suggestions for the authors, and Lydia Pulsipher and Don Meinig for suggesting that the Seeds of Change museum exhibit be reviewed. Patricia Gilmartin and Ted Steinke deserve high marks as cartography editors, in their work with authors and their commitment to high-quality cartography. I consider the photographs, maps, and graphics, and the cover (prepared by Ted) essential parts of the contents. I enjoyed working with all the authors and found them a cooperative and committed group with strong interests in seeing that the issue be of highest quality. I also thank Bill Denevan and Neal Lineback, as Publications Committee chairs, and the AAG Council for supporting this effort. Finally, I wish to thank my editorial assistant, Rose Canon, for her many extra hours during the weeks before materials were due at the printer and her cooperation in working with authors, cartographers, the editorial team, and the printer. Her own interest in and commitment to this project made the difficulties seem minor. Her contributions have been invaluable.

I consider it imperative that the North American geography community contribute to our knowledge and understanding of the worlds before and after 1492. The quincentennial offered that opportunity and challenge. We have met that challenge through the contributions in this issue by leading world scholars addressing major and important issues and themes. I am very pleased with the results. I believe we can all take pride in having our discipline's contributions placed alongside those quincentennial efforts of our colleagues in other disciplines. I feel confident that this issue will be used in seminars and subsequent research in Europe and in North and South America for decades.   SDB

Articles

The Americas before and after 1492: An Introduction to Current Geographical Research

Karl W. Butzer

Department of Geography, University of Texas at Austin, Austin, TX 78712,

FAX 512-471-5049

Abstract. The controversy over the Columbian Quincentenary identifies two broad issues of fundamental interest to geography: (a) the decimation and displacement of indigenous peoples, leading to creation of new human and cultural landscapes; and (b) the relative ecological impacts of indigenous and Colonial land use, as a prelude to the global environmental transformation introduced by the Industrial Revolution. This introductory essay outlines the contributions of ten critical or synthetic reviews, setting them in a wider context of contemporary research, as a web of related themes focused on the Americas before and after 1492. These themes include: (a) pre-Columbian population densities, environmental impact, and the myth of the Indian as Ecologist; (b) the labor intensity and technological sophistication of pre-Columbian agriculture in many areas; (c) the human implications and landscape impact of catastrophic indigenous depopulation; (d) the process of Spanish settlement and landscape transformation; (e) diffusion, continuity, and syncretism in the residual indigenous landscapes; (f) the divergent policies and impacts of French and British colonization, and the comparatively limited attention given to Native American and African contributions to the North American cultural landscape; and (g) the different perceptions, cartographies, and geographies of the explorers, the indigenous peoples, and the European scholars engaged in the Columbian Encounter. The final discussion identifies themes that can-not yet be adequately reviewed, especially the impact of Colonial settlement upon the environment, as distinct from the consequences of the Industrial Era, its technology, and its demand for raw materials. The debate raised by the Encounter can and should refocus geographical research on related cultural and environmental questions that require fresh attention.

Key Words: Precolumbian agriculture, indigenous cartography, environmental degradation, depopulation, diffusion, Colonial landscapes, ecological myths, European perceptions, the Quincentenary.

From Polemics to New Research Perspectives

CELEBRATION and anti-celebration. For several years the media have played up the polemic of the Quincentenary, pitting Columbus the icon against Columbus the symbol of New World genocide and environmental destruction. While one group celebrates the Columbian voyage and the creation of a new Euro-American world, the other laments the depopulation and deculturation of the Americas. Pickets, mainly organized by American Indian organizations, greet visitors at museums displaying artifacts or maps from the period of 1492, or interact with the smallish crowds watching the arrival of replicas of Columbus's ships in Miami or Galveston.

But there is little evidence of a groundswell

Annals of the Association of American Geographers. 82(3), 1992, pp. 345–368
© Copyright 1992 by Association of American Geographers

of American interest in the ongoing debate, let alone of any emerging position as to whether the "Discovery" was a good thing or not. Perhaps the continuing media hype has led to a premature sense of fatigue. Perhaps, too, the issues raised do not seem relevant for Americans today, since Columbus was an Italian and the arguments seem to concern Spaniards and Native Americans. In contrast to the hoopla of 1892, which Chicago, somewhat misguidedly, celebrated as the birthday of the New World, contemporary Anglo-Americans may have scaled back their historical horizons to Plymouth Rock and 1776, leaving 1492 for Hispanics to worry about.

But the Quincentenary cannot be dismissed that conveniently. The year 1492 dramatically changed intellectual conceptions of the world. It brought the peoples of two semi-isolated hemispheres into confrontation, creating new "realities," the moral implications of which cannot be ignored indefinitely. It also opened the way for biological and technological transfers on a vast scale, creating novel cultural, economic, and biotic configurations in the "New" World, with significant repercussions on the "Old." In an increasingly integrated world system, the growing momentum of intercontinental energy flows favored the Industrial Revolution, with its once almost unimaginable impact on the quality of global environments. The Columbian Encounter set in motion immense social and environmental changes that will continue in the future, and which affect the lives of all Americans, whether they are aware of them or not.

Amid the flurry of ideological controversy, glossy picture books, and surrealistic media events, a coherent current of analytical studies has begun to emerge. This is reflected in the publications accompanying the museum exhibits *Seeds of Change* (reviewed in this volume) and *Circa 1492* (Levenson 1991), or in the special issue of *Newsweek* entitled *When Worlds Collide* (Fall 1991). It is also documented in the Smithsonian trilogy *Columbian Consequences* (Thomas 1989–91), sponsored by the Society for American Archaeology, a special issue of *Historical Archaeology* (Vol. 26, No. 1, 1992), and in the Islamic perspective of Lunde (1992), works that provide critical and informative perspectives on the Encounter. Geographers were involved in several projects,

including the versatile volumes of *North American Exploration* (Allen 1992). Geographers also organized and contributed invited papers to the 1992 scientific symposium of SCOPE—an international agency dominated by biologists—devoted to the global legacies of the Columbian Encounter (Turner 1992).

Not surprisingly, historians have been prominent in reevaluation of stereotypic and entrenched ideas (Axtell 1992). Anticipating the current disgrace of inaccurate high school textbooks, Axtell (1987) reviewed the mass of half-truths about "other" Europeans, Indians, and the Age of Discovery that mark such books. A comprehensive study of the historical context of Columbus (Phillips and Phillips 1992) offers a welcome antidote to both the acid and the saccharine (mis)representations of that ambiguous figure now in circulation.

Contrary to what one might assume, the Quincentenary has also prompted sober introspection among Spanish historians, and a recent congress in Sevilla focused on the social context of growing intolerance for ethnic diversity on the Iberian peninsula during the century before 1492 (Benito et al. 1991). Throughout the U.S., students are engaged in public debate, and panels of invited speakers argue among themselves or try to address searching questions from the floor. Critical classroom screenings of films such as *Dances with Wolves* and *Black Robe* are heightening awareness of the value of cultural diversity. In anthropology, geography, and history departments, existing course listings are being coopted to hold seminars or give courses on the Columbian Encounter. The themes discussed are not about the Columbian diaries or landfalls on some obscure island, but about cultural diversity or transformation of the world we now live in.

It is commonplace that the controversy and debate raised by important issues serve to refocus research on questions that require new or renewed attention. That is precisely what the contributors to this volume have attempted to do, in writing ten critical or synthetic reviews related to the impact of 1492 on human landscapes of the Americas. The focus of the collection is on principles, processes, and perceptions. One pertinent question is the myth or reality of a pristine American wilderness before the arrival of Columbus; the resulting discussion brings together a body of contemporary research on Prehispanic demography, agro-technology, and resource management. A second question concerns the human impact of the Encounter; here attention focuses on the demographic collapse that followed the introduction of Old World epidemic disease, which demands attention to the scale of the human tragedy it represents, as well as an examination of its implications for settlement discontinuity and transformation of the human and cultural landscape. A third question centers on the new societies that emerged in the Colonial world; how did they shape and manage their diverse cultural landscapes? A fourth and final question comprises the different perceptions, cartographies, and geographies—of the explorers, of the Native Americans, and of the scholars engaged in the Encounter. Geography encompasses a broad spectrum of environmental and cultural, as well as interconnective and integrative concerns. We hope that the papers will prove innovative and provocative to other disciplines as well as our own.

Constraints of space and time have set limits to the number of authors, to the temporal focus, and to the depth at which specific problems could be explored. Within these constraints, the individual papers form a web of interlinked contributions, selected as examples from a wide spectrum of current research. They address, often in unconventional ways, conceptual issues underemphasized in the specialist literature. They also illustrate research methodologies and implicitly identify potential resources in libraries, in archives, or in the field. The authors represent American, Canadian, and German universities, and include one anthropologist. Finally, the bibliographies are broad and current, and include works in languages other than English.

This introductory essay attempts to set a wider context of contemporary research for the individual papers, in addition to highlighting their contributions. Themes that could not be covered by our collection of essays are sketched out in the accompanying discussion, to facilitate a broader overview of the Americas before and after 1492. Some basic questions, such as the environmental impact of European settlement, cannot yet be resolved, because the requisite database is not available; they will require many more research projects in the coming years. Long after the polemics have died down, the search to understand the questions raised will go on.

A Persistent Myth: The Indian as Ecologist

One of the fundamental questions brought into focus by the Columbian controversy concerns what William Denevan (this volume) calls the myth of a pristine New World landscape in 1492. The idea goes back at least as far as the romantic primitivists of the nineteenth century, but has recently been given new meaning. Sale (1990) claims that New World peoples lived in harmony with nature and refrained deliberately from altering their environments, to the degree that they were somehow able to maintain an idyllic ecological equilibrium. Europeans, by contrast, had a ruthless land ethic, were driven only by materialistic goals, and introduced an agrosystem that was, by definition, harmful. Sale believes the result was environmental destruction of apocalyptic proportions.

The central issues thus are twofold: (a) whether Native American peoples did or did not alter or degrade their environment; and (b) whether or not European settlers had an immediate and drastically negative impact on the environment (Butzer and Butzer 1992). The first entails an assessment of aboriginal technology, land use, and population levels, as prerequisite for evaluating their environmental impact.

The New World was not an empty land. As Denevan argues, the Americas at the end of the 1400s supported a population of 43–65 million inhabitants distributed as follows: close to four million people for North America, almost 20 million in Mexico and Central America, three million on the Caribbean islands, and 24 million in South America, two-thirds of whom lived in the Andean region. Most of these depended on agriculture of varying degrees of technical sophistication. Prehispanic built environments remain conspicuous in the landscape today, ranging from the ruins of great cities and monumental ceremonial centers, to field patterns in eastern North America or Amazonia and traces of road systems in New Mexico or Peru. Some of the most convincing evidence to this effect, namely extensive agricultural landforms such as raised fields or terraces in now-uncultivated areas, has been compiled by geographers since the landmark observations of Denevan in the early 1960s. In this context, the expanded field researches of Denevan and Turner, and also those of Tichy (1974), Donkin (1979), and Siemens (1989), find one of their several practical applications.

A wide range of ethnohistorical, biotic, and paleobotanical arguments are reviewed by Denevan to demonstrate ecological modifications of the temperate and tropical woodlands as well as the prairies and savannas of the New World. To some degree these biomes were humanized in terms of physiognomy, species composition, and reduced biodiversity—long before the arrival of Europeans. Native American use of fire, clearance for cultivation, and other forms of manipulation or exploitation had left an unambiguous imprint: the forests of eastern North America were relatively open, the prairies of Indiana and Illinois were unable to return to a woodland-grass mosaic despite the shifts to moister climate during the later Holocene, and the Amazon rainforest was (and remains) anything but virgin.

These thematic and regional arguments could be complemented by abundant references to specialized diachronic studies, such as palynology and limnology, which directly identify long periods of deforestation and soil erosion in prehistoric times. The implications of such studies in Mexico, Guatemala, and Honduras are profound. They corroborate Denevan's evidence that "primeval" vegetation, even complex rainforests, can regenerate in several centuries, given complete settlement abandonment. They also show that indigenous agriculture and high populations have invariably led to fundamental biotic change and frequently to significant soil erosion. Populated landscapes must generally have been open landscapes, if not degraded ones. Such intensive disturbance can be documented not only across many centuries, but even for time spans as long as two millennia. One may also wonder whether the Maya population collapse in Guatemala ca. A.D. 1000 was facilitated by unsustainable kinds of land use.

For several generations, leading palynologists insisted that prehistoric land use could not be detected in pollen profiles anywhere in the eastern U.S. The problem was that they concentrated on bog sites rather than settlement areas. By changing that strategy, Delcourt et al. (1986) were able to demonstrate that pre-

historic settlement in Tennessee was also accompanied by forest clearance and weed explosions, coeval with pollen and macrobotanical remains of maize and other cultivated plants. But the continuing prominence of tree pollen suggests much more localized deforestation in Tennessee than in Middle America.

In effect, indigenous land use before 1492 has left a very tangible record of ecological impact in the pollen and soil record, much as it did in prehistoric Europe (see Butzer 1982, chap. 8). That is surprising in one sense, since Native Americans lacked the large domesticated animals commonly assumed to have had major repercussions on ecological equilibrium in the Old World. The empirical evidence therefore contradicts the romantic notion that Native Americans had some auspicious recipe to use the land without leaving a manifest and sometimes unsightly imprint upon it. As Denevan argues convincingly, the "pristine Precolumbian landscape" is indeed a myth. That has direct and indirect implications for contemporary ecological management, as discussed below.

Reconstructing Pre-Columbian Agriculture

Exactly how did Native American farmers use the land in Precolumbian times? William Doolittle (this volume) and Thomas Whitmore and Billie Turner (this volume) marshal a suite of cogent arguments as to the intensity of indigenous agriculture and the sophistication of many of its technologies.

Agriculture was practiced in two major regions of North America, in the eastern woodlands and in the Southwest and the adjacent parts of Northwest Mexico. But depicting agriculture on a map is complicated by the gradational nature of dependence on cultivated food plants as well as by changing patterns over time. Maps for A.D. 1200, 1500, and 1750 would show different distributions. The ethnographic record includes: (a) hunter-foragers without agriculture, primarily in California, the Pacific Northwest, and in the boreal woodlands of Canada; (b) hunter-foragers who planted supplementary crops, mainly in the center of the continent; and (c) Indians who depended primarily on domesticated plants, but who also used a substantial component of wild animal and plant foods, as in the eastern U.S. and in parts of the Southwest (Butzer 1990).

Doolittle deals with the group (c) and focuses on potential criteria to identify degrees of agricultural intensification, i.e., greater labor inputs to increase crop yields per unit area over a particular span of time. Intensification is particularly relevant to the potential impact on the environment, because it is linked to the persistence of agricultural efforts in a specified area. For example, was a particular plot cleared and cultivated once every twenty or thirty years, or was it permanently kept open and planted every other year? The former would characterize extensive, slash-and-burn agriculture, while the latter would represent a form of intensive agriculture. People also select among their options according to the quality of soil, while agricultural activities can vary considerably during the course of a century or two.

To deal with such problems realistically, Doolittle chooses to use surrogate data that can either be derived from early ethnohistorical reports or identified in the field. These include physical evidence for canal irrigation, terraced fields or terrace-like check dams (in channels or across valley floors) in the Southwest, or ethnohistorical evidence for large cultivated areas amid permanently cleared lands in the eastern U.S., a record that is complemented by visible traces of systematic field-surface modification such as ridging or hilling (small, regular planting-mounds). Household or house-lot gardens, with careful tending of a diversified array of plants, were reported in both the East and Southwest.

All these features imply special efforts and a considerable investment of labor; they can therefore be considered as proxy evidence for intensification. Most examples of this kind were reported from or are found on better floodplain or valley-floor soils, and observations by early explorers suggest that such cultivation was effectively permanent. But this does not clarify whether large, rather than limited areas, were cultivated every year, or every other year, or whether such practices could be sustained indefinitely.

The problem is that on all but the most fertile soils, yearly cropping is almost impossible to sustain without application of fertilizer, or rotation of grains with legumes, or both. Traditional agriculture in the Mediterranean Basin and Europe was overwhelmingly based on a two-year cycle of crops and fallow, with productivity maintained by animal manure, that accumulated during four–six months of grazing on stubble, grass, and weedy plants (Spurr 1986; Vassberg 1984; Butzer 1992c). The so-called three-field system improved productivity in some areas during the Middle Ages, by inserting a year of legume cultivation, which helped restore soil nitrogen.

What remains uncertain in the New World is the range of *alternative* methods devised to maintain productivity without manure. For example, ridging or hilling, which involves removal of topsoil that was piled up on linear or round surfaces, is equivalent to deep mixing by a plow, and it can double the thickness of topsoil. Household wastes and night soil are limited, but permanent intercropping of beans with maize may have been practiced on a large scale during late prehistoric times, a method that would retard soil depletion.[1] One study in central Mexico suggests that the size of house gardens, presumably devoted to complex intercropping, ranged from 0.3–0.9 ha per household during the early 1500s (Williams n.d.). Such remarkably expansive "gardening" could represent one possible solution to the problem.

These open questions notwithstanding, the criteria proposed by Doolittle imply a measure of intensification as well as permanent clearings in at least some areas, an argument consonant with the botanical and pollen evidence from the Little Tennessee River Valley (Delcourt et al. 1986). Since the ethnographic record is finite, Doolittle urges considerably more field research devoted to recording agricultural landforms so as to add detail to the map. More paleobotanical studies are also needed, both within and outside of archaeological excavations (see Hastorf and Popper 1988), as are analyses of soil nutrients (see Sandor 1992). These may eventually afford a fuller understanding of cropping practices, of the spatial extent and permanence of clearance and cultivation, or the degree to which cultivation every other year, for example, may have been sustainable. Attention must also be paid to possible evidence for pre-European soil erosion, potentially preserved in the record of slope and stream deposits along North American valley floors.[2]

Whitmore and Turner employ criteria similar

to those of Doolittle, but they focus on three mesocale environmental transects in Mexico and Guatemala. The "Cortés transect," following that conquistador's route from the coast at Veracruz to Mexico City on the high plateau, is an obvious choice. For the tropical lowlands, these authors single out raised fields, ditches, and canals preserved in the coastal wetlands, and the subtle but visible patterning of fields and embankments on higher ground. Ethnographic analogy is used to infer a complementarity of rain-fed and seasonal wetland cultivation, in addition to household gardens and orchards of fruit trees or cacao, at or before the time of Conquest. On the piedmont of the plateau escarpment, there are terraces and remains of dams; at higher levels, less permanent forms of agriculture are posited in the cloud forest ecozone. The semiarid climate and frost hazards of the plateau favored a patchwork of rain-fed cultivation on slopes modified by rock-faced terraces or vegetated berms (*metepantli*), interspersed with irrigated tracts, fed by floodwaters, small dams, or canals. Wetlands in the basin centers were partly converted into elaborate hydraulic systems, with cultivation on raised *chinampa* surfaces.

The "Montejo transect" cuts across the subhumid Yucatan Peninsula, where two mesoenvironments are distinguished: karstic plains with orchard-gardens and rain-fed maize on thick soils, and rolling karstic hills, with slash-and-burn agriculture on shallow soils. The "Alvarado transect" cuts across Guatemala from the humid Pacific coast to the *tierra fría* of the highlands. Agriculture in the uplands was intensive, with evidence of terracing, hilling, and possibly raised fields, while the piedmont was used for irrigated gardens and cacao plantations.

Spanish intrusion and depopulation by disease left the tropical lowlands of the Cortés and Alvarado transects empty; the Gulf Coast was converted to Spanish livestock raising, the Pacific sector to small-scale Spanish commercial plantations. In the high country as well as on the plains of Yucatan, the Spaniards introduced the plow and Old World livestock, and competed with the residual indigenous population. These issues are developed and discussed further below.

The approach proposed by Whitmore and Turner resembles the vertical ecozonation model, but emphasizes different patchworks of agricultural microsystems that were attuned to small-scale environmental variation within each elevation zone. Collectively these adaptations represented a complex human landscape, in which large areas were often substantially modified in order to produce food for large populations.

Given a denser database and greater vertical differentiation of agricultural land use than in North America, this three-dimensional model is particularly suitable to synthesize several mosaics of indigenous land use. As a heuristic device, it presents an inviting challenge for field and documentary studies to flesh out at the micro- and mesoscale. Such research could also contribute to interrelated issues such as the benefits and drawbacks of traditional ethnoagriculture, the possibility of excessive stress on resources during periods of peak pre-Conquest population, and the comparative productivity of Precolumbian and Postconquest agrosystems.

The papers of Doolittle and Whitmore-Turner are both directed toward indigenous agriculture at or shortly before the Contact Period. They represent complementary methodologies to reconstruct the human landscapes of the New World, by means of case studies, for about the year 1492. Synchronic in focus, they provide methodologies for delineating varying levels of prehistoric population pressure and the extent to which specific environments were humanized or even degraded. But the diachronic perspective remains important. Thematic historical studies, such as the evolution of irrigation technology (e.g., Doolittle 1990), or detailed local studies of smaller areas over time, such as the work of Veblen (1975) on the forests of Totonicapan, draw attention to processes such as incremental change, longer-term adaptation, and response to crises. Such historical monitoring of land use and landscape change can provide a critical tool to examine the long-term impacts of traditional agriculture or to anticipate the hidden costs of high-technology development (Butzer 1992a).

Depopulation and Discontinuity

The conquest of one society by another is inevitably brutal, whether it be the Spanish subjugation of the Taíno or Aztecs, or the Puritan elimination of the Pequod. The conquered are traumatized and the conquerors dehumanized, both by the killings and by the subsequent uprooting of people and the violations of human dignities and freedoms. Hundreds of culture groups disappeared in the aftermath of 1492, and dozens of other societies were significantly changed. Displacement or elimination did not even end with the Colonial era, as the expulsion of the Cherokee or the shooting of women and children at Wounded Knee remind us, without the need to invoke similar atrocities in independent Latin America. But no purpose is served by special pleading or assessing culpability. Conquest is horrible and all participants are guilty of excess, Spanish or British, European or Native American.

The human tragedy of the European conquest, however, was unprecedented in scale, not because of its unquestionable brutality, but primarily through the spread of epidemic disease. By an accident of geographic isolation, the pathogens that evolved in the Old World, and which repeatedly wreaked havoc there, were excluded from the New World for many millennia. This battery of Old World epidemic diseases had several origins, but most were the result of coevolution between people and domesticated livestock.[3]

Early European contacts with the New World introduced new epidemics, in rapid succession, to populations without immunity, as George Lovell shows in his paper. Influenza, smallpox, measles, mumps, and pneumonic plague arrived first, followed by typhus, diphtheria, malaria, and yellow fever. The result of each pandemic was disastrous, and before a population could rebound demographically, a new epidemic struck, so that the "die off" became cumulative, eventually leading to demographic collapse (Whitmore 1991).

Lovell deals with both the demographic and human dimensions of the tragedy, as documented in five representative areas: Hispaniola, central and northwestern Mexico, Guatemala, and Peru. He evaluates a vast body of literature to demonstrate (a) the scale and universality of the disaster; (b) the trauma and significance of the first pandemic in each area, either in destroying an entire population or in breaking the resistance of indigenous peoples; (c) the advance of disease, even ahead of the invading Spaniards; and (d) the persistent problems of diagnosing exactly what diseases were responsible.

Lovell employs an unusual body of medical writings to show that clinical diagnoses are difficult at best. Disease symptoms change their characteristic form over time, e.g., hemorrhagic smallpox or pneumonic, rather than bubonic plague. Compound epidemics also cannot be excluded.[4]

Given the fragmentary demographic information for the early contact period, the computer simulations of Whitmore (1991) offer an alternative perspective, anchored as they are in more reliable population data of the late 1500s, and predicated on contemporary epidemiological indices, flexible demographic profiles, and further mortality through postepidemic famine. For the Basin of Mexico, Whitmore (1991) arrives at an 89 percent reduction from 1.59 million inhabitants in 1519 to 180,000 in 1607. Denevan (this volume) estimates a 74 percent decline in North America, 1492–1800, and 89 percent for the hemisphere as a whole from 1492–1650.

The numbers do matter, as Lovell contends. They matter, above all, because they set parameters for a demographic disaster that remains unparalleled in human history. Whether we favor the lower or upper part of Denevan's estimates for a New World population in 1492, we must still deal with the appalling implications of between 40–60 million people succumbing to disease and famine as a result of the Columbian Encounter. Lovell suggests that this disaster contributed to the military defeat of the indigenous peoples of the New World.[5] Some entire societies, such as the Taíno, disappeared as a result. But numbers provide only an unsatisfactory surrogate for the scale of the human tragedy involved. Lovell is keenly aware of this and introduces a sampling of poignant human testimony from the period. This allows us to appreciate, in some small way, the horror of what transpired.

The numbers also matter from an environmental perspective, because they have to be reasonable for an overwhelmingly agricultural population, given the technology, communications, and limited sources of fertilizer in 1492. For the Basin of Mexico, the 1.6 million figure of Whitmore is a third higher than the 0.8–1.2 million estimate of Sanders (1981), based on archaeological survey. Presenting an exemplary case study, B. Williams (1989) concludes that Sanders's assumptions would require annual cropping on thin soils with little or no irrigation. That is not very reasonable.

The archaeologically inferred population trace of the Basin of Mexico prior to 1519 raises another red flag: the reconstructed population increased from 160,000 in A.D. 1350 to 1.2 million in 1519 (Sanders 1981), which requires a sustained annual growth rate of 1.0 percent over a span of 150 years; subsequent to the demographic collapse, the indigenous population fluctuated from 1600–1750 at low levels that were similar to those maintained prior to A.D. 1350. Expanding the suggestions of B. Williams (1989), it is indeed possible that population pressure in the Basin of Mexico was placing demands on the agricultural resource base that simply were not sustainable. If this is correct, the demographic collapse in Aztec Mexico may have camouflaged an interrelated ecological disaster.

The loss of some 90 percent of a population within a century would also lead to widespread abandonment of agricultural landscapes. In North America this accelerated a process of population decline and land abandonment, already visible in the archaeological record since A.D. 1400 (see Butzer 1990). Abandonment was particularly conspicuous in the tropical lowlands, which lost 95 percent of their population. Even in highland areas with a 15-percent survivor rate, there was insufficient labor to work the existing fields. According to Whitmore (1991, fig. 5), the "dependency ratio" would have fluctuated near 0.85 for many decades, accentuating the labor shortage. Denevan points out that almost all of the vast tracts of terraced hillsides and raised fields in the New World were laid waste. Even the irrigated floodplains of the Basin of Mexico were almost deserted by the 1590s, so that Spaniards were allowed to buy them up from the indigenous survivors (Butzer and Butzer 1992).

Demographic collapse, in short, led to widespread settlement discontinuity. To grasp the implications of such discontinuity, one must imagine what almost total depopulation would mean in Italy or Spain ca. 1500—silent villages, decaying cities, fields lying waste, orchards overgrown with brush. Such desolation set the stage for landscape transformation, within a new Colonial context.

From Spanish Land Grants to a Colonial Landscape

Colonization presupposes a niche for immigrants and the resulting patterns of settlement reflect occupation, opportunity, and prior experience. Most colonial enterprises began with exploitation of expensive raw materials. But control through conquest or military presence is not always followed by systematic permanent settlement. But agricultural and urban settlement was a striking characteristic of Spanish, French, and British colonization in the Americas, transforming the cultural landscape of the New World. The appropriation of land consequently assumes central importance in understanding the process of settlement: the availability of and competition for land, the means of acquisition, the related policies and legal context, and any past experience in domestic settlement expansion or international conquest.

In the case of Spain, the long reconquest of the Islamic-controlled South provided abundant historical experience. The basic principles were to govern and populate: (a) to strive for settlement continuity among the conquered people, so as to maintain economic productivity; and (b) to settle colonists on abandoned or unused agricultural land, so as to ensure control and increase productivity (Burns 1973; López de Coca 1977). These goals are clear in the abortive settlement of Hispaniola 1493 and its more successful follow-up in 1502, as well as in the instructions given to subsequent conquistadors (see Solano 1991). But there was as yet no precedent for permanent overseas settlement, and the slow and unsatisfactory means of communication made supervision of such projects difficult. Until the 1540s, when an adequate legal framework had been set up, Spanish colonization was to some degree experimental or spontaneous, based on principles derived from historical experience.

The key instrument of Spanish settlement became the land grant (merced), awarded throughout the Spanish Colonial realm, including the American borderlands, until the early nineteenth century. Although this institution changed over time, both the principles and the significance remained similar (Ebright 1988). The paper by Hanns Prem (this volume) focuses on these grants, how they worked in general, and what impact they had in Mexico during the first century of settlement. The land grants are indispensable to understanding how Spain fashioned a new Colonial landscape. Indirectly they serve as a vehicle to explain the nature of the relationship between the colonizers and the indigenous peoples in the rural world. In regard to urban policies, see Butzer (this volume).

A fundamental feature of the land grant policy was that it favored prominent citizens who had rendered service to the government, specifically officials and officers, rather than common immigrants with farming backgrounds. Titles were also secured by the religious institutions, the friends and relatives of the powerful, or "front men" for wealthy public officials engaged in accumulating larger holdings—contrary to the formal policy of awarding limited parcels of land to any one person. Even when titles were given to common settlers, in outlying areas such as the Bajío (after 1570), such land tended to be sold off to the expanding estates (Murphy 1986). As a result, institutional structures in the Spanish New World were heavily weighted against a small freehold tradition (also Butzer 1992b).

Land grants began to be awarded in numbers during the early 1560s, which steadily put Indian properties at risk from Spanish acquisition. Traditional Indian lands were sacrosanct under Spanish law, but only as long as they were cultivated. Indian depopulation in Mexico, underway since 1520, took on alarming proportions after the pandemic of 1545, and was transformed into a demographic collapse by the epidemic disaster of 1576. By 1580 there simply were insufficient numbers of Indians to cultivate all the village fields. Indian settlement amalgamation (congregación), begun in the late 1540s, resumed in the late 1580s to aggregate the few surviving families of many villages into new nuclei. Although congregación did not generally alter the surviving Indian landscape as much as might be expected, primarily because compliance was incomplete, it did lead to significant abandonment of Indian lands in some areas.[6] But nucleation in new towns was also weakened by a steady migration of Indian wage labor to live on Spanish farms, locally or in other districts such as the Bajío. This again reduced the work force of traditional communities.

It was depopulation and congregación, and outmigration from Indian communities, that accelerated the expansion of Spanish landholdings. As Prem explains, the archival documentation for land grants can be used not only to reconstruct the procedure of land allocation, but also to identify regional settlement histories and the different roles of the Spaniards and the Indian elites in this process. Prem presents that information in a systematic context, by comparing Spanish acquisition in three major regions of central Mexico, based on a number of supporting studies. Several major conclusions emerge:

(a) The alienation of traditional Indian land holdings began on a large scale after 1580, indirectly through awards of abandoned lands, or directly through purchase.

(b) By the early 1600s, the great majority of Indian properties west of Puebla and in the Basin of Mexico had been acquired by Spaniards. Sheep raising, restricted to rough terrain and mountain slopes, was much less important than agriculture; Indian irrigation networks were coopted with little change in some areas (Butzer and Butzer 1992), while in others irrigation was expanded or introduced, based on Spanish initiative.

(c) Indian wage labor provided the work force on Spanish farms, operated by managers for owners living in Mexico City or Puebla. Farm holdings were steadily expanded through purchase and other methods, leading to the consolidation of relatively large estates.

(d) In more peripheral areas, such as the valleys of Toluca, Mezquital, San Pablo, and Oaxaca, Spanish acquisition of Indian property was far less complete, while livestock raising increased in importance with greater distance from Mexico City.

The first century of Spanish settlement created a rural landscape in central Mexico that was largely, but by no means exclusively, controlled by Spaniards, many of them wealthy. Agriculture produced large quantities of wheat for urban Spaniards, but maize retained its prominence as the staple of the Indian majority, apart from the fact that wheat, as a winter crop, did not thrive without irrigation (Butzer 1992b). Introduced livestock, mainly sheep, grazed on uncultivated land, beyond the former limits of Indian agriculture. In addition, overstocking of dormant winter pastures, reflecting recurrent frost and drought, was mitigated by well-organized transhumance patterns, as sheep were driven to public lands in the tropical low country or far to the semiarid north (Butzer and Butzer 1992).

Beyond the heartland of central Mexico, regional settlement histories were very different (Butzer and Butzer 1992). A second nucleus of Spanish agriculture developed in the Bajío lowlands, with livestock economies dominant further north. The Gulf lowlands included large tracts dominated by Spanish cattle raising, while transhumant sheep were grazed on winter pastures, primarily on the piedmont. At the same time, old centers of Indian agriculture in Michoacan, Oaxaca, and along the plateau escarpment northeast of Mexico City remained overwhelmingly in Indian hands. For the administrative region of New Spain, which excludes the west and north of Mexico, Spaniards controlled about 25 percent of the land in the 1640s; they farmed some 4000 km^2 and ran perhaps 6–8 million sheep and 1.5–2 million cattle (Butzer and Butzer 1992). The Indian agricultural domain probably represented about 45 percent of New Spain, with the remaining 30 percent constituting what by Spanish law was public land.

In sum, there was a considerable degree of continuity in terms of Indian ownership. But the large or small nodes of Colonial settlement, the new market orientation for wheat and animal products, the introduction of domesticated stock as a major element of the rural landscape, the recasting of Indian settlement in the form of new gridiron towns, and the partial elimination of dispersed settlement, all serve to highlight a fundamental discontinuity. New Spain had also become a dual society, with separate Spanish and Indian towns, and residential segregation in the cities—not in order to "exclude" the Indian population, but to preserve a degree of Indian local autonomy and avoid intrusion by Spaniards into the Indian domestic sphere (Butzer 1992b).

This new cultural landscape of Colonial Mexico evidently continued to evolve. By the 1700s, great estates dominated much of the countryside, and palatial residences were built on some of them. A century later, most rural Indians lived in new satellite hamlets around such haciendas. But the great estates only reached their zenith on the eve of the Mexican Revolution, in 1910. By then, most rural Mexicans, Indian and Mestizo alike, had been reduced to a dependent class (Nickel 1978).

This overview of Spanish colonization outlines discontinuity and change in the cultural landscape of New Spain. Many of the principles and processes are also applicable, in general terms, to other parts of the Spanish Americas. Yet each region provided a unique context, with divergent development. The best Spanish administrators were sent to Mexico and Peru, and it was here that the legal safeguards for indigenous rights were most consistently enforced. In the other colonies, Spanish officials tended to be less competent, enlightened, or incorruptible. As a result, some colonies had a sorry history of abuse, and others were totally dominated by entrenched Colonial elites. These differences in socioeconomic evolution during three centuries of Colonial rule contributed significantly to the fragmentation of Latin America after independence.

Diffusion, Continuity, and Syncretism in the Indigenous Landscape

Our focus now shifts from the active role of the Spaniards to that of the indigenous people. Native American languages continue to be prominent in the highlands of Middle America and the Central Andes, and a wealth of Prehispanic cultural traits has been reported from some areas by anthropological investigations. Do such cultural landscapes reflect continuity into the present from a Tarascan, Zapotec, Mayan, or Inca past?

Daniel Gade (this volume) examines that proposition for the seemingly intact indigenous society still ensconced in the mountain redoubts of the Central Andes. Instead of emphasizing the negative impacts of the Conquest, he examines the ability of Andean peasants to manipulate and incorporate elements of Spanish culture into their lifeways. Diffusion of information was a key component of the Columbian Encounter, but rudimentary lists of plants or animals transferred from one hemisphere to another convey little information and also do injustice to the complexity of cultural screening or ecological adaptation. Studies of diffusion should therefore consider how new traits were tested, and accepted or rejected, and what the consequences of incorporation were.

Spanish introductions had their greatest impact in accessible valleys and basins at intermediate elevations of 2500–3500 m, where the climate was temperate and the ecology analogous to that of upland Spain. Gade distinguishes between the many Spanish traits introduced by the new settlers and the limited selection of such traits that found approval among the indigenous people. This second repertoire is of interest here. Wheat, barley, broad beans, and a number of condiments, including onions and garlic, were tested and found to be advantageous plants to incorporate within the existing agrosystem. Mediterranean fruit trees did not do well in the montane climate, but Old World bananas and oranges or Mexican *capulí* cherries did.

Spanish livestock gave greater subsistence security and proved to be more important than the Old World plants. In the wake of depopulation and increasing labor shortage, they provided food with relatively little work or facilitated transport and plowing. Donkeys, as well as mules and horses, were superior to llamas as beasts of burden. Sheep were acquired by 1560, with large flocks verified by the 1590s; they provided meat and sometimes milk, and their soft wool could be interwoven in textiles. Unlike in Mexico, distinctive transhumance patterns did not develop on a large scale. Goats proved to be versatile grazers on very steep slopes, just as pigs became waste processors in the villages. Castilian chickens were good producers of eggs, and displaced the domesticated muscovy duck. But grazing sheep and goats could also lead to soil erosion, and their intrusion into fields of standing crops periodically led to damages.

The light Andalusian plow, pulled by oxen, provided distinct advantages over traditional spades or digging sticks to cultivate relatively level terrain and less stony soils. With only one plow team and plowshare per village, collective or open-field cultivation of crops was introduced. Wheat was threshed by means of animal trampling. Simple Spanish gristmills were also incorporated, while ovens replaced baking pits. Construction with adobe or *tapia*, a puddled-mud technique, expanded greatly because of the Spanish introduction of wooden molds to preshape adobe bricks, while a mix of lime-rich mud and straw could now be poured, as tapia, into box-like wooden frames. Jointed beams simplified roof construction, roof tiles were more durable than thatching, and wooden doors set in wood frames provided greater security.

As in Mexico, the Spaniards tried to remodel the indigenous settlement pattern, moving people from scattered farmsteads or loose hamlets, next to their fields, into new gridiron towns. The native population again resisted nucleation, so avoiding assimilation to Spanish urban living.

Gade argues that the indigenous people of the central Andean world selected ideas and material traits that served to enhance family security, reduce subsistence risk, and offer a broader and more versatile diet. Spanish traditions were simplified and then recombined within the Inca agrosystem. Such syncretism is evident in the agricultural components, diet and folk medicine, settlement patterns and clothing, as well as in spheres such as religion and language that are beyond the scope of Gade's paper. Taking its present shape about 1650, this modified and enriched Andean lifeway has remained remarkably stable across three centuries, presenting an increasingly archaic cast over time. Many originally Spanish components today are perceived to be indigenous. But they demonstrate that the visible cultural landscape is not a simple legacy of the Inca past.

The selective acculturation described here was limited to a particular vertical ecozone. At lower elevations, Spanish transformation was more or less complete, while at higher elevations indigenous patterns of land use and settlement proved their competitive value and still persist. This is an exemplary study of information diffusion and adaptive change, that suggests a methodology to examine persistence and change in the cultural landscape. The evidence for selective acceptance of Spanish crops, animals, and management techniques among the indigenous peoples of Mexico implies a similar pattern of qualified acculturation (Butzer 1992b).

Diffusion after 1492 was a two-way street. A number of New World plants were disseminated in the Old World rapidly, others more slowly. Maize promptly displaced several species of millet, becoming a key fodder crop in southern Europe, and a major source of human nutrition in West Africa, India, and China. Potatoes became a staple in many parts of Europe during the 1700s. Cassava roots (manioc) spread through West Africa and southern Asia. These three food sources remain a cornerstone for the livelihood of more than a billion people in the eastern hemisphere.

Other New World cultigens also enjoyed success overseas: sunflowers, for the oils and chewiness of their seeds; several varieties of beans; the tomatoes, without which Italian cuisine would be flat; the popular vices of cacao and tobacco; as well as chili peppers, pineapples, vanilla, peanuts, and quinine. European colonists in the New World adopted the same plants, after some initial reluctance. That is one meaning of the Columbian Exchange (Crosby 1972), the beginning of a global migration of foods that has generally improved the quality of human life (See Langer 1975; Lunde 1992, 47–55).

The scope of this exchange requires a second look at the implications of adopting new plants and management techniques into an existing agrosystem, or new foods into a traditional cuisine. Do wheat, sheep, and garlic make the Inca more Spanish, or do tomatoes and maize make Italians more Mexican? Such questions are sufficiently disconcerting to demand another look at acculturation.

Maize in Mesoamerica or wheat, wine, and olive oil in the Mediterranean world are more than foods. They carry additional levels of meaning in the symbolic and ideological sphere. Such cultural interpretations are lost when they become part of an alien cultural repertoire, in which they may or may not acquire new symbolic meaning. The acceptance of isolated new traits also differs from acceptance of a "package" of traits. Testing and eventual acceptance of a single new food plant at a particular time requires a perceived equivalence in form or function, and perhaps substitution for an indigenous "equivalent" with little or no symbolic significance. The acceptance of a whole array of new traits at once is another matter. In the Andean example, it would certainly require considerable structural readjustment in terms of work scheduling, resource management, and dietary strategies, if not also in perception, social norms, or cultural values. The modern Andean conviction that their adopted elements are *criollo*, or autochthonous, underscores the point.

Andean or Mesoamerican syncretism does indeed suggest a reduction of cultural distance between Indian and Spaniard (see Graham et al. 1989), as does the Spanish acceptance of maize, adobe housing, Indian mates and early marriage patterns, or a large indigenous vocabulary (Butzer 1992b). Such changes argue for a degree of acculturation.

British and French Colonization

France and Britain had little experience in colonization when they entered the American theater a century later than Spain. By then, epidemic disease in North America had taken a heavy toll. Agriculture had retracted in some areas and indigenous populations had been generally thinned, so that there was little immediate conflict over land. But French and British policies and expedients for settlement differed, as they also differed from those of Spain, reflecting particular circumstances and historical precedents.

Although the immense estuary of the St. Lawrence River invited exploration as a potential water route to Asia (see Allen, this volume), control over the fur trade may have been a key motive for French engagement in 1605; there also were fishing rights to secure (Harris and Warkentin 1974; also Harris 1987). Settlement was initially placed in the hands of *seigneurs*, who played a similar role in the French countryside to an English squire. The seigneurs assigned land to groups of colonists as permanent leaseholds in return for a variety of rents and tithes on production. Beyond providing some minimal services such as a gristmill, the seigneur normally lived in a larger settlement and played no direct role in the development of land use patterns (Harris 1984). Distinct regional solutions were found, tuned to the local ecology, and based on French and central European experience (Harris and Warkentin 1974, chap. 2).

In Acadia, coincident with the later Canadian maritime provinces, soils were poor except in the coastal valleys. The high tides of the Bay of Fundy generate diurnal surges of water far upstream, converting the valleys into wetlands. These were reclaimed by French settlers who built dikes to restrain the daily tidal bore, while profiting from the fresh increments of fertile flood silt to create a kind of mini-polder landscape along the valley bottoms (Harris and Warkentin 1974, 28–29).

Another remedy was found along the St. Lawrence River and its main, south bank tributaries, in present-day Québec. Here clusters of farms were aligned along Pleistocene shoreline ridges, immediately above the floodplain meadows. Long lots, ten times as long as their width, stretched back across the old alluvium at right angles to the ridges. This long-lot system was developed in eleventh-century Europe to colonize unutilized floodplains and forested watersheds. During the 1700s, it also became a hallmark of French settlement in Louisiana and around French fur-trading posts at strategic river or lakeshore sites in the American Midwest. By about 1800, the striking long lots began to interfinger with irregularly-shaped properties measured by the British (and Spanish) metes and bounds system along the Mississippi River (Harris 1990). The imprint of France remains visible today in field patterns that record the properties and the toil of its pioneer settlers across the interior of North America (also Walthall 1991).

Given the initial abundance of land and weak market demand, French settlers in the New World abandoned familiar labor-intensive forms of agriculture, such as three-course rotation of crops, heavy manuring, and improved stockbreeding (Harris 1984). Tree stumps were left to rot in the ground, manure was rarely used, and a two-course crop rotation substituted. Such extensive agriculture gave mediocre yields, but disintensification with respect to European antecedents also characterized the Thirteen Colonies.

The British settlement experience, outlined by Carville Earle (this volume), was more complex than that of France, reflecting distinct but homogenous socioeconomic groups of immigrants from different parts of England ("ethnocultural pluralism"). The first tentative probings of the Atlantic Seaboard were linked to sixteenth-century piracy ("privateering") on Spanish shipping. Reluctant to engage directly in American settlement, the British Crown awarded concessions ("monopolies") to chartered companies, who sought new investments on the Atlantic Seaboard, where the Hakluyts had pronounced the "mediterranean latitudes" of Virginia and North Carolina optimal for settlement. This decentralized strategy spawned semiautonomous colonies, each centered on a key town that served as administrative center and economic entrepôt. Each colony also drew on a different reservoir of immigrants: Puritans from East Anglia in New England, Quakers from northern England in Pennsylvania, aristocratic planters from southern England around Chesapeake Bay. The first two areas attracted immigrant families, while the plantation colonies had the capital and the incentive to bring in single males, too poor to pay for the voyage, as indentured servants.

Reflecting the immigrants and their economic goals, contrasting rural economies developed on the Eastern Seaboard: (a) small-scale agriculture, primarily designed to meet household subsistence needs in New England and overseas grain markets in the Middle colonies; and (b) commercial agriculture, successively emphasizing tobacco, indigo, tidewater rice, sugar cane, and ultimately cotton, from Chesapeake Bay to Charleston. The northern sector experienced population growth and urban expansion, benefitting from immigrant surges from several dissenting groups from Great Britain and later, Germany. By 1700, Boston had close to 7000 inhabitants, New York 4500, and Philadelphia 3000, while the largest town in the southern sector, Charleston, had only 2000.

With little female immigration and a less healthy climate, demographic expansion was slow in the south, and labor scarce. Indians were enslaved, but they were quickly displaced by white indentured servants and, after 1680, by African slaves imported from the West Indies and Africa. Planters and merchants, in turn, collected the produce of these bonded laborers and rice, tobacco, and indigo were exported directly to England and the Continent—all of which accorded nicely with the Crown's mercantilist aims. Plantation crops gave out north of the Chesapeake, and farmers there turned toward mixed farming systems which accented wheat and corn for export in the Middle Colonies and localized subsistence in the less hospitable environs of New England. Northern merchants directed grain exports among the various markets in the Atlantic economy and, led by Bostonians, assumed control of the intercolony trade linking the various economic sectors and regions. These vigorous coastal enclaves were filling up by the early 1700s, and soon after Scots-Irish, German, English, and Welsh settlers spilled over into the less desirable piedmont to the rear of the plantations around the Chesapeake estuary. The rapid pace of interior expansion between 1700–50 tested the Empire, occasioning, among other things, hostile Indian responses, French fears of British colonial pretensions, confusion over titles to land, and sectional strife between interior settlements and colonial administrations based along the coast.

Characteristic of the decentralized and multiethnic British colonial enterprise was its diversity, reflected not only in its varied economic pursuits, but also in its imprint on the landscape (see Mitchell and Groves 1987). River-front, long-lot field patterns are mainly found in New England and other patterns of long lots around Philadelphia; these generally date to the initial settlements. Metes-and-bounds surveying became dominant, however, and town plans increasingly regular. Subsistence-oriented agriculture disintensified, with two-course crop rotation increasingly common. The German settlers retained their three-field system, but the Finns and Swedes on the Delaware followed a more familiar shifting pattern of clearance and bush fallow, akin to that of the local indigenous peoples; this was subsequently adopted by the Scots-Irish settlers that spearheaded settlement beyond the Appalachian perimeter (Jordan and Kaups 1989). Further south, tobacco producers also deployed shifting cultivation for maintaining soil fertility in the Chesapeake, while rice planters in the Carolina low country engaged in microreclamations of estuarine marsh (Hilliard 1978).

Although latecomers to the colonial process, the British colonies on the mainland enjoyed spectacular, if often cyclical, advances. Fueled by the export of plantation crops and grains to eager Atlantic markets, population and economy on the seaboard grew by more than three percent per annum, the area of settlement by more than two percent. The infrastructure of trade and commerce which sustained these advances, in turn, enabled these colonies to take the lead in movements of independence and industrialization during the Age of Revolution (1770–1830).

Rates of immigration were by no means proportional to the subsequent size of European populations in the New World. Table 1 compares Spanish, French, and British colonization, using the first century of immigration and

Table 1. Demographic Patterns of Key European Colonies during the First Century of Settlement

	Population (in thousands)	
	Immigrants	Europeans
Spanish Colonies to 1600		
Mexico	90	92
Central America		20
Caribbean	22	12
South America	63	116
Total	175	240
French Colonies to 1700		
Quebec	7	13
Acadia		2
Caribbean	38	6
Total	45	21
British Colonies to 1700		
Newfoundland	39	3
New England		93
Mid-Atlantic region	116	54
Southern region		104
Caribbean	222	36
Total	377	290

Sources: Based on Boyd-Bowman (1976), Butzer (1992b), Gemery (1980), Mitchell and Groves (1987).

settlement as a reference point. Caribbean settlement evidently met with little demographic success, as a result of disease, low birth rates, and low life expectancies (see Gemery 1980; Curtin 1989). Surprisingly, many more British and French emigrants went to the Caribbean than to mainland North America. New England had greater demographic success than the Chesapeake region or the tidewater south. Spanish population growth with respect to immigration was twice that of its British counterpart. Although Spanish regions of immigration are obscured by a lack of separate data for Central America, and by a steady stream of transmigrants from Mexico and Central America to Peru, demographic growth was greatest on the Mexican Plateau and in the dry, temperate lowlands of Peru.

A notable difference between the different colonial systems is that 48 percent of the Spanish settlers lived in towns with more than 2500 Europeans at the end of the first century (Butzer 1992b), while only 5 percent of the population in the British colonies would qualify for such a definition of "urban" in 1700. This not only reflects different social preferences, but also the limited opportunities for small freeholders in Spanish Colonial agriculture. The colonies of these three powers evidently were very different.

Although there finally are two good historical texts on the Caribbean world (Watts 1987; Richardson 1992, chaps. 2–3), that region tends to fall between the cracks for American historical geographers and their Latin Americanist counterparts. But as Table 1 suggests, North America was at first little more than an adjunct to the British and French colonial enterprises in the Caribbean, at least in regard to financial returns (see Meinig 1986). The southern Atlantic Seaboard begs to be studied in conjunction with the Caribbean. It also bears mention that the African role in the circum-Caribbean plantation complex (Curtin 1990) has been comparatively neglected by geographers. For example, *Historical Archaeology* recently devoted an issue to Southern plantations that examines the cultural record and livelihood of African slaves (Vol. 24, No. 4, 1990). The volume of involuntary African immigration (Table 2) consistently exceeded that of European colonists. Some 8.8 million African slaves were imported to the New World by 1810 (Rawley 1981), compared with roughly 1.8 million European emigrants. But death outnumbered births among African slaves, as a result of epidemics, famine, malnutrition, suicide, a deficit of women, and high infant mortality. Consequently their numbers had to be constantly replenished through "imports," even when the plantation economy was not expanding. More attention needs to be devoted by historical geographers to the links between Africa and the

New World as manifest in the cultural imprint.

The integration of Native American themes into the repertoire of American historical geography is more advanced, but it remained for a historian, William Cronon (1983), to highlight the competition and complementarity of Euro-American and Native American subsistence ecologies. Some examples of related research by geographers can be cited. Ray and Freeman (1978, 231–60) illustrate how the "frontier" can be seen as an arena of interaction, even beyond the periphery of European settlement. Similarly, Albers and Kay (1987) sketch a startling alternative scenario for the Native American presence by showing that indigenous peoples had a remarkable capacity for multiethnic coexistence. Contrary to the stereotypic view, a sizeable number of early settlers did take Indian mates, as Jordan and Kaups (1989, 87–92) argue from historical and contemporary evidence. The large French-speaking minority of the Canadian Plains, the Métis, are mixed-blood descendants of French fur traders (Brown 1983). There also were smaller and little known multicultural communities among the trappers who began the settling of the Mountain West (Lecompte 1978, 62–67, 221). Beyond the genetic contribution to American bloodlines, there are good grounds to posit that Indian women facilitated frontier expansion and shaped its society.

European settlers moving inland from the coast, and their descendants crossing the mountain passes to the interior, continued to encounter settled or recently-abandoned agricultural landscapes. Aided by Indian guides and surviving on Indian foods, the pioneers at the head of the Euro-American advance followed the signposts of cleared fields and orchards that recorded the long experience of Native Americans in selecting good soils and managing local ecologies with a similar technology (Butzer 1990). As the Spaniards in another time and place, British and American settlers followed readily in the tracks of indigenous farmers, only to be frustrated where these gave way to mobile hunters or foragers. A new cultural landscape was built on the traces of an older one, regardless of whether abandoned or functional. These perspectives of interaction, ecological convergence, and superimposition imply a less ethnocentric vision of America's past. They do need to be investi-

Table 2. African Slave Imports to the European Colonies during the First Century of Settlement

	Number of imports (in thousands)
Thirteen Colonies (to 1700)	29
British Caribbean (to 1700)	264
French Caribbean (to 1700)	156
Dutch Caribbean (to 1700)	120
Spanish Colonies[a] (to 1600)	75
(1600–1700)	295
Portuguese Brazil (to 1600)	50
(1600–1700)	560
Total to 1700	1,553[b]

Sources: Based on Curtin (1969), Rawley (1981), and Klein (1986).
[a]Primarily for mining in Mexico and Colombia and for agriculture in lowland Peru and the Gulf-Caribbean region.
[b]Includes 4000 to Danish Antilles.

gated, sooner rather than later, by a new generation of geographers.

Multiple Perceptions, Cartographies, and Geographies

The very terms "New" World and "discovery" highlight the dialectic between Europe and the Americas. The irony has not escaped a succession of humorists who describe the Indians greeting the landfall of 1492 with comments such as "we have been discovered!" or "You must be Columbus." Three of the papers in this volume explore perceptions, cartographies, and geographies, well-documented in the case of the Europeans, fragmentarily preserved in the case of the indigenous peoples.

If Columbus had not crossed the Ocean Sea in 1492, another explorer would have done so within a very few years. Ship construction, nautical skills, and knowledge of the ocean currents and wind patterns had improved dramatically during the fifteenth century, setting the stage for bold voyages into the open sea. But captains did not set sail into the unknown without a body of empirical and nonempirical information sufficient to convince them that such a venture promised success.

The vision of Columbus, in expecting to find Asia in the west, was built on his interpretation of flotsam washing up on the beaches of the Madeiras, his reading of Medieval travelers' accounts and fables, his belief in Ptolemy's incorrect estimate of the earth's circumference, and the conviction that he had a divine mission (see Phillips and Phillips 1992, 100–11). The paper by John Allen (this volume) takes the premise that Europe was conceptually and operationally prepared for the eventual discovery of new lands to the west. He argues that the initial voyages of exploration were based on existing geographical lore and on observation and experience, as well as on myth, legend, and rumor. In their turn, the subsequent voyages were influenced by the accumulating experience of earlier ventures and the evolving geographical images of the New World.

Allen reviews the many categories of lore available before 1492, including: ocean voyages in classical antiquity; legends of early Medieval, Celtic exploration in the North Atlantic, based in part on Irish knowledge of Iceland prior to Viking (Norse) discovery and settlement; surviving information about the Viking settlement of Vinland (Newfoundland) ca. A.D. 1000, and recurrent Medieval tales about mid-Atlantic islands or voyages into the unknown. On our part we continue to speculate whether some of the Portuguese, British, and Breton fishermen known to have fished off the Newfoundland banks after 1500 may have stumbled upon North America some twenty years earlier. Allen traces the information for the voyages of the Cabots—Genoese navigators sailing with Bristol sailors in the service of England—who rediscovered Newfoundland in 1497 and explored parts of the Atlantic Seaboard from 1498–1509. Unlike Columbus, the Cabots followed the trajectory of their Celtic and Viking precursors, by steering out to the northwest. Thus the notion of a Northwest Passage to Asia was born.

Following the British initiative, France engaged the Florentine navigator Verrazzano to explore the Atlantic coast of North America in 1523, leading Cartier to explore the St. Lawrence River in 1534 and 1535, with an unsuccessful attempt to found a first settlement at Québec 1541–42. Cartier's penetration upstream to present-day Montréal not only had a revolutionary impact on cartography, but directed the later French Colonial enterprise to the river and lake systems of the continental interior, to establish the theoretical and experimental basis for North American exploration during the next three centuries. The remarkable resolution of the Mercator map of 1569 reflects these feats.

Brian Harley (this volume) reverses the perspective by critically examining the historical claims of these maps to "truth." The Renaissance revolution in cartographic knowledge and cognition coincided with a fundamental shift from portolan charts, designed as aids for navigation, to documents increasingly used for geopolitical ends. Decorated with national flags, coats of arms, and the names or portraits of discoverers, some maps became a visible record of conquest and imperial claims, demarcating national boundaries. Other ideological statements include crosses and religious inscriptions or portraits. In one form or other, maps had begun to represent reified symbols of power—a tradition continued until after World War II by the use of distinctive colors on maps and globes to represent the overseas possessions of the imperial powers.

By the early 1500s, maps can also be seen as media to present the New World as a "theater" for European colonization. Indeed, a second level of symbolic intent can be inferred. The imposition of European place-names and the engraving of a Christian, European landscape with churches and a europeanized environment can be viewed as a means of cultural appropriation and transfer. In order to attract settlers or console emigrants with memories of the Old World, such maps, deliberately or not, projected a new geographical "reality." Maps became tools with which Europe could impose its own image, values, and aspirations on the newly discovered world. Finally, maps based on exploration could precede actual colonization, thus anticipating and even shaping government policy. This explicitly revisionist stance shatters ethnocentric preconceptions, allowing us to see the Age of Discovery in a more objective light (see also Axtell 1992).

At the same time, Harley raises the matter of indigenous cartographies, noting that histories of cartography and published collections of historical charts tend to ignore Native American maps. Such maps of indigenous origin, mainly dating to the early Colonial period, are well-documented in Mexico. Harley explores this arena briefly, arguing that, like some Medieval maps, their Middle American counterparts projected space and time onto the same two-dimensional plane, to create "spatial histories" that combine geographical perceptions, ancestral migrations, and dynastic histories. On a much broader level, Indian geographical knowledge was also incorporated into European maps of the period. It is known that explorers used Indian guides, that some Europeans commented on Indian mapping abilities, and that a few mapmakers of European origin specifically acknowledge Indian contributions to their charts. Finally, on more tenuous grounds, Harley suggests that Indians may have reappropriated European cartographic traditions as tools of resistance.

The three maps added after Brian Harley's sudden and premature death are accompanied by an addendum by Karl Butzer and Barbara Williams that explains and suggests a first level of interpretation of the superimposed perceptual and conceptual landscapes the maps illustrate. These maps, dating from ca. 1580, suggest a transition between indigenous and European cartographic traditions and therefore serve to introduce the reader, in stages, to the unfamiliar form of spatial representation discussed by Harley.

Integrating the two main thrusts of his paper, Harley reveals the coexistence and dialectic of indigenous and European cartographies. The purpose of his revisionism is not to denigrate the feats of the individuals central to the Age of Discovery, nor to impugn the strength of intellect and will reflected in the European achievements of the period. Rather it is to open our vision to a broader context that allows greater analytical facility. Only by removing the introverted blinders imposed by ethnocentrism—an adaptive feature of all cultures—can we appreciate the wealth of skill and experience embodied in another cartographic tradition or even hope to understand the perceptions of Native Americans in 1492.

The intellectual confrontation of Europeans with the environment and the peoples of the New World posed a similar problem, compounded by dogmatic world views inherited from a Classical and Medieval past. That particular Encounter provoked novel methods of empirical description, organization, analysis, and synthesis that mainline historians have been unable to fully appreciate. As a result the impact of the Encounter on science in general, and geography in particular, has been understated and overlooked or largely forgotten. The paper by Karl Butzer (this volume) examines seven methodological spheres: observational skills, environmental analysis, classification of biota, ethnography, town planning, geographical synthesis, and a scientific framework for the natural history and peoples of the New World. The presentation centers on exemplary individuals, who illustrate the diverse backgrounds, abilities, and interests of the period. Many came from rural backgrounds and had little formal education, but this may have been advantageous in examining New World phenomena, both in their own right and in comparison with similar categories in the Old World. Geography itself was the unifying theme for these diversified strands of scientific analysis, which illustrate the intellectual prowess of Spain during the century from 1492–1590.

A comparative study of the observational skills and geographical sophistication of indigenous Americans must await further research along promising avenues for investigation. The opportunities identified by Harley represent one such window, and a comprehensive study of the environmental and cultural content of the maps accompanying the *relaciones geográficas* of Mexico (see Butzer, this volume) is a must. But proper symbolic and historical interpretation require special skills, as Rincón-Mautner (1990) points out, in studying the *pinturas* preserved in villages of the Mixteca. A second window is suggested by Barbara Williams's examination of Aztec soil taxonomy and comprehension, measured against contemporary folk soil taxonomies (B. Williams and Ortíz-Solorio 1981; B. Williams 1982). Yet another window is suggested by the first-hand indigenous information recorded in the sixteenth century by Bernadino de Sahagún (see Butzer, this volume). His linguistic analyses allowed him to recognize the links between the world of appearances and the cognitive structures underlying it. A study of indigenous conceptualization of culture and landscape in semiotic terms is indeed possible, based on Sahagún's rich materials.

In such a context the Renaissance myth of the American Noble Savage and its latter-day counterpart, the Indian as Primitive Ecologist, appear grossly reductionistic. Denevan's quotation from Shetler envisions Native Americans as "transparent" in the landscape, "living as natural elements of the ecosphere." This is a perception as tenacious and just as ridiculous as the British view of North America as a "howling wilderness" (Bowden 1992). Such myths are pejorative to Native Americans by reinforcing an image of technologically primitive aborigines, blending into the forest. Conservationist attitudes toward resources and nature do not guarantee that "working with nature" will be possible in practice (Tuan 1968), especially in the face of subsistence stress.

A Devastated Colonial Landscape and Other Open Questions

From the myth of the Indian as Ecologist, we come full circle to the issue of a "Devastated Colonial Landscape." That question has little direct connection with the concerns of contemporary ecologists about deforestation, endangered species, and air or water pollution. A global Industrial Revolution intervened between the twentieth century and the landing at Plymouth Rock, and from 1776–1821 the New

World colonies moved to independence. The parameters and perspectives for what transpired after 1776 are different, reflecting a spate of technological innovations, accelerating demand for distant raw materials, rapid population growth, and a more complex global network integrating raw materials, industrial production, and markets.

The precise question in regard to a hypothetical Devastated Colonial Landscape centers on: (a) the livestock, domesticated plants, and weeds introduced by Colonial settlers, in conjunction with particular management techniques and a plow technology; and (b) whether or not European land use and resource management were exploitative and destructive. Several potential lines of investigation can be followed up, at the local or regional level:

(1) palynological, ethnobotanical, and archival research on local vegetation change during the last five centuries or so;
(2) field investigation of slope soils and sediments as well as alluvial microhistories, tied into an informed diachronic context for land tenure, land use, and management techniques in a particular watershed; and
(3) documentary research on regional land use and management, and on contemporaneous evidence for soil depletion or erosion, deforestation or woodland regeneration, flood events and their recurrence intervals, rural population pressure or depopulation, and so forth.

This type of environmental history requires sustained study and cannot be proclaimed from a hilltop by the sweep of a hand. No wonder that this "chapter" cannot yet be written and, in fact, no single person can assemble the scattered pieces of evidence that currently are available, often in scattered and unpublished reports.

The degree to which disintensified European agriculture in eastern North America had serious ecological consequences before 1776 appears to be an open question (M. Williams 1989). Nor is it clear what impact reintensification had, beginning anywhere between the late 1700s and the late 1800s. Plantation agriculture did lead to soil erosion, when cotton cultivation was initiated on the southern piedmonts during the late 1700s, but that pertains to another era (Trimble 1974, 1985; Earle 1988). The vast clear-cuttings across the eastern woodlands, to feed the ovens of the early iron mills, reached their climax in the Upper Midwest during the 1830s, and soil erosion, not surprisingly, followed in their wake (Knox 1987). There is as yet no case to accuse Colonial settlers of the Atlantic Seaboard or the St. Lawrence Valley of landscape devastation. If anything, as Denevan argues, the forests of eastern North America regenerated between 1500–1750.

For Mexico, it is popular to point to the introduction of Spanish livestock as an agent of ecological deterioration, but here again the evidence is far from convincing, at least for a general indictment. A reconstruction of vegetation from documentary evidence for the Bajío ca. 1590 shows that riparian forests were still essentially intact, woodlands on watersheds were at least as extensive as during the present century, and any evidence for degradation was limited to old areas of Indian agriculture (Butzer and Butzer 1992). Along the watersheds of the Basin of Mexico, despite extensive documented cutting of timbers for construction, mountain streams continued to provide reliable sources of water not only for irrigation, but also for the operation of grist and fulling mills, at least until the 1630s (Butzer and Butzer 1992). None of the available pollen profiles from Mexico show evidence of active devegetation or weed explosion during the Colonial era, although resolution is low, and livestock grazing may have slowed forest regeneration in the wake of Indian depopulation.

There is conspicuous evidence of Prehispanic soil erosion in central Mexico (Werner 1986), but little to support a Colonial counterpart. At Tula, Hidalgo state, the rate of valley sedimentation was cut by 75 percent following Indian depopulation, although at some later point the river did cut down its channel (Butzer 1992a). Near San Miguel Allende, north of the Bajío, there were no extreme flood events from well before 1500 until after about 1750, when flood silts began to accumulate on the Río Laja floodplain (Charles Frederick 1992); this matches the absence of historical records for destructive floods in the Bajío before 1750. In the Mixteca of Oaxaca, cited by Lovell (this volume) as an example in point, landscape devastation is better correlated with the deep channel trenching which followed somewhat later than an increase in stream alluviation during early Colonial times (Rincón-Mautner

1992). Such examples warrant much greater caution in drawing intuitive conclusions.

The continuing absence of evidence for at least a general trend to environmental disturbance in Mexico before the mid-1700s probably has an explanation. Livestock were deliberately managed in a highly mobile fashion; based on older Iberian experience, overstocking on confined dry-season pastures was avoided by long-distance transhumance for sheep and medium-distance mobility for cattle (Butzer and Butzer 1992). This goes to the heart of Sale's (1990) indictment of the European land ethic.

The empirical evidence shows that European land use was overwhelmingly conservationist since prehistoric times, despite periodic local or regional crises in environmental stability (Butzer 1982, chap. 8). If anything, one must be impressed that the agricultural productivity of the Mediterranean Basin has been sustained through more than 6000 years of farming and pastoral land use. Livestock can indeed be very destructive to the environment, when poorly managed. But the mounting biophysical evidence shows that, historically, equilibrium management was the rule rather than the exception (Butzer and Martí 1991). Perhaps a different question is in order: When, where, and why was conservationist European agriculture abandoned in the New World?

This brief sketch is designed to show that the case for a devastated Colonial landscape is neither proven nor evident before the mid-1700s. But that does not preclude future demonstration that some areas were indeed degraded and at an early date, a development that seems more probable than not. The discussion has also been limited to visible environmental impacts. More subtle changes, such as reduced diversity or species replacement in the tree or ground cover, will certainly have taken place as a result of livestock activities or settlement expansion; but these can only be detected by more fine-grained methodologies. What the evidence outlined here does make clear is that *assumptions* about European land use practices are unwarranted.

Environmental history is a scientific endeavor, as was understood by those innovative historians who founded the journal *Environmental Review*. Its purpose is to test hypotheses empirically, and to seek explanation for observed phenomena. The history of New World biota and soils, in relation to human land use and modification, is of singular importance and deserves a new round of attention by geographers, especially in North America. Demanding good temporal controls for observed change, and distinguishing processes before and after 1776—for example—is not at all specious: the methods and motivations of concurrent land use must be understood. The complexity of deforestation and forest regeneration, with different plant successions and dominants, is illustrated by the Harvard Forest Program (Schoonmaker and Foster 1991; Foster forthcoming). Does the closing of a forest preserve to human use today, with inhibition of forest fires, promote a different species composition from that of 1750 or 1400 (Heinselman 1981)? Environmental dynamics have important implications for contemporary ecological management, and simplistic myths, however appealing, can only muddy the waters at a time when critical conservationist decisions must be made for the future.

In closing, two basic issues stand out as the challenge of the Columbian Encounter to geographers: (1) the changing history of land use and attitudes to land, as reflected in the environmental history of the many regions of the New World during the last millennium or so; and (2) the interactive role of Native Americans, European settlers, and Africans in shaping the human and cultural landscapes of the Americas. The myths and polarities proposed by some of the revisionists lack conviction or reality, but they do make the case that there is much more to be learned by examining the record more closely, and by paying greater attention to the indigenous peoples as well as to the Africans, as important participants in the drama and contributors to the outcome. The implications go well beyond an understanding of the past, by placing contemporary questions of ecology, traditional land use, and cultural diversity into sharper focus.

Acknowledgments

First and foremost I am grateful to Stanley D. Brunn, editor of the *Annals of the Association of American Geographers,* for his vision in sponsoring a special issue, devoted to the Columbian Encounter and documenting current geographical research. His support never faltered, and was critical, given the tight schedule of twelve months between the initial request for abstracts and shipment of the manuscripts to the printer. William Denevan could always be depended on for sound advice and essential support. Bill Turner's grasp of the importance of the Encounter remained a source of inspiration, and Carville Earle's professional skills helped refine many of the papers. I also owe a debt to the many referees in the U.S., Canada, Colombia and Europe who gave their advice. Laura Gutiérrez-Witt made it possible to include copies of indigenous maps. Judy S. White and Beverly Benadom word-processed five of the manuscripts through multiple editions with infinite patience and care, making it possible to meet the final deadlines. The endowment of the R.C. Dickson Professorship of Liberal Arts at the University of Texas covered the substantial, cumulative costs of multiple copying, redrafting, telephone calls, faxes, postage, and express mail.

Notes

1. Available analyses of stable isotopes (carbon and nitrogen) from human bone suggest that beans were not yet an important dietary component during the thirteenth century (Schwarcz et al. 1985).
2. In the case of a preagricultural site in Illinois, human disturbance on an adjacent slope composed of erodible loess led to a substantial increase in sedimentation rates during the two major periods of site occupation, about 8500 and 5200 years ago (Butzer 1977).
3. Smallpox, measles, mumps, diphtheria, and influenza evolved from cattle or sheep viruses, which emerged as deadly human infections among prehistoric animal-breeders in the Near East or Europe. They presumably created catastrophic pandemics in prehistoric times, slowly increasing immunity among generational survivors, but continued to sweep off countless children every 10–30 years until the nineteenth century. Influenza still caused 20 million deaths worldwide in 1918. The bacteria responsible for plague, typhoid fever, typhus, and cholera emerged later, probably in overcrowded settlements, mainly in Asia. Plague swept the Roman Empire in the 540s, sharply reducing populations and flaring up anew for several centuries. After a 600-year break, it reappeared as the "Black Death" of 1347, with echoes into the 1720s. By 1492, most European populations had been genetically selected and were less vulnerable to plague or to typhus, which had provoked an epidemic during the 1470s. Yellow fever, an epidemic disease, and malaria, an endemic one, were both transmitted by mosquitoes and expanded in the Old World tropics through population growth and increasing human mobility. The literature on historical epidemiology in the Old World is hopelessly fragmentary, and cannot be cited here. A partial introduction to the issues can be found in Brothwell and Sandison (1967). General overviews of the Old World antecedents, with limited detail and documentation, include Cartwright (1972), Crosby (1972), and McNeill (1976).
4. José López Piñero (Valencia), a leading historian

of medicine, informs me that a more secure identification of the New World epidemics of the sixteenth century would require substantial archival research, not only to document the temporal evolution of a particular outbreak, but also to understand the changing vocabulary used to describe symptoms.

5. Without the demographic collapse, it seems improbable that the Spaniards would have been able to control the populous highland peoples of Middle America and the Andes, thus limiting assimilation and accelerating the decolonization process. The implications of such a scenario, perhaps modeled on Western "intervention" in China (1841–1949), are provocative.

6. *Congregación* was designed to (a) replace Indian population centers with planned, gridiron towns (see Butzer, this volume), a goal that was achieved to some degree, and (b) to eliminate dispersed Indian settlement, by nucleation in such new towns. Success or failure of the latter can be estimated from the prominence or absence of small farm clusters or loose hamlets shown on the 1:50,000 topographic maps that cover the traditional agricultural domain of central and southern Mexico. Swarms of farmsteads or hamlets remain conspicuous in the Otomí areas of Hidalgo state, among the Nahuatl-speaking mountain settlements of northeastern Hidalgo or the adjacent tropical lowlands belonging to San Luís Potosí, and in many parts of Oaxaca. By contrast, the ethnic Nahua heartland of central Mexico generally lacks dispersed settlement, as does most of the former Huastec domain in the Pánuco lowlands. It remains to be tested whether high indices of settlement dispersal help identify areas where Indian settlement retained a degree of continuity or whether such landscapes were remodeled after the European intrusion, in the wake of indigenous resistance to *congregación*. A study of Nahuatl (Aztec) toponyms in the area northwest of Puebla suggests that many, if not most, of these place names are "new," i.e., younger than the mid-1500s (Dyckerhoff 1984). For a detailed analysis of the process of *congregación* in Guatemala, see Lovell (1990).

References

Albers, P., and Kay, Jeanne. 1987. Sharing the land: A study in American Indian territoriality. In *A cultural geography of North American Indians*, ed. T. E. Ross and T. G. Moore, pp. 47–91. Boulder, CO: Westview Press.

Allen, John L., ed. 1992. *North American exploration*. Lincoln: University of Nebraska Press. 2 vols.

Axtell, James. 1987. Europeans, Indians, and the Age of Discovery in American history textbooks. *American Historical Review* 92:621–32.

———. 1992. Columbian encounters: Beyond 1992. *William and Mary Quarterly* 49:335–60.

Benito Ruano, Elroy, et al. 1991. *La península ibérica en la era de los descubrimientos 1391–1492*, III. Jornadas Hispano-Portuguesas de Historia Medieval, Sevilla, 25–30 November 1991 (Book of Abstracts).

Bowden, Martin J. 1992. The invention of American tradition. *Journal of Historical Geography* 18:3–26.

Boyd-Bowman, Peter. 1976. Patterns of Spanish emigration to the Indies until 1600. *Hispanic American Historical Review* 56:580–604.

Brothwell, Don, and Sandison, A. T., eds. 1967. *Diseases in antiquity*. Springfield, IL: Thomas.

Brown, J. S. H. 1983. Women as center and symbol in the emergence of Métis communities. *Canadian Journal of Native Studies* 3:39–46.

Burns, Robert I. 1973. *Islam under the crusaders: Colonial survival in the thirteenth-century kingdom of Valencia*. Princeton, NJ: Princeton University Press.

Butzer, Karl W. 1977. *Geomorphology of the lower Illinois Valley as a spatial-temporal context for the Koster Archaic site*. Reports of Investigations 34. Springfield: Illinois State Museum.

———. 1982. *Archaeology as human ecology*. New York: Cambridge University Press.

———. 1990. The Indian legacy in the American landscape. In *The making of the American landscape*, ed. M. Conzen, pp. 27–50. Boston: Unwin Hyman.

———. 1992a. Ethno-agriculture and cultural ecology in Mexico: Historical vistas and modern implications. In *Geographers' research on Latin America: Benchmark 1990*, Yearbook, Conference of Latin Americanist Geographers 17: forthcoming.

———. 1992b. Spanish conquest society in the New World: Ecological readaptation and cultural transformation. In *Person, place, thing*, ed. S. T. Wong. Baton Rouge: Louisiana State University, Geoscience and Man, forthcoming.

———. 1992c. The Classical and Islamic agronomic traditions. In *Science in the early Middle Ages*, ed. P. L. Butzer and D. Lohrmann. Basel: Birkhaeuser, forthcoming.

——— and Butzer, Elisabeth K. 1992. Transfer of the Mediterranean livestock economy to New Spain: Adaptation and consequences. In *Legacies of the Columbian Encounter*, ed. B. L. Turner II. Madrid: Consejo Superior de Investigaciones Científicas, forthcoming.

———. Forthcoming. The sixteenth-century environment of the central Mexican Bajío: Archival reconstruction from Spanish land grants. In *Culture, form, and place*, ed. Kent Mathewson. Baton Rouge, LA: Louisiana State University, Geoscience and Man.

——— and Martí, Bernardo, organizers. 1992.

Arqueología: La huella del hombre en el ecosistema mediterráneo. Symposium, Universidad Internacional Menéndez-Pelayo, Valencia, July 1–5, 1991.

Cartwright, Frederick F. 1972. *Disease and history*. London: Rupert Hart-Davis.

Cronon, William. 1983. *Changes in the land: Indians, colonists, and the ecology of New England*. New York: Hill and Wang.

Crosby, Alfred W. 1972. *The Columbian Exchange: Biological and cultural consequences of 1492*. Westport, CT: Greenwood.

Curtin, Philip D. 1969. *The Atlantic slave trade: A census*. Madison: University of Wisconsin Press.

———. 1989. *Death by migration: The European encounter with the tropical world in the nineteenth century*. New York: Cambridge University Press.

———. 1990. *The rise and fall of the plantation complex*. New York: Cambridge University Press.

Delcourt, Paul A.; Delcourt, Hazel R.; Cridlesbaugh, P. A.; and Chapman, J. 1986. Holocene ethnobotanical and paleoecological record of human impact on vegetation in the Little Tennessee River Valley, Tennessee. *Quaternary Research* 25:330–49.

Denevan, William M., ed. 1992. *The native population of the Americas in 1492*, 2nd ed. Madison: University of Wisconsin Press.

Donkin, R. A. 1979. *Agricultural terracing in the New World*. Viking Fund Publications in Anthropology 56. Tucson: University of Arizona Press.

Doolittle, William E. 1990. *Canal irrigation in prehistoric Mexico: The sequence of technological change*. Austin: University of Texas Press.

Dyckerhoff, Ursula. 1984. Mexican toponyms as a source on regional ethnohistory. In *Explorations in ethnohistory: Indians of central Mexico in the sixteenth century*, ed. H. R. Harvey and H. J. Prem, pp. 229–52. Albuquerque: University of New Mexico Press.

Earle, Carville V. 1988. The myth of the Southern soil miner: Macrohistory, agricultural innovation, and environmental change. In *The ends of the earth: Perspectives on modern environmental history*, ed. D. Worster, pp. 195–210. New York: Cambridge University Press.

Ebright, Malcolm, ed. 1988. Spanish and Mexican land grants and the law. Journal of the West 27(3).

Foster, David R. Forthcoming. Land-use history and forest transformations in central New England. In *Human impacts on the environment*, ed. S. Pickett and M. McDonnell. New York: Springer.

Frederick, Charles. 1992. Personal communication.

Gemery, Henry A. 1980. Emigration from the Brit-

ish Isles to the New World, 1630–1700: Inferences from Colonial populations. *Research in Economic History* 5:179–231.

Graham, Elizabeth; Pendergast, David M.; and Jones, Grant D. 1989. On the fringes of conquest: Maya-Spanish contact in Colonial Belize. *Science* 246:1254–59.

Harris, R. Cole. 1984. *The seigneurial system in early Canada*, 2nd ed. Montreal: McGill-Queen's University Press.

———, ed. 1987. *Historical atlas of Canada*, vol. 1, *From the beginnings to 1800*. Toronto: University of Toronto Press.

———. 1990. French landscapes in North America. In *The making of the American landscape*, ed. M. P. Conzen, pp. 63–79. Boston: Unwin Hyman.

——— and Warkentin, John. 1974. *Canada before Confederation: A study in historical geography*. New York: Oxford University Press.

Hastorf, Christine A., and Popper, Virginia S., eds. 1988. *Current paleoethnobotany: Analytical methods and cultural interpretations of archaeological plant remains*. Chicago: University of Chicago Press.

Heinselman, M. L. 1981. Fire and succession in the conifer forests of northern North America. In *Forest succession*, ed. D. C. West, H. H. Shugart, and D. B. Botkin, pp. 374–405. New York: Springer.

Hilliard, Sam. 1978. Antebellum tidewater rice culture in South Carolina and Georgia. In *European settlement and development in North America*, ed. James R. Gibson, pp. 91–115. Toronto: University of Toronto Press.

Jordan, Terry G., and Kaups, Matti. 1989. *The American backwoods frontier: An ethnic and ecological interpretation*. Baltimore: Johns Hopkins University Press.

Klein, Herbert S. 1986. *African slavery in Latin America and the Caribbean*. New York: Oxford University Press.

Knox, James C. 1987. Historical valley floor sedimentation in the upper Mississippi Valley. *Annals of the Association of American Geographers* 77:224–44.

Langer, William L. 1975. American foods and Europe's population growth, 1750–1850. *Journal of Social History* 8:51–66.

Lecompte, Janet. 1978. *Pueblo, hardscrabble, greenhorn: The Upper Arkansas, 1832–1856*. Norman: University of Oklahoma Press.

Levenson, Jay A., ed. 1991. *Circa 1492: Art in the Age of Exploration*. New Haven, CT: Yale University Press.

López de Coca, José E. 1977. *La tierra de Malaga a fines del siglo XV*. Granada: Universidad de Granada.

Lovell, W. George. 1990. Mayans, missionaries, evidence and truth: The polemics of native resettlement in sixteenth-century Guatemala. *Journal of Historical Geography* 16:277–94.

Lunde, Paul. 1992. The Middle East and the Age of Discovery. *Aramco World* 43 (3).

McNeill, William H. 1976. *Plagues and people.* Garden City, NY: Anchor.

Meinig, Donald W. 1986. *The shaping of America. A geographical perspective on 500 years of history,* vol. 1, *Atlantic America, 1492–1800.* New Haven, CT: Yale University Press.

Mitchell, Robert D., and Groves, Paul A., eds. 1987. *North America: The historical geography of a changing continent.* Totowa, NJ: Rowman and Littlefield.

Murphy, Michael E. 1986. *Irrigation in the Bajío region of Colonial Mexico.* Dellplain Latin American Series 19. Boulder, CO: Westview Press.

Nickel, Herbert J. 1978. *Soziale Morphologie der mexikanischen Hacienda.* Wiesbaden: F. Steiner.

Phillips, William D., and Phillips, Carla Rahn. 1992. *The worlds of Christopher Columbus.* New York: Cambridge University Press.

Rawley, James A. 1981. *The Transatlantic slave trade.* New York: Norton.

Ray, Arthur J., and Freeman, Donald. 1978. *"Give us good measure": An economic analysis of relations between the Indians and the Hudson's Bay Company before 1763.* Toronto: University of Toronto Press.

Richardson, Bonham C. 1992. *The Caribbean in the wider world, 1492–1992: A regional geography.* New York: Cambridge University Press.

Rincón-Mautner, Carlos. 1990. The territory and environment of San Miguel Tulancingo, Coixtlahuaca, Mexico. Abstract, Annual Meeting, Association of American Geographers, Toronto 1990, p. 208.

———. 1992. Historic human environmental impact in the Mixteca region of Oaxaca, Mexico. Abstracts, Annual Meeting, Association of American Geographers, San Diego, p. 204.

Sale, Kirkpatrick. 1990. *The Conquest of Paradise: Christopher Columbus and the Columbian Legacy.* New York: Knopf.

Sanders, William T. 1981. Ecological adaptation in the Basin of Mexico: 23,000 B.C. to the present. In *Archaeology: Supplement to the handbook of Middle American Indians,* ed. J. A. Sabloff, pp. 147–97. Austin: University of Texas Press.

Sandor, Jonathan A. 1992. Long-term effects of prehistoric agriculture on soils: Examples from New Mexico and Peru. In *Soils in archaeology,* ed. Vance T. Holliday, 217–46. Washington: Smithsonian Institution Press.

Schoonmaker, Peter K. and Foster, David R. 1991. Some implications of paleoecology for contemporary ecology. *The Botanic Review* 57:204–45.

Schwarcz, Henry P.; Melbye, J.; Katzenberg, M. A.; and Knyf, M. 1985. Stable isotopes in human skeletons of southern Ontario: Reconstructing paleodiet. *Journal of Archaeological Science* 12:187–206.

Siemens, Alfred H. 1989. *Tierra configurada.* Mexico City: Consejo Nacional para la Cultura y las Artes.

Solano, Francisco de. 1991. *Cedulario de tierras (1497–1820): Compilación de legislacion agraria colonial,* 2nd ed. Mexico City: Universidad Nacional Autónoma de México, Instituto de Investigaciones Jurídicas.

Spurr, M. S. 1986. *Arable cultivation in Roman Italy c. 200 B.C.–c. A.D. 100.* London: Society for the Promotion of Roman Studies.

Thomas, David Hurst, ed. 1989–91. *Columbian consequences: Archaeological and historical perspectives on the Spanish borderlands.* 3 vols. Washington: Smithsonian Institution Press.

Tichy, Franz. 1974. Deutung von Orts- und Flurnetzen in Hochland von Mexiko als kulturreligiöse Reliktformen altindianischer Besiedlung. *Erdkunde* 28:194–207.

Trimble, Stanley W. 1974. *Man-induced soil erosion in the Southern Piedmont, 1700–1970.* Ankeny, IA: Soil Conservation Society of America.

———. 1985. Perspectives on the history of soil erosion control in the eastern United States. *Agricultural History* 59:162–80.

Tuan, Yi-Fu. 1968. Discrepancies between environmental attitude and behavior: Examples from Europe and China. *Canadian Geographer* 12:176–89.

Turner, B. L. II, ed. 1992. *Legacies of the Columbian Encounter.* Madrid: Consejo Superior de Investigaciones Científicas.

Vassberg, David E. 1984. *Land and society in Golden Age Castile.* New York: Cambridge University Press.

Veblen, Thomas T. 1975. The ecological, cultural, and historical bases of forest preservation in Totonicapan, Guatemala. Ph.D. Dissertation, Department of Geography, University of California, Berkeley.

Walthall, John A., ed. 1991. *French colonial archaeology: The Illinois country and the Western Great Lakes.* Urbana: University of Illinois Press.

Watts, David. 1987. *The West Indies: Patterns of development, culture, and environmental change since 1492.* New York: Cambridge University Press.

Werner, G. 1986. Landschaftsumgestaltung als Folge von Besiedlung, Vegetationsänderung und Landnutzung durch die altindianische Bevölkerung im Staat Tlaxcala, Mexicko. *Erdkunde* 40:262–70.

Whitmore, Thomas M. 1991. A simulation of the sixteenth-century population collapse in the

Basin of Mexico. *Annals of the Association of American Geographers* 81:464–87.

Williams, Barbara J. 1982. Aztec soil glyphs and contemporary Nahua soil classification. In *The Indians of Mexico in pre-Columbian and modern times*, ed. M. E. R. Jansen and T. J. J. Leyenaar, pp. 206–22. Leiden, the Netherlands: Rutgers.

——. 1989. Contact period rural overpopulation in the Basin of Mexico: Carrying-capacity models tested with documentary data. *American Antiquity* 54:715–32.

——. n.d. Ethnohistorical rural settlement data compared with archaeological surface remains: A test of preservation from Contact Period Tepetlaoztoc. Manuscript in preparation.

—— and **Ortíz-Solorio, Carlos.** 1981. Middle American folk soil taxonomy. *Annals of the Association of American Geographers* 71:335–58.

Williams, Michael. 1989. *Americans and their forests: An historical geography.* New York: Cambridge University Press.

The Pristine Myth: The Landscape of the Americas in 1492

William M. Denevan

Department of Geography, University of Wisconsin, Madison, WI 53706

Abstract. The myth persists that in 1492 the Americas were a sparsely populated wilderness, "a world of barely perceptible human disturbance." There is substantial evidence, however, that the Native American landscape of the early sixteenth century was a humanized landscape almost everywhere. Populations were large. Forest composition had been modified, grasslands had been created, wildlife disrupted, and erosion was severe in places. Earthworks, roads, fields, and settlements were ubiquitous. With Indian depopulation in the wake of Old World disease, the environment recovered in many areas. A good argument can be made that the human presence was less visible in 1750 than it was in 1492.

Key Words: Pristine myth, 1492, Columbus, Native American settlement and demography, prehistoric New World, vegetation change, earthworks.

"This is the forest primeval . . . "

Evangeline: A Tale of Acadie
(Longfellow, 1847).

WHAT was the New World like at the time of Columbus?—"Geography as it was," in the words of Carl Sauer (1971, x).[1] The Admiral himself spoke of a "Terrestrial Paradise," beautiful and green and fertile, teeming with birds, with naked people living there whom he called "Indians." But was the landscape encountered in the sixteenth century primarily pristine, virgin, a wilderness, nearly empty of people, or was it a humanized landscape, with the imprint of native Americans being dramatic and persistent? The former still seems to be the more common view, but the latter may be more accurate.

The pristine view is to a large extent an invention of nineteenth-century romanticist and primitivist writers such as W.H. Hudson, Cooper, Thoreau, Longfellow, and Parkman, and painters such as Catlin and Church.[2] The wilderness image has since become part of the American heritage, associated "with a heroic pioneer past in need of preservation" (Pyne 1982, 17; also see Bowden 1992, 22). The pristine view was restated clearly in 1950 by John Bakeless in his book *The Eyes of Discovery*:

> There were not really very many of these redmen . . . the land seemed empty to invaders who came from settled Europe . . . that ancient, primeval, undisturbed wilderness . . . the streams simply boiled with fish . . . so much game . . . that one hunter counted a thousand animals near a single salt lick . . . the virgin wilderness of Kentucky . . . the forested glory of primitive America (13, 201, 223, 314, 407).

But then he mentions that Indian "prairie fires . . . cause the often-mentioned oak openings . . . Great fields of corn spread in all directions . . . the Barrens . . . without forest," and that "Early Ohio settlers found that they could drive about through the forests with sleds and horses" (31, 304, 308, 314). A contradiction?

In the ensuing forty years, scholarship has shown that Indian populations in the Americas were substantial, that the forests had indeed been altered, that landscape change was commonplace. This message, however, seems not to have reached the public through texts, essays, or talks by both academics and popularizers who have a responsibility to know better.[3]

Kirkpatrick Sale in 1990, in his widely reported *Conquest of Paradise*, maintains that it was the Europeans who transformed nature, following a pattern set by Columbus. Although Sale's book has some merit and he is aware of large Indian numbers and their impacts, he nonetheless champions the widely-held dichotomy of the benign Indian landscape and

Annals of the Association of American Geographers. 82(3), 1992, pp. 369–385
© Copyright 1992 by Association of American Geographers

the devastated Colonial landscape. He over-states both.

Similarly, *Seeds of Change: Christopher Co-lumbus and the Columbian Legacy,* the popular book published by the Smithsonian Institution, continues the litany of Native American passivity:

> pre-Columbian America was still the First Eden, a pristine natural kingdom. The native people were transparent in the landscape, living as natural elements of the ecosphere. Their world, the New World of Columbus, was a world of barely perceptible human disturbance (Shetler 1991, 226).

To the contrary, the Indian impact was neither benign nor localized and ephemeral, nor were resources always used in a sound ecological way. The concern here is with the form and magnitude of environmental modification rather than with whether or not Indians lived in harmony with nature with sustainable systems of resource management. Sometimes they did; sometimes they didn't. What they did was to change their landscape nearly everywhere, not to the extent of post-Colonial Europeans but in important ways that merit attention.

The evidence is convincing. By 1492 Indian activity throughout the Americas had modified forest extent and composition, created and expanded grasslands, and rearranged microrelief via countless artificial earthworks. Agricultural fields were common, as were houses and towns and roads and trails. All of these had local impacts on soil, microclimate, hydrology, and wildlife. This is a large topic, for which this essay offers but an introduction to the issues, misconceptions, and residual problems. The evidence, pieced together from vague ethnohistorical accounts, field surveys, and archaeology, supports the hypothesis that the Indian landscape of 1492 had largely vanished by the mid-eighteenth century, not through a European superimposition, but because of the demise of the native population. The landscape of 1750 was more "pristine" (less humanized) than that of 1492.

Indian Numbers

The size of the native population at contact is critical to our argument. The prevailing position, a recent one, is that the Americas were well-populated rather than relatively empty lands in 1492. In the words of the sixteenth-century Spanish priest, Bartolomé de las Casas, who knew the Indies well:

> All that has been discovered up to the year forty-nine [1549] is full of people, like a hive of bees, so that it seems as though God had placed all, or the greater part of the entire human race in these countries (Las Casas, in MacNutt 1909, 314).

Las Casas believed that more than 40 million Indians had died by the year 1560. Did he exaggerate? In the 1930s and 1940s, Alfred Kroeber, Angel Rosenblat, and Julian Steward believed that he had. The best counts then available indicated a population of between 8–15 million Indians in the Americas. Subsequently, Carl Sauer, Woodrow Borah, Sherburne F. Cook, Henry Dobyns, George Lovell, N. David Cook, myself, and others have argued for larger estimates. Many scholars now believe that there were between 40–100 million Indians in the hemisphere (Denevan 1992). This conclusion is primarily based on evidence of rapid early declines from epidemic disease prior to the first population counts (Lovell, this volume).

I have recently suggested a New World total of 53.9 million (Denevan 1992, xxvii). This divides into 3.8 million for North America, 17.2 million for Mexico, 5.6 million for Central America, 3.0 million for the Caribbean, 15.7 million for the Andes, and 8.6 million for lowland South America. These figures are based on my judgment as to the most reasonable recent tribal and regional estimates. Accepting a margin of error of about 20 percent, the New World population would lie between 43–65 million. Future regional revisions are likely to maintain the hemispheric total within this range. Other recent estimates, none based on totaling regional figures, include 43 million by Whitmore (1991, 483), 40 million by Lord and Burke (1991), 40–50 million by Cowley (1991), and 80 million for just Latin America by Schwerin (1991, 40). In any event, a population between 40–80 million is sufficient to dispel any notion of "empty lands." Moreover, the native impact on the landscape of 1492 reflected not only the population then but the cumulative effects of a growing population over the previous 15,000 years or more.

European entry into the New World abruptly reversed this trend. The decline of native American populations was rapid and severe, probably the greatest demographic disaster ever (Lovell, this volume). Old World diseases were the primary killer. In many regions, particularly the tropical lowlands, populations fell by 90 percent or more in the first century after contact. Indian populations (estimated) declined in Hispaniola from 1 million in 1492 to a few hundred 50 years later, or by more than 99 percent; in Peru from 9 million in 1520 to 670,000 in 1620 (92 percent); in the Basin of Mexico from 1.6 million in 1519 to 180,000 in 1607 (89 percent); and in North America from 3.8 million in 1492 to 1 million in 1800 (74 percent). An overall drop from 53.9 million in 1492 to 5.6 million in 1650 amounts to an 89 percent reduction (Denevan 1992, xvii–xxix). The human landscape was affected accordingly, although there is not always a direct relationship between population density and human impact (Whitmore, et al. 1990, 37).

The replacement of Indians by Europeans and Africans was initially a slow process. By 1638 there were only about 30,000 English in North America (Sale 1990, 388), and by 1750 there were only 1.3 million Europeans and slaves (Meinig 1986, 247). For Latin America in 1750, Sánchez-Albornoz (1974, 7) gives a total (including Indians) of 12 million. For the hemisphere in 1750, the *Atlas of World Population History* reports 16 million (McEvedy and Jones 1978, 270). Thus the overall hemispheric population in 1750 was about 30 percent of what it may have been in 1492. The 1750 population, however, was very unevenly distributed, mainly located in certain coastal and highland areas with little Europeanization elsewhere. In North America in 1750, there were only small pockets of settlement beyond the coastal belt, stretching from New England to northern Florida (see maps in Meinig 1986, 209, 245). Elsewhere, combined Indian and European populations were sparse, and environmental impact was relatively minor.

Indigenous imprints on landscapes at the time of initial European contact varied regionally in form and intensity. Following are examples for vegetation and wildlife, agriculture, and the built landscape.

Vegetation

The Eastern Forests

The forests of New England, the Midwest, and the Southeast had been disturbed to vary-ing degrees by Indian activity prior to European occupation. Agricultural clearing and burning had converted much of the forest into successional (fallow) growth and into semi-permanent grassy openings (meadows, barrens, plains, glades, savannas, prairies), often of considerable size.[4] Much of the mature forest was characterized by an open, herbaceous understory, reflecting frequent ground fires. "The de Soto expedition, consisting of many people, a large horse herd, and many swine, passed through ten states without difficulty of movement" (Sauer 1971, 283). The situation has been described in detail by Michael Williams in his recent history of American forests: "Much of the 'natural' forest remained, but the forest was not the vast, silent, unbroken, impenetrable and dense tangle of trees beloved by many writers in their romantic accounts of the forest wilderness" (1989, 33).[5] "The result was a forest of large, widely spaced trees, few shrubs, and much grass and herbage . . . Selective Indian burning thus promoted the mosaic quality of New England ecosystems, creating forests in many different states of ecological succession" (Cronon 1983, 49–51).

The extent, frequency, and impact of Indian burning is not without controversy. Raup (1937) argued that climatic change rather than Indian burning could account for certain vegetation changes. Emily Russell (1983, 86), assessing pre-1700 information for the Northeast, concluded that: "There is no strong evidence that Indians purposely burned large areas," but Indians did "increase the frequency of fires above the low numbers caused by lightning," creating an open forest. But then Russell adds: "In most areas climate and soil probably played the major role in determining the precolonial forests." She regards Indian fires as mainly accidental and "merely" augmental to natural fires, and she discounts the reliability of many early accounts of burning.

Forman and Russell (1983, 5) expand the argument to North America in general: "regular and widespread Indian burning (Day 1953) [is] an unlikely hypothesis that regretfully has been accepted in the popular literature and consciousness." This conclusion, I believe, is unwarranted given reports of the extent of prehistoric human burning in North America and Australia (Lewis 1982), and Europe (Patterson and Sassaman 1988, 130), and by my own and other observations on current Indian and peasant burning in Central America and South America; when unrestrained, people burn frequently and for many reasons. For the Northeast, Patterson and Sassaman (1988, 129) found that sedimentary charcoal accumulations were greatest where Indian populations were greatest.

Elsewhere in North America, the Southeast is much more fire prone than is the Northeast, with human ignitions being especially important in winter (Taylor 1981). The Berkeley geographer and Indianist Erhard Rostlund (1957, 1960) argued that Indian clearing and burning created many grasslands within mostly open forest in the so-called "prairie belt" of Alabama. As improbable as it may seem, Lewis (1982) found Indian burning in the subarctic, and Dobyns (1981) in the Sonoran desert. The characteristics and impacts of fires set by Indians varied regionally and locally with demography, resource management techniques, and environment, but such fires clearly had different vegetation impacts than did natural fires owing to differences in frequency, regularity, and seasonality.

Forest Composition

In North America, burning not only maintained open forest and small meadows but also encouraged fire-tolerant and sun-loving species. "Fire created conditions favorable to strawberries, blackberries, raspberries, and other gatherable foods" (Cronon 1983, 51). Other useful plants were saved, protected, planted, and transplanted, such as American chestnut, Canada plum, Kentucky coffee tree, groundnut, and leek (Day 1953, 339–40). Gilmore (1931) described the dispersal of several native plants by Indians. Mixed stands were converted to single species dominants, including various pines and oaks, sequoia, Douglas fir, spruce, and aspen (M. Williams 1989, 47–48). The longleaf, slash pine, and scrub oak forests of the Southeast are almost certainly an anthropogenic subclimax created originally by Indian burning, replaced in early Colonial times by mixed hardwoods, and maintained in part by fires set by subsequent farmers and woodlot owners (Garren 1943). Lightning fires can account for some fire-climax vegetation, but Indian burning would have extended and maintained such vegetation (Silver 1990, 17–19, 59–64).

Even in the humid tropics, where natural fires are rare, human fires can dramatically influence forest composition. A good example is the pine forests of Nicaragua (Denevan 1961). Open pine stands occur both in the northern highlands (below 5,000 feet) and in the eastern (Miskito) lowlands, where warm temperatures and heavy rainfall generally favor mixed tropical montane forest or rainforest. The extensive pine forests of Guatemala and Mexico primarily grow in cooler and drier, higher elevations, where they are in large part natural and prehuman (Watts and Bradbury 1982, 59). Pine forests were definitely present in Nicaragua when Europeans arrived. They were found in areas where Indian settlement was substantial, but not in the eastern mountains where Indian densities were sparse. The eastern boundary of the highland pines seems to have moved with an eastern settlement frontier that has fluctuated back and forth since prehistory. The pines occur today where there has been clearing followed by regular burning and the same is likely in the past. The Nicaraguan pines are fire tolerant once mature, and large numbers of seedlings survive to maturity if they can escape fire during their first three to seven years (Denevan 1961, 280). Where settlement has been abandoned and fire ceases, mixed hardwoods gradually replace pines. This succession is likely similar where pines occur elsewhere at low elevations in tropical Central America, the Caribbean, and Mexico.

Midwest Prairies and Tropical Savannas

Sauer (1950, 1958, 1975) argued early and often that the great grasslands and savannas of the New World were of anthropogenic rather than climatic origin, that rainfall was generally sufficient to support trees. Even nonagricultural Indians expanded what may have been pockets of natural, edaphic grasslands at the expense of forest. A fire burning to the edge of a grass/forest boundary will penetrate the drier forest margin and push back the edge, even if the forest itself is not consumed (Mueller-Dombois 1981, 164). Grassland can therefore advance significantly in the wake of hundreds of years of annual fires. Lightning-set fires can have a similar impact, but more slowly if less frequent than human fires, as in the wet tropics.

The thesis of prairies as fire induced, primarily by Indians, has its critics (Borchert 1950; Wedel 1957), but the recent review of the topic by Anderson (1990, 14), a biologist, concludes that most ecologists now believe that the eastern prairies "would have mostly disappeared if it had not been for the nearly annual burning of these grasslands by the North American Indians," during the last 5,000 years. A case in point is the nineteenth-century invasion of many grasslands by forests after fire had been suppressed in Wisconsin, Illinois, Kansas, Nebraska, and elsewhere (M. Williams 1989, 46).

The large savannas of South America are also controversial as to origin. Much, if not most of the open vegetation of the Orinoco Llanos, the Llanos de Mojos of Bolivia, the Pantanal of Mato Grosso, the Bolívar savannas of Colombia, the Guayas savannas of coastal Ecuador, the *campo cerrado* of central Brazil, and the coastal savannas north of the Amazon, is of natural origin. The vast *campos cerrados* occupy extremely senile, often toxic oxisols. The seasonally inundated savannas of Bolivia, Brazil, Guayas, and the Orinoco owe their existence to the intolerance of woody species to the extreme alternation of lengthy flooding or waterlogging and severe desiccation during a long dry season. These savannas, however, were and are burned by Indians and ranchers, and such fires have expanded the savannas into the forests to an unknown extent. It is now very difficult to determine where a natural forest/savanna boundary once was located (Hills and Randall 1968; Medina 1980).

Other small savannas have been cut out of the rainforest by Indian farmers and then maintained by burning. An example is the Gran Pajonal in the Andean foothills in east-central Peru, where dozens of small grasslands (*pajonales*) have been created by Campa Indians—a process clearly documented by air photos (Scott 1978). *Pajonales* were in existence when the region was first penetrated by Franciscan missionary explorers in 1733.

The impact of human activity is nicely illustrated by vegetational changes in the basins of the San Jorge, Cauca, and Sinú rivers of northern Colombia. The southern sector, which was mainly savanna when first observed

in the sixteenth century, had reverted to rainforest by about 1750 following Indian decline, and had been reconverted to savanna for pasture by 1950 (Gordon 1957, map p. 69). Sauer (1966, 285–88; 1976, 8) and Bennett (1968, 53–55) cite early descriptions of numerous savannas in Panama in the sixteenth century. Balboa's first view of the Pacific was from a "treeless ridge," now probably forested. Indian settlement and agricultural fields were common at the time, and with their decline the rainforest returned.

Anthropogenic Tropical Rain Forest

The tropical rain forest has long had a reputation for being pristine, whether in 1492 or 1992. There is, however, increasing evidence that the forests of Amazonia and elsewhere are largely anthropogenic in form and composition. Sauer (1958, 105) said as much at the Ninth Pacific Science Congress in 1957 when he challenged the statement of tropical botanist Paul Richards that, until recently, the tropical forests have been largely uninhabited, and that prehistoric people had "no more influence on the vegetation than any of the other animal inhabitants." Sauer countered that Indian burning, swiddens, and manipulation of composition had extensively modified the tropical forest.

"Indeed, in much of Amazonia, it is difficult to find soils that are not studded with charcoal" (Uhl, et al. 1990, 30). The question is, to what extent does this evidence reflect Indian burning in contrast to natural (lightning) fires, and when did these fires occur? The role of fire in tropical forest ecosystems has received considerable attention in recent years, partly as result of major wild fires in East Kalimantan in 1982–83 and small forest fires in the Venezuelan Amazon in 1980–84 (Goldammer 1990). Lightning fires, though rare in moist tropical forest, do occur in drier tropical woodlands (Mueller-Dombois 1981, 149). Thunderstorms with lightning are much more common in the Amazon, compared to North America, but in the tropics lightning is usually associated with heavy rain and noncombustible, verdant vegetation. Hence Indian fires undoubtedly account for most fires in prehistory, with their impact varying with the degree of aridity.

In the Río Negro region of the Colombian-Venezuelan Amazon, soil charcoal is very common in upland forests. C-14 dates range from 6260–250 B.P., well within human times (Saldarriaga and West 1986). Most of the charcoal probably reflects local swidden burns; however, there are some indications of forest fires at intervals of several hundred years, most likely ignited by swidden fires. Recent wild fires in the upper Río Negro region were in a normally moist tropical forest (3530 mm annual rainfall) that had experienced several years of severe drought. Such infrequent wild fires in prehistory, along with the more frequent ground fires, could have had significant impacts on forest succession, structure, and composition. Examples are the pine forests of Nicaragua, mentioned above, the oak forests of Central America, and the babassu palm forests of eastern Brazil. Widespread and frequent burning may have brought about the extinction of some endemic species.

The Amazon forest is a mosaic of different ages, structure, and composition resulting from local habitat conditions and disturbance dynamics (Haffer 1991). Natural disturbances (tree falls, landslides, river activity) have been considerably augmented by human activity, particularly by shifting cultivation. Even a small number of swidden farmers can have a widespread impact in a relatively short period of time. In the Río Negro region, species-diversity recovery takes 60–80 years and biomass recovery 140–200 years (Saldarriaga and Uhl 1991, 312). Brown and Lugo (1990, 4) estimate that today about forty percent of the tropical forest in Latin America is secondary as a result of human clearing and that most of the remainder has had some modification despite current low population densities. The species composition of early stages of swidden fallows differs from that of natural gaps and may "alter the species composition of the mature forest on a long-term scale" (Walschburger and Von Hildebrand 1991, 262). While human environmental destruction in Amazonia currently is concentrated along roads, in prehistoric times Indian activity in the upland (interflueve) forests was much less intense but more widespread (Denevan forthcoming).

Indian modification of tropical forests is not limited to clearing and burning. Large expanses of Latin American forests are humanized forests in which the kinds, numbers, and distributions of useful species are managed by human populations. Doubtless, this applies to the past as well. One important mechanism in forest management is manipulation of swidden fallows (sequential agroforestry) to increase useful species. The planting, transplanting, sparing, and protection of useful wild, fallow plants eliminates clear distinctions between field and fallow (Denevan and Padoch 1988). Abandonment is a slow process, not an event. Gordon (1982, 79–98) describes managed regrowth vegetation in eastern Panama, which he believes extended from Yucatán to northern Colombia in pre-European times. The Huastec of eastern Mexico and the Yucatec Maya have similar forms of forest gardens or forest management (Alcorn 1981; Gómez-Pompa 1987). The Kayapó of the Brazilian Amazon introduce and/or protect useful plants in activity areas ("nomadic agriculture") adjacent to villages or camp sites, in foraging areas, along trails, near fields, and in artificial forest-mounds in savanna (Posey 1985). In managed forests, both annuals and perennials are planted or transplanted, while wild fruit trees are particularly common in early successional growth. Weeding by hand was potentially more selective than indiscriminate weeding by machete (Gordon 1982, 57–61). Much dispersal of edible plant seeds is unintentional via defecation and spitting out.

The economic botanist William Balée (1987, 1989) speaks of "cultural" or "anthropogenic" forests in Amazonia in which species have been manipulated, often without a reduction in natural diversity. These include specialized forests (babassu, Brazil nuts, lianas, palms, bamboo), which currently make up at least 11.8 percent (measured) of the total upland forest in the Brazilian Amazon (Balée 1989, 14). Clear indications of past disturbance are the extensive zones of terra preta (black earth), which occur along the edges of the large floodplains as well as in the uplands (Balée 1989, 10–12; Smith 1980). These soils, with depths to 50 cm or more, contain charcoal and cultural waste from prehistoric burning and settlement. Given high carbon, nitrogen, calcium, and phosphorus content, terra preta soils have a distinctive vegetation and are attractive to farmers. Balée (1989, 14) concludes that "large portions of Amazonian forests appear to exhibit the continuing effects of past human interference." The same argument has been made for the

Maya lowlands (Gómez-Pompa, et al. 1987) and Panama (Gordon 1982). There are no virgin tropical forests today, nor were there in 1492.

Wildlife

The indigenous impact on wildlife is equivocal. The thesis that "overkill" hunting caused the extinction of some large mammals in North America during the late Pleistocene, as well as subsequent local and regional depletions (Martin 1978, 167–72), remains controversial. By the time of the arrival of Cortéz in 1519, the dense populations of Central Mexico apparently had greatly reduced the number of large game, given reports that "they eat any living thing" (Cook and Borah 1971–79, (3) 135, 140). In Amazonia, local game depletion apparently increases with village size and duration (Good 1987). Hunting procedures in many regions seem, however, to have allowed for recovery because of the "resting" of hunting zones intentionally or as a result of shifting of village sites.

On the other hand, forest disturbance increased herbaceous forage and edge effect, and hence the numbers of some animals (Thompson and Smith 1970, 261–64). "Indians created ideal habitats for a host of wildlife species . . . exactly those species whose abundance so impressed English colonists: elk, deer, beaver, hare, porcupine, turkey, quail, ruffed grouse, and so on" (Cronon 1983, 51). White-tailed deer, peccary, birds, and other game increases in swiddens and fallows in Yucatán and Panama (Greenberg 1991; Gordon 1982, 96–112; Bennett 1968). Rostlund (1960, 407) believed that the creation of grassy openings east of the Mississippi extended the range of the bison, whose numbers increased with Indian depopulation and reduced hunting pressure between 1540–1700, and subsequently declined under White pressure.

Agriculture

Fields and Associated Features

To observers in the sixteenth century, the most visible manifestation of the Native American landscape must have been the cultivated fields, which were concentrated around villages and houses. Most fields are ephemeral, their presence quickly erased when farmers migrate or die, but there are many eye-witness accounts of the great extent of Indian fields. On Hispaniola, Las Casas and Oviedo reported individual fields with thousands of *montones* (Sturtevant 1961, 73). These were manioc and sweet potato mounds 3–4 m in circumference, of which apparently none have survived. In the Llanos de Mojos in Bolivia, the first explorers mentioned *percheles,* or corn cribs on pilings, numbering up to 700 in a single field, each holding 30–45 bushels of food (Denevan 1966, 98). In northern Florida in 1539, Hernando de Soto's army passed through numerous fields of maize, beans, and squash, their main source of provisions; in one sector, "great fields . . . were spread out as far as the eye could see across two leagues of the plain" (Garcilaso de la Vega 1980, (2) 182; also see Dobyns 1983, 135–46).

It is difficult to obtain a reliable overview from such descriptions. Aside from possible exaggeration, Europeans tended not to write about field size, production, or technology. More useful are various forms of relict fields and field features that persist for centuries and can still be recognized, measured, and excavated today. These extant features, including terraces, irrigation works, raised fields, sunken fields, drainage ditches, dams, reservoirs, diversion walls, and field borders number in the millions and are distributed throughout the Americas (Denevan 1980; see also Doolittle and Whitmore and Turner, this volume). For example, about 500,000 ha of abandoned raised fields survive in the San Jorge Basin of northern Colombia (Plazas and Falchetti 1987, 485), and at least 600,000 ha of terracing, mostly of prehistoric origin, occur in the Peruvian Andes (Denevan 1988, 20). There are 19,000 ha of visible raised fields in just the sustaining area of Tiwanaku at Lake Titicaca (Kolata 1991, 109) and there were about 12,000 ha of *chinampas* (raised fields) around the Aztec capital of Tenochtitlán (Sanders, et al. 1979, 390). Complex canal systems on the north coast of Peru and in the Salt River Valley in Arizona irrigated more land in prehistory than is cultivated today. About 175 sites of Indian garden beds, up to several hundred acres each, have been reported in Wisconsin (Gartner 1992). These various remnant fields probably represent less than 25 percent of what once existed, most being buried under sediment or destroyed by erosion, urbanization, plowing, and bulldozing. On the other hand, an inadequate effort has been made to search for ancient fields.

Erosion

The size of native populations, associated deforestation, and prolonged intensive agriculture led to severe land degradation in some regions. Such a landscape was that of Central Mexico, where by 1519 food production pressures may have brought the Aztec civilization to the verge of collapse even without Spanish intervention (Cook and Borah 1971–79 (3), 129–76).[6] There is good evidence that severe soil erosion was already widespread, rather than just the result of subsequent European plowing, livestock, and deforestation. Cook examined the association between erosional severity (gullies, barrancas, sand and silt deposits, and sheet erosion) and pre-Spanish population density or proximity to prehistoric Indian towns. He concluded that "an important cycle of erosion and deposition therefore accompanied intensive land use by huge primitive populations in central Mexico, and had gone far toward the devastation of the country before the white man arrived" (Cook 1949, 86).

Barbara Williams (1972, 618) describes widespread *tepetate*, an indurated substrate formation exposed by sheet erosion resulting from prehistoric agriculture, as "one of the dominant surface materials in the Valley of Mexico." On the other hand, anthropologist Melville (1990, 27) argues that soil erosion in the Valle de Mezquital, just north of the Valley of Mexico, was the result of overgrazing by Spanish livestock starting before 1600: "there is an almost total lack of evidence of environmental degradation before the last three decades of the sixteenth century." The Butzers, however, in an examination of Spanish land grants, grazing patterns, and soil and vegetation ecology, found that there was only light intrusion of Spanish livestock (sheep and cattle were moved frequently) into the southeastern Bajío near Mezquital until after 1590 and that any degradation in 1590 was "as much a matter of long-term Indian land use as it was of Spanish intrusion" (Butzer and Butzer forthcoming). The relative roles of Indian and early Spanish

impacts in Mexico still need resolution; both were clearly significant but varied in time and place. Under the Spaniards, however, even with a greatly reduced population, the landscape in Mexico generally did not recover due to accelerating impacts from introduced sheep and cattle.[7]

The Built Landscape

Settlement

The Spaniards and other Europeans were impressed by large flourishing Indian cities such as Tenochtitlán, Quito, and Cuzco, and they took note of the extensive ruins of older, abandoned cities such as Cahokia, Teotihuacán, Tikal, Chan Chan, and Tiwanaku (Hardoy 1968). Most of these cities contained more than 50,000 people. Less notable, or possibly more taken for granted, was rural settlement—small villages of a few thousand or a few hundred people, hamlets of a few families, and dispersed farmsteads. The numbers and locations of much of this settlement will never be known. With the rapid decline of native populations, the abandonment of houses and entire villages and the decay of perishable materials quickly obscured sites, especially in the tropical lowlands.

We do have some early listings of villages, especially for Mexico and Peru. Elsewhere, archaeology is telling us more than ethnohistory. After initially focusing on large temple and administrative centers, archaeologists are now examining rural sustaining areas, with remarkable results. See, for example, Sanders et al. (1979) on the Basin of Mexico, Culbert and Rice (1991) on the Maya lowlands, and Fowler (1989) on Cahokia in Illinois. Evidence of human occupation for the artistic Santarém Culture phase (Tapajós chiefdom) on the lower Amazon extends over thousands of square kilometers, with large nucleated settlements (Roosevelt 1991, 101–02).

Much of the rural precontact settlement was semi-dispersed (*rancherías*), particularly in densely populated regions of Mexico and the Andes, probably reflecting poor food transport efficiency. Houses were both single-family and communal (pueblos, Huron long houses, Amazon malocas). Construction was of stone, earth, adobe, daub and wattle, grass, hides, brush, and bark. Much of the dispersed settlement not destroyed by depopulation was concentrated by the Spaniards into compact grid/plaza style new towns (*congregaciones, reducciones*) for administrative purposes.

Mounds

James Parsons (1985, 161) has suggested that: "An apparent 'mania for earth moving, landscape engineering on a grand scale runs as a thread through much of New World prehistory." Large quantities of both earth and stone were transferred to create various raised and sunken features, such as agricultural landforms, settlement and ritual mounds, and causeways.

Mounds of different shapes and sizes were constructed throughout the Americas for temples, burials, settlement, and as effigies. The stone pyramids of Mexico and the Andes are well known, but equal monuments of earth were built in the Amazon, the Midwest U.S., and elsewhere. The Mississippian period complex of 104 mounds at Cahokia near East St. Louis supported 30,000 people; the largest, Monk's Mound, is currently 30.5 m high and covers 6.9 ha. (Fowler 1989, 90, 192). Cahokia was the largest settlement north of the Río Grande until surpassed by New York City in 1775. An early survey estimated "at least 20,000 conical, linear, and effigy mounds" in Wisconsin (Stout 1911, 24). Overall, there must have been several hundred thousand artificial mounds in the Midwest and South. De Soto described such features still in use in 1539 (Silverberg 1968, 7). Thousands of settlement and other mounds dot the savanna landscape of Mojos in Bolivia (Denevan 1966). At the mouth of the Amazon on Marajó Island, one complex of forty habitation mounds contained more than 10,000 people; one of these mounds is 20 m high while another is 90 ha in area (Roosevelt 1991, 31, 38).

Not all of the various earthworks scattered over the Americas were in use in 1492. Many had been long abandoned, but they constituted a conspicuous element of the landscape of 1492 and some are still prominent. Doubtless, many remain to be discovered, and others remain unrecognized as human or prehistoric features.

Roads, Causeways, and Trails

Large numbers of people and settlements necessitated extensive systems of overland travel routes to facilitate administration, trade, warfare, and social interaction (Hyslop 1984; Trombold 1991). Only hints of their former prominence survive. Many were simple traces across deserts or narrow paths cut into forests. A suggestion as to the importance of Amazon forest trails is the existence of more than 500 km of trail maintained by a single Kayapó village today (Posey 1985, 149). Some prehistoric footpaths were so intensively used for so long that they were incised into the ground and are still detectable, as has recently been described in Costa Rica (Sheets and Sever 1991).

Improved roads, at times stone-lined and drained, were constructed over great distances in the realms of the high civilizations. The Inca road network is estimated to have measured about 40,000 km, extending from southern Colombia to central Chile (Hyslop 1984, 224). Prehistoric causeways (raised roads) were built in the tropical lowlands (Denevan 1991); one Maya causeway is 100 km long, and there are more than 1,600 km of causeways in the Llanos de Mojos. Humboldt reported large prehistoric causeways in the Orinoco Llanos. Ferdinand Columbus described roads on Puerto Rico in 1493. Gaspar de Carvajal, traveling down the Amazon with Orellana in 1541, reported "highways" penetrating the forest from river bank villages. Joseph de Acosta (1880, (1) 171) in 1590 said that between Peru and Brazil, there were "waies as much beaten as those betwixt Salamanca and Valladolid." Prehistoric roads in Chaco Canyon, New Mexico are described in Trombold (1991). Some routes were so well established and located that they have remained roads to this day.

Recovery

A strong case can be made for significant environmental recovery and reduction of cultural features by the late eighteenth century as a result of Indian population decline. Henry Thoreau (1949, 132–37) believed, based on his reading of William Wood, that the New England forests of 1633 were more open, more park-like, with more berries and more wildlife, than Thoreau observed in 1855. Cronon (1983, 108), Pyne (1982, 51), Silver (1990, 104), Martin (1978, 181–82), and Williams (1989, 49) all maintain that the eastern forests recovered and filled in as a result of Indian depopulation, field abandonment, and reduction in burning. While probably correct, these writers give few specific examples, so further research is needed. The sixteenth-century fields and savannas of Colombia and Central America also had reverted to forest within 150 years after abandonment (Parsons 1975, 30–31; Bennett 1968, 54). On his fourth voyage in 1502–03, Columbus sailed along the north coast of Panama (Veragua). His son Ferdinand described lands which were well-peopled, full of houses, with many fields, and open with few trees. In contrast, in 1681 Lionel Wafer found most of the Caribbean coast of Panama forest covered and unpopulated. On the Pacific side in the eighteenth century, savannas were seldom mentioned; the main economic activity was the logging of tropical cedar, a tree that grows on the sites of abandoned fields and other disturbances (Sauer 1966, 132–33, 287–88). An earlier oscillation from forest destruction to recovery in the Yucatán is instructive. Whitmore, et al. (1990, 35) estimate that the Maya had modified 75 percent of the environment by A.D. 800, and that following the Mayan collapse, forest recovery in the central lowlands was nearly complete when the Spaniards arrived.

The pace of forest regeneration, however, varied across the New World. Much of the southeastern U.S. remained treeless in the 1750s according to Rostlund (1957, 408, 409). He notes that the tangled brush that ensnarled the "Wilderness Campaign of 1864 in Virginia occupied the same land as did Captain John Smith's 'open groves with much good ground between without any shrubs'" in 1624; vegetation had only partially recovered over 240 years. The Kentucky barrens in contrast were largely reforested by the early nineteenth century (Sauer 1963, 30). The Alabama Black Belt vegetation was described by William Bartram in the 1770s as a mixture of forest and grassy plains, but by the nineteenth century, there was only 10 percent prairie and even less in some counties (Rostlund 1957, 393, 401–03). Sections of coastal forests never recovered, given colonist pressures, but Sale's (1990, 291) claim that "the English were well along in the

process of eliminating the ancient Eastern woodlands from Maine to the Mississippi" in the first one hundred years, is an exaggeration.

Wildlife also partially recovered in eastern North America with reduced hunting pressure from Indians; however, this is also a story yet to be worked out. The white-tailed deer apparently declined in numbers, probably reflecting reforestation plus competition from livestock. Commercial hunting was a factor on the coast, with 80,000 deer skins being shipped out yearly from Charleston by 1730 (Silver 1990, 92). Massachusetts enacted a closed season on deer as early as 1694, and in 1718 there was a three-year moratorium on deer hunting (Cronon 1983, 100). Sale (1990, 290) believes that beaver were depleted in the Northeast by 1640. Other fur bearers, game birds, elk, buffalo, and carnivores were also targeted by white hunters, but much game probably was in the process of recovery in many eastern areas until a general reversal after 1700–50.

As agricultural fields changed to scrub and forest, earthworks were grown over. All the raised fields in Yucatán and South America were abandoned. A large portion of the agricultural terraces in the Americas were abandoned in the early colonial period (Donkin 1979, 35–38). In the Colca Valley of Peru, measurement on air photos indicates 61 percent terrace abandonment (Denevan 1988, 28). Societies vanished or declined everywhere and whole villages with them. The degree to which settlement features were swallowed up by vegetation, sediment, and erosion is indicated by the difficulty of finding them today. Machu Picchu, a late prehistoric site, was not rediscovered until 1911.

The renewal of human impact also varied regionally, coming with the Revolutionary War in North America, with the rubber boom in Amazonia, and with the expansion of coffee in southern Brazil (1840–1930). The swamp lands of Gulf Coast Mexico and the Guayas Basin of Ecuador remained hostile environments to Europeans until well into the nineteenth century or later (Siemens 1990; Mathewson 1987). On the other hand, Highland Mexico-Guatemala and the Andes, with greater Indian survival and with the establishment of haciendas and intensive mining, show less evidence of environmental recovery. Similarly, Indian fields in the Caribbean were rapidly replaced by European livestock and sugar plantation systems, inhibiting any sufficient recovery. The same is true of the sugar zone of coastal Brazil.

Conclusions

By 1492, Indian activity had modified vegetation and wildlife, caused erosion, and created earthworks, roads, and settlements throughout the Americas. This may be obvious, but the human imprint was much more ubiquitous and enduring than is usually realized. The historical evidence is ample, as are data from surviving earthworks and archaeology. And much can be inferred from present human impacts. The weight of evidence suggests that Indian populations were large, not only in Mexico and the Andes, but also in seemingly unattractive habitats such as the rainforests of Amazonia, the swamps of Mojos, and the deserts of Arizona.

Clearly, the most humanized landscapes of the Americas existed in those highland regions where people were the most numerous. Here were the large states, characterized by urban centers, road systems, intensive agriculture, a dispersed but relatively dense rural settlement pattern of hamlets and farmsteads, and widespread vegetation and soil modification and wildlife depletion. There were other, smaller regions that shared some of these characteristics, such as the Pueblo lands in the southwestern U.S., the Sabana de Bogotá in highland Colombia, and the central Amazon floodplain, where built landscapes were locally dramatic and are still observable. Finally, there were the immense grasslands, deserts, mountains, and forests elsewhere, with populations that were sparse or moderate, with landscape impacts that mostly were ephemeral or not obvious but nevertheless significant, particularly for vegetation and wildlife, as in Amazonia and the northeastern U.S. In addition, landscapes from the more distant past survived to 1492 and even to 1992, such as those of the irrigation states of north coast Peru, the Classic Maya, the Mississippian mound builders, and the Tiwanaku Empire of Lake Titicaca.

This essay has ranged over the hemisphere, an enormous area, making generalizations about and providing examples of Indian landscape transformation as of 1492. Examples of some of the surviving cultural features are shown in Figure 1. Ideally, a series of hemispheric maps should be provided to portray the spatial patterns of the different types of impacts and cultural features, but such maps are not feasible nor would they be accurate given present knowledge. There are a few relevant regional maps, however, that can be referred to. For example, see Butzer (1990, 33, 45) for Indian settlement structures/mounds and subsistence patterns in the U.S.; Donkin (1979, 23) for agricultural terracing; Doolittle (1990, 109) for canal irrigation in Mexico; Parsons and Denevan (1967) for raised fields in South America; Trombold (1991) for various road networks; Hyslop (1984, 4) for the Inca roads; Hardoy (1968, 49) for the most intense urbanization in Latin America; and Gordon (1957, 69) for anthropogenic savannas in northern Colombia.

The pristine myth cannot be laid at the feet of Columbus. While he spoke of "Paradise," his was clearly a humanized paradise. He described Hispaniola and Tortuga as densely populated and "completely cultivated like the countryside around Cordoba" (Colón 1976, 165). He also noted that "the islands are not so thickly wooded as to be impassable," suggesting openings from clearing and burning (Columbus 1961, 5).

The roots of the pristine myth lie in part with early observers unaware of human impacts that may be obvious to scholars today, particularly for vegetation and wildlife.[8] But even many earthworks such as raised fields have only recently been discovered (Denevan 1966; 1980). Equally important, most of our eyewitness descriptions of wilderness and empty lands come from a later time, particularly 1750–1850 when interior lands began to be explored and occupied by Europeans. By 1650, Indian populations in the hemisphere had been reduced by about 90 percent, while by 1750 European numbers were not yet substantial and settlement had only begun to expand. As a result, fields had been abandoned, while settlements vanished, forests recovered, and savannas retreated. The landscape did appear to be a sparsely populated wilderness. This is the image conveyed by Parkman in the nineteenth century, Bakeless in 1950, and Shetler as recently as 1991. There was some European impact, of course, but it was localized. After 1750 and especially after 1850, populations greatly expanded, resources were more intensively exploited, and European modification of the environment accelerated, continuing to the present.

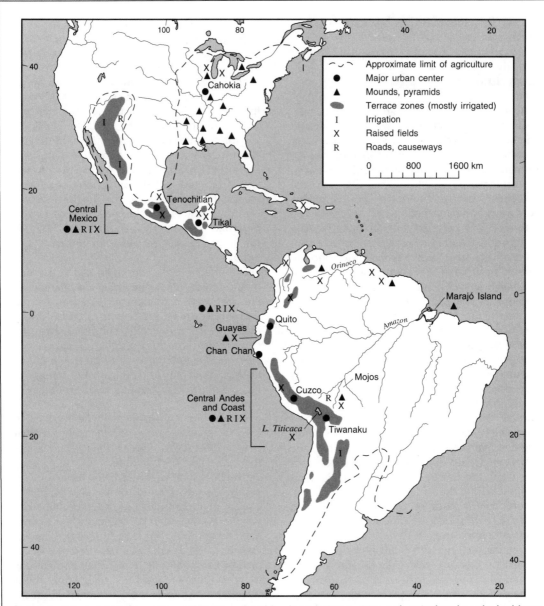

Figure 1. Selected features of the prehistoric cultural landscape. Some cities and agricultural works had been abandoned by 1492. The approximate limit of agriculture and the distribution of terraces is based on Donkin (1979, 23); other features were mapped by the author.

It is possible to conclude not only that "the virgin forest was not encountered in the sixteenth and seventeenth centuries; [but that] it was invented in the late eighteenth and early nineteenth centuries" (Pyne 1982, 46). However, "paradoxical as it may seem, there was undoubtedly much more 'forest primeval' in 1850 than in 1650" (Rostlund 1957, 409). Thus the "invention" of an earlier wilderness is in part understandable and is not simply a deliberate creation which ennobled the American enterprise, as suggested by Bowden (1992, 20–23). In any event, while pre-European landscape alteration has been demonstrated previously, including by several geographers, the case has mainly been made for vegetation and mainly for eastern North America. As shown here, the argument is also applicable to most of the rest of the New World, including the humid tropics, and involves much more than vegetation.

The human impact on environment is not simply a process of increasing change or degradation in response to linear population growth and economic expansion. It is instead interrupted by periods of reversal and ecological rehabilitation as cultures collapse, populations decline, wars occur, and habitats are abandoned. Impacts may be constructive, benign, or degenerative (all subjective concepts), but change is continual at variable rates and in different directions. Even mild impacts and slow changes are cumulative, and the long-term effects can be dramatic. Is it possible that the thousands of years of human activity before Columbus created more change in the visible landscape than has occurred subsequently with European settlement and resource exploitation? The answer is probably yes for most regions for the next 250 years or so, and for some regions right up to the present time. American flora, fauna, and landscape were slowly Europeanized after 1492, but before that they had already been Indianized. "It is upon this imprint that the more familiar Euro-American landscape was grafted, rather than created anew" (Butzer 1990, 28). What does all this mean for protectionist tendencies today? Much of what is protected or proposed to be protected from human disturbance had native people present, and environmental modification occurred accordingly and in part is still detectable.

The pristine image of 1492 seems to be a myth, then, an image more applicable to 1750, following Indian decline, although recovery had only been partial by that date. There is some substance to this argument, and it should hold up under the scrutiny of further investigation of the considerable evidence available, both written and in the ground.

Acknowledgments

The field and library research that provided the background for this essay was undertaken over many years in Latin America, Berkeley, and Madison. Mentors who have been particularly influential are Carl O. Sauer, Erhard Rostlund, James J. Parsons, and Woodrow Borah, all investigators of topics discussed here.

Notes

1. Sauer had a life-long interest in this topic (1963, 1966, 1971, 1980).
2. See Nash (1967) on the "romantic wilderness" of America; Bowden (1992, 9–12) on the "invented tradition" of the "primeval forest" of New England; and Manthorne (1989, 10–21) on artists' images of the tropical "Eden" of South America. Day (1953, 329) provides numerous quotations from Parkman on "wilderness" and "vast," "virgin," and "continuous" forest.
3. For example, a 1991 advertisement for a Time-Life video refers to "the unspoiled beaches, forests, and mountains of an earlier America" and "the pristine shores of Chesapeake Bay in 1607."
4. On the other hand, the ability of Indians to clear large trees with inefficient stone axes, assisted by girdling and deadening by fire, may have been overestimated (Denevan forthcoming). Silver (1990, 51) notes that the upland forests of Carolina were largely uninhabited for this reason.
5. Similar conclusions were reached by foresters Maxwell (1910) and Day (1953); by geographers Sauer (1963), Brown (1948, 11–19), Rostlund (1957), and Bowden (1992); and by environmental historians Pyne (1982, 45–51), Cronon (1983, 49–51), and Silver (1990, 59–66).
6. B. Williams (1989, 730) finds strong evidence of rural overpopulation (66 percent in poor crop years, 11 percent in average years) in the Basin of Mexico village of Asunción, ca. A.D. 1540, which was probably "not unique but a widespread phenomenon." For a contrary conclusion, that the Aztecs did not exceed carrying capacity, see Ortiz de Montellano (1990, 119).
7. Highland Guatemala provides another prehistoric example of "severe human disturbance" involving deforestation and "massive" soil erosion (slopes) and deposition (valleys) (Murdy 1990, 186). For the central Andes there is some evidence that much of the *puna* zone (3200–4500 m), now grass and scrub, was deforested in prehistoric times (White 1985).
8. The English colonists in part justified their occupation of Indian land on the basis that such land had not been "subdued" and therefore was "land free to be taken" (Wilson 1992, 16).

References

Acosta, Joseph [José] de. 1880 [1590]. *The natural and moral history of the Indies.* Trans. E. Gimston, Hakluyt Society, vols. 60, 61. London.

Alcorn, J. B. 1981. Huastec noncrop resource management: Implications for prehistoric rain forest management. *Human Ecology* 9:395–417.

Anderson, R. C. 1990. The historic role of fire in the North American grassland. In *Fire in North American tallgrass prairies,* ed. S. L. Collins and

L. L. Wallace, pp. 8–18. Norman: University of Oklahoma Press.

Bakeless, J. 1950. *The eyes of discovery: The pageant of North America as seen by the first explorers.* New York: J. B. Lippincott.

Balée, W. 1987. Cultural forests of the Amazon. *Garden* 11:12–14, 32.

———. 1989. The culture of Amazonian forests. In *Advances in Economic Botany,* vol. 7, pp. 1–21. New York: New York Botanical Garden.

Bennett, C. F. 1968. *Human influences on the zoogeography of Panama.* Ibero-Americana 51. Berkeley: University of California Press.

Borchert, J. 1950. Climate of the central North American grassland. *Annals of the Association of American Geographers* 40:1–39.

Bowden, M. J. 1992. The invention of American tradition. *Journal of Historical Geography* 18:3–26.

Brown, R. H. 1948. *Historical geography of the United States.* New York: Harcourt, Brace.

Brown, S., and Lugo, A. 1990. Tropical secondary forests. *Journal of Tropical Ecology* 6:1–32.

Butzer, K. W. 1990. The Indian legacy in the American landscape. In *The making of the American landscape,* ed. M. P. Conzen, pp. 27–50. Boston: Unwin Hyman.

———, **and Butzer, E. K.** Forthcoming. The sixteenth-century environment of the central Mexican Bajío: Archival reconstruction from Spanish land grants. In *Culture, form, and place,* ed. K. Mathewson. Baton Rouge, LA: Geoscience and Man.

Colón, C. 1976. *Diario del descubrimiento,* vol. 1, ed. M. Alvar. Madrid: Editorial La Muralla.

Columbus, C. 1961. *Four voyages to the New World: Letters and selected documents,* ed. R. H. Major. New York: Corinth Books.

Cook, S. F. 1949. *Soil erosion and population in Central Mexico.* Ibero-Americana 34. Berkeley: University of California Press.

———, **and Borah, W.** 1971–79. *Essays in population history.* 3 vols. Berkeley: University of California Press.

Cowley, G. 1991. The great disease migration. In *1492–1992, When worlds collide: How Columbus's voyages transformed both East and West.* Newsweek, Special Issue, Fall/Winter, pp. 54–56.

Cronon, W. 1983. *Changes in the land: Indians, colonists, and the ecology of New England.* New York: Hill and Wang.

Culbert, T. P., and Rice, D. S., eds. 1990. *Precolumbian population history in the Maya lowlands.* Albuquerque: University of New Mexico Press.

Day, G. M. 1953. The Indian as an ecological factor in the northeastern forest. *Ecology* 34:329–46.

Denevan, W. M. 1961. The upland pine forests of Nicaragua. *University of California Publications in Geography* 12:251–320.

———. 1966. *The aboriginal cultural geography of the Llanos de Mojos of Bolivia.* Ibero-Americana 48. Berkeley: University of California Press.

———. 1980. Tipología de configuraciones agrícolas prehispánicas. *América Indígena* 40:619–52.

———. 1988. Measurement of abandoned terracing from air photos: Colca Valley, Peru. *Yearbook, Conference of Latin Americanist Geographers* 14:20–30.

———. 1991. Prehistoric roads and causeways of lowland tropical America. In *Ancient road networks and settlement hierarchies in the New World,* ed. C. D. Trombold, pp. 230–42. Cambridge: Cambridge University Press.

———, ed. 1992 [1976]. *The native population of the Americas in 1492,* 2nd ed. Madison: University of Wisconsin Press.

———. Forthcoming. Stone vs. metal axes: The ambiguity of shifting cultivation in prehistoric Amazonia. *Journal of the Steward Anthropological Society.*

———, **and Padoch, C., eds.** 1988. *Swidden-fallow agroforestry in the Peruvian Amazon.* Advances in Economic Botany, vol. 5. New York: New York Botanical Garden.

Dobyns, H. F. 1981. *From fire to flood: Historic human destruction of Sonoran Desert riverine oases.* Socorro, NM: Ballena Press.

———. 1983. *Their number become thinned: Native American population dynamics in eastern North America.* Knoxville: University of Tennessee Press.

Donkin, R. A. 1979. *Agricultural terracing in the aboriginal New World.* Viking Fund Publications in Anthropology 56. Tucson: University of Arizona Press.

Doolittle, W. E. 1990. *Canal irrigation in prehistoric Mexico: The sequence of technological change.* Austin: University of Texas Press.

Forman, R. T. T., and Russell, E. W. B. 1983. Evaluation of historical data in ecology. *Bulletin of the Ecological Society of America* 64:5–7.

Fowler, M. 1989. *The Cahokia atlas: A historical atlas of Cahokia archaeology.* Studies in Illinois Archaeology 6. Springfield: Illinois Historic Preservation Agency.

Garren, K. H. 1943. Effects of fire on vegetation of the southeastern United States. *The Botanical Review* 9:617–54.

Gartner, W. G. 1992. The Hulbert Creek ridged fields: Pre-Columbian agriculture near the Dells, Wisconsin. Master's thesis, Department of Geography, University of Wisconsin, Madison.

Garcilaso de la Vega, The Inca. 1980 [1605]. *The Florida of the Inca: A history of the Adelantado,*

Hernando de Soto. 2 vols. Trans. and ed. J. G. Varner and J. J. Varner. Austin: University of Texas Press.

Gilmore, M. R. 1931. Dispersal by Indians a factor in the extension of discontinuous distribution of certain species of native plants. *Papers of the Michigan Academy of Science, Arts and Letters* 13:89–94.

Goldammer, J. G., ed. 1990. *Fire in the tropical biota: Ecosystem processes and global challenges.* Ecological Studies, vol. 84. Berlin: Springer-Verlag.

Gómez-Pompa, A. 1987. On Maya silviculture. *Mexican Studies* 3:1–17.

———; Salvador Flores, J.; and Sosa, V. 1987. The "pet kot": A man-made forest of the Maya. *Interciencia* 12:10–15.

Good, K. R. 1987. Limiting factors in Amazonian ecology. In *Food and evolution: Toward a theory of human food habitats,* ed. M. Harris and E. B. Ross, pp. 407–21. Philadelphia: Temple University Press.

Gordon, B. L. 1957. *Human geography and ecology in the Sinú country of Colombia.* Ibero-Americana 39. Berkeley: University of California Press.

———. 1982. *A Panama forest and shore: Natural history and Amerindian culture in Bocas del Toro.* Pacific Grove: Boxwood Press.

Greenberg, L. S. C. 1991. Garden-hunting among the Yucatec Maya. *Etnoecológica* 1:30–36.

Haffer, J. 1991. Mosaic distribution patterns of neotropical forest birds and underlying cyclic disturbance processes. In *The mosaic-cycle concept of ecosystems,* ed. H. Remmert, pp. 83–105. Ecological Studies, vol. 85. Berlin: Springer-Verlag.

Hardoy, J. 1968. *Urban planning in pre-Columbian America.* New York: George Braziler.

Hills, T. L., and Randall, R. E., eds. 1968. *The ecology of the forest/savanna boundary.* Savanna Research Series 13. Montreal: McGill University.

Hyslop, J. 1984. *The Inka road system.* New York: Academic Press.

Kolata, A. L. 1991. The technology and organization of agricultural production in the Tiwanaku state. *Latin American Antiquity* 2:99–125.

Lewis, H. T. 1982. Fire technology and resource management in aboriginal North America and Australia. In *Resource managers: North American and Australian hunter-gatherers,* ed. N. M. Williams and E. S. Hunn, pp. 45–67. AAAS Selected Symposia 67. Boulder, CO: Westview Press.

Lord, L., and Burke, S. 1991. America before Columbus. *U.S. News and World Report,* July 8, pp. 22–37.

McEvedy, C., and Jones, R. 1978. *Atlas of world population history.* New York: Penguin Books.

MacNutt, F. A. 1909. *Bartholomew de las Casas: His life, his apostolate, and his writings.* New York: Putnam's.

Manthorne, K. E. 1989. *Tropical renaissance: North American artists exploring Latin America, 1839–1879.* Washington: Smithsonian Institution Press.

Martin, C. 1978. *Keepers of the game: Indian-animal relationships and the fur trade.* Berkeley: University of California Press.

Mathewson, K. 1987. Landscape change and cultural persistence in the Guayas wetlands, Ecuador. Ph. D. dissertation, Department of Geography, University of Wisconsin, Madison.

Maxwell, H. 1910. The use and abuse of forests by the Virginia Indians. *William and Mary College Quarterly Historical Magazine* 19:73–103.

Medina, E. 1980. Ecology of tropical American savannas: An ecophysiological approach. In *Human ecology in savanna environments,* ed. D. R. Harris, pp. 297–319. London: Academic Press.

Meinig, D. W. 1986. *The shaping of America. A geographical perspective on 500 years of history,* vol. 1, *Atlantic America, 1492–1800.* New Haven: Yale University Press.

Melville, E. G. K. 1990. Environmental and social change in the Valle del Mezquital, Mexico, 1521–1600. *Comparative Studies in Society and History* 32:24–53.

Mueller-Dombois, D. 1981. Fire in tropical ecosystems. In *Fire regimes and ecosystem properties: Proceedings of the Conference,* Honolulu, 1978, pp. 137–76. General Technical Report WO-26. Washington: U.S. Forest Service.

Murdy, C. N. 1990. Prehispanic agriculture and its effects in the valley of Guatemala. *Forest and Conservation History* 34:179–90.

Nash, R. 1967. *Wilderness and the American mind.* New Haven, CT: Yale University Press.

Ortiz de Montellano, B. R. 1990. *Aztec medicine, health, and nutrition.* New Brunswick, NJ: Rutgers University Press.

Parsons, J. J. 1975. The changing nature of New World tropical forests since European colonization. In *The use of ecological guidelines for development in the American humid tropics,* pp. 28–38. International Union for Conservation of Nature and Natural Resources Publications, n.s., 31. Morges.

———. 1985. Raised field farmers as pre-Columbian landscape engineers: Looking north from the San Jorge (Colombia). In *Prehistoric intensive agriculture in the tropics,* ed. I. S. Farrington, pp. 149–65. International Series 232. Oxford: British Archaeological Reports.

———, and Denevan, W. M. 1967. Pre-Columbian ridged fields. *Scientific American* 217 (1):92–100.

Patterson, W. A., III, and Sassaman, K. E. 1988.

Indian fires in the prehistory of New England. In *Holocene human ecology in northeastern North America,* ed. G. P. Nicholas, pp. 107–35. New York: Plenum.

Plazas, C., and Falchetti, A. M. 1987. Poblamiento y adecuación hidráulica en el bajo Río San Jorge, Costa Atlantica, Colombia. In *Prehistoric agricultural fields in the Andean region,* ed. W. M. Denevan, K. Mathewson, and G. Knapp, pp. 483–503. International Series 359. Oxford: British Archaeological Reports.

Posey, D. A. 1985. Indigenous management of tropical forest ecosystems: The case of the Kayapó Indians of the Brazilian Amazon. *Agroforestry Systems* 3:139–58.

Pyne, S. J. 1982. *Fire in America: A cultural history of wildland and rural fire.* Princeton, NJ: Princeton University Press.

Raup, H. M. 1937. Recent changes in climate and vegetation in southern New England and adjacent New York. *Journal of the Arnold Arboretum* 18:79–117.

Roosevelt, A. C. 1991. *Moundbuilders of the Amazon: Geophysical archaeology on Marajo Island, Brazil.* San Diego: Academic Press.

Rostlund, E. 1957. The myth of a natural prairie belt in Alabama: An interpretation of historical records. *Annals of the Association of American Geographers* 47:392–411.

———. 1960. The geographic range of the historic bison in the southeast. *Annals of the Association of American Geographers* 50:395–407.

Russell, E. W. B. 1983. Indian-set fires in the forests of the northeastern United States. *Ecology* 64:78–88.

Saldarriaga, J. G., and West, D. C. 1986. Holocene fires in the northern Amazon Basin. *Quaternary Research* 26:358–66.

———, and Uhl, C. 1991. Recovery of forest vegetation following slash-and-burn agriculture in the upper Río Negro. In *Rainforest regeneration and management,* ed. A. Gómez-Pompa, T. C. Whitmore, and M. Hadley, pp. 303–12. Paris: UNESCO.

Sale, K. 1990. *The conquest of paradise: Christopher Columbus and the Columbian legacy.* New York: Alfred A. Knopf.

Sánchez-Albornoz, N. 1974. *The population of Latin America: A history.* Berkeley: University of California Press.

Sanders, W. T.; Parsons, J. R.; and Santley, R. S. 1979. *The Basin of Mexico: Ecological processes in the evolution of a civilization.* New York: Academic Press.

Sauer, C. O. 1950. Grassland climax, fire, and man. *Journal of Range Management* 3:16–21.

———. 1958. Man in the ecology of tropical America. *Proceedings of the Ninth Pacific Science Congress, 1957* 20:104–10.

———. 1963 [1927]. The barrens of Kentucky. In *Land and life: A selection from the writings of Carl Ortwin Sauer,* ed. J. Leighly, pp. 23–31. Berkeley: University of California Press.

———. 1966. *The early Spanish Main.* Berkeley: University of California Press.

———. 1971. *Sixteenth-century North America: The land and the people as seen by the Europeans.* Berkeley: University of California Press.

———. 1975. Man's dominance by use of fire. *Geoscience and Man* 10:1–13.

———. 1980. *Seventeenth-century North America.* Berkeley: Turtle Island Press.

Schwerin, K. H. 1991. The Indian populations of Latin America. In *Latin America, its problems and its promise: A multidisciplinary introduction,* ed. J. K. Black, 2nd ed., pp. 39–53. Boulder, CO: Westview Press.

Scott, G. A. J. 1978. *Grassland development in the Gran Pajonal of eastern Peru.* Hawaii Monographs in Geography 1. Honolulu: University of Hawaii.

Sheets, P., and Sever, T. L. 1991. Prehistoric footpaths in Costa Rica: Transportation and communication in a tropical rainforest. In *Ancient road networks and settlement hierarchies in the New World,* ed. C. D. Trombold, pp. 53–65. Cambridge: Cambridge University Press.

Shetler, S. 1991. Three faces of Eden. In *Seeds of change: A quincentennial commemoration,* ed. H. J. Viola and C. Margolis, pp. 225–47. Washington: Smithsonian Institution Press.

Siemens, A. H. 1990. *Between the summit and the sea: Central Veracruz in the nineteenth century.* Vancouver: University of British Columbia Press.

Silver, T. 1990. *A new face on the countryside: Indians, colonists, and slaves in South Atlantic forests, 1500–1800.* Cambridge: Cambridge University Press.

Silverberg, R. 1968. *Mound builders of ancient America: The archaeology of a myth.* Greenwich, CT: New York Graphic Society.

Smith, N. J. H. 1980. Anthrosols and human carrying capacity in Amazonia. *Annals of the Association of American Geographers* 70:553–66.

Stout, A. B. 1911. Prehistoric earthworks in Wisconsin. *Ohio Archaeological and Historical Publications* 20:1–31.

Sturtevant, W. C. 1961. Taino agriculture. In *The evolution of horticultural systems in native South America, causes and consequences: A symposium,* ed. J. Wilbert, pp. 69–82. Caracas: Sociedad de Ciencias Naturales La Salle.

Taylor, D. L. 1981. Fire history and fire records for Everglades National Park. Everglades National Park Report T-619. Washington: National Park Service, U.S. Department of the Interior.

Thompson, D. Q., and Smith, R. H. 1970. The forest primeval in the Northeast—a great myth? *Pro-*

ceedings, Tall Timbers Fire Ecology Conference 10:255–65.

Thoreau, H. D. 1949. The journal of Henry D. Thoreau, vol. 7, September 1, 1854–October 30, 1855, ed. B. Torrey and F. H. Allen. Boston: Houghton Mifflin.

Trombold, C. D., ed. 1991. Ancient road networks and settlement hierarchies in the New World. Cambridge: Cambridge University Press.

Uhl, C.; Nepstad, D.; Buschbacher, R.; Clark, K.; Kauffman, B.; and Subler, S. 1990. Studies of ecosystem response to natural and anthropogenic disturbances provide guidelines for designing sustainable land-use systems in Amazonia. In Alternatives to deforestation: Steps toward sustainable use of the Amazon rain forest, ed. A. B. Anderson, pp. 24–42. New York: Columbia University Press.

Walschburger, T., and von Hildebrand, P. 1991. The first 26 years of forest regeneration in natural and man-made gaps in the Colombian Amazon. In Rain forest regeneration and management, ed. A. Gómez-Pompa, T. C. Whitmore, and M. Hadley, pp. 257–63. Paris: UNESCO.

Watts, W. A., and Bradbury, J. P. 1982. Paleoecological studies at Lake Patzcuaro on the west-central Mexican plateau and at Chalco in the Basin of Mexico. Quaternary Research 17:56–70.

Wedel, W. R. 1957. The central North American grassland: Man-made or natural? Social Science Monographs 3:39–69. Washington: Pan American Union.

White, S. 1985. Relations of subsistence to the vegetation mosaic of Vilcabamba, southern Peruvian Andes. Yearbook, Conference of Latin Americanist Geographers 11:3–10.

Whitmore, T. M. 1991. A simulation of the sixteenth-century population collapse in the Basin of Mexico. Annals of the Association of American Geographers 81:464–87.

———; Turner, B. L. II; Johnson, D. L.; Kates, R. W.; and Gottschang, T. R. 1990. Long-term population change. In The earth as transformed by human action, ed. B. L. Turner II, et al., pp. 25–39. Cambridge: Cambridge University Press.

Williams, B. J. 1972. Tepetate in the Valley of Mexico. Annals of the Association of American Geographers 62:618–26.

———. 1989. Contact period rural overpopulation in the Basin of Mexico: Carrying-capacity models tested with documentary data. American Antiquity 54:715–32.

Williams, M. 1989. Americans and their forests: A historical geography. Cambridge: Cambridge University Press.

Wilson, S.M. 1992. "That unmanned wild countrey": Native Americans both conserved and transformed New World environments. Natural History, May:16–17.

Wood, W. 1977 [1635]. New England's prospect, ed. A. T. Vaughan. Amherst: University of Massachusetts Press.

Agriculture in North America on the Eve of Contact: A Reassessment

William E. Doolittle

Department of Geography, University of Texas, Austin, TX 78712

FAX 572/471-5049

In honor of Campbell W. Pennington

Abstract. Despite countless archaeological excavations at prehistoric agricultural sites, understanding of the cultivation practices of native North Americans ca. 1492 remains imperfect, and regional syntheses of agricultural patterning elusive. The problem remains that excavations and surveys focus more on site function than on food production; more on the remains of plants than on cultivation practices; more on socioeconomic hypotheses than on human-environmental or spatial implications. This paper uses extensive ethnohistorical accounts of early European explorers that help to identify five different types of agricultural methods in use during the Contact period. I argue that the agroecological landscapes of both the Southwest and Eastern Woodlands were quite complex, in response to mosaic environments, and that labor-intensive agriculture was as common in the East as in the Southwest. Subtleties in irrigation strategies were of equal if not greater importance than the obvious function of simply providing water in arid environments. Pre-European cultivators built terraces in the mountainous Southwest, in part to halt environmental degradation. I question the dominance of shifting cultivation in the Eastern Woodlands. Large, permanently cultivated cleared areas, raised fields, and mounding indicate that intensive practices were common and widespread here. Lastly, I argue that house-lot gardens across the continent may have been critical, rather than merely supplemental, in the overall scheme of indigenous food production. Much work remains to be done before the many residual questions about native agriculture can be resolved.

Key Words: Native American agriculture, irrigation, terracing, shifting cultivation, raised fields, gardens.

AGRICULTURE may well be the most comprehensive of geographical topics. It involves modification of both the biological (plants) and physical (soils-landforms) components of the environment (e.g., Johannessen 1966; Johnston 1977), and it incorporates social and economic components with distinctive spatial manifestations (e.g., Stevens and Lee 1979; Visser 1982). It also is dynamic, playing a major role in recent human history (Doolittle 1984; Wallach 1985). With good reason several geographers have directed their attention to issues of growing food in prehistoric times. Some studies have been undertaken for academic reasons (Donkin 1979), but lessons learned from earlier successes and failures may help in selecting future food production strategies, especially in the Third World (Denevan, et al. 1987).

Much of the research conducted on ancient agriculture by geographers, especially those based in North America, has focused on Latin America. Here geographers were responsible for singling out important problems such as the subsistence base for prehistoric high cultures with large populations (Parsons 1969; Siemens 1980; Turner 1974), segments of which were engaged in government, craft production, trade, and other nonagricultural activities. Latin America has also provided opportunities to ex-

Annals of the Association of American Geographers. 82(3), 1992, pp. 386–401
© Copyright 1992 by Association of American Geographers

amine how indigenous people used pre-industrial tools and techniques to coax a livelihood from marginal or fragile habitats (Wilken 1987; Browder 1989).

By comparison, relatively few geographers have studied pre-Contact agriculture in North America. Almost all knowledge of this topic comes from archaeological work beginning in the nineteenth century (Lapham 1855, Bandelier 1890–92). Virtually thousands of subsequent projects have resulted in the collection of an impressive body of data on cultigens (Ford 1985) and agricultural landforms (Glassow 1980). But there are important shortcomings in understanding indigenous North American agriculture, reflecting the traditional preoccupation of archaeology with sites and the limited participation by geographers, who are particularly skilled in dealing with the spatial components and dynamics of land use and agroecology.

First, data were collected largely as a by-product of projects with other goals (see Haury 1976); few archaeologists focus primarily on food production. Second, archaeological evidence of agriculture frequently consists of plant remains encountered during site excavations or pollen of cultigens found while examining sediments for evidence of environmental change (Struever 1968); too much importance was placed on crops and far too little on the fields that must have produced them. Third, those studies of relict agricultural features and landforms that have been conducted were designed mainly to understand how such features fit into the broader social, political, and economic structures of the culture (see Vivian 1990), not for their inherent human-environmental or spatial implications. Fourth, ethnographic analogs from surviving indigenous Americans were often accepted uncritically, so that their applications may have been faulty (Cordell and Plog 1979; Sullivan 1982). Fifth, and perhaps most important, few syntheses have been attempted, and such efforts have tended to be overgeneralized (Hurt 1987).

As a result, many scholars and lay readers alike have an oversimplified image of native agriculture at the time when Europeans first set foot on North America. A common scenario envisions agriculture as "extensive" in the humid Eastern Woodlands, involving mainly slash-and-burn shifting cultivation and producing relatively low yields per unit area, and "intensive" in the arid Southwest, requiring irrigation to overcome moisture deficits and produce relatively high yields per unit area (e.g., Butzer 1990, 45). To be sure, these forms of agriculture were practiced in the respective areas. But they were not necessarily the most common nor the most important practices. Such a simple dichotomy between agricultural practices or levels of agricultural intensity belies the biophysical diversity of both regions, and reflects the underinvolvement of geographers.

This paper has a threefold purpose. First, it argues that the agroecological landscapes of both the Southwest and Eastern Woodlands were quite complex in response to mosaics of diverse biophysical environments. This is demonstrated by discussing five general types of agricultural methods, or types of fields and related features, that were in use at Contact and which are elucidated here. Second, it demonstrates that intensive practices were as common in the East as in the Southwest. Third, it identifies gaps in our understanding and suggests some problems for further exploration.

Published accounts of early European expeditions, such as the Gentleman of Elvas's (1946) chronicle of Hernando De Soto's travels, constitute the principal data relied upon here. Such evidence is, of course, imperfect. Some areas, such as the Atlantic coast, were visited repeatedly and reported on in detail, whereas others, for instance the Ohio Valley, were seen and described less frequently. Similarly, areas such as the Southwest were visited early, before fundamental cultural changes took place, whereas others, including the Plains, were visited late, after native populations had been reduced by disease and had acquired European tools, techniques, and crops. Beyond such spatial and temporal discrepancies, the descriptions also exhibit biases. Europeans experienced philosophical, cultural, and linguistic difficulties in comprehending and discussing much of what they encountered in what to them was truly a New World (Franklin 1979).

Although the published documentation has its shortcomings, it is of sufficient quality that one prominent geographer, Carl Sauer (1971, 1980), was able to use it in reconstructing the continent's environments and land use during the sixteenth and seventeenth centuries. Many of the reports certainly contain descriptions of indigenous agriculture that seem to be accurate. Areas much visited and described by Europeans were places where agriculture was an important way of life to the Indians; areas less visited and described tended to be regions where agriculture was not important. Confronted by unfamiliar phenomena such as maize and digging stick cultivation, the explorers typically went to great lengths to provide meticulously detailed descriptions. Accounts by various writers also tend to corroborate each other. On the whole, the early European accounts provide a valuable source of information about indigenous American agriculture during the early Contact period. Those written in languages other than English have been translated a sufficient number of times to extract their original meanings. When the explorers' descriptions are examined as a whole, a fairly complete and accurate picture of pre-European agriculture on the continent begins to come into focus. In those cases

where documentary data are lacking, but archaeological data are available, the latter are used. Bearing in mind these considerations, I examine the native agricultural landscape of North America at the time of the European encounter.

The Southwest

Native agriculture in the Southwest at and before Contact has been considered "intensive," requiring considerable labor or substantial landscape modification, because the biophysical environments are envisioned as so harsh and rugged that there is little land suitable for cultivation. Two types of land are characteristic of the southwestern agricultural landscape, (a) the floodplains of low-lying desert streams, with deep and fertile soils that are highly localized, and (b) upland slopes, where rainfall may be sufficient but soils are thin and of poor quality. To cope with these conditions,

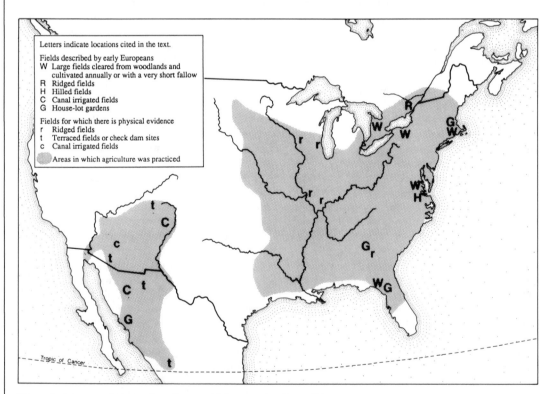

Figure 1. Patterns of Native American agriculture at the time of European contact.

natives of the Southwest employed canal irrigation, terraces, and checkdams (Fig. 1).

Irrigation

Archaeologists interested in indigenous subsistence in the American Southwest and northwestern Mexico have long focused their attention on canals, which are found in numerous places and may have rich histories. Physical evidence of canal irrigation in that region dates back to as early as A.D. 130 (Henderson 1989, 194). Documentary evidence confirms that Indians were irrigating at the time of Contact, and ethnographic studies indicate that irrigation remains important for many of these people, including the Pima, Hopi, and Zuni. Although indigenous irrigation in the Southwest has been the subject of much study, and the function of gravity-flow canals seems straightforward, many subtleties need to be recognized or questions answered. One nuance and one gap in our understanding of irrigation will suffice as examples.

Early Spanish explorers did not report seeing irrigation in every part of the wider Southwest. Only two areas stood out by having canals worthy of mention, eastern Sonora and northern New Mexico (Fig. 1). Writing of people who inhabited valleys in the former area, Baltasar de Obregón, chronicler for Francisco de Ibarra, noted in 1565 that "their plantations are well provided with canals used for irrigating them" (Hammond and Rey 1928, 160). Antonio de Espejo reported that in 1582, people of the Río Grande pueblos had

> fields planted with corn, beans, calabashes, and tobacco (piciete) in abundance. These crops are seasonal, dependent on rainfall, or they are irrigated by means of good ditches (Hammond and Rey 1966, 220).

The irrigation systems described in these two accounts appear to be similar in form, but their functions were different, especially in respect to environmental conditions.

For the New Mexican pueblos, the growing season averages between 120–140 days, depending on locale. This is sufficient to raise a single crop. Since summer is the rainy season, irrigation was employed mainly to offset periodic dry spells. In eastern Sonora, by contrast, the growing season ranges from 220–260 days, or nearly twice as long. Much of the region's annual precipitation falls between July and September, but hardly any rain is received from March through June. Documentary evidence for Sonora indicates that two crops per year were grown (Doolittle 1988, 45). The later crop undoubtedly benefitted from irrigation, but the earlier one was totally dependent on it. Double cropping sustained a large number of people in eastern Sonora, and its dependence on canal irrigation required a level of social organization that may well have been more elaborate than that of the pueblos of New Mexico (C. Riley 1987, 39–96). Furthermore, it has been recently argued that the indigenous agricultural and social systems of eastern Sonora were sufficiently similar to those introduced by the Jesuits throughout northern Mexico that, following the massive societal problems resulting from introduced disease, they actually facilitated acculturation and contributed to the assimilation and eventual disappearance of the region's native people (Reff 1991, 249–71). This, of course, stands in stark contrast to events in New Mexico where pueblo Indians still retain their identity.

Indigenous irrigation systems in the Southwest evidently varied in their functional complexity. They also varied in scale and sustainability. Some canal networks were very large and others quite small. Some were used for relatively brief periods, while others functioned for long time spans. Is there a correlation between size and sustainability? The answer to this question is probably yes.

The prehistoric Hohokam people who lived in the Salt and Gila river valleys distinguished themselves by developing some very large canal irrigation systems (Fig. 2). Main canals ranged up to 10 m wide and 4 m deep. Some extended in length up to 30 km, had hundreds of smaller branch canals, and irrigated thousands of hectares (Masse 1981). Recent studies, conducted principally to mitigate the loss of sites during the construction of highways in the Phoenix area, have demonstrated that canals were affected by seasonal floods and that they were not all used contemporaneously (Ackerly et al. 1987). As maintenance problems increased, ancient people systematically abandoned one canal system, moved further away from the river, and constructed another (Howard and Huckleberry 1991). In many cases, sediment removed from canals during periodic

Figure 2. An ancient irrigation canal in the Park of Four Waters, Phoenix, Arizona. The spoil banks on each side of the canal are the largest prehistoric agricultural earthworks remaining in North America.

cleaning may have accumulated sufficiently to appear today as distinct mapping units (phases) on government soil surveys (Dart 1986). It is clear that the Hohokam struggled constantly to manage their hydraulic resources. They may have finally lost the battle, since their culture eventually collapsed.

In contrast, there are scores, if not hundreds, of small irrigation systems throughout the region. These have main canals that rarely exceed 10 km in length, 2 m in width, and 0.5 m in depth, and branch canals that provide water to a maximum of a few hundred hectares. Many of these systems, for example those associated with some of the pueblos in New Mexico, have remained in continuous use for at least several centuries (Tyler 1986). Others, such as some of those of eastern Sonora, may have been used without serious problems for upwards of 700 years (Doolittle 1988, 47). The remarkable durability of such irrigation systems has often been overlooked.

Terraces and Check Dams

The modification of slopes for agricultural purposes was neither widespread in North America prior to the arrival of Europeans, nor was it something that drew the attention of explorers. Physical evidence of slope modification is limited to the arid and mountainous southwestern quadrant of the continent (Fig. 1). There are no written accounts of the practice by the early chroniclers. In spite of their relatively limited spatial extent and their lack of mention by Spaniards who traversed the region in the sixteenth century, features known generally as terraces and check dams have significant implications.

A number of terms, including *trincheras* and linear borders, have been used in discussing slope modifications that involve rows of rocks placed in series perpendicular to slope (Woodbury 1961). A number of functions have been ascribed to these features (Woosley 1980;

Figure 3. Prehistoric agricultural terraces located on Mesa Verde, Colorado.

Di Peso 1984). In general, they fall into two classes, terraces and check dams. Terraces were built primarily to create level planting surfaces with deep, fertile soils that have high water-retention properties (Sandor, et al. 1986). They often have risers or facing walls that consist of several courses of rock stacked on each other, retaining sediment that either accumulated naturally or was carried in manually (Fig. 3). Some terraces are found on slopes of up to 20 percent, but others lie across the channels of intermittent streams in narrow, steep canyons, especially in higher elevations; some also cross the floors of broad valleys (Donkin 1979, 32–33). Check dams were built primarily to slow and spread runoff to protect fields downslope from excessive flooding and sediment deposition (Doolittle 1985). Also constructed of rocks stacked no more than a few courses high, check dams indirectly serve to trap sediment eroded from upslope. Check dams are found across the channels of all types of small intermittent streams.

At the time of Contact, terraces and check dams were especially common near the large site of Casas Grandes in Chihuahua, Mexico. Detailed studies of these features in, and on the flanks of, the Sierra Madre Occidental originally concluded that they were used between A.D. 1100–1450 (Herold 1965, 1). These dates, however, were based on affiliations with cultures that more recent studies have demonstrated were later than previously thought (Dean and Ravesloot forthcoming). In other parts of the Southwest, terraces and check dams are thought to be older, but the few systematic studies done to date suggest that such slope modifications were not uncommon in the few centuries immediately prior to the arrival of Europeans; no such features have been dated earlier than A.D. 1000.

The area of pre-Columbian slope modification in North America is large and diverse, both biologically and physically. Relict features have been found as far north as Mesa Verde in Southern Colorado (Rohn 1963), and as far south as the Rió Tunal in Durango, Mexico (Kelley 1956, 129). Although limited largely to the sierras and surrounding foothills, slope modification was also practiced as far west as the Sonoran Desert (Fish 1985). Terraces and check dams are found in environments ranging from pine forests in high elevations, with abundant rainfall and short growing seasons, to hot and dry locales only a few hundred meters above sea level. They are found on a variety of geological formations and soil types (Schmidt and Gerald 1988).

The idea that terraces and check dams built in diverse environments during pre-Contact times served a number of functions warrants more consideration than it has received. Some terraces clearly contributed to a remarkably sustainable subsistence base. The area in which remnants of ancient terraces are found remains the homeland of many indigenous people. In some cases, such as the Rarámuri (Tarahumar) and the Tepehuan, terraces used for the cultivation of food crops today appear to have been used continuously since before the arrival of Europeans (Pennington 1963, 48; 1969, 59). The mechanics and ecology whereby these fields have not been depleted of soil fertility remain unknown. Conversely, the reasons why long-abandoned terraces have not continued to be used need to be determined. Some ancient check dams may have alleviated runoff problems associated with agriculture, but some may also have helped control erosion on steep slopes, after trees were cut for building materials or fuel wood. Perhaps this explains why indigenous peoples of the Southwest are not usually considered agents of deforestation, even though populations were high and timber was in demand (C. Riley 1987; Betancourt et al. 1986). Some check dams may have facilitated the regeneration of forests by retaining soil that otherwise would have been eroded away. In that case, some check dams would have constituted critical components in a rudimentary form of tree farming, a practice corroborated by other evidence (Nichols and Smith 1965).

The Eastern Woodlands

Native agriculture in eastern North America has long been considered "extensive," probably because the biophysical environments are typically envisioned as expansive and homogeneous. Indeed, the term "woodlands" connotes a uniform environment and "eastern" refers to no less than half of the continent. In reality, the region is ecologically quite varied. For example, soils tend to be deep and fertile along rivers, but sometimes sandy with limited fertility on uplands. They also tend to be neutral in the north but acidic in the south. Temperatures also vary latitudinally, hence the growing season is barely sufficient to raise even one crop per year in parts of southeastern Canada, but is long enough to raise two crops annually in the south. Given this diversity, it is difficult to generalize about the agricultural landscape. There also is reason to question whether agriculture across the region typically was extensive; indeed, there is evidence of intensive practices in many areas.

Slash-and-Burn Shifting Cultivation?

Prevailing thought holds that shifting cultivation involving long fallows and slash-and-burn techniques was widespread, even dominant (e.g., Williams 1989, 39). Most authors who draw such conclusions rely almost exclusively on reports of native forest clearing. Frequently used is an account of 1612, written in Virginia by John Smith (1907, 95), which states that:

> The greatest labor they take, is in planting their corn, for the country is naturally overgrown with wood. To prepare the ground they bruise the bark of the trees neare the roote, then do they scortch the roots with fire that they grow no more.

The similarities with clearing tropical forests in the practice of shifting cultivation are evident (Ruthenberg 1976, 333), but absent in statements such as Smith's are references to field rotation, a key component in any shifting cultivation system. Granted, there are numerous references to field abandonment, but explanatory factors other than weed encroachment and decreases in fertility are frequently cited, including pest infestation (Elvas 1946, 173), and above all, depopulation due to diseases (Dermer 1905, 251), migration (Bradford and Winslow 1974, 59), or warfare (Champlain 1907, 203).

Fallowing is specifically mentioned in only a few documents, but such descriptions do not fit the normal picture of slash-and-burn shifting cultivation. Most such systems involve brief periods of cultivation, one to three years, followed by a longer period of fallow, more than twenty years. Early accounts of native North American agriculture, however, refer to cropping for extended periods of time, with very brief fallows. One case for long cultivation periods is reported by Francois du Peron (1898, 153), a Jesuit missionary, who wrote on Huronia in 1639, that:

> the land . . . produces for only ten or twelve years at most; and when ten years have expired, they are obliged to move their village to another place.

An example of short fallow comes from Samuel de Champlain (1907, 71), who noted that around Boston Bay in 1605:

> there were also several fields entirely uncultivated, the land being allowed to remain fallow. When they wish to plant it, they set fire to the weeds, and then work it over with their wooden spades.

The key point here is *weed-covered* fallowed land, contradicting the notion that forests were cleared for long-fallow shifting cultivation.

Early European accounts of indigenous North American agriculture differ from descriptions of present-day slash-and-burn cultivation in at least two other aspects, the degree of clearing and the size of fields. Typically, slash-and-burn fields have stumps left in the fields, and they are small, less than a few hectares in extent. Yet several early observers (Champlain 1907, 92, Smith 1907, 95) reported that after the forest was cut and burned and the fields planted, stumps of the remaining trees were eventually dug up and removed. Equally so there are reports of very large fields. Writing of Florida in 1539, Garcilaso de la Vega (1951, 182), one of De Soto's chroniclers, noted for example that:

> the Spaniards marched on through some great fields of corn, beans, and squash and other vegetables which had been sown on both sides of the road and were spread out as far as the eye could see across two leagues of plain.

Taken in their totality, the accounts do not portray a typical scenario of extensive shifting cultivation involving slash-and-burn techniques (Woods 1987). References to complete clearing, long periods of cultivation, and large fields, all point to a system of agriculture that approaches annual cultivation: the mention of weed burning suggests that fallows were very short. Intercropping and the rotation of maize and beans can compensate for a lack of manure and facilitate nearly continuous cultivation (Francis, et al. 1978). References to the girdling, cutting, and burning of trees indicate forest clearance, but do not necessarily support the case for long-fallow, shifting cultivation. Instead, early writers repeatedly referred to how difficult it was for Indians to clear the forest. As Gabriel Sagard-Theodat (1964, 8) wrote of the Iroquois in 1623, "clearing is very troublesome for them, since they have no proper tools."

Recently Denevan (1991) has posited that long-fallow slash-and-burn agriculture in the Amazon Basin was a post-Spanish practice, adopted only when metal axes were made available. He argues that because it was so difficult to clear forests with stone tools, farmers maintained fields for long periods of time before abandoning them. The same appears to be true in North America. Detailed first-hand accounts of unambiguous, long-fallow, slash-and-burn agriculture practiced by Native Americans are late, from the eighteenth century (Kalm 1972, 299–300). Such accounts may well reflect what has been called "disintensification" (Brookfield 1972), in response to native depopulation, or the cultivation of previously little-used, marginal upland environments, to which indigenous people were relegated after European settlers took over fertile bottom lands (Jordan and Kaups 1989, 100–05, 127–29). It is unlikely that agricultural changes were linked to climate, which did not change significantly during this period. In sum, agriculture in the Eastern Woodlands of North America ca. 1492 appears to have been more intensive than is commonly thought (Fig. 1), an alternative hypothesis that warrants further study, following several possible lines of evidence. One of these is systematic attention to old agricultural landforms.

Raised Fields

Support for the argument that agriculture in eastern North America at the time of European contact was relatively intensive is supported by relict raised fields in diverse parts of the region (Fig. 1). Raised fields are agricultural landforms constructed by piling earth, excavated nearby, into hills, platforms, or ridges. Typical raised fields of the ridged variety are found in series, separated by canals or furrows, not unlike a giant wash board. Studies conducted in other parts of the world, where ridged fields remain in use, show that such features involve much labor, produce large yields, and are normally used in environments marginal for agriculture (e.g., Waddell 1972).

Documentary evidence that ridged fields were used in North America ca. 1492 is scant, although one account contains a wealth of information. Writing of Quebec in 1749, Peter Kalm (1972, 421–22) noted:

> that there were many great plains destitute of trees, where the land was furrowed, as if it had been ploughed. In what manner this happened no one knows, for the corn-fields of a great village, or town, of the *Indians* are scarce above four or six of our acres in extent; whereas those furrowed plains sometimes continue for several days journey.

Although Kalm's description is rather late, the reference to a different set of fields under cultivation at the time implies earlier abandonment of ridged field cultivation (see also Kalm 1972, 218). Archaeological research confirms such a conclusion. Numerous vestiges of ridged fields have been revealed by excavation through much of the Great Lakes area (Fox 1959), in the Ohio and Mississippi river valleys (Muller 1986, 196; Gallagher et al. 1985), and in at least one case in the Southeast (Kelly 1938, 10, 69, 70). Such ridged fields have been specifically dated as early as A.D. 1000 (Peske 1966) and as late as the fifteenth century (Gallagher 1989).

Different explanations have been offered for the purposes or advantages offered by such ridged fields. It has been argued that some were constructed in order to expand cultivation into wetlands, by elevating planting surfaces or a waterlogged subsoil above the water surface (Fowler 1969). Others, particularly those on well-drained uplands between the 120–150-day frost-free isograms, may have been built to raise the planting surface and reduce frost hazards from cold air drainage and collection; this would also extend the growing season (Riley and Freimuth 1979). On a more comprehensive level, other authors argue that ridging may have served several tillage functions, such as thickening or replenishing topsoil along planting lines (Gallagher and Sasso 1987). More work evidently needs to be done in order to better understand the ecology of these fields.

Beyond the function of ridged fields, there also are questions about origin, cultural affiliation, and abandonment. Similarities with ridged fields in parts of South America have prompted suggestions that North American ridged fields involved technology that was diffused through the Caribbean, into the Southeast, and then into the Midwest (T. Riley 1987). The discovery of prehistoric ridged fields in northern Veracruz, Mexico (Siemens 1989), suggests alternative contacts, if indeed diffusion is a preferred hypothesis. More important than origins, however, are sociocultural associations, since relict ridged fields are found in those parts of the continent inhabited by peoples long identified by monumental earthworks, a correlation that has simply been too easy to pass up (see Fowler 1969). Chronological data certainly confirm the association, but an interesting geographical question remains. If the ridged fields were constructed by the various mound-building people, why have ridged fields not been reported in proximity to many of the large sites, such as Seip Mound, Ohio and Moundville, Alabama? Some such sites are surrounded by low-lying, often inundated, lands that are marginal for agriculture. They appear to have involved large populations, yet not a single trace of a raised field has been archaeologically confirmed in the vicinity of some major sites, whereas they are present near other, less spectacular mound sites in the Midwest.

Related to the question of fields in association with sites is the special problem of the Ocmulgee mounds at Macon, Georgia. There, archaeologists accidentally discovered remnants of ridged fields on well-drained hills *under* an earthen pyramid (Kelly 1938). The superposition of the pyramid indicates that ridged fields were not used *on* the site when the pyramids were in use. But, were they used in areas surrounding the site, especially the floodplain of the river? When he passed the site in 1773, William Bartram (1940, 68) noted that:

> On the east banks of the Oakmulge, this trading road runs nearly two miles through ancient Indian fields, which are called the Oakmulge fields: they are the rich low lands of the river . . . .Their old fields and planting land extend up and down the river, fifteen or twenty miles from the site.

Unfortunately, Bartram did not describe the topographical characteristics of the fields, but given that ridged fields were used in the area earlier, it is possible that the fields he saw were ridged.

For many known mound sites, the lack of ridged fields may be more a result of poor research design than reality: a function of not searching systematically. Scholars working in

Figure 4. Ancient corn hills on the campus of Carroll College, Waukesha, Wisconsin, 1902. Source: State Historical Society of Wisconsin, used by permission.

eastern North America have tended to assume that vestiges of ancient fields were destroyed by more recent human activities. To be sure, historic erosion on uplands and accompanying sedimentation of low-lying areas (Trimble 1974), in addition to present-day cultivation practices, have obscured many old native fields. But there is perhaps no place that has been as intensively worked over for so long as England, yet prehistoric agricultural features remain most evident on the landscape there today. Perhaps we have been remiss with prospecting in this country, especially given available remote sensing capabilities.

Many early writers have described the mounding of soil into hills—as opposed to ridging—on native North American fields (Fig. 4). In reference to indigenous cultivation practices in Virginia in 1609, Marc Lescarbot (1977, 274) wrote:

> they heape their ground in small heapes two foote distant one from another . . . they set their Corne in those heapes of earth as wee doe plant beans.

Individual, small mounds such as these are sufficiently distinct from ridged fields, but potentially different functions of fields with different topographical expression has yet to be determined. As a working hypothesis, it can be suggested that mounded fields are associated with regular dry farming, while the latter are most commonly linked with the specific cultivation of wet or cold micro-habitats. It is curious that hilling or mounding continued to be widespread during the post-Contact period whereas ridging was abandoned. To date, only one scholar has addressed this question (Gallagher forthcoming). His tentative explanation is also limited to disintensification resulting from population decline: ridging was abandoned because it was labor intensive, requiring a large population, while hilling or mounding involved little work and few people. At first glance, this argument seems plausible. Nonetheless, many of the explorers who noted corn planted on mounded beds also described very large fields, that both supported and required large populations. This inconsistency begs resolution.

Gardens Everywhere

A number of geographers are interested in house-lot or dooryard gardens, one of the most intensive forms of agriculture. For the most part, they are biogeographers (Kimber 1966) or cultural geographers (Herlihy 1984), who focus on tropical regions with a high diversity of plants and have limited their discussion to modern contexts. Given this regional and temporal focus, the existence and importance of gardens in North America before and at the time of Contact has been underappreciated. This is surprising since dooryard-type gardens were used in the Southwest by 2000 B.C. (Woodbury and Zubrow 1979, 44), earlier still in the Eastern Woodlands (Fowler 1971, 125–26), and some special forms are still used by Native Americans today (Fig. 5).

Documentary descriptions of gardens are early, numerous, and come from most parts of the continent (Fig. 1). These accounts, though uneven in the amount of information provided, indicate that small household plots were intensive, botanically diverse, and culturally and economically important. They also varied from place to place. For example, writing about Plymouth Harbor in 1603, Martin Pring (1905, 58–59) noted that near the houses of natives "we beheld their Gardens and one among the rest of an Acre of ground, and in the same was sowne Tobacco, Pompions, Cowcumbers and such." In discussing indigenous people of southern Sonora between 1617–19, Andrés Pérez de Ribas (1944, 150) wrote that "they used to plant next to their houses a kind of vineyard of a plant that the Spaniards call lechuguilla, because its form resembles that of lettuce." Further information in the same document suggests that the plant described is agave (Dobyns 1988, 50).

In addition to gardens in proximity to dwellings, several documents mention fields located

Figure 5. A house-lot garden at Zuni Pueblo, New Mexico. Only two of these famous so-called "waffle gardens" remain today.

at some distance. Two cases serve as illustrations. Describing conditions in Florida in 1563, Jean Ribaut (1927, 73) wrote:

> About there howses they laboure and till there ground, sowing there fildes with a grayn called Mahis, whereof the[y] make there meale, and in their gardens the[y] plant beans, gourds, cowekcumbers, citrons, peasen, and many other simples and rootes unknon to us.

William Bartram (1940, 169) wrote of native peoples in the Southeast in 1773 that:

> They plant but little here about the town; only a small garden plot at each habitation, consisting of a little Corn, Beans, Tobacco, Citruls, &c. Their plantation, which supplies them with the chief of their vegetable provisions, such as Zea, Convolvulus batata, Cucurbita citrulus, Cuc. lagenaria, Cuc. pepo, Cuc. melopepo, Cuc. verrucosa, Dolichos varieties, &c. lies on the rich prolific lands bordering on the great Alachua savanna about two miles distant.

Although these accounts are similar in some respects, there is fundamental difference. Ribaut indicates vegetables were grown in residential gardens, while the staple grain was grown in distant fields; Bartram, on the other hand, reveals that many of the crops grown in large fields were also grown in small plots near houses.

The first situation, involving spatial zonation, was probably a function of variable labor inputs and yields per unit area. The documents thus suggest spatial gradients of agricultural intensification (see Chisholm 1968). Although geographers interested in modeling the economies of agricultural land use practices tend to focus on modern, mechanized systems, more might also be learned about the patterning of farming activities from early documentary accounts of indigenous cultivation.

The second case, involving crop redundancy, may reflect a strategy to insure against crop losses in consecutive years. House-lot gardens as small as those described clearly cannot produce a sufficient amount of food to feed many people. Large fields are essential, but they are much more susceptible to crop failures than gardens. Field problems include frosts, pests, droughts, and even human destruction. Gardens, on the other hand, not only reduce risk by greater crop diversity, but they can also be protected and the individual plants nurtured. For example birds can be frightened away, plants can be hand-watered or covered to avoid frost damage, while soils can be fertilized with household wastes. As a result of the care that gardens tend to receive, a dependable seed crop can be produced each year. Even if a field crop was totally destroyed, the garden could provide seed for next year's planting (Fish et al. 1983, 69–70). These notions are provisional, but they offer interesting perspectives for further attention.

Numerous documentary accounts refer to indigenous people transplanting crops from seed beds located within residential gardens (Lindestrom 1925, 181, Lafitau 1974, 55). It is reasonable to assume that Native American cultivators prior to 1492 employed a strategy of seed production in gardens.

Conclusions

The early European explorers provided numerous descriptions of North America and its indigenous inhabitants. These accounts have long been used to reconstruct scenarios of ancient native lifeways. Unfortunately, the passages that focus on food production systems have been considered somewhat casually by scholars whose concern is with culture history; they have been little scrutinized by scholars primarily interested in agriculture. As a result, highly generalized visions of cultivation have been offered and accepted as truth. In reality, we do not know as much about North American Indian agriculture at the time of the great cultural encounter as we have led ourselves to believe. This is especially true in regard to regional characterizations, which tend to be overly simplistic; native practices were more complex than the convenient formula of intensive in the Southwest and extensive in the Eastern Woodlands.

This paper provides a sample of the numerous, diverse, and complex ways in which this continent's inhabitants were able to modify their biophysical environments, in order to sustain themselves. The materials and arguments here also show that, by A.D. 1492, these people had developed highly complex agricultural systems. Native North American farmers took advantage of environmental opportunities and found ways to compensate for or overcome environmental shortcomings. As the evidence of irrigation and terracing in the Southwest shows, each system had nuances that most scholars have not considered. Indeed, they probably had some characteristics that await discovery.

In addition to its ecological components, agriculture practiced by Indians across the continent also reflected social and economic factors. The intensity of agriculture did vary from place to place, at the time of Contact, as well as before and after. In part, such differences were a function of local variations in the demand for food. Agricultural intensity was usually high in places where populations were dense and where some portion of the population was engaged in activities other than subsistence farming. Conversely, intensity was low in less densely inhabited places. As descriptions provided by explorers in the Eastern Woodlands show, agricultural practices tended to be intensive; extensive agriculture merited little mention.

The social and economic aspects of native North American agriculture also had a spatial component that has been neglected. As is seen in the accounts of gardens, agriculture was more intensive near houses and towns than in more distant locales. Theories applied to modern agricultural land use may help explain this phenomenon (Henshall 1967). Future studies of indigenous American agriculture may also contribute insights for land use theory: the documentary evidence, in combination with ethnographic and archaeological data, provides a temporal dimension that would allow modeling of long-term change.

The study of how inhabitants of this continent produced food prior to the arrival of Old World domesticates and technology also is important in cultural ecological terms. Many of the agricultural systems described in early ethnological documents had been in use for centuries. In some cases they continue to be used. Archaeological data show that many prehistoric systems functioned for several hundred years, but were eventually abandoned for reasons yet to be understood. The evidence suggests that some agricultural systems were, over extended periods, incompatible with long-term ecological equilibrium. Lessons remain to be learned from both the past successes and failures of this continent's native farmers.

Acknowledgments

The research on which this paper is based was funded by a grant from the National Endowment for the Humanities (RO-21458-87), and a Faculty Research Assignment Award of the University Research Institute of the University of Texas at Austin. I thank all the students who, in 1987 and 1990, participated in my graduate seminars on North American agriculture in 1492, especially Michael D. Myers, B. J. Perkins, and Michael D. Pool.

References

Ackerly, Neal W.; Howard, Jerry B.; and McGuire, Randall H. 1987. *La Ciudad canals: A study of Hohokam irrigation systems at the community level.* Anthropological Field Studies 17. Tempe: Arizona State University.

Bandelier, A. F. 1890–92. *Final report of investigations among the Indians of the southwestern United States carried on mainly in the years from 1880 to 1885.* Papers of the Archaeological Institute of America, Americana Series 3 and 4. Cambridge, MA.

Bartram, William. 1940. *The travels of William Bartram,* ed. Mark Van Doren. New York: Facsimile Library.

Betancourt, Julio L.; Dean, Jeffrey S.; and Hull, Herbert M. 1986. Prehistoric long-distance transport of construction beams, Chaco Canyon, New Mexico. *American Antiquity* 51:370–75.

Bradford, William, and Winslow, Edward. 1974. *A relation . . . of the beginning and proceedings of the English plantation settled at Plimoth in New England.* Norwood, MA: Walter J. Johnson, Inc.

Brookfield, H. C. 1972. Intensification and disintensification in Pacific agriculture: A theoretical approach. *Pacific Viewpoint* 13:30–48.

Browder, John O. 1989. *Fragile lands of Latin America: Strategies for sustainable development.* Boulder, CO: Westview Press.

Butzer, Karl W. 1990. The Indian legacy in the American landscape. In *The Making of the American Landscape,* ed. Michael P. Conzen, pp. 27–50. Boston: Unwin Hyman.

Champlain, Samuel de. 1907. *Voyages of Samuel de Champlain,* ed. W. L. Grant. New York: Charles Scribner's Sons.

Chisholm, Michael. 1968. *Rural settlement and land use: An essay in location.* London: Hutchinson University Library.

Cordell, Linda S., and Plog, Fred. 1979. Escaping the confines of normative thought: A reevaluation of Puebloan prehistory. *American Antiquity* 44:405–29.

Dart, Allen. 1986. Sediment accumulation along Hohokam canals. *The Kiva* 51:63–84.

Dean, Jeffrey S., and Ravesloot, John C. Forthcoming. The chronology of cultural interaction in the Gran Chichimeca. In *Culture and contact: Charles C. DiPeso's Gran Chichimeca,* ed. Anne I. Woosley and John C. Ravesloot. Albuquerque: University of New Mexico Press.

Denevan, William M. 1991. Stone vs. steel: Was

shifting cultivation a post-European Amazon adaptation? Paper presented at the annual meeting of the Association of American Geographers, Miami.

————; **Mathewson, Kent; and Knapp, Gregory,** eds. 1987. *Pre-Hispanic agricultural fields in the Andean region.* International Series 359 (i). Oxford: British Archaeological Reports.

Dermer, Thomas. 1905. To his worshipful friend M. Samual Purchas, preacher of the Word, at the Church a little within Ludgate, London. In *Sailors' narratives of voyages along the New England coast, 1524–1564,* ed. George Parker Winship, pp. 249–58. New York: Burt Franklin.

DiPeso, Charles C. 1984. The structure of the eleventh century Casas Grandes agricultural system. In *Prehistoric agricultural strategies in the Southwest,* ed. Suzanne K. Fish and Paul R. Fish, pp. 261–69. Anthropological Research Papers 33. Tempe: Arizona State University.

Dobyns, Henry F. 1988. Pima Indian historic agave cultivation. *Desert Plants* 2:49–53.

Donkin, R. A. 1979. *Agricultural terracing in the New World.* Viking Fund Publications in Anthropology 56. Tucson: University of Arizona Press for the Wenner-Gren Foundation for Anthropological Research.

Doolittle, William E. 1984. Agricultural change as an incremental process. *Annals of the Association of American Geographers* 74:124–37.

————. 1985. The use of check dams for protecting downstream agricultural lands in the prehistoric Southwest: A contextual analysis. *Journal of Anthropological Research* 41:279–305.

————. 1988. *Pre-Hispanic occupance in the Valley of Sonora, Mexico: Archaeological confirmation of early Spanish reports.* Anthropological Papers of the University of Arizona 48. Tucson.

Elvas, the Gentleman of. 1946. The narrative of the expedition of Hernando de Soto. In *Spanish explorers in the southern United States 1528–1543,* ed. Theodore H. Lewis, pp. 127–272. New York: Barnes and Noble.

Fish, Suzanne K. 1985. Prehistoric disturbance floras of the Lower Sonoran Desert and their implications. In *Late Quaternary vegetation and climates of the American Southwest,* ed. Bonnie F. Jacobs, Patricia L. Fall, and Owen K. Davis, pp. 77–88. Contribution Series 16. Tucson: American Association of Stratigraphic Palynologists.

————; **Fish, Paul R.; and Downum, Christian.** 1983. Hohokam terraces and agricultural production in the Tucson Basin. In *Prehistoric agricultural strategies in the Southwest,* ed. Suzanne K. Fish and Paul R. Fish, pp. 55–72. Anthropological Research Papers 33. Tempe: Arizona State University.

Ford, Richard I., ed. 1985. *Prehistoric food production in North America.* Anthropological Papers

75. Ann Arbor: University of Michigan Museum of Anthropology.

Fowler, Melvin. 1969. Middle Mississippian agricultural fields. *American Antiquity* 34:365–75.

————. 1971. The origin of plant cultivation in the central Mississippi valley: A hypothesis. In *Prehistoric agriculture,* ed. Stuart Struever, pp. 122–28. Garden City, NY: Natural History Press.

Fox, George R. 1959. The prehistoric garden beds of Wisconsin and Michigan and the Fox Indians. *The Wisconsin Archaeologist* 40:1–19.

Francis, C. A.; Prager, M.; and Laing, D. R. 1978. Genotype by environment interactions in climbing bean varieties in monoculture and associated with maize. *Crop Science* 18:242–46.

Franklin, Wayne. 1979. *Discoverers, explorers, settlers: The diligent writers of early America.* Chicago: University of Chicago Press.

Gallagher, James P. 1989. Agricultural intensification and ridged-field cultivation in the prehistoric upper Midwest of North America. In *Foraging and farming: The evolution of plant exploitation,* ed. David R. Harris and Gordon C. Hillman, pp. 572–84. London: Unwin and Hyman.

————. Forthcoming. Prehistoric field systems in the upper Midwest. In *Late prehistoric agriculture: Observations from the Midwest,* ed. William I. Woods. Studies in Illinois Archaeology 7. Springfield: Illinois Historic Preservation Agency.

————; **Boszhardt, Robert F.; Sasso, Robert F.; and Stevenson, Katherine.** 1985. Oneota ridged field agriculture in southwestern Wisconsin. *American Antiquity* 50:605–12.

———— **and Sasso, Robert F.** 1987. Investigations into Oneota ridged field agriculture on the northern margin of the prairie peninsula. *Plains Anthropologist* 32:141–51.

Garcilaso de la Vega, I. 1980 [1605]. *The Florida of the Inca: A history of the adelantado Hernando de Soto.* Trans. and ed. John Grier Varner and Jeanette Johnson Varner. Austin: University of Texas Press.

Glassow, Michael A. 1980. *Prehistoric agricultural development in the northern Southwest: A study in changing patterns of land use.* Anthropological Papers 16. Socorro, NM: Bellena Press.

Hammond, George P., and Rey, Agapito, trans. and eds. 1928. *Obregón's history of sixteenth century explorations in western America.* Los Angeles: Wetzel Publishing Co.

———— **and ————, trans. and eds.** 1966. *The discovery of New Mexico 1580–1594: The explorations of Chamuscado, Espejo, Castaño de Sosa, Morlete, and Leyva de Bonilla and Humaña.* Albuquerque: University of New Mexico Press.

Haury, Emil W. 1976. *The Hohokam: Desert farmers and craftsman, excavations at Shaketown 1964–1965.* Tucson: University of Arizona Press.

Henderson, T. Kathleen. 1989. The chronology of the Las Acequias canals. In *Prehistoric agricultural activities on the Lehi-Mesa terrace: Perspectives on Hohokam irrigation cycles,* ed. Neal W. Ackerly and T. Kathleen Henderson, pp. 184–99. Flagstaff, AZ: Northland Research Inc.

Henshall, Janet D. 1967. Models of agricultural activity. In *Models in geography,* ed. Richard J. Chorley and Peter Haggett, pp. 425–58. London: Methuen and Co.

Herlihy, Peter H. 1984. The Maya dooryard orchard-garden: An ancient and contemporary agricultural system. Paper presented at annual meeting of the Conference of Latin Americanist Geographers, Ottawa, Canada.

Herold, Laurance C. 1965. *Trincheras and physical environment along the Río Gavilan, Chihuahua, Mexico.* Department of Geography, Publications in Geography, Technical Paper 65-1. Denver: University of Denver.

Howard, Jerry B., and Huckleberry, Gary. 1991. *The operation and evolution of an irrigation system: The East Papago canal study.* Phoenix: Soil Systems Publications in Archaeology 18.

Hurt, R. Douglas. 1987. *Indian agriculture in America: Prehistory to the present.* Lawrence: University Press of Kansas.

Johannessen, Carl L. 1966. The domestication process in trees reproduced by seed: The Pejibaye palm in Costa Rica. *Geographical Review* 56:363–76.

Johnston, Kirsten. 1977. Disintegration of a traditional resource-use complex: The Otomí of the Mezquital Valley, Hidalgo, Mexico. *Economic Geography* 53:364–67.

Jordan, Terry G., and Kaups, Matti. 1989. *The American backwoods frontier: An ethnic and ecological interpretation.* Baltimore: Johns Hopkins University Press.

Kalm, Peter. 1972. *Travels into North America,* trans. John R. Forster. Barre, VT: Imprint Society.

Kelley, J. Charles. 1956. Settlement patterns in North-central Mexico. In *Prehistoric settlement patterns in the New World,* ed. Gordon R. Willey, pp. 128–39. Viking Fund Publications in Anthropology 23. New York.

Kelly, A. R. 1938. *A preliminary report on archaeological explorations at Macon, GA.* Smithsonian Institution Bureau of American Ethnology, Bulletin 119. Washington.

Kimber, Clarissa T. 1966. Dooryard gardens of Martinique. *Yearbook of the Association of Pacific Coast Geographers* 28:97–118.

Lafitau, Joseph Francois. 1974. *Customs of the American Indians compared with the customs of the primitive times,* ed. and trans. William N. Fenton and Elizabeth L. Moore. Toronto: Champlain Society.

Lapham, I. A. 1855. *The antiquities of Wisconsin.* Washington: Smithsonian Institution.

Lescarbot, Marc. 1977. *Nova Francia.* Norwood, NJ: Walter J. Johnson.

Lindestrom, Peter. 1925. *Geographia Americae with an account of the Delaware Indians based on surveys and notes made in 1654–1656,* trans. Amandus Johnson. Philadelphia: Swedish Colonial Society.

Masse, Bruce W. 1981. Prehistoric irrigation systems in the Salt River valley, Arizona. *Science* 214:408–15.

Muller, Jon. 1986. *Archaeology of the lower Ohio river valley.* Orlando, FL: Academic Press.

Nichols, Robert F., and Smith, David G. 1965. Evidence of prehistoric cultivation of Douglas-fir trees at Mesa Verde. In *Contributions of the Wetherill Mesa archaeological project,* assembled by Douglas Osborne, pp. 57–64. Salt Lake City: *Memoirs of the Society for American Archaeology* 19.

Parsons, James J. 1969. Ridged fields in the Río Guayas Valley, Ecuador. *American Antiquity* 34:76–80.

Pennington, Campbell W. 1963. *The Tarahumar of Mexico: Their environment and material culture.* Salt Lake City: University of Utah Press.

———. 1969. *The Tepehuan of Chihuahua: Their material culture.* Salt Lake City: University of Utah Press.

Pérez de Ribas, Andrés. 1944. Triunfos de nuestra santa fé entre gentes las más bárbaras y fieras del Nuevo Orbe consequidos por los soldados de la milicia de la Compañía de Jesus en las misiones de la provincia de Nueva España. Mexico City: Editoral Layac.

Peron, Francois du. 1898. Letter of Father Francois du Peron of the Society of Jesus, to Father Joseph Imbert du Peron, his Brother, religious of the same society. In *The Jesuit Relations and Allied Documents,* ed. Reuben Gold Thwaites, pp. 149–89. Cleveland: Burrows Brothers.

Peske, G. R. 1966. Oneota settlement patterns and agricultural patterns in Winnebago County. *The Wisconsin Archaeologist* 47:188–95.

Pring, Martin. 1905. Plymouth Harbor. In *Sailors narratives of voyages along the New England coast: 1524–1624,* ed. George Parker Winship, pp. 51–63. New York: Burt Franklin.

Reff, Daniel T. 1991. *Disease, depopulation, and cultural change in northwestern New Spain, 1518–1764.* Salt Lake City: University of Utah Press.

Ribaut, Jean. 1927. *The whole & true discouerye of terra Florida.* Deland, FL: Florida State Historical Society.

Riley, Carroll L. 1987. *The frontier people: The greater Southwest in the protohistoric period.* Albuquerque: University of New Mexico Press.

Riley, Thomas J. 1987. Ridged-field agriculture and the Mississippian economic pattern. In *Emergent horticultural economies of the Eastern Woodlands,* ed. William F. Keegan, pp. 295–304. Occasional Paper 7. Carbondale: Southern Illinois University, Center for Archaeological Investigations.

—— **and Freimuth, Glen.** 1979. Field systems and frost drainage in the prehistoric agriculture of the upper Great Lakes. *American Antiquity* 44:271–85.

Rohn, Arthur H. 1963. Prehistoric soil and water conservation on Chapin Mesa, southwestern Colorado. *American Antiquity* 28:441–55.

Ruthenberg, Hans. 1976. *Farming systems in the tropics.* Oxford: Clarendon Press.

Sagard-Theodat, Gabriel. 1964. Sagard-Theodat's description of Iroquoian agriculture. In *The valley of the six nations: A collection of documents on the Indian lands of the Grand River,* ed. Charles M. Johnson, pp. 7–11. Toronto: University of Toronto Press.

Sandor, J. A.; Gersper, P. L.; and Hawley, J. W. 1986. Soils at prehistoric agricultural terracing sites in New Mexico: 1. Site placement, soil morphology, and classification. *Soil Science Society of America Journal* 50:166–73.

Sauer, Carl Ortwin. 1971. *Sixteenth century North America: The land and the people as seen by the Europeans.* Berkeley: University of California Press.

——. 1980. *Seventeenth-Century North America.* Berkeley: Turtle Island.

Schmidt, Robert H., and Gerald, Rex E. 1988. The distribution of conservation-type water-control systems in the northern Sierra Madre Occidental. *The Kiva* 53:165–79.

Siemens, Alfred H. 1980. Indicios de aprovechamiento agrícola prehispánico de tierras inundables en el centro de Veracruz. *Biotica* 5:83–92.

——. 1989. *Tierra configurada: Investigaciones de los vestigios de agricultura precolumbina en tierras inundables costeras desde el norte de Veracruz hasta Belice.* Mexico City: Consejo Nacional para la Cultura y las Artes.

Smith, John. 1907. Description of Virginia and proceedings of the colonie. In *Narratives of early Virginia,* ed. Lyon Gardiner Tyler, pp. 73–204. New York: Charles Scribner's Sons.

Stevens, Richard, and Lee, Yuk. 1979. A spatial analysis of agricultural intensity in a Basotho village of southern Africa. *The Professional Geographer* 31:177–83.

Struever, Stuart. 1968. Woodland subsistence-settlement systems in the lower Illinois Valley. In *New perspectives in archaeology,* ed. Sally R. Binford and Lewis R. Binford, pp. 285–312. Chicago: Aldine.

Sullivan, Alan P. 1982. Mogollon agrarian ecology. *The Kiva* 48:1–15.

Trimble, Stanley W. 1974. *Man-induced soil erosion on the Southern Piedmont, 1700–1970.* Ankeny: Soil Conservation Service of America.

Turner, B. L., II. 1974. Prehistoric intensive agriculture in the Mayan Lowlands. *Science* 195:118–24.

Tyler, Daniel. 1986. Dating the Caño ditch: Detective work in the Pojoaque Valley. *New Mexico Historical Review* 61:14–25.

Visser, Sent. 1982. On agricultural location theory. *Geographical Analysis* 14:167–76.

Vivian, R. Gwinn. 1990. *The Chacoan prehistory of the San Juan Basin.* San Diego: Academic Press.

Waddell, Eric. 1972. *The mound builders: Agricultural practices, environment, and society in the central highlands of New Guinea.* Seattle: University of Washington Press.

Wallach, Bret. 1985. British irrigation works in India's Krishna Basin. *Journal of Historical Geography* 11:155–73.

Wilken, Gene C. 1987. *Good farmers: Traditional agricultural management in Mexico and Central America.* Berkeley: University of California Press.

Williams, Michael. 1989. *Americans and their forests: A historical geography.* Cambridge: Cambridge University Press.

Woodbury, Richard B. 1961. Prehistoric agriculture at Point of Pines. In *Memoirs of the Society for American Archaeology* 17, ed. Raymond H. Thompson, pp. 1–48. *American Antiquity* 26:3.2.

Woodbury, Richard B., and Zubrow, Ezra B. W. 1979. Agricultural beginnings, 2000 B.C.–A.D. 500. In *Handbook of North American Indians,* vol. 9, ed. William C. Sturtevant, pp. 43–60. Washington: Smithsonian Institution.

Woods, William I. 1987. Maize agriculture and the late prehistoric: A characterization of settlement location strategies. In *Emergent horticultural economies of the Eastern Woodlands,* ed. William F. Keegan, pp. 275–94. Occasional Paper 7. Carbondale: Southern Illinois University, Center for Archaeological Investigations.

Woosley, Ann I. 1980. Agricultural diversity in the prehistoric Southwest. *The Kiva* 45:317–35.

Landscapes of Cultivation in Mesoamerica on the Eve of the Conquest

Thomas M. Whitmore* and B. L. Turner II**

*Department of Geography, University of North Carolina, Chapel Hill, NC 27599,
e-mail tmwhitmo@uncvx1.oit.unc.edu

**Graduate School of Geography, George Perkins Marsh Institute,
Clark University, Worcester, MA 01610,

Fax 508/793-7780, e-mail bTurner@uax.clark.edu, omnet B.Turner

Abstract. Pre-Columbian Amerindian agriculturalists developed technologies and management practices with which to crop a wide range of ecological conditions, giving rise to a multiplicity of cultivated landscapes. This variety was particularly evident in Mesoamerica, where agricultural practices ranged from swiddening to multicropped, hydraulically transformed wetlands. Here we explore these indigenous cultivated landscapes as they existed about the time of the Columbian Encounter. We illustrate them through the examination of three transects approximating the courses of the initial Spanish *entradas* through this diverse region: the first extends from the Gulf coast to central Mexico; the second traverses the Yucatán peninsula from north to south; and the third climbs into highland Guatemala from the Pacific coastal plain.

Second, we broadly sketch the major changes that took place in these landscapes during the first phase of Spanish domination and some of the forces that shaped these changes. Three processes were especially significant: the Amerindian depopulation, the introduction of exotic biota and technologies, and the reordering of land and the rural economy. Ultimately, however, reconfigured "hybrid" landscapes resulted that reflected the union of cultures.

Last, we argue that the scale of environmental transformation of Amerindian agriculture has not always been fully appreciated, the scale of environmental degradation associated with Spanish introductions has been overstated at times, and the contrasting ideologies of nature between the two cultures has been oversimplified.

Key Words: Amerindian agriculture, Mesoamerica, sixteenth century, Columbian Encounter.

THE Columbian Encounter opened the world to the treasures of Amerindian plant domestication, the impacts of which would be global in reach and range far beyond agriculture per se. The potato, for example, increased the caloric base of northern Europe, facilitating its exponential population growth after 1750, while maize, manioc, sweet potato, and peanut became dietary mainstays for much of the rest of the world (Hamilton 1976, 856–57, 860). Amerindian cotton was literally the fabric of the industrialization of textiles (Sauer 1976, 818), and tobacco claims the dubious distinction of "vice of choice" for much of the world.

Less well known is that these and other Amerindian domesticates of global significance (e.g., avocado, bean, cacao, chile, papaya, squash, and tomato) coevolved with equally impressive systems of cultivation. Long before the Columbian Encounter, Amerindian agriculturalists had developed technologies and management practices with which to crop a wide range of environments and ecological conditions, giving rise to a variety of landscapes of cultivation. This variety was particularly evident in Mesoamerica, where advanced material culture and state organization extended from the southern border of the Bajío in Central Mexico southeastward to Guatemala, including parts of Belize, Honduras, Nicaragua, and Costa Rica (Fig. 1). Some of these cultivated landscapes consisted of intermingled or patchwork-like microsystems, fine-tuned to small-scale environmental variations, while others were dominated by zonal patterns keyed to the broad environmental zones created by elevation, aspect, and slope.

The *conquistadores* marveled at these landscapes, even as they sowed the seeds of change. A new rendering of the land emerged at a pace only slightly slower than that of the conquest itself. Within fifty years of Columbus's initial landfall, Spanish hegemony over Middle America (the Caribbean, Mexico, and Central America) was complete and, in the course of the sixteenth century, most of the cultivated landscapes of Mesoamerica had been forever altered from their former condition. This alteration followed not only from changes in control of the land, but from the introduction of exotic biota, technologies, and management practices as well.

The cultivated landscapes of the preconquest Amerindians and the implications of their transformation, especially in Mesoamerica, have been the subject of rather polarized views, many of which have been empirically uninformed (see Denevan, this volume and Doolittle, this volume). Amerindian agriculture has not always been fully appreciated, the scale of environmental degradation associated with Spanish transformation of this agriculture has been overstated at times, and the contrasting ideologies of nature between the two cultures has been oversimplified.

Here we explore the indigenous cultivated landscapes that were witnessed by the Spanish adventurers as they existed about the time of the Columbian Encounter. Our primary objective is to illustrate the variety of these landscapes through the examination of three transects traversing different environmental and sociopolitical terrain. Each transect approximates the course of one of the initial Spanish *entradas* through this diverse region: the "Cortés transect" extends to central Mexico from the Gulf coast, the "Montejo transect" traverses the Yucatán peninsula from north to south, and the "Alvarado transect" climbs into highland Guatemala from the Pacific coastal plain (Fig. 1). Second, we broadly sketch the major changes that took place in these landscapes during the first phase of Spanish domination and some of the forces that shaped these changes. Our intent is neither to mythologize the accomplishments of the Amerindians nor to vilify the conquerors, but to illustrate the magnitude and breadth of the changes that took place in the cultivated landscapes of Mesoamerica as a result of the Columbian Encounter.

The Cortés Transect

Cortés and his small band probably first saw the snowcapped summit of Orizaba (5,639 m) from ship's deck in the vicinity of modern Veracruz, Mexico. From that vantage point, they were observing the eastern flanks of the Aztec empire, a domain that stretched east-west from the Gulf of Mexico to the Pacific Ocean and north-south from the Bajío to the Isthmus of Tehuantepec (Figs. 1, 2). More properly identified with the "Triple Alliance" of the city states of Tenochtitlán, Texcoco, and Tacuba in the Basin of Mexico (Gibson 1964, 17), the empire has taken its popular name from the dominant Mexica (Tenochtitlán) and their mythical homeland, Aztlan. The Alliance commanded a political and economic realm unparalleled in Mesoamerican history, complete with a supreme ruler, professional armies and merchants, and a system of taxation and marketing that siphoned the wealth of the empire into its lacustrine heart. Population estimates for Central Mexico, roughly corresponding with the empire, range from <10 million–>50 million (Denevan 1976, 77–84; 1992).

This transect parallels the Cortés route and crosses virtually every major climatic and agroecological zone in Mesoamerica: the hot and humid *tierra caliente* of the Gulf Coast Plains, the *tierra templada* (temperate land) of the coastal piedmont and the basins on the *altiplano* or Mesa Central, and the upper reaches of the sierras that separate the basins from one another (Figs. 2, 3). Each of these broad realms, with the exception of the cold lands and steep slopes of the sierras, was or-

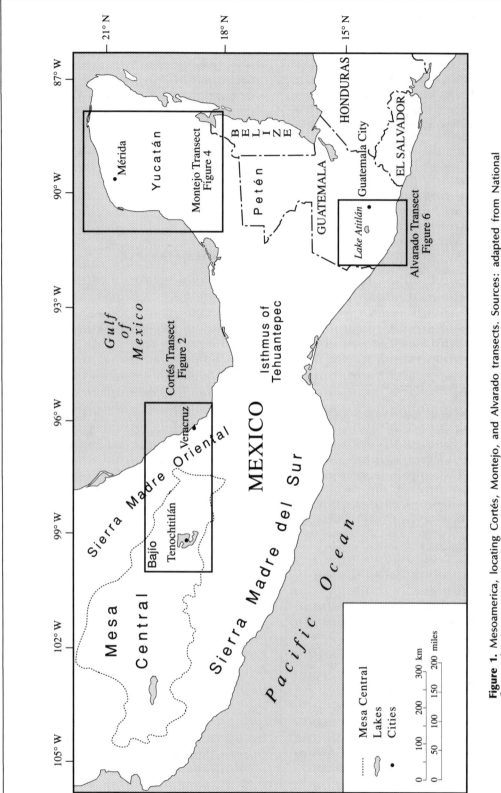

Figure 1. Mesoamerica, locating Cortés, Montejo, and Alvarado transects. Sources: adapted from National Geographic Society (1980) as base map only and West (1964a) for other locational information.

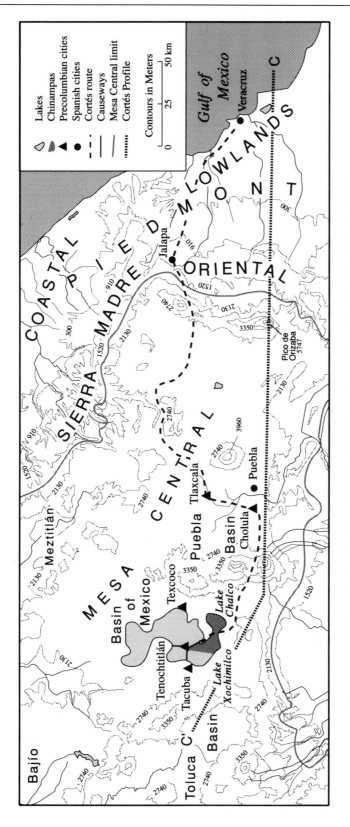

Figure 2. Cortés Transect, showing Central Mexico, Cortés's route, and the path of the Cortés Profile C-C' (see Fig. 3). Sources: adapted from U.S. Defense Mapping Agency (1965) as a base map and West (1964a) for other locational information.

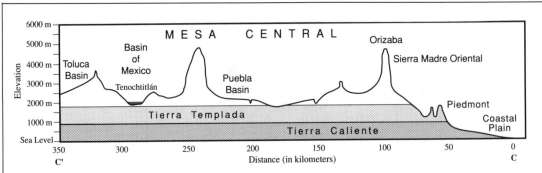

Figure 3. Cortés Profile, showing vertical relief along C-C' transect, as noted in Fig. 2. Sources: based on Fig. 2.

chestrated and transformed into landscapes of cultivation.

Gulf Coastal Plain and Piedmont

The area of the Spaniards landfall was inhabited by the Totonac who mastered the seasonal rhythm and environmental variation of the coastal plain and piedmont to produce crops for local subsistence as well as tribute, and possible commerce, with the Aztec empire (Barlow 1949; Hassig 1985, 114, 115; Stark 1990, 269). The coastal plains and hills offered a complex mosaic of microenvironmental opportunities and constraints for agriculture. The cultivated landscapes encountered in this complex natural terrain consisted of a patchwork of different cultivation types interspersed with forests and scrub land. It is even likely that the forests were managed and may have sheltered orchards. The Totonac orchestrated their year-round cultivation with the spatial and temporal variations in soil-water conditions, working the well-drained lands during the rainy season, and the inundated lands in the dry season (Siemens 1988, 1992; Wilkerson 1983, 58). The landscape configured by these practices led Spaniards to describe the lowlands around Zempoala as "a garden with luxuriant vegetation" (Diaz del Castillo 1956, 87).

The mainstay of Totonac (and Mesoamerican agriculture generally) was rainfed cultivation or *temporal*. In the Gulf Coast area, such cultivation dominated the well-drained, usually sloping, terrain and incorporated terraces with rock-walled, earthen, and probably also earth and *maguey* (*metepantli*) embankments (Rojas

Rabiela 1988, 118; Sluyter 1990, 20–37, 51–53; Wilkerson 1983, 64, 76).

Perhaps as important, however, were a variety of wetland adaptations that allowed cultivation during the marked dry season (Siemens 1983, 87; 1990, 117; Vivió Escoto 1964, 212; West 1964b, 58). In some instances, the margins of wetlands and levees were cultivated as water receded in the dry season, facilitated by the use of small drainage ditches. In others, more elaborate networks of canals were used to create field systems in wetlands proper. Siemens (1982, 1983) believes that these more elaborate networks may also have functioned in a flood-recessional manner. Contemporary flood-recessional cultivation in the Gulf Coast (and elsewhere) does not employ the elaborate and major canal networks found in the relics of the ancient systems. Thus we suspect that the cultivation associated with wetlands proper may have functioned through most of the year rather than only during recession of the floods.

Relics of walls and embankments on drylands and fields and canals in wetlands are abundant in the Gulf Coast area, although dating their continued use up to the eve of conquest is difficult to establish (Sluyter 1990; Siemens 1982, 1983). Indeed, Siemens et al. (1988, 107) found evidence that at least one wetland system in Veracruz was probably abandoned 500–700 years before the Columbian Encounter. Further southeast, however, Spanish accounts describe conditions that imply wetland cultivation in the sixteenth century (Pohl 1985). This evidence, the relatively large populations along portions of the Gulf Coast (López de Gómara 1964, 91; Stark 1978, 214–19; Wilkerson 1983, 55), and the amount of tribute extracted by the

Aztec from the area (Barlow 1949), lead us to suspect that many of the relic agricultural features found throughout the Gulf Coast zone may have been operating at the time of Spanish contact. These issues require further investigation. In addition, Wilkerson (1983, 81) speculates that runoff and other types of irrigation were used in the area.

It can also be presumed that two types of orchard-gardens were found in the area: the ubiquitous *solar* or *calmil,* carefully tended household gardens providing vegetables, fruits, condiments, medicinals, and fiber products (Siemens 1983, 97); and orchards, especially of cacao and various fruits grown for commercial purposes and tribute (Bergmann 1969, 86, 88; Millon 1955, 705; Schmidt 1977, 57; Stark 1974, 204, 210; 1978, 215). Orchard species may have been cultivated as special plots (see Montejo Transect), and/or they may have been integrated within managed forests as described by Alcorn (1984) for the modern Huastec.

Field management practices were probably similar to those used in the *altiplano,* including *montones* (mounded soil) or *camellones* (ridged or furrowed soil) and possibly transplanting from seedbeds (*almácigos* or *tlalacalli*) (Rojas Rabiela 1988, 33, 74–75, 82; Schmidt 1977, 57). While maize dominated, ethnohistorical and ethnographic analogs suggest that fields were intercropped with beans, squash, cotton, maguey (*Agave spp.*), *tuna* (*Opuntia spp.*) or root crops (Rojas Rabiela 1988, 93; Sluyter 1990, 56, 62; Stark 1974, 205; 1978, 216).

Sierra Madre Oriental

The eastern versant of the Sierra Madre Oriental presented a formidable escarpment separating the Gulf Coastal Plains and Piedmont from the mineral wealth and cooler climates on the *altiplano.* Its ascent took the Spaniards from the *tierra caliente* to the *tierra templada* and, ultimately the *tierra fría* beyond the 2000–3000 m saddle of the range (Fig. 2). The slope is steep and rugged throughout, dissected by the deep, narrow canyons of the Gulf-bound streams (West 1964b, 52–53). Much of the mountain slope receives large amounts of orographically-induced rainfall (2000 mm–3000 mm annually), giving rise to cloud forests near the crest (Vivió Escoto 1964, 201).

This escarpment was an agricultural transi-

tion zone perhaps shaped less by agroecological conditions than by declining population pressures between the piedmont and the upper slopes. The piedmont apparently was a landscape of terraces, and Siemens (1990, 145) quotes a nineteenth-century German resident who described "terraces . . . on every slope." As slopes grew steeper, however, the intensity of cultivation diminished to a shifting type, although fog moisture in the dry season supported two maize crops annually in a single field in some locations (Rojas Rabiela 1988, 78). Gutiérrez Ruvalcaba (forthcoming) notes sixteenth-century cultivation frequencies in the Sierra Madre Oriental of 1:8–1:10 (i.e, one year of cultivation and eight–ten years of fallow for each *milpa* plot). Another source notes shorter cycle periods (1:4–1:5) for the same region (the Colonial-era province of Meztitlán on the present-day Hildago-Veracruz border [Rojas Rabiela 1988, 62]).[1] Local inhabitants also may have employed a vertical zonation strategy, cultivating plots at different elevations to reduce risk and augment production (Gutiérrez Ruvalcaba forthcoming; Siemens 1990, 144).

Mesa Central

Crossing the Sierra, the Spaniards entered the great semiarid volcanic basins and ranges of the Mesa Central, encountering landscapes that they found more familiar and appealing than those of the *tierra caliente* (Figs. 2, 3). Here, a large Amerindian population was arranged in settlement hierarchies dominated by city-states whose hinterlands spread across basin floors and up the surrounding slopes. Agriculture formed the basis of subsistence and commerce among city-states and was central to the tribute extracted by the Aztec.

The Mesa Central is composed of broad, flat-floored basins ringed by imposing volcanoes and broad slopes (West 1964b, 42, 47), many of which offered fertile soils for agriculture (Stevens 1964, 195–296; West 1964b, 47). Most of this area is above 1800 m (Figs. 2, 3). Here, Mesoamerican crop production was limited by recurrent frosts and low levels of precipitation (Sanders et al. 1979, 230) (mean annual precipitation ranges from 250 mm–1000 m) combined with high annual variability (Vivió Escoto 1964, 199). Paradoxically, poor interior drainage gave rise to various wetlands on the basin floors.

While each basin differed according to its

features and occupation, commonality of use gave rise to a characteristic pattern of cultivated landscapes.[2] The upper *sierras* remained in forest, a source of wood and regulator of water. Below the forest line, rainfed terraced and semiterraced cultivation dominated. Various forms of floodwater irrigation were pursued within ephemeral water courses and along lands adjacent to them, including the edges of the basins' floors into which the drainages emptied. On the basin floor proper, where poor drainage was common, various kinds of wetland cultivation were adapted to the perihumid conditions.

Small clusters of villages and hamlets were scattered across the landscape. Their intensively cultivated gardens produced food crops, condiments, ornaments, and medicinal plants (Evans 1990, 117, 126; Palerm 1955; Rojas Rabiela 1988, 92–93; forthcoming). Specialized orchards of avocado, *nopal de grana* (the cacti hosting the cochineal insect used for red dye, *Opuntina spp.*), *maguey* (agave or century plant, *Agave spp.*), *tejocote* (Mexican hawthorn, *Crataegus mexicana*), *capulín* (capulin cherry, *Prunus capuli*) and other fruits occupied favored niches (Rojas Rabiela 1988, 93: forthcoming).

Rainfed cultivation dominated spatially, although its forms were adapted to the varying terrain.[3] Upper and lower slopes were embraced by flights of sloping *metepantli* (semiterraces) which preserved soil and soil moisture (Donkin 1979, 131; Patrick 1985; Rojas Rabiela 1988: 118–19; Sanders 1981, 192). More than a simple slope adjustment, *metepantli* incorporated food and fiber production into the terrace by using *maguey* or *nopal* cacti as berm anchors (Evans 1990, 125; Patrick 1985, 542; Wilken 1979). Maize, beans, and squash were the mainstays of slope cultivation, but Mesoamerican cultivators grew a large variety of other cultigens, including amaranth (*Amaranthus annuus*), *chía* (*Salvia hispanica*), tomato, beans, squash, and chiles.

Perhaps the most common irrigation works were weirs or check dams that captured silt and water within intermittent drainages, or that spread water onto adjacent lands for floodwater irrigation (Donkin 1979, 42, 44; García Cook 1985; Parsons 1971, 220; Rojas Rabiela 1988, 120; 1985, 202; forthcoming; Sanders et al. 1979, 222–81; Wolf and Palerm 1955, 266). Perhaps it was these features in Cholula that Cortés described in 1520: "the farmlands are very fertile and they have much land and the greater part is irrigated" (1945, 146). In some cases, this technique was extended to valley floors, which were straddled by broad terraces that could be fed by channel runoff water (Donkin 1979, 44; Rojas Rabiela 1988, 120; Sanders et al. 1979, 253; Wolf and Palerm 1955).

Small dams and diversion weirs coupled with canals provided permanent irrigation water from springs or permanent streams in selected locations (Armillas et al. 1956; Doolittle 1990, 115; Millon 1957; Rojas Rabiela 1985, 198; 1988, 121; Sanders et al. 1979, 260–62). Thousands of small contour bench terraces in the Basin of Mexico are thought to have been irrigated in this way (Donkin 1979, 44; Sanders et al. 1979, 251–52). In some cases, lengthy canals, complete with aqueducts that spanned intervening *barrancas* (gullies), attest to the use of permanent irrigation (Doolittle 1990, 127; Donkin 1979, 42, 44; Parsons 1971, 220; Wolf and Palerm 1955, 266). At least one instance of the canalization and relocation of the flow of a large stream for irrigation is known in the Basin of Mexico (Doolittle 1990, 115–20). While terracing was located throughout the Mesa Central, its association with elaborate irrigation infrastructures has only been well documented for the Basin of Mexico.

Many of the seasonal and permanent wetlands and shallow lakes in the interior of the valleys of Tlaxcala, Mexico, and perhaps Puebla were transformed into a network of canals and planting surfaces (wetland fields) on which year-round cultivation could be practiced (Parsons 1971, 220; Rojas Rabiela 1985, 208; Sanders 1972, 131–32; Sanders et al. 1979, 275; Wilken 1969, 1987). In some cases, hierarchial systems of canals channeled excessive water to the interior, creating drained fields along the periphery of lakes or wetlands.

The latter form of wetland cultivation reached its zenith among the *chinampas*, or "floating gardens," of the Basin of Mexico, occupying thousands of hectares of the southern freshwater lakes of Chalco and Xochimilco (Armillas 1971, 653; Sanders et al. 1979, 275; West and Armillas 1952, 171) (Fig. 2). The actual *chinampa* was a narrow artificial island (a raised field), anchored by trees along its edges, and constructed from lake muck and biotic materials dredged from the shallow lakes themselves (Wilken 1985, 42). The effect was to raise the planting surface relative to the water in the bordering canals, providing subsurface irrigation at all times, but also facilitating surface irrigation if needed. Canals were regularly cleaned, and the aquatic muck was used to fertilize the fields (Armillas 1971, 653; Palerm 1973; West and Armillas 1952, 171; Wilken 1985, 42).[4]

By the sixteenth century, *chinampas* were part of a state-designed and controlled hydraulic system that included dikes and sluice gates controlling water level and quality in the southern parts of the lacustrine network (Palerm 1973). Not only did dikes protect the two southern lakes from brackish Lake Texcoco, but an adjacent section of that lake was diked as well, making chinampa agriculture possible on the islands of the Aztec capital (Fig. 2) (Calneck 1972; Parsons 1976, 253; Sanders et al. 1979, 154).

Individually and as a system, *chinampas* required significant labor input to construct and maintain, but they combined very high productivity with risk-reduction (Armillas 1971, 660; Coe 1964, 98; Moriarty 1968, 473; Parsons 1976, 244–46; Sanders 1972, 133; Sanders et al. 1979, 390). Irrigation reduced problems of drought, and the presence of water mitigated frost hazard. *Chinampas* were probably double-cropped, using different cultigens and transplantation from seedbeds (Rojas Rabiela 1985, 165; 1988, 79–80). Few cultivation systems in the world could match their sustained level of productivity.

The Montejo Transect

The Yucatán Peninsula, home to the lowland Maya, provided a radically different experience for the Spaniards (Figs. 1, 4). As in the Mexican case, the northern Yucatán was well peopled, and the Maya were both skilled cultivators and active in long-distance trade (Andrews 1983; Chamberlain 1948; Farriss 1984). Nevertheless, by such measures as the number and spatial domain of city-states, and level of sociopolitical organization and affluence (as measured by the scale and quality of monumental architecture), the condition of the lowland Maya in

Yucatán at the time of contact was not on par with that of their Classic Period ancestors of some 500–700 years earlier (Chase and Rice 1985; Jones 1989; Turner 1983a, b).

The Yucatán is composed of two environmental domains (Figs. 4, 5) over which a common set of cropping practices were differentially employed in association with differing intensities of occupation. The peninsula is a large limestone shelf with extreme karst conditions, dominated by a tropical wet-dry climate (*tierra caliente*) in which rainfall increases considerably from the northwest to the southeast (Finch 1965; Wilhelmy 1981; Wilson 1980). The northern periphery of the peninsula is a relatively flat, lowly elevated plain, but starting with the Puuc Hills (Figs. 3, 4), a rolling hill or upland area extends southward into the *Péten* (Guatemala). Everywhere in the north, extremely shallow and rocky soils, an absence of surface water, and a pronounced dry season impeded agriculture.

At the time of the Columbian Encounter, the northern low plains were moderately to heavily occupied. In contrast, the central and southern uplands, an area that was once the heart of the Classic Maya civilization (Culbert 1973; Turner 1990a), were very sparsely settled in 1492 (Jones 1989; Means 1917; Scholes and Roys 1968; Turner 1990a, b).

Northern and Coastal Plains

Spaniards officially discovered the Yucatán in 1517 (Chamberlain 1948, 61–64; Clendinnen 1987, 17–18; Means 1917) only to find that at least two Spaniards, survivors of a shipwreck, were present among the Maya. One of these men refused to return to his former comrades, but led the Maya in subsequent military encounters against them (Chamberlain 1948, 61–64; Means 1917). The Spaniards bypassed the Yucatán for Mexico, so that the initial conquest awaited 1527, while subjugation of the peninsula followed some twenty years later (Farriss 1984, 12). Led by Francisco de Montejo (the Elder), the first *entrada* began on the northeastern coast of the peninsula and marched inland. The transect that we follow here roughly corresponds to the north-south course of Montejo's route, with some liberties taken to include the interior uplands which Montejo's

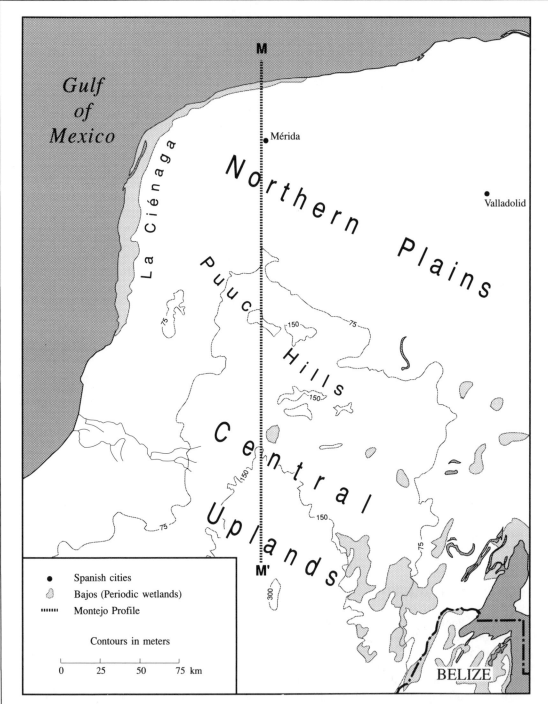

Figure 4. Montejo Transect, showing the Northern Yucatán, and the path of the Montejo Profile, M-M' (see Fig. 5). Sources: adapted from U.S. Defense Mapping Agency (1974) and National Geographic Society (1969) as base maps and West (1964a) for other locational information.

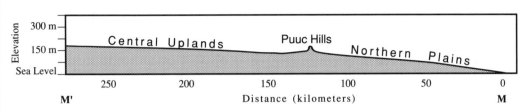

Figure 5. Montejo Profile, showing vertical relief along M-M′ transect, as noted in Fig. 4. Sources: based on Fig. 4.

party apparently avoided because of its sparse occupation.

The littoral of northern Yucatán was extremely important economically to the Maya, who had converted coastal wetlands (the *ciénaga*) into the center of Mesoamerican salt production and trade. Salt was apparently transported by canoe along the coasts to Mexico and Central America (Andrews 1983). The settlements controlling salt production lay inland, spread throughout the northern plains, as was most of the Maya population. Here the Spaniards encountered large numbers of Maya, arranged in small-sized polities consisting of sizable villages and well-tended landscapes.

These villages and their lands had a common morphology. A small plaza and public monument, usually a small pyramid or some other shrine, marked the center of a village, from which homesteads, each demarcated by stone walls enclosing orchard-gardens, radiated outward (the elite lived closest to the center) (Clendinnen 1987; Gómez-Pompa et al. 1987). Homesteads gave way to open- or outfields in various stages of fallow, which in turn gave way to forest, much of which may have been managed. Here, culling and related activities may have supported forms of agroforestry (*pet kot*) (Gómez-Pompa et al. 1987). This spatial arrangement was repeated across the northern plains, with the apparent exception of savanna areas.

Spanish documents refer to both "plantations" and "orchard-gardens" in the area, using the former designation frequently for elite-owned "cacao" stands situated on the edges of Maya towns (Tozzer 1941, 194–95; Scholes and Roys 1968, 171–72).[5] The spatial arrangement and concentration of these plots

may have given the impression of extensive orchards. Maya horticultural practices were not well documented by the Spaniards, other than reports that the elite used slaves and servants to care for their orchards, and evidence of monocropping or plantation-like labor organization is lacking (Scholes and Roys 1968, 171–72).

Orchard-gardens played an important role among the Maya and the Amerindians of *tierra caliente* in general (Killion forthcoming). Much of the Maya food supply was grown in orchard-gardens, as testified by their spatial extent and the quantity of remains of orchard-gardens species taken from excavations of Maya middens (Turner and Miksicek 1984). Indeed, Gómez-Pompa and colleagues (1987) argue that the unusual distribution of useful species currently found within ancient walled plots throughout Yucatán are remnants of ancient orchard-gardens (see also Folan et al. 1979). Individual trees and groves were apparently privately owned and inherited (Millon 1955, 700; Scholes and Roys 1968, 171–72).

Landa referred to the use of agaves, chiles, beans, and cotton in house gardens (Tozzer 1941, 194–95). Maya orchard-gardens included a large variety of native trees, shrubs, and other species adapted to the wet-dry tropical climate of the plains (Clendinnen 1987, 141; Chamberlain 1968, 52; Scholes and Roys 1968, 171–72, 328; Tozzer 1941, 179, 230). These included agave and cotton, avocado, *nance* (*Brysonima crassifolia*), allspice (*Pimenta dioica*), guava (*Psidium guajava*), sapodilla (*Manilkara zapote*), and *mamey zapote* (*Calocarpum mammosum*).

The prevalence of orchard-gardens notwithstanding, the staple crop of the northern Maya at the time of the Columbian Encounter was maize. Considerable documentation by earlier chroniclers indicates that the bulk of it was produced in fields distant from the walled homesteads and orchard-gardens, although walls may have been present in these "outfields" (walls without occupation structures are common; see Freidel and Leventhal 1975). The cultivation practices in these "outfields" are uncertain, as is the intensity of cultivation. In the mid-1500s, Landa noted that the Maya prepared the land from January to April (in the dry season), planted with a digging stick, and cultivated by "collect[ing] together refuse and burn[ing] it in order to sow" (indicating shifting cultivation?); but they also had "improved" lands and "kept the land well cleared and free from weeds" (indicating nonshifting cultivation?) (Tozzer 1941, 62, 64, 97; Landa 1937, 38).

Because of the level of population and the well-defined boundaries of villages and provinces in the north, we suspect that a short-fallow rotational system was used in which plot preparation focused on burning collected and dried vegetation in order to provide essential phosphorus for the soil before the rains began in April. Plots were first sowed to maize and subsequently intercropped with squash and nitrogen fixing beans.[6] Interestingly, the region was known for its cotton and hemp production at the time of conquest, although virtually no descriptions of its cultivation exist. Weeding dominated the growing season labor until the fall harvest.

The outfields of each village were apparently separated from those of the next by forest which, in addition to possible agroforestry activities, formed a reserve for wood fuel, hunting, and tame animals. Deer were, perhaps, the most important of the semitame animals, apparently controlled from birth through biological imprinting, and later herded from the village to feed in the forest (Means 1917, 30; Tozzer 1941, 127).

The Uplands

Compared to the northern plains, the rolling karst hills of the central peninsular area must have been a disappointment and aggravation to the Spaniards, for here the population thinned dramatically (Means 1917; Scholes and Roys 1968, 333), and the tropical forest provided a frontier refuge for Maya fleeing Spanish control. The distinctive cultivated landscape of the northern plain was replaced in the uplands by extensive swidden systems, possibly similar to those described by ethnographers in the nineteenth and twentieth centuries.[7] This slash-and-burn or *milpa* (literally cornfield) method involved basically the same tools and crops as in the north, but utilized longer fallow cycles and lower labor inputs, especially for weeding. New plots were cut in January to allow the woody species to dry sufficiently for burning before the rains of April. After several seasons of cultivation, a plot was abandoned for a protracted period to escape the concentration of pests and weeds there and to allow regrowth of a secondary forest.

The role of orchard-gardens in the uplands during this period is not clear. They may have existed around larger settlements, but references to activity of this kind are sparse. House gardens were undoubtedly common. The forests were very much the product of past Maya activities and were well stocked with economic species from which extensive collecting took place.

Alvarado Transect

Pedro de Alvarado led the Spanish *entrada* into the highland Maya realm of Guatemala in 1524, charting a route southeastward from the Mesa Central, following the Pacific coastal plain, before turning northward into the well-defended highlands of present day Guatemala (Figs. 1, 6). Following the experience of Cortés, Alvarado brought thousands of Aztec and Tlaxcalan warriors to subdue the Maya, who fought the invasion in a series of bloody battles. The Spaniards found a populous highlands divided into provinces of different ethnolinguistic Maya stock. Each province had hereditary rulers, but no overarching state was present, nor were there many large cities of the material majesty found in the Aztec realm. The region, however, contained some of the finest agricultural soils in Mesoamerica and the lowlands of its Pacific versant gave the Spaniards a preview of yet another source of wealth—estate production of cacao.

The climb from the Pacific Coast to the homelands of the highland Maya transverses an array of broad agroecological zones associated with elevation (West 1964a, 373). The Coastal Plain (*La Costa*) and the Boca Costa or piedmont comprise a 40–50 km-wide strip between the ocean and highlands proper (Figs. 6, 7).

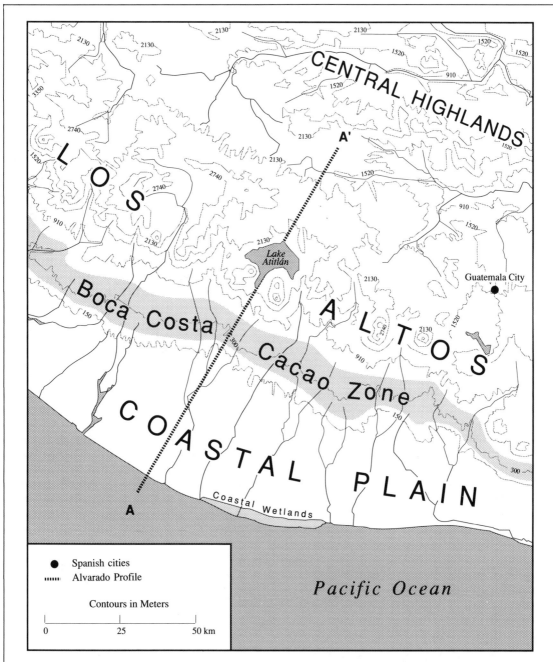

Figure 6. Alvarado Transect, showing southwestern Guatemala, and the path of the Alvarado Profile, A-A' (see Fig. 7). Sources: adapted from U.S. Defense Mapping Agency (1978) as a base map and Bergmann (1969) and Orelanna (1984) for other locational information.

The coastal plain (up to about 100 m elevation) and the lower Boca Costa (about 100 m–460 m elevation) are *tierra caliente* while the upper Boca Costa (about 460—1500 m elevation) is *tierra templada*. Precipitation increases inland and with elevation, such that portions of the Boca Costa receive in excess of 2000 mm annually (Vivó Escoto 1964, fig. 10). Around 1000 m elevation, the mountain front rises steeply to cinder cones and composite volcanos, some of

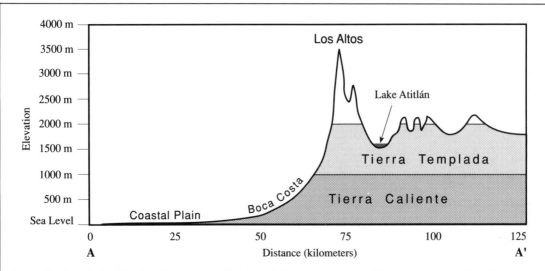

Figure 7. Alvarado Profile, showing vertical relief along A-A' transect, as noted in Fig. 6. Sources: based on Fig. 6.

which exceed 3000 m. Above the 1500 m contour and to the interior of the versant is *Los Altos,* the highland volcanic axis, composed of small depressions and calderas surrounded by volcanoes (more than twenty in Guatemala alone). Lake Atitlán occupies such a caldera at 1566 m. The peaks are in clouds and mist much of the time and average annual precipitation there reaches 3000 mm–4000 mm. To the northern end of the Alvarado transect the volcanic axis gives way to the lower-elevated and drier central highlands.

Boca Costa

Very little is known about Amerindian agriculture on the narrow coastal plain proper. In contrast, the Boca Costa was a zone so prized for its agricultural fertility that Amerindian groups vied with one another for its control. The southwest portion of the Boca Costa was part of the greater Soconusco (also spelled Soconosco, Xoconusco, and Xoconocho) region, extending into southeastern Chiapas state in Mexico. This region was renowned for producing and widely exporting the finest cacao in Mesoamerica (Bergmann 1969, 86; Gasco and Voorhies 1989, 289; MacLeod 1973, 68–79; Millon 1955, 702). Cacao is a delicate species that requires moist but well-drained soils, shade, protection from high winds, and warm temperatures (mean temperatures be-

tween 18° C and 32° C, without frost) (Gasco 1987, 157). Owing to these needs, major orchard zones were below 650 m (Orellana 1984, 70) where annual precipitation totals ranged between 1150 mm–2500 mm. Pronounced dry seasons necessitated irrigation. Cacao was commonly germinated using seedbeds (*almácigos*) and replanted to orchards (Rojas Rabiela 1988, 82). Another species, *Theobroma tricolor,* is hardier, but it is not clear that it was grown extensively in the Boca Costa. Major cacao began about 30 km inland on the alluvial fans. Bergmann (1969, 89) suggests that this interior location was a response to the drier conditions approaching the ocean, but it also corresponds with the well-drained agricultural soils of the alluvial fans characteristic of this piedmont.

Cacao was produced over a wide area, perhaps in an orchard or plantation-like pattern. The Spaniards referred to estates and gardens or orchards of cacao, terms that imply not only monocropping conditions but possibly irrigation as well (Armillas 1949, 88; Bergmann 1969, 90; Millon 1955; Rojas Rabiela 1988, 92; Zamora Acosta 1985, 182). Cacao was intensively tended, its care including the use of shade trees (e.g., *madera negra* [*Gliricidia maculata* H. B. and K.] or *coxote* [*G. sapium*]) and protection from predators and theft (Lange 1971, 240–44; Millon 1955, 704; Orellana 1984, 70; Stone 1977, 85–86; Rojas Rabiela 1988, 92).

The immense value of the cacao to Mesoamericans was in its use as a thick beverage or gruel. Such was the importance of this food that the cacao bean served as a medium of exchange in Mesoamerica, used in virtually any commodity or service transaction (Millon 1955; Bergmann 1969, 85–86). Elites controlled the production of and trade in cacao in the Boca Costa, although this control did not require actual occupation of the piedmont. Highland Maya communities governed some of the production in the Boca Costa, while Náhuatl-speaking groups within the piedmont may have served to ensure the flow of cacao to Aztec Mexico (Bergmann 1969, 89; Orellana 1984). At the time of the Spanish conquest, the Aztec extracted tribute from Soconusco and Boca Costa by taxing the towns controlling production, regardless of their location.

The Boca Costa also offered a full array of agriculture, producing other foods and fibers. Maize was double and even tripled-cropped in some locales (Fuentes and Guzmán 1882, 64; Zamora Acosta 1985, 182), undoubtedly through the use of irrigation. It is also possible that orchards producing other crops than cacao were present. The spatial extent of this production onto the southern versant proper (between the cacao zone and Los Altos) is not well understood. The slope is very steep and rugged, and it appears to have been sparsely occupied at contact relative to the lands above and below. The southern versant may have been used for extensive cultivation as a "spill-over" zone for farmers ascending from the Boca Costa or descending from Los Altos.

Los Altos

In addition to the ubiquitous house gardens, rainfed cultivation was practiced on both terraced and nonterraced fields in the slopes and depressions of Los Altos. Many slopes were intensively cultivated without terracing, particularly where mounding (*montones*) or ridging (*camellones* contouring the slope) were apparently sufficient to impede erosion (see Wilken 1987, 129–144). Although Alvarado spoke of a highly developed agriculture, Spanish descriptions of practices associated with *temporal* are vague, making it difficult to distinguish shifting from permanent cultivation (Zamora Acosta 1985, 178; Palerm and Wolf 1962, 336). The *Annals of the Cakchiquels* (ca. 1559–81) mentions cut-and-burn techniques, but not rotation of fields, leading to various interpretations about the implied frequency of cultivation (Feldman 1985, 29; Orellana 1984, 69). The apparently extensive use of mounding, along with the use of a hoe-like instrument and a scraper-like rake for weeding, led Feldman (1985, 29–30) to conclude that a rainfed system, more intensive than slash and burn, was prevalent in Los Altos.

Terracing was practiced throughout the highlands (Orellana 1984, 27–29), although specific references to Los Altos are few. Remnants of pre-Hispanic terracing exist in the central highlands, and the practice may have been followed at the time of conquest (Guzmán 1962, 398). The distribution of the relic features may reflect soil distinctions between the volcanic axis of Los Altos and the more northerly central highlands or it may reflect differential Spanish impacts. Documentation of terrace remains in the volcanic axis zone is slim, however. Lothrop (1933) found relic terraces around Lake Atitlán but did not designate their function for agriculture as opposed to house sites.

Highland Maya terracing, in general, served the same functions as described in the Cortés transect. Where associated with the *tablón*, however, irrigation was common. The *tablón* (literally, plank) is a raised-garden plot (20–65 cm in height), usually rectangular in shape with inwardly sloping sides, accompanied by irrigation channels (Mathewson 1984; Wilken 1971, 435). If on a sufficient slope, the *tablón* is constructed on terraces with the irrigation channel located at the base of each terrace wall. *Tablones* in use today are especially frequent around the edges of Lake Atitlán and on the northern slopes above the lake, although they can be found elsewhere in the highlands (Altee 1968; Wilken 1987). While no direct evidence yet confirms the use of *tablones* in the pre-Hispanic highlands, two facts strongly suggest that they were a major component of highland Maya agriculture. The first is that each of the structural elements of *tablones* was known and used by the Maya; the second is that the current distribution coincides with contact-era social and environmental conditions that would have promoted their use (Mathewson 1984, 17–20; Orellana 1984, 69; Wilken 1971, 435–36). It is likely that *tablón* systems constituted many of the gardens described in Spanish accounts.

The principal crops grown were those prevalent throughout the highlands of Mesoamerica. According to Feldman (1985, 26), at least seven varieties of maize, three of squash, nine of beans, tobacco, and, perhaps, sweet potato have been identified in Los Altos in prehistoric context. Studies of highland Maya communities by Stadelman (1940) and others indicate the presence of a much greater variety of maize, much of which is assumed to have been present in antiquity.

The Lake Atitlán Basin was a microcosm of the highland landscapes in general at contact times, including its occupation by at least three Maya groups: the Cakchiquel in the north and east sides, the Tzutujuil on the south side and Pacific slopes, and the Quiché on the north and west sides (Lothrop 1933, 3). The cultivated landscape here appeared as a mosaic of practices associated more with slope than with climatic variation or with elevation. The upper, broad slopes of the basin were apparently under intensive rainfed cultivation, complete with cascading *monotones* and *camellones*. Further down the basin, where drainage systems facilitated irrigation but the steepness of slope increased significantly (particularly on the northern side of the lake), ranks of terraced *tablones* continued down towards the lake. Near lake level, almost all the small deltas of the drainages were also converted into *tablones* (see Mathewson 1984).

The Fate of the Cultivated Landscapes

The repercussions of the Conquest spread swiftly throughout Mesoamerica during the first century of the Hispanic era, leaving few, if any, cultivated landscapes untouched (Butzer 1991). The conquerors reapportioned land and labor under conditions of rapid Amerindian depopulation and reconstituted agriculture through the introduction of European technologies and biota. The conquered retained, where possible and appropriate, their crops and cropping techniques. Ultimately, however, both conquerors and conquered borrowed extensively, if differentially, from one another, and the reconfigured landscapes that resulted were not so much one culture's cultivated landscape replacing another's but their union on "hybrid" landscapes.[8]

Causes of the Transformations

The Conquest of Mesoamerica set in motion a series of processes, intentional and otherwise, that penetrated every facet of the physical and spiritual world of the Amerindian, with many of the results having significant ramifications on cultivated landscapes. We cannot treat all of these processes here, but focus on three clusters of them that were especially significant in a direct way: the Amerindian depopulation, the introduction of exotic biota and technologies, and the reordering of land and the rural economy.

The scale of Amerindian depopulation that accompanied the introduction of Old World pathogens by the Spaniards is nothing short of phenomenal, remaining unparalleled in demographic history (see Lovell this volume).[9] This demographic tragedy affected agriculture in at least two ways. The landesque capital (terracing, irrigation, wetland systems) of the intensive cropping systems of the Amerindian could not be sustained with such losses in labor, leading to the decay of many cultivated landscapes (Cook and Borah 1979, 169), with the concomitant environmental degradation that typically follows from the lack of upkeep. This decay contributed to the larger process of land abandonment which, in turn, weakened Amerindian claims to land and led to Spanish land appropriation (e.g., Licate 1981).

The introduction of Old World biota and technologies, part of what Crosby (1972) calls the Columbian Exchange, had wide-ranging impacts on the landscape because of the new land-uses associated with them and the expansion of these uses into areas extensively utilized by Amerindians. Among the most dramatic were those of range livestock, previously unknown in Mesoamerica. The population explosion of grazing animals early in the sixteenth century is claimed by many to have contributed to accelerated erosion on agricultural lands, increased siltation, more frequent and profound flooding, and losses of harvests due to predatory herds and the physical trampling of the fields (Brand 1961, 133; Chevalier 1963, 93; Cook and Borah 1979, 169; Crosby, 1972, 76–77; Gibson 1964, 305; Morrisey 1951, 116; Simpson 1952; Super 1988, 26). Chevalier (1963, 93) claims that entire communities in the Mesa Central were forced to move, in part because of livestock damage to croplands, and the land so abandoned may well have contributed to the growth in cattle and sheep *estancias* (ranches) during the early sixteenth century (Chevalier 1963, 83; Licate 1981, 114–15).

Such impacts may have been more short-lived than conventional wisdom asserts. Gibson (1964, 281), among others (e.g., Butzer and Butzer, personal communication), notes that the Spanish Crown invoked law and policy directed at preserving Amerindian lands and cultivation, although these efforts were apparently at odds with the forces of depopulation, resettlement, land abandonment, and local appropriation (Licate 1981, 113). Discovery of silver in the north and the cattle producers' adaptions of their production strategies to the new lands, led to a livestock industry that spread northward into lands that were less intensively used in pre-Columbian times, producing an economy that was relatively in tune with the environments in question (Butzer and Butzer).

The critical point for our discussion is that much land that was once under Amerindian cultivation (in the highland domain) or was sparsely utilized (north of Mesoamerica proper or in lands abandoned because of depopulation) was rapidly put to a new, exotic use. The land-cover impacts associated with this land-use change are vividly illustrated in the Gulf Coast area, where cattle and sheep production was pursued on pastures created by burning forest and on former wetland fields; in either case, these were formerly Amerindian cultivated landscapes, altered to new use (Siemens 1992).

Hispanic crop introductions also redefined the lands to be cultivated and the form of cultivation on them (Hassig 1985, 221). The use of plow and draft animals, for example, placed a premium on level or gently sloped lands with good soil depth and drainage and large field size (Cook and Borah 1979, 171). In contrast, pre-Columbian *coa*-based cultivation was particularly suitable for use in shallow soils and small fields, and on steep slopes.[10] The shift to plow cultivation and the abandonment of cultivated lands owing to depopulation and resettlement may have altered the overall proportion of valley bottom to upper slope cultivation relative to pre-Hispanic times.

Spanish preferences for European foods also played a part. Wheat cultivation was carried across the *altiplano* from the Puebla basin to the northern silver mines (Gibson 1964, 322;

Chevalier 1963, 51–54; Super 1988, 32) because of the demand for wheat bread. This pursuit led the Spaniards to introduce irrigation in the Bajío and other arid lands on the margins of Mesoamerica, and to rework Amerindian irrigation in the Basin of Mexico to allow winter (dry season) cultivation (Chevalier 1963, 70; Butzer and Butzer; Davis 1990). The environmental impacts of these shifts in agriculture are insufficiently documented so that more pointed assessments constitute speculation.

Plantation crops for trans-Atlantic commerce emerged in the lowlands, although large-scale plantations were not the norm (Butzer 1991, 210). The most important of the crops in terms of landscape change was sugarcane, which the Spaniards introduced wherever ecologically suitable (Chevalier 1963, 74). Cortés himself established a sugarcane plantation in the lowlands west of Tuxtla as early as 1528 (Barrett 1970, 11). For the most part, sugarcane production in the *tierra caliente* was undertaken on small estates, as was Spanish-controlled production of cacao, cotton, tobacco, and dyes (MacLeod 1973, 220–24). By the close of the sixteenth century, sugarcane production also spread into warmer upland locales, such as in Morelos where large-scale plantations were established (Barrett 1970, 4; Super 1988, 37), and where it may have helped to displace Amerindian cultivation (Chevalier 1963, 82).

These changes were intertwined with those stemming from the reordering of land and labor. By the mid-sixteenth century, significant land holdings had accrued to the Spaniards and, interestingly, to Amerindian elites in some areas (Gibson 1964; Licate 1981; Simpson 1952). Amerindian labor was siphoned off for work on large Spanish estates, and the *encomienda* (grants for the control of Amerindian labor) refocused production goals, and in some cases, the location of Amerindian settlements. After mid-century, full-blown resettlement schemes (the *congregación*) relocated much of the remaining rural population (Cline 1949). The impacts of these activities were to reduce Amerindian cultivation in some locales and increase land pressures on others.

Landscapes Transformed and Traditions Retained

Three very broad patterns of transformation of cultivated landscapes followed throughout

Mesoamerica and beyond. The humid *tierra caliente* (save the northern Yucatán) was virtually abandoned, allowing major forest regeneration. The few remaining Amerindians in these lowlands, armed with the introduction of steel cutting tools, increasingly moved towards labor-saving swidden cultivation. The Spaniards, on the other hand, introduced small-scale estates devoted to plantation crops, both introduced and native, followed by livestock production. The *tierra templada* witnessed wide-spread abandonment and destruction of Amerindian agricultural landscapes and the emergence of new ones. The general pattern of this transformation involved the disuse of some land, the disproportional redistribution of other lands to the Spaniards, and an investment in large-scale plow and wheat cultivation and livestock production drawing on Amerindian labor (see Prem, this volume). Finally, cultivation and livestock rearing expanded into the more arid segments of Mesoamerica and the lands beyond, especially to the north, and later into Central America.

Indigenous landscapes dominated by labor-intensive cultivation, especially terraces and wetland systems, were particularly affected. Terrace systems were abandoned throughout the upper piedmonts of the Mesa Central of Mexico (Cortés transect), Los Altos of Guatemala (Alvarado transect), and somewhat later in the piedmont of the Gulf Coast (Cortés transect) (Donkin 1979, 35–36). These extensively distributed systems of slope modification simply could not be maintained in the face of Amerindian depopulation and relocation (Cook and Borah 1979, 168; Donkin 1979, 36) and with the increasing focus of cultivation in valleys and lower basins.

Similarly, wetland agriculture, the productive heart of some pre-Columbian landscapes, also faded in significance. It did so for several reasons beyond those of population collapse and labor shortage. Indigenous wetland agriculture was not well understood by the Spaniards, was not central to their vision of appropriate land use, and was not suited for plow or wheat production. Moreover, it occupied lands potentially suitable for plow and livestock production, if properly drained (Cook and Borah 1979, 171; Hassig 1985, 221). Interestingly, deterioration of the Amerindian systems upslope lead to increased sedimentation and other problems that apparently de-

graded some wetland systems below (Gibson 1964, 305; López Ríos 1988). Owing to these and other factors, wetland agriculture almost disappeared from the Mesa Central (Cortés transect), except for the *chinampas* of Lakes Chalco and Xochimilco in the Basin of Mexico (which would decay slowly) and the drained fields in the Tlaxcalan valley. Wetland systems, other than ephemeral flood-recessional practices, also disappeared in the Gulf Coast Plain (Cortés transect), although their demise may have been underway previous to the Conquest.

In the Yucatán (Montejo transect), the Spaniards developed extensive cattle estates, utilizing both Maya agricultural lands and forest (Farriss 1984, 32).[11] This not only disrupted the well-developed cultivated landscape of the Maya, but, along with depopulation, the introduction of steel cutting tools, and Maya "escape" to the forests outside of Spanish control, probably led to the disintensification of Maya cultivation from rotational to shifting cultivation.[12] The rearranged landscape was composed of large estates interspersed with small villages, following a form of *milpa* cultivation that has continued to the present.

Most of the cultivated landscapes that escaped major change lay on the margins of Spanish interests or control. For example, agriculture in the expanse of the lowland tropical forest between the Maya highlands (Alvarado transect) and northern Yucatán (Montejo transect) remained more or less as it had been at contact, that is extensive swidden cultivation. One landscape prized by the Spaniards that survived more or less in its pre-Hispanic form, at least under the first phase of Spanish domination, was that of the cacao-producing Boca Costa and Soconusco (Alvarado transect). The Spaniards were quick to realize the importance of cacao among Mesoamericans and, later, its value for international trade (Hamilton 1976, 860–61). They took control of cacao producing zones largely through the *encomienda*, the effect of which was to leave the form of production largely intact.

The reconfiguring of the cultivated landscapes did not mean that Amerindian agricultural practices and technologies were lost; many survived as integral components of the new landscapes. Perhaps the most important of these was the omnipresent *calmil*. Small household gardens remained central to Amerindian and peasant agriculture throughout the contact and colonial periods (and are still maintained), albeit with European additions. Field-scale surface modifications, especially *camellones* and *montones,* also endured well, especially where maize cultivation persisted without the plow. These features were so common in the *Mesa Central* in the sixteenth century that any parcel of cultivated land was referred to as a *camellón* and even abandoned lands were known as *"acamellonada"* (i.e., filled with planting mounds) (Rojas Rabiela 1988, 42–43). The *metapantli* (maguey-anchored terraces) also survived (Patrick 1977), perhaps because of the ease of upkeep of the retaining wall, although it was much more spatially restricted than in precontact times (Donkin 1979). Vestiges of drained fields, raised fields, and *tablones* also weathered the conquest, but in highly localized areas. The survival of the *tablón* in Guatemala (Alvarado transect) was due in part to its use on steep and narrow lands not suited for other forms of cultivation, and, as Mathewson (1984, 24–25) implies, because it may have been appropriated by the Spaniards for their own horticultural needs. Finally, various extensive rotational systems continued to be employed, especially in the *tierra caliente* and in areas that were and remained sparsely utilized. In some cases, extensive agriculture may have been introduced anew in so-called refuge areas—regions where the indigenous population fled to avoid Spanish laws, taxes, or culture, such as the sparsely inhabited interior of the Maya lowlands.

These Amerindian systems were combined with Hispanic ones to create the new cultivated landscapes of New Spain. In some cases, systems of either origin were distributed across a landscape according to the differing socioeconomic and environmental circumstances present (e.g., Spanish-dominated bottom lands and Amerindian-dominated slope lands). More common, however, the various systems themselves were modified by exchanges in biota and technology. The new cultivated landscapes, therefore, were a product of agricultural systems lost, added, modified through exchange, and redistributed across the terrain.

Transformations in Perspective

What became known as *La leyenda negra* (the Black Legend) encapsulated long-standing beliefs about Spanish civilization and its conquests in the New World, perhaps overstating its barbarism and brutality relative to other societies. In recent years, another legend related to the Columbian Encounter has emerged: what might be called *La leyenda verde.* This Green Legend mythologizes the achievements and qualities of Amerindian cultures, especially their agriculture. Such interpretations, especially in the popular literature (e.g., Sale 1990; Weatherford 1988), attribute Amerindian decision making in agriculture and landscape alterations to cultural values placed on the conservation of nature or on the need for harmony with nature as much as or more than to the need for food, fiber, and tribute, the desire for wealth, or the response to sociopolitical conflict and change. An idealized Amerindian experience of using nature in a benign way is contrasted with a European penchant for controlling or raping nature for profit. This polarization errs in several fundamental ways as applied to the cultivated landscapes of Mesoamerica and New Spain. It fails to appreciate sufficiently the nature and scale of agricultural production in preconquest Mesoamerica and, hence, the scale and magnitude of its associated environmental changes, and it tends to inflate the environmental damage associated with the cultivated landscapes of New Spain.

The peoples of Mesoamerica engineered nature into regional mosaics comprised of diverse systems of cultivation which contributed to extensive land modification and conversion. The particular systems and the landscapes in which they were embedded were the result of real and perceived needs in the context of the cultural and environmental constraints and opportunities. These systems served first to feed the large populations, but also to sustain elites and oppressive political structures, engage in commerce, and pay tribute. Polities fought one another for the control of the land and the wealth that came from its cultivation. Production shortfalls, even prolonged famines, were common throughout Mesoamerica (e.g., Hassig 1981), and changes in socioeconomic conditions led to localized decay, abandonment, and replacement of particular agricultural landscapes, ofttimes leading to environmental degradation (e.g., see Williams 1972).

The Columbian Encounter constituted an abrupt, even brutal, change in population, biota, technological capacity (especially in transportation), and, to a much lesser extent, political economy that recast Amerindian cultivated landscapes. The swiftness of change as well as the changes themselves exacerbated environmental damage as some systems were abandoned and others reconstituted, but ultimately a series of "*mestizo*" cultivated landscapes emerged that were more or less ecologically sustainable. It is difficult to compare these pre- and post-Columbian landscapes in terms of such attributes as land and labor productivity or environmental damage. In general however, Amerindian systems may have been more land productive (output per unit area and time), while Spanish systems were higher in labor productivity. The exception to this characterization, of course, was Amerindian shifting cultivation.

This reality does not demean the accomplishments of the Amerindian cultivator, nor does it diminish the impact of the Columbian Encounter. Rather, it directs us to understand the Encounter from a position of balance. Both the pre- and postcontact landscapes of cultivation were constructed for the purpose of extracting from nature, and as the pressures for this extraction varied, so did the kind and scale of local landscape transformation. Where and when these pressures were high in Mesoamerica, extensive alterations of environments took place. The denudation of the tropical forests of the Maya lowlands before 1000 A.D. and the complete transformation of the Basin of Mexico, especially during Aztec times, are clear examples. We can assign the negative environmental impacts of the emergent landscapes of New Spain to an inherent view of nature embedded within Hispanic and European culture, only in a polemic that fails to understand the material circumstances that drive agricultural change. A more balanced view of this collision of worlds forces us to recognize that environmental degradation invariably follows the abandonment of well-adjusted intensive systems and the experimentation with rapidly evolving new systems. This was so before the Columbian Encounter and remains so today.

Acknowledgments

Much of the research behind this work was supported by a grant from the National Endowment for the Humanities. We are indebted to Karl W. Butzer, William M. Denevan, William E. Doolittle, Kent Mathewson, William B. Meyer, Ylena Ogneva, Alfred Siemens, Andrew Sluyter, and the anonymous reviewers for their comments and critiques of this manuscript during various stages of preparation. We thank Heather Henderson for assistance in preparing the final manuscript, and Patti Neumann for preparing the maps and figures.

Notes

1. See the Montejo Transect for descriptions of swidden or slash-and-burn cultivation (also called *tumba y roza,* signifying long fallow, and *barbecho,* signifying short fallow).
2. This section is based largely on information from two large city-state provinces encountered along the Cortés route, Tlaxcala and Cholua (in the present Mexican states of Tlaxcala and Puebla), and from the Basin of Mexico (including parts of the present day Mexican states of México and the Distrito Federal) (Fig. 2).
3. For the details of the construction, morphology, and functioning of most the systems described for the Mesa Central, see Wilken's (1987) thorough assessment of modern-day systems, many, if not most, of which have their origins in pre-Columbian times, and Rojas Rabiela's (1988) excellent treatment of early postcontact indigenous systems.
4. The construction of *chinampas* has been the subject of considerable discussion, because few, if any, have been built in modern times. No less an authority than Humboldt refers to "the chinampas, that Europeans call floating gardens. There are two types: some are moveable . . . others are closely fixed to the margins" (1966, 134). Some have interpreted references to "floating gardens" as references to *chinampas* proper, while others believe that they refer to the canoes filled with transplantings (on route to *chinampas*) or to gathered vegetation floated across the lakes for various purposes. See the following for details and more on the *chinampa* dispute: Apenas 1943, Bancroft 1914 [1887], Bernal 1973, de Acosta 1604, Gibson 1964, Leicht 1937, López Ríos 1988, and Wilken 1985.
5. Spanish documents notwithstanding, the northern Yucatán is not generally considered to have been a major source of cacao (*Theobroma cacao* or *T. bicolor*) at contact times (Bergmann 1969). Indeed, the Yucatán's hydrological conditions seem unsuitable for extensive production. The sole direct evidence of cacao from the Yucatán is a rare variety only known in the Lacandon region of Mexico (Gómez-Pompa, et al. 1990).
6. Landa (Tozzer 1941, 196) mentioned the presence of root crops, probably *jicama (Pachyrihizus erosus* L.), but the significance of root crops in the north at contact times is suspect. The soils of the plains are extremely thin, incapable of supporting adequate root and tuber growth. No reports of the use of mounding (*montones*), which might indi-

cate major root crop cultivation, exist for the lowland Maya realm at this time.

7. For descriptions of contemporary swidden agriculture throughout the Maya lowlands, see Carter 1969; O. Cook 1921; Emerson and Kempton 1935; Hester 1954; Higbee 1948; Redfield and Avilla 1934; Roys 1943.

8. Licate (1981, 1, 133) refers to this hybridization as giving rise to "Mexican" landscapes in the Mesa Central. We have refrained from using this term because two of our transects deal with cultural or political units that are not Mexican.

9. Perhaps fueled by the controversy that still surrounds the scale of the Amerindian depopulation, the literature related to the Amerindian population decline is too large to fully cite here. See Denevan (1976, 1992) for a useful bibliography and a thorough overview of the issue. Simulation exercises indicate that depopulation probably approached 90 percent by 1600 (Whitmore 1991, 1992).

10. A prevalent theme asserts that Amerindians typically favored wetlands and slopes because noninundated, level terrain (between slope and shore) was not suited to their nonplow cultivation technologies. This assessment is too simple. Nonplow cultivators are known to have cultivated almost every conceivable terrain (Turner and Brush 1987), given the need to do so.

11. The development of agricultural estates for the monocropping of henequen (sisal) did not emerge in the Yucatán until the nineteenth century (Farriss 1984, 34).

12. We are not certain of the impact of metal tools on the frequency of swidden or milpa cultivation in the region. One argument holds that the ease of cutting trees with steel tools promoted more extensive systems of cultivation, and that the more strenuous labor involved in felling trees with stone tools would have favored more frequent cultivation of the same plot. Incidentally, Landa (Tozzer 1941, 121) reported that the Maya had metal hatchets, but it is not certain that they were used in agriculture.

References

Acosta, Joseph de. 1880 [1590]. The natural and moral history of the Indies. London: Hakluyt Society. 1880.

Alcorn, Janice B. 1984. Haustec Mayan ethnobotany. Austin: University of Texas Press.

Altee, Charles B., Jr. 1968. Vegetable production in Guatemala. Washington: U.S. Agency for International Development.

Andrews, Anthony P. 1983. Maya salt production and trade. Tucson: University of Arizona Press.

Apenas, Ola. 1943. The pond in our backyard. Mexican Life 19(60):15–18.

Armillas, Pedro. 1949. Notas sobre sistemas de cultivo en Mesoamérica. Anales del Instituto Nacional de Anthropología e Historia 3:85–113.

——. 1971. Gardens on swamps. Science 174(4010):653–61.

——; Palerm, Angel; and Wolf, Eric R. 1956. A small irrigation system in the valley of Teotihuacan. American Antiquity 21(4):396–99.

Bancroft, Hubert H. 1914 (1887). The history of Mexico, being a popular history of the Mexican people from earliest primitive civilization to the present time. San Francisco: Bancroft Co.

Barlow, R. H. 1949. The extent of the empire of the Culhua Mexica. Ibero-Americana 28. Berkeley: University of California Press.

Barrett, Ward. 1970. The sugar hacienda of the Marqueses del Valle. Minneapolis: University of Minnesota Press.

Bergmann, John F. 1969. The distribution of cacao cultivation in pre-Columbian America. Annals of the Association of American Geographers 59:85–96.

Bernal, Ignacio. 1973. Mexico before Cortez: Art history and legend. New York: Doubleday Anchor Press.

Brand, Donald D. 1961. The early history of the range cattle industry in northern mexico. Agricultural History 35(3):132–39.

Butzer, Karl W. 1991. Spanish colonization of the new world: Cultural continuity and change in Mexico. Erdkunde 45(3):204–19.

——. 1992. Transfer of the Mediterranean livestock economy to New Spain: Adaptations and consequences. Paper presented at the SCOPE Scientific Symposium on Principles, Patterns, and Processes: Some Legacies of the Columbian Encounter, Sevilla, Spain.

—— and Butzer, Elisabeth. 1992. Personal communication, January.

Calneck, Edward E. 1972. Settlement patterns and chinampa agriculture at Tenochtitlán. American Antiquity 37(1):104–15.

Carter, William E. 1969. New lands and old traditions: Kekchi cultivators in the Guatemalan lowlands. Latin American Monograph 6. Gainesville: University of Florida Press.

Chamberlain, Robert S. 1948. The conquest and colonization of Yucatan, 1517–1550. Publication 582. Washington: Carnegie Institution of Washington.

Chase, Arlen F., and Rice, Prudence M. 1985. The lowland Maya postclassic. Austin: University of Texas Press.

Chevalier, F. 1963. Land and society in colonial America, ed. L. B. Simpson; trans. by A. Eustis. Berkeley: University of California Press.

Clendinnen, Inga. 1987. Ambivalent conquests: Maya and Spaniard in Yucatan, 1517–1570. Cambridge: Cambridge University Press.

Cline, H. F. 1949. Civil congregations of the Indians in New Spain, 1598–1606. The Hispanic American Historical Review 29(3):349–69.

Coe, M. D. 1964. The chinampas of Mexico. *Scientific American* 211(1):90–98.

Cook, O. F. 1921. Milpa agriculture: A primitive tropical system. *Annual Report of the Smithsonian Institution,* 1919:302–26.

Cook, Sherburne F., and Borah, W. 1979. Indian food production and consumption in Central Mexico before and after the conquest (1500–1650). In *Essays in population history, Mexico and California.* vol. 3. Berkeley: University of California Press.

Cortés, Hernán. 1945. *Cartas y relaciones.* Buenos Aires: Emecé Editores, S.A.

Crosby, Alfred W., Jr. 1972. *The Columbian exchange: Biological and cultural consequences of 1492.* Contributions in American Studies 2. Westport, CT: Greenwood.

Culbert, T. Patrick. 1973. *The classic Maya collapse.* Albuquerque: University of New Mexico Press.

Davis, Clint. 1990. Water control and settlement in colonial Mexico's first frontier: The bordo system of the eastern Bajío. *Yearbook, Conference of Latin Americanist Geographers* 16:73–81.

Denevan, W. M. 1992 [1976]. *The native population of the Americas in 1492.* Madison: University of Wisconsin Press.

Diaz del Castillo, Bernal. 1956. *The discovery and conquest of Mexico,* trans. A. P. Maudslay. New York: Farrar, Straus and Giroux.

Donkin, R. A. 1979. *Agricultural terracing in the aboriginal New World.* Tucson, AZ: University of Arizona Press for the Wenner-Gren Foundation for Anthropological Research, Inc.

Doolittle, William E. 1990. *Canal irrigation in prehistoric Mexico. The sequence of technological change.* Austin: University of Texas Press.

Emerson, R. A., and J. H. Kempton. 1935. Agronomic investigations in Yucatan. *Yearbook of the Carnegie Institution of Washington* 34:138–42.

Evans, Susan T. 1990. The productivity of maguey terrace agriculture in central Mexico during the Aztec period. *Latin American Antiquity* 1(2):117–32.

Farriss, Nancy M. 1984. *Maya society under colonial rule: The collective enterprise of survival.* Princeton, NJ: Princeton University Press.

Feldman, Lawrence H. 1985. *A tumpline economy. Production and distribution systems in sixteenth-century eastern Guatemala.* Culver City, CA: Labyrinthos.

Finch, William A. Jr. 1965. The karst landscape of Yucatan. Ph.D. dissertation, University of Illinois.

Folan, W. J.; Fletcher, L. A.; and Kintz, E. R. 1979. Fruit, fiber, bark, and resin: social organization of a Maya urban center. *Science* 204:697–701.

Freidel, David A., and Leventhal, Richard M. 1975.

The settlement survey. In *A study of changing pre-Columbian commercial systems: The 1972–1973 season at Cozumel, Mexico,* ed. J. A. Sabloff, and W. L. Rathje, pp. 60–76. Monograph 3. Peabody Museum of Archaeology and Ethnology. Cambridge: Harvard University.

Fuentes y Guzmán, D., and de Francisco, Antonio. 1882. *Historia de Guatemala, o recordation florida. Natural vecino y regidor perpetuo de la cindad de Guatemala.* Madrid: Biblioteca de los Americanistas.

García Cook, Angel. 1985. Historia de la tecnología agrícola en el altiplano central desde el principio de la agricultura hasta el siglo XIII. In *Historia de la agricultura. Epoca prehispánica-siglo XVI,* ed. Teresa Rojas Rabiela, and William T. Sanders, pp. 7–75. Mexico City: Instituto Nacional de Antropología e Historia.

Gasco, Janine. 1987. Cacao and the economic integration of native society in colonial Soconusco, New Spain. Ph.D. dissertation, University of California, Santa Barbara.

——— and Barbara Voorhies. 1989. The ultimate tribute: The role of the Soconusco as an Aztec tributary. In *Ancient trade and tribute,* ed. by Barbara Voorhies, pp. 48–94. Provo: University of Utah Press.

Gibson, Charles. 1964. *The Aztec under Spanish rule: A history of the Indians of the valley of Mexico 1519–1810.* Stanford, CA: Stanford University Press.

Gómez-Pompa, Arturo; Flores, Jose Salvador; and Sosa, Victoria. 1987. The "pet kot": A manmade tropical forest of the Maya. *Interciencia* 12(1):10–15.

———; ———; and Aliphat Fernández, Mario. 1990. The sacred cacao groves of the Maya. *Latin America Antiquity* 1(3):247–57.

Gutiérrez Ruvalcaba, Ignacio. Forthcoming. Ecología y agricultura en Metztitlán, siglos XVI y XVII. In *Agricultura indígena: Pasado y presente,* ed. by Teresa Rojas Rabiela. Mexico City: CIESAS, Editiones de las Casa Chata.

Guzmán, Louis E. 1962. Las terrazas de los antiguos mayas montañeses. *Revista Interamerican de Ciencias Sociales,* 2nd epoch, vol. 1(3):398–406.

Hamilton, Earl J. 1976. What the new world gave the economy of the old. In *First images of America,* vol. 2, ed. Fredi Chiappelli, Michael J. B. Allen, and Robert L. Benson, pp. 853–84. Berkeley: University of California Press.

Hassig, Ross. 1981. The famine of one rabbit: Ecological causes and social consequences of a pre-Columbian calamity. *Journal of Anthropological Research* 37:171–82.

———. 1985. *Trade, tribute, and transportation. The sixteenth-century political economy of the valley of Mexico*. Norman: University of Oklahoma Press.

Hester, Joseph A. 1954. Natural and cultural bases of ancient Maya subsistence. Ph.D. dissertation, University of California, Los Angeles.

Higbee, Edward. 1948. Agriculture in the Mayan homeland. *Geographical Review* 48:457–64.

Humboldt, Alexander von. 1966. *Ensayo politico sobre el reino de la nueva España*, ed. Juan A. Ortega y Medina. Mexico City: Editorial Porrua, S.A.

Jones, Grant D. 1989 *Maya resistance to Spanish rule: Time and history on a colonial frontier*. Albuquerque: University of New Mexico Press.

Killion, T. Forthcoming. *Gardens in prehistory*. University, AL: University of Alabama Press.

Landa, Diego de. 1937 [1566]. *Yucatán before and after the conquest*. Trans. W. Gates. New York: Dover Publications.

Lange, Frederick W. 1971. *Culture history of the Sapoa river valley of Costa Rica*. Occasional Papers in Anthropology 4. Beloit, WI: Logan Museum of Anthropology, Beloit College.

Leicht, Hugo. 1937. Chinampas y almácigos flotantes. *Anales del Instituto de Biología (UNAM)* 5(3):375–86.

Licate, Jack A. 1981. *Creation of a Mexican landscape: Territorial organization and settlement in the eastern Puebla basin 1520–1605*. Department of Geography Research Papers 201. Chicago: University of Chicago.

López de Gómara, Francisco. 1964. *Cortés. The life of the conqueror by his secretary*. Trans. and ed. Lesley Byrd Simpson. Berkeley: University of California Press.

López Ríos, Georgina Florencia. 1988. *Sistema agrícola de chinampa: Perspectiva agroecológica*. Mexico City: Universidad Autonoma Chapingo.

Lothrop, Samuel K. 1933. *Atitlán. An archaeological study of ancient remains on the borders of Lake Atitlán, Guatemala*. Publication 444. Washington: Carnegie Institute of Washington.

MacLeod, Murdo J. 1973. *Spanish central America: Socioeconomic history, 1520–1720*. Berkeley: University of California Press.

Mathewson, Kent. 1984. *Irrigation horticulture in highland Guatemala: The tablón system of Panajachel*. Boulder, CO: Westview.

Means, Philip A. 1917. *History of the Spanish conquest of Yucatán and of the Itzás*. Papers of the Peabody Museum of American Archaeology and Ethnology, Harvard University, vol. 8. Cambridge, MA.

Millon, René F. 1957. Irrigation systems in the valley of Teotihuacán. *American Antiquity* 23(2):160–66.

———. 1955. Trade, tree cultivation, and the development of private property in land. *American Anthropologist* 57(4):698–712.

Moriarty, J. R. 1968. Floating gardens (chinampas) agriculture in the old lakes of Mexico. *America Indígena* 28(2):461–84.

Morrisey, Richard J. 1951. The northward expansion of cattle ranching in New Spain, 1550–1600. *Agricultural History* 25(3):115–21.

National Geographic Society. 1989. *Land of the Maya* (map). Washington.

———. 1980. *Mexico and Central America* (map). Washington.

Orellana, Sandra L. 1984. *The Tzutujil Mayas. Continuity and change, 1250–1630*. Norman: University of Oklahoma Press.

Palerm, Angel. 1955. The agricultural bases of urban civilization in Mesoamerica. In *Irrigation civilizations: A comparative study*, ed. by J. H. Steward, pp. 28–42. Pan American Union Social Science Monographs 1. Washington.

———. 1973. *Obras hidráulicas prehispánicas en el sistema lacustre del valle de Mexico*. Cordoba, Mexico: Instituto Nacional de Anthropología e Historia.

——— **and Wolf, Eric.** 1962. Potencial ecológico y desarrollo cultural de mesoamerica. *Revista Interamericana de Ciencias Sociales,* 2nd epoch, 1(2):322–45.

Parsons, Jeffery R. 1971. *Prehistoric settlement patterns in the Texcoco region, Mexico*. Memoirs of the Museum of Anthropology 3. Ann Arbor: University of Michigan.

———. 1976. The role of chinampa agriculture in the food supply of Aztec Tenochtitlán. In *Cultural change and continuity: Essays in honor of James Bennett Griffin*, ed. by Charles E. Cleland, pp. 233–57. New York: Academic Press.

Patrick, L. 1985. Agave and zea in highland central Mexico: The ecology and history of the Metepantli. In *Prehistoric intensive agriculture in the tropics*, vol. 2, ed. I. S. Farrington, pp. 539–46. Oxford: B.A.R. International Series, 232.

———. 1977. A cultural geography of the use of seasonally dry, sloping terrain: The metepantli crop terraces of central Mexico. Ph.D. dissertation, University of Pittsburgh.

Pohl, Mary. 1985. An ethnohistorical perspective on ancient Maya wetland fields and other cultivation systems in the lowlands. In *Prehistoric lowland Maya environment and subsistence economy*, ed. M. D. Pohl, Papers of the Peabody Museum of Archaeology and Ethnology, Harvard University, vol. 77, pp. 35–45. Cambridge, MA.

Redfield, Robert, and Avila, R. 1934. *Chan Kom: A Maya village*. Publication 488. Washington: Carnegie Institution of Washington.

Rojas Rabiela, Teresa. 1985. La technología agrícola mesoamericana en el Siglo XVI. In *Histo-*

ria de la agricultural epoca prehispánica-siglo XVI, ed. Teresa Rojas Rabiela and William T. Sanders, pp 129–232. Mexico City: Instituto Nacional de Antropología e Historia.

———. 1988. *Las siembras de ayer: La agricultura indígena del siglo XVI.* Mexico City: Secretaría de Educación Pública y Centro de Investigaciones y Estudios Superiores en Antropología Social.

———. Forthcoming. Historia de la agricultura. Epoca prehispanica. In *La agricultura en tierras mexicanas. De las origenes del siglo XX.* Mexico City: Editorial Grijalbo S.A.

Roys, Ralph L. 1943. *The Indian background of colonial Yucatan.* Publication 548. Washington: Carnegie Institution of Washington.

Sale, Kirkpatrick. 1990. *The conquest of paradise: Christopher Columbus and the Columbian legacy.* New York: A. Knopf.

Sanders, William T. 1972. The agricultural history of the basin of Mexico. In *The valley of Mexico,* ed. Eric R. Wolf, pp. 101–59. Albuquerque: University of New Mexico Press.

———. 1981. Ecological adaptation in the basin of Mexico: 23,000 BC to present. In *Archaeology. Handbook of middle American Indians,* ed. J. A. Sabloff, pp. 147–97. Austin: University of Texas Press.

———; **Parsons, J. R.; and Santley, R. S.** 1979. *The basin of Mexico: Ecological processes in the evolution of a civilization.* New York: Academic Press.

Sauer, Jonathan D. 1976. Changing perception and exploitation of New World plants in Europe, 1492–1800. In *First images of America* vol. 2, ed. Fredi Chiappelli, pp. 813–32. Berkeley: University of California Press.

Schmidt, Peter J. 1977. Un sistema de cultivo intensivo en la cuenca del río Nautla, Veracruz. *Boletín del Instituto Nacional de Antropología e Historia* 3(20):50–60.

Scholes, France V., and Roys, Ralph L. 1968 [1948]. *The Maya Chontal Indians of Acalan-Tixchel: A contribution to the history and ethnography of the Yucatan peninsula.* Norman: University of Oklahoma Press.

Siemens, Alfred H. 1982. Modelling pre-hispanic hydroagriculture on levee backslopes in northern Veracruz, Mexico. In *Drained field agriculture in Central and South America,* ed. J. P. Darch, pp. 27–54. Oxford: British Archaeological Reports International Series 189.

———. 1983. Oriented raised fields in central Veracruz. *American Antiquity* 48(1):85–102.

———. 1990. *Between summit and sea. Central Veracruz in the nineteenth century.* Vancouver: University of British Columbia Press.

———. 1992. Land use succession in the Gulf lowlands on Mexico: A long view. Paper presented at the SCOPE Scientific Symposium on Principles, Patterns, and Processes: Some Legacies of the Columbian Encounter. Sevilla, Spain.

———, **et al.** 1988. Evidence for a cultivar and a chronology from patterned wetlands in central Veracruz, Mexico. *Science* 242:105–07.

Simpson, L. B. 1952. *Exploitation of land in central Mexico in the sixteenth century.* Ibero-Americana 36. Berkeley: University of California Press.

Sluyter, Andrew. 1990. Vestiges of upland fields in central Veracruz: A new perspective on its Precolumbian human ecology. M.A. thesis, University of British Columbia.

Stadleman, Raymond. 1940. *Maize cultivation in northwestern Guatemala.* Contributions to American Anthropology and History. Publication 523, pp. 83–263. Washington: Carnegie Institution of Washington.

Stark, Barbara L. 1974. Geography and economic specialization in the lower Papaloapan, Veracruz, Mexico. *Ethnohistory* 21(3):199–221.

———. 1978. An ethnohistoric model for native economy and settlement patterns in southern Veracruz, Mexico. In *Prehistoric coastal adaptation: The economy and ecology of maritime Central America,* ed. Barbara L. Stark and Barbara Voorhies, pp. 211–38. New York: Academic Press.

———. 1990. The Gulf coast and central highlands of Mexico: Alternative methods for interaction. *Research in Economic Anthropology* 12:243–85.

Stevens, Rayfred L. 1964. The soils of Middle America and their relation to Indian people and cultures. In *Natural environments and early cultures,* vol. 1, Handbook of Middle American Indians, ed. Robert C. West, pp. 265–315. Austin: University of Texas Press.

Stone, Doris. 1977. *Pre-Columbian man in Costa Rica.* Cambridge: Harvard University Peabody Museum Press.

Super, John C. 1988. *Food, conquest, and colonization in sixteenth-century Spanish America.* Albuquerque: University of New Mexico Press.

Tozzer, Alfred M. 1941. *Landa's relación de las cosas de Yucatán.* Peabody Museum, Paper 18 (translation). Cambridge: Harvard University.

Turner, B. L. II. 1983a. Comparisons of agrotechnologies in the Basin of Mexico and central Maya lowlands: Formative to the classic Maya collapse. In *Highland-lowland interaction in Mesoamerica. Interdisciplinary approaches* ed. A. G. Miller, pp. 13–47. Washington: Dunbarton Oaks Research Library and Collection.

———. 1983b. *Once beneath the forest: Prehistoric terracing in the Río Bec region of the Maya lowlands.* Dellplain Latin American Series 13, Boulder, CO: Westview Press.

———. 1990a. Population reconstruction for the central Maya lowlands: 1000 BC to AD 1500. In

Precolumbian population history in the Maya lowlands, ed. T. P. Culbert and D. S. Rice pp. 301–24. Albuquerque: University of New Mexico Press.

——. 1990b. The rise and fall of population and agriculture in the central Maya lowlands: 300 BC to present. In *Hunger in history: Food shortage, poverty, and deprivation,* ed. L. F. Newman, pp. 178–211. Cambridge, MA: Basil Blackwell.

—— and Brush, S. B. 1987. *Comparative farming systems.* New York: Guilford Press.

—— and Miksicek, Charles H. 1984. Economic plant species associated with prehistoric agriculture in the Maya lowlands. *Economic Botany* 38:179–93.

U.S. Defense Mapping Agency. 1978. *Operational navigational chart, K-25.* Washington.

——. 1974. *Operational navigational chart, J-24.* Washington.

——. 1965. *Operational navigational chart, J-25.* Washington.

Vivió Escoto, Jorge A. 1964. Weather and climate of Central Mexico. In *Natural environment and early cultures,* vol. 1, Handbook of Middle American Indians, ed. Robert C. West, pp. 187–215. Austin: University of Texas Press.

Weatherford, Jack. 1988. *Indian givers: How the Indians of the Americas transformed the world.* New York: Fawcett Columbine.

West, Robert C. 1964a. The natural regions of middle America. In *Natural environments and early cultures.* vol. 1, Handbook of Middle American Indians, pp. 363–83. Austin: University of Texas Press.

——. 1964b. Surface configuration and associated geology of Middle America. In *Natural environments and early cultures,* vol. 1, Handbook of Middle American Indians, pp. 33–83. Austin: University of Texas Press.

—— and Pedro Armillas. 1952. Las chinampas de México. Poesía realidad de los "jardines flontates." *Cuadernos Americanos* 50:165–82.

Whitmore, Thomas M. 1991. A simulation of the sixteenth-century population collapse in the Basin of Mexico. *Annals of the Association of American Geographers* 81(3):464–87.

——. 1992. *Disease and death in early colonial Mexico: Simulating Amerindian depopulation.* Dellplain Latin American Geography Series. Boulder, CO: Westview Press.

Wilhelmy, Herbert. 1981. *Welt und umwelt der Maya.* Munich: R. Piper and Co. Verlag.

Wilken, Gene C. 1969. Drained field agriculture: An intensive farming system in Tlaxcala, Mexico. *The Geographical Review* 59:215–41.

——. 1971. Food-producing systems available to the ancient Maya. *American Antiquity* 36:xx.

——. 1979. Traditional slope management: An analytical approach. In *Hill lands: Proceedings of an international symposium,* pp. 416–21. Morgantown: West Virginia University Books.

——. 1985. A note on bouyancy and other dubious characteristics of the "floating" chinampas of Mexico. In *Prehistoric intensive agriculture in the tropics,* ed. I. S. Farrington, pp. 31–48. International Series 232. Oxford: British Archaeological Reports.

——. 1987. *Good farmers: Traditional agricultural resource management in Mexico and Central America.* Berkeley: University of California Press.

Wilkerson, S. Jeffrey K. 1983. So green like a garden: Intensive agriculture in ancient Veracruz. In *Drained field agriculture in Central and South America,* ed. J. P. Darch, pp. 55–90. International Series 189. Oxford: British Archaeological Reports.

Williams, Barbara J. 1972. Tepetate in the Valley of Mexico. *Annals of the Association of American Geographers* 62(4):618–26.

Wilson, Eugene M. 1980. Physical geography of the Yucatán peninsula. In *Yucatán, a world apart,* ed. E. H. Moseley and E. D. Terry, pp. 5–40. University, AL: University of Alabama Press.

Wolf, Eric C., and Palerm, Angel. 1955. Irrigation in the old Acolhua domain, Mexico. *Southwestern Journal of Anthropology* 11:265–81.

Zamora Acosta, Elias. 1985. *Los Mayas de las tierras altas en el siglo XVI. Tradición y cambio en Guatemala.* Sevilla: Diputación Provincial de Sevilla.

"Heavy Shadows and Black Night": Disease and Depopulation in Colonial Spanish America

W. George Lovell

Department of Geography, Queen's University at Kingston, Ontario, Canada K7L 3N6

FAX 613-545-6122

Abstract. A substantive body of scholarship now recognizes that Native American populations declined precipitously in size following European conquest and colonization. The precise magnitude of demographic collapse continues to spark heated debate, but consensus is emerging where dissent prevailed before. That consensus attributes Indian depopulation in large part to the introduction of Old World disease. Many factors besides imported sickness caused aboriginal demise, but disease proved the most destructive agent of a fatal complex. This paper examines the role disease played in depopulating the Spanish Indies, from first contact to the early seventeenth century. Analysis focuses on five distinct geographical settings: Hispaniola, central Mexico, northwestern Mexico, Guatemala south of the Petén rainforest, and the central Andes. For each of these settings, literature is reviewed that illuminates problems of data, chronology, impact, and identification that have charged discussion of the issues for some time. An attempt is made to situate regional findings in hemispheric context and to appraise the status of the disease factor in quincentennial consciousness.

Key Words: Old World disease, Native American depopulation, colonial Spanish America, Hispaniola, Mexico, Guatemala, central Andes.

Little by little heavy shadows and black night enveloped our fathers and grandfathers and us also, oh, my sons! All of us were thus. We were born to die!

Annals of the Cakchiquels (ca. 1559–81)

WHOEVER watched as Columbus came ashore, if any natives did, witnessed the beginning of a conquest that would eventually cause the greatest destruction of lives in history. We will never know precisely how many died, but it is now possible, even in the midst of ongoing controversy about the numbers involved, to distinguish which factor out of a tragic and potent mix proved the most destructive. That factor is disease (N. D. Cook and Lovell 1992). Whether the theater of disaster was the Canadian west or the Chilean south, European intrusion unleashed on Native American peoples abrupt and unprecedented collapse by exposing their immune systems to hitherto unknown forms of sickness.

It was, to be sure, a variable encounter, for some Indian groups fared much better than others in the face of sustained European expansion. Period by period, place by place, no two experiences were exactly alike, for regional and local circumstances differed markedly across the Americas. The Taino of Hispaniola, for example, have disappeared, as have the Beothuk of Newfoundland and the Yahi of California. In sharp contrast, more than twenty distinct Maya cultures endure in Guatemala, albeit under considerable duress. Many factors besides disease must be examined in order to explain patterns of survival or demise (Newson 1985; Lutz and Lovell 1990), but the key to comprehending the scale and rapidity of native depopulation, especially in the years immediately following contact, lies in the role played by Old World disease. Europeans fell sick and died from illness too, just as countless Indians perished by fire and sword or from trauma and exploitation, reasons connected more to ideology and power than to genetics and germs. But disease ranks first, at least in terms of the intellectual discourse that generally prevails, in learned journals if not in the popular imagination, five centuries after conquest was begun.

It was not always so. Until early this century, Spain's American exploits continued to be viewed in the English-language world through the lens of the Black Legend. That view attributes native loss-of-life primarily to demoniacal acts of cruelty, a vision promoted from 1514 on in the works of the Dominican friar Bartolomé de las Casas (1957–61). It befell an American geographer, Carl O. Sauer, to be among the first of modern scholars to call attention to the impact of Old World disease on Native American life (1935), a relationship Las Casas apparently understood but chose not to emphasize. While the Black Legend, as Charles Gibson (1964) aptly observed, also reflects the hideous truth of a Black Reality, its overall portrayal is crude and simplistic, its representations stark and unrefined. Sauer was certainly no apologist for Spanish colonialism, as his views of Columbus and the Columbus legacy clearly attest (1966). He was, if anything, like Las Casas a "defender of the Indians," calling for greater recognition of the worth of their cultures and more sympathetic appreciation of their fate (1939). Three of Sauer's Berkeley associates—Woodrow Borah, Sherburne F. Cook, and Lesley B. Simpson—pursued this interest, revolutionizing not only the way we think about the size of Precolumbian native populations but also the ranking of factors most responsible for post-conquest decline (Denevan, forthcoming). Although the "Berkeley School" of historical demography has its articulate detractors, even they would concede that an impressive body of work has shaped the agenda of current debate.

This paper seeks to illuminate the role disease played in depopulating the Spanish Indies, primarily from first contact to the early seventeenth century. That period is important,

for its temporal span is one in which epidemics that originated as "visiting people" (Greek *epidemos*) eventually became endemic, ones that stayed among or "in people" (Greek *endemos*), for most parts of the empire at any rate. Five vignettes—for Hispaniola, central Mexico, northwestern Mexico, Guatemala south of the Petén rainforest, and the central Andes—illustrate the problems encountered with data, chronology, impact, and identification. A concluding section situates the regional discussions in hemispheric context and appraises the status of the disease factor in quincentennial consciousness.

"Who Will Believe This?": Hispaniola, 1493–1518[1]

In terms of conquest demography, no single outcome provokes such heated debate, nor such vast disagreement in terms of aboriginal numbers, as Hispaniola, the Caribbean island today shared by Haiti and the Dominican Republic. Hispaniola's notoriety involves (1) the Admiral of the Ocean Sea, Cristóbal Colón, the name by which Columbus (baptized Cristoforo Colombo in his native Genoa) is known in the Spanish-speaking world; (2) the equally controversial figure of Bartolomé de las Casas, who went to Hispaniola in 1502 as a young man in search of fortune, mended his ways at age 40, and thereafter, as a member of the Church, denounced the behavior of fellow Spaniards and campaigned relentlessly to better the native lot; and (3) the first known casualties of the European conquest of America, the Taino or Island Arawaks.[2]

The range of contact population estimates, given that all scholars manipulate essentially the same sources, is remarkable. At the low end, Verlinden (1968) suggests a mere 60,000, roughly half the figures put forward by Amiama (1959) and Rosenblat (1976). In the middle range, Córdova (1968) reckons 500,000, compatible with the uppermost statistic in a series calculated by Lipschutz (1966); Moya Pons (1971, 1987) advances 375,000–600,000; and Zambardino (1978) and Guerra (1985) favor approximately one million. At the high end, S. F. Cook and Borah (1971, 407) project eight million. Sauer (1966, 65–69), shrewdly noncommittal, refers to an "oft-repeated figure" of 1,100,000, the number that Las Casas was told by Archbishop Deza of Seville that Columbus had mentioned to him in conversation. Skeptical of the whole business, Henige (1978, 237) concludes that "it is futile to offer any numerical estimates at all on the basis of the evidence now before us." Others press on, evaluating eyewitness testimony for new evidence and insight (Watts 1987, 71–75).

Numbers clearly matter. In the case of Hispaniola, however, whatever estimate one contemplates is but a prelude to extinction. Criticized for promoting his low estimate "in order to defend the enterprises of Columbus," Rosenblat (1976, 45) observes that "it scarcely seems that explaining the extinction of 100,000, instead of 3,000,000, implies a glorification of colonization." Regardless of the numbers involved, Hispaniola and neighboring islands had been reduced by 1519 to what Sauer (1966, 294) described as "a sorry shell." What could have caused such drastic, irreversible depopulation?

Until recently, the disease factor could not be invoked with confidence because most scholars believed that the first major outbreak of Old World sickness was smallpox, which did not appear in Hispaniola until December 1518 (N. D. Cook and Lovell 1992, 221). Sauer (1966, 204) called that outbreak "the first epidemic of record." More categorically, Henige (1986, 19) declares that his perusal of sources revealed "no serious or epidemic incidence of infectious disease in Hispaniola before late 1518." S. F. Cook and Borah (1971, 1:409–10), however, argue for a much earlier introduction of disease than 1518, mindful that the timing of occurrence directly affects the credibility of their estimates. They contend that "from the first voyage on, there was disease among the Spaniards," a circumstance that made it "most unlikely that the sick would have been kept so isolated that the natives would not have picked up any disease of epidemic possibility." Their contention now has the independent support of a seductive piece of analysis by Francisco Guerra (1985), who suggests that there was an outbreak of influenza in Hispaniola, from which considerable numbers died, following the return of Columbus on his second voyage in 1493.

What is striking about the evidence marshalled by Guerra is its unanimity with respect to when and where the disease broke out, its clinical characteristics, and the impact it had on Spaniards as well as Indians. This last point is important, for Guerra makes it clear that, while natives suffered "infinitely," the invaders were also affected. Of the 1500 men who sailed from Cádiz on September 25, 1493, scarcely 200 were alive a decade later. Among the first to fall sick, in fact, was Columbus, laid low on December 10, one day after the illness appeared in the newly-founded Isabela. The Admiral eventually recovered, but other Spaniards and many more Indians did not.

Guerra uses his medical training to discount diagnosis as malaria or yellow fever, opting instead for an almost textbook identification of influenza.[3] Diagnosis is based on source descriptions that mention acute infection, extreme contagion, high fevers, prostration, aches and pains, and general malaise. Guerra argues that a virulent strain of influenza developed among humans after people came in contact with pigs carrying swine fever. Eight sows, his sources indicate, had been taken aboard ship during a provisioning call *en route* to the Indies at La Gomera in the Canary Islands between October 5–7, 1493. Swine fever, Guerra notes, was the source of the influenza pandemic that in 1918 resulted in more than ten million deaths. His depiction of Indian depopulation in Hispaniola from around 1506 on (Guerra 1985, 341) is every bit as precipitous as that of S. F. Cook and Borah (1971, 1:401, 407), although his contact estimate is considerably less. From Hispaniola, Guerra argues, influenza would have spread to other islands and eventually the mainland.

One particularly interesting feature of Guerra's analysis is his presentation of data for the Philippine Islands as a comparative frame of reference against which to measure native population dynamics in the West Indies. He first draws attention to geographical similarities (area, climate, latitude) and the common historical denominator of Spanish conquest and colonization. The key difference between the two island groups at contact, Guerra asserts, is that native peoples in the Philippines lived alongside domesticated animals, whereas those in the West Indies did not. This meant that humans in the former archipelago had adjusted biologically to the presence among them of diseases originating in animals, including swine fever. The population of the latter had not. Contact with mainland China ensured that the Philippines were incorporated early on into the Old World disease pool. Landfall there by Magellan, in 1521, and exposure thereafter not only to Spaniards but also to the assorted paraphernalia of empire, thus had radically different consequences for native ecology from the arrival and reappearance in the West Indies of Columbus (Watts 1987). The founding of Manila in 1571 was not accompanied by the disease and depopulation that followed the founding of Isabela in 1493. From the sixteenth century on, the native population of the Philippines increased steadily, the experience in reverse of the aboriginal peoples of Hispaniola and surrounding islands.

By 1518, then, when smallpox is usually first considered to have entered the American scene, a pestilence that may have been influenza had already gutted the West Indies. Ambitious Spaniards wanted nothing more to do with the ruin they, their actions, and their imported sickness had created. Wealth lay on the mainland to the west, towards which sailed an expedition led by Hernán Cortés. In its wake followed smallpox.

"Not Forever on Earth": Central Mexico, 1518–1605[4]

Spaniards under the leadership of Cortés landed on the Mexican coast at Veracruz on Good Friday, 1519. They soon became aware that they had entered a world organized and settled very differently from the Caribbean islands they had been anxious to leave. We know it today as Mesoamerica, a term used to define a far-flung area embraced by central and southern Mexico, Guatemala, Belize, El Salvador, the westernmost parts of Honduras and Nicaragua, and the Nicoya peninsula of Costa Rica. At the time of the Cortés landfall, Mesoamerica was home to scores of cultures capable of meeting basic human needs and replete with remarkable accomplishments in art and architecture, astronomy, mathematics and the measurement of time, plant domestication, environmental management, written and pictographic communication, and the building of towns and cities. The splendors of Mesoamerica were many, but none was more impressive nor offered as much possibility for enrichment than the Aztec (Mexica) capital of Tenochtitlán, which the Spaniards entered, mortals mistaken for gods, on November 8,

1519 (León-Portilla 1962; 1984). They arrived as guests, watchful and inquisitive, taking measure. Later they were driven out after their motives became apparent; almost two years passed before they and their allies forced the surrender of Tenochtitlán. Of day One Serpent in the year Three House, an Aztec poem laments:

> Our spears lie broken in the streets.
> We have torn our hair in our grief.
> Gone are the roofs of our houses
> Their walls red with blood.
>
> Worms crawl across the streets and squares.
> The walls are splattered with gore.
> Red are the waters lurid as tan bark,
> And when we drink the water tastes of brine.
>
> Against the adobe walls
> We have pounded our hands in despair,
> For our city is no more.
> The shields of our warriors were its defense,
> But not even they could save it.[5]

Tenochtitlán fell on August 13, 1521, but between the time the Spaniards were first repelled and their final victory, an event occurred that bears directly on the outcome of military confrontation. Just as the Aztecs could not have been defeated without the participation, under Spanish command, of warriors furnished by the city state of Tlaxcala, so also is victory impossible to imagine without the turmoil set loose in Tenochtitlán by an outbreak of smallpox, which worked to the invaders' advantage. Once again, a native text provides mournful commentary:

> While the Spaniards were in Tlaxcala, a great plague broke out here in Tenochtitlán. It began to spread during the thirteenth month [September 30–October 19, 1520] and lasted for seventy days, striking everywhere in the city and killing a vast number of our people. Sores erupted on our faces, our breasts, our bellies; we were covered with agonizing sores from head to foot.
> The illness was so dreadful that no one could walk or move. The sick were so utterly helpless that they could only lie on their beds like corpses, unable to move their limbs or even their heads. They could not lie face down or roll from one side to the other. If they did move their bodies, they screamed with pain.
> A great many died from this plague, and many others died of hunger. They could not get up to search for food, and everyone else was too sick to care for them, so they starved to death in their beds.[6]

Scholars generally agree that the plague so graphically described was, in fact, smallpox, and that its effects on the Aztecs and other Mesoamerican peoples, whom it lashed under "virgin soil" conditions, was devastating (Borah 1992, 7–10). Disagreement, however, persists as to how many perished and how many were alive to begin with.

Like Hispaniola, the range of contact population estimates is immense. S. F. Cook and Simpson (1948) first volunteered 11 million for central Mexico, a figure Borah and S. F. Cook (1963) later raised to 25.2 million. Rosenblat (1954) reckoned 4.5 million for all of Mexico, an estimate close to that of Sanders's (1972) 5–6 million inhabitants for the Aztec empire. Sanders and archaeologist Barbara Price (1968) favor 12–15 million for all of Mesoamerica. For the Basin of Mexico, Sanders (1976, 149) calculates 1–1.2 million, with roughly one-third to one-quarter that number resident in the "metropolitan area and satellite villages and towns" of Tenochtitlán and 150,000–200,000 in the island city proper, twelve square kilometers in extent. Also for the Basin of Mexico, Whitmore (1991, 477) advances 1.59 million as a figure he believes conforms to the "moderate historical estimates" of Sanders and others. Whitmore (1991, 483) champions an "all-Mexico total" of 16 million, based on a "scaling procedure" that extends his computer simulations for the Basin of Mexico farther afield.[7] Like Whitmore, Zambardino concerns himself more with methodological procedure than source interpretation, offering a contact figure of 5–10 million for central Mexico, which for him "matches the evidence gathered and presented by Borah and Cook far more accurately than their estimate of 25 million" (Zambardino 1980, 22). Following Sanders, Slicher van Bath (1978) scrutinizes Borah, Cook, and Simpson's conversion of diverse socioeconomic categories into total population and then shaves their count by 15 percent to arrive at 21.4 million for central Mexico.

This region is the unit of analysis most often investigated by the provocative Berkeley trio, two of whom (S. F. Cook and Borah 1971, 1:viii) compute native depopulation there between 1518–1605, in millions, as follows:

1518	25.2
1532	16.8
1548	6.3
1568	2.7
1580	1.9
1595	1.4
1605	1.1

Zambardino (1980) argues that, from a mathematical standpoint, each of these estimates conceals a significant margin of error, having been calculated for an extensive area from data which, for the most part, are indirect, incomplete, and locally specific, a criticism leveled earlier by Sanders (1976). Fully aware that the debate is far from resolved, S. F. Cook and Borah (1979, 3:102) conclude that "the Indian population of central Mexico, under the impact of factors unleashed by the coming of the Europeans, fell by 1620–1625 to a low of approximately 3% of its size at the time the Europeans first landed on the shores of Veracruz." Even if one is inclined not to accept the figures put forward by Cook and Borah, their work has served as a catalyst for much recent work in historical demography, to the advancement of the field as a whole.

Attributing demographic collapse in the century following conquest primarily to the disease factor, as the "Berkeley School" always has done, leads logically to discussion of particular epidemic episodes. The convergence of opinion that identifies the first major bout of sickness as smallpox—we even know the name of the black slave, Francisco de Eguía, held responsible for transferring infection from ship to shore in 1520—does not extend to the second outbreak (1531–32), nor most subsequent outbreaks between 1538 and the early seventeenth century. This lack of agreement is addressed in the recent work of H. J. Prem (1992), whose analysis of native health and welfare, like that of A. López Austin (1988), evaluates rich Aztec testimony that augments better-known, though not always carefully consulted, Spanish texts. Prem dissects relevant sources with considerable prudence before venturing an opinion as to what possible diseases match the symptoms and characteristics described. Two of his conclusions are of special interest: (1) that the manner in which a disease is presently thought to behave may not correspond to its manifestation in the past; and (2) that only the very earliest epidemics, few in number, involved one specific pathogen, the greater likelihood being that outbreaks of sickness involved what Borah (1992, 7) calls "compound epidemics." Prem suggests that while one principal agent may be singled out, its predominance does not preclude other forms of sickness. The incidence of measles and typhus at roughly thirty-year intervals is striking in Prem's sequence. He also contends, as do Slicher van Bath (1978) and Whitmore (1991), that depopulation occurred in a series of abrupt, irregular drops, rather than the smooth, gradual progression depicted in the work of S. F. Cook and Borah (1971, 1:80–81).

What did follow an upward, exponential trajectory was the population of introduced livestock. As Indians disappeared, herds of cattle, sheep, and goats became a prominent feature of the rural landscape; Old World animals were roughly nine times more numerous than native inhabitants by the early seventeenth century (Simpson 1952, frontispiece). The ecological consequences of this four-legged invasion continue to be poorly understood and improperly represented (Butzer forthcoming). S. F. Cook (1949) observed that, in some parts of central Mexico, erosion sequences point to ground cover and topsoil having been removed in Precolumbian times, an observation borne out by recent pollen analysis (Brown 1985; González and Montúfar 1980). These studies, however, also indicate that processes of deterioration occurred or were accelerated under Spanish domination, even if Old World livestock offered native communities increased subsistence options and afforded their fields a hitherto unknown source of fertilizer. More informed awareness of regional variation is in order. The "Simpson scenario" of vanishing Indians and multiplying livestock is perhaps nowhere more vividly etched than in the eroded terrain of the Mixteca Alta (S. F. Cook and Borah 1968; Lovell 1975). Disease and depopulation, there as elsewhere, helped fuel a process of environmental degradation that scars the landscape still.

"A Long Series of Encounters": Northwestern Mexico, 1519–1653[8]

That part of Mexico lying beyond the northern perimeter of Mesoamerica, from the Pacific lowlands of Sonora and Sinaloa up through the canyon country of Chihuahua and on towards the open plains cut by the Río Grande, presented yet another cultural arrangement for Spaniards to contemplate. No *conuco* mounds here, the large earthen piles

characteristic of the islands, nor manicured *chinampas*, the "floating gardens" Cortés and his men marveled at in the waters surrounding Tenochtitlán. Favorable pockets did exist, where intensive agriculture was practiced and where towns and villages flourished, but the cultural whole, with important exceptions, lacked the political, social, and technological sophistication found farther south. Population levels at contact, therefore, could not possibly have been comparable to those of central Mexico, but even in this daunting periphery, indications are that human numbers were still impressively large.

A fundamentally different view of the meaning of conquest, and bold advocacy of higher estimates than most scholars hitherto had advanced, begins in the 1930s with the pioneering work of Sauer, for it is in the regional setting of northwestern Mexico that prevailing scholarly attitudes about aboriginal culture and demography were first seriously challenged. In their study of Aztatlán, Sauer and Brand (1932) combine perusal of documentary sources with field observation to assert that, at the time of Spanish intrusion, the area of the Pacific coast under examination supported a population roughly the same size as the one living there in the early twentieth century, which in 1920 was 225,000. They caution at the outset that "statements we present herewith are anything but conclusive," instead asking that "certain discoveries" be treated "in terms of a tentative thesis" (Sauer and Brand 1932, 3). Crucial though the disease factor is, other reasons must be sought to account for native decline in Aztatlán; slave raids, pillage, and wanton destruction, for example, Sauer and Brand (1932, 41) recognize as the acts of "about as hard a gang of killers as Spain let loose anywhere in the New World." Three years later, Sauer (1935, 32) published another monograph in which the same analytical approach was applied to a much more extensive territory, resulting in a similar finding as at Aztatlán:

The record, as interpreted, gives an aboriginal population between Gila and Río Grande de Santiago in excess of half a million, almost three-fourths of the number now living in this part of Mexico. Bit by bit, the theme has obtruded itself that aboriginal rural populations and present ones are much the same. This, I believe, is not a sensational conclusion, but a quite natural one.[9]

What struck the mind of Sauer as "quite natural" was, in fact, "a sensational conclusion" for others less inclined to look closely at subsistence possibilities and thereby gain some insight into potential carrying capacity, an insight that would then allow the historical record to be read either with justifiable skepticism or with greater credibility. One scholar who must have found Sauer's proposition difficult to accept was the Berkeley anthropologist Alfred Kroeber, who had earlier estimated the contact population of northwestern Mexico at 100,000, less than one-fifth the number calculated tribe by tribe, region by region, by his colleague in geography (Kroeber 1934).

Sauer's influence is apparent in much of the literature on Latin American historical demography, even if the field is not one customarily associated with his expertise (Denevan forthcoming). For northwestern Mexico, two recent contributions help complete the picture. The "north frontier" that forms the third component of Peter Gerhard's monumental New Spain trilogy (1972; 1979; 1982) includes entire colonial jurisdictions (Nueva Galicia, Alta and Baja California) not incorporated by Sauer's spatial orbit, but the former's population estimates indicate the variable extent of Indian decline particularly well. The experience of Nueva Galicia conforms to the demographic trajectory of central Mexico, with a sixteenth-century collapse, a seventeenth-century nadir, and an eighteenth-century recovery. Alta and Baja California, on the other hand, resemble a delayed variant of the West Indies, with aboriginal inhabitants dwindling to extinction. Gerhard (1982, 24) observes that "whereas in central and southern Mexico the native population may have dropped 95 percent in the sixteenth century, on the northern frontier the loss, while drastic, was less pronounced and, as might be expected, occurred later." He also notes (1982, 23) that "native populations here sometimes were fatally infected with European disease before they came under Spanish control," a circumstance that both Sauer (1935) and S. F. Cook (1937) failed to take into consideration.

Gerhard's figures take on added significance for "north frontier" territory today comprised by Sonora, Sinaloa, Durango, and Chihuahua in Mexico, and Arizona, New Mexico, and Texas in the U.S., when viewed alongside the elaborate disease chronology reconstructed by Daniel Reff (1991, 97–179). For different areas of northwestern Mexico, with some overlap into the southwestern U.S., Reff reconstructs the events surrounding sixteen disease episodes between 1530–1653. He divides his chronology into two periods that fall before and after the arrival of Jesuit fathers in the region in 1591. The coming of the "Black Robes," with their instructions to keep records and write annual reports, means that post-Jesuit epidemics can be pieced together with greater attention to detail than pre-Jesuit epidemics. Unlike Dobyns (1983), Reff (1991, 102) considers that "native exchange networks" were not sufficiently organized to facilitate diffusion into northwestern Mexico of the smallpox epidemic that caused so much destruction elsewhere between 1518–25. He does, however, contend that at least four outbreaks of sickness occurred before Father Gonzalo de Tapia and Father Martín Pérez made their way to Villa San Felipe in 1591. This leads Reff (1991, 15) to conclude that "the Jesuits found only vestiges of once populous and developed cultures" and that the discrepancy between accounts of explorers and missionaries may be ascribed to "significant disease-induced changes" between the time of penetration by the first contingent of Spaniards and arrival on the scene by the second.

Discussion of the demographic consequences of disease outbreaks complements without duplicating Gerhard's treatment of the matter. Reff (1991, 16) estimates that "most native populations were reduced by 30 percent to over 50 percent prior to sustained contact with the Jesuits." In the wake of the order's missionization program, which sought to gather formerly dispersed, mobile groups together in a single, fixed location, "native populations were reduced by upwards of 90 percent." Depopulation is viewed as the result of "a complex set of demographic factors, but particularly an exceedingly high infant mortality rate." While cognizant of the devastating role of disease, Reff acknowledges, like Sauer and Brand, that certain goals and policies pursued by Spain helped accelerate the process of decline. He argues that mining activity in Durango and southern Chihuahua forged "routes of contagion" south to north from about 1546 on and that missionization, by nucleating Indians and thereby increasing the likelihood of greater mortality when disease broke out, in fact killed the very Indians whose souls it was designed to save. The latter scenario, not surprisingly, resulted in widespread mission abandonment and the terrifying correlation of sickness with foreign presence. A backlash was inevitable. Father Gonzalo de Tapia met his martyr's death (a severed head, a dismembered arm) when Indians who believed that it was he who had infected their communities took revenge during a pastoral visit to Tovoropa on July 11, 1594. After setting the church on fire, they stuck Father Gonzalo's head on a pole and paraded it on a circuit of neighboring settlements.

Reff's work is a creative example of what can be gained by diligent and persistent application, particularly *not* accepting what other scholars say about a source but instead consulting that source first-hand in order to judge, interpret, accept or reject information for oneself. Reff's thorough combing of the history written in the mid-seventeenth century by the Jesuit father Andrés Pérez de Ribas is a case in point, for it "abounds with references to disease" that previous researchers apparently missed. Reff (1991, 281–82) also makes the point that "fundamental acceptance of European techno-economic superiority" frustrates accurate representation of aboriginal patterns of land and life. His stricture applies with equal force to interpretations of the contact situation in Guatemala.

"Great Was the Stench of the Dead": Guatemala, 1519–1632[10]

In Guatemala, more than in any other Latin American country of comparable territorial extent, physical and cultural diversity lend themselves to a regional investigative approach, an approach governed by awareness of place-to-place variation even over short distances. This reality is reflected in all sorts of intellectual enterprises, in anthropology and linguistics, in archaeology and human ecology, but espe-

cially in historical geography (Lovell 1990, 1992b). Gaps in our knowledge abound. For Guatemala, however, a mosaic can be assembled that addresses, region by region, the combination of factors responsible for catastrophic depopulation in the century or so following conquest.

Of the five sets of figures recorded in Table 1, those suggested by Denevan (1976) and by Lovell, Lutz, and Swezey (1984) pertain to all or a sizeable portion of the present-day republic of Guatemala. The calculation of Sanders and Murdy (1982) refers to highland Guatemala only, while Zamora's (1983) covers both highland and lowland areas in the western half of the country. The spatial compass of Solano (1974) is never clearly defined, but his figures relate to most of Guatemala lying south of the Petén lowlands. Differences in the size of territory appraised, therefore, must be borne in mind when comparisons are made. Zamora's contact estimate of 315,000, for example, at first glance appears to be in agreement with Solano's tally of 300,000. When, however, the spatial bases of reckoning are taken into account, Zamora's figure more closely coincides with the 500,000–800,000 advanced by Sanders and Murdy, and in fact is not entirely out of line with the 2 million favored by Denevan or by Lovell, Lutz, and Swezey.

Solano's statistics are more difficult to reconcile. Even his low contact estimate, when viewed in relation to figures put forward for 1550 and 1575, indicates a "massive collapse" (1974, 61). For the last quarter of the sixteenth century, however, Solano champions a population increase that conflicts with abundant contemporary testimony (Lovell 1992a). In a field of study where emotions are known to run high, Solano (1974, 61) claims that the "Berkeley School" is driven by "a secret passion," the goal of which is "to blame Spanish actions as the direct cause" of drastic native depopulation.

Table 1. Native Population Size in Sixteenth-Century Guatemala

Year	Denevan (1976)	Lovell, Lutz, and Swezey (1984)	Sanders and Murdy (1982)	Zamora (1983)	Solano (1974)
ca. 1520	2,000,000	2,000,000	500–800,000	315,000	300,000
ca. 1550		427,850		121,000	157,000
ca. 1575				75,000	148,000
ca. 1600				64,000	195,000

Table 2. Contact Estimates and Native Depopulation by Region for Guatemala, 1520–75

Region	1520	1525	1550	1575
Northwest	260,000	150,000	73,000	47,000
Verapaz	208,000		52,000	
Northeast	17,500			524
Southwest	33,000		8,250	
Totonicapán	105,000	75,000		13,250
Center-South (Quiché)	823,000			
Center-South (Cakchiquel)	250,000			
East Central (Pocoman)	58,000			14,500
East Central (Chortí)	120,000			
Atitlán (Tzutuhil)	72,000	48,000	5,600	5,300
Southeast (Pipil)	100,000			

Source: Lovell and Lutz (forthcoming).

If Solano's *hispanidad* tirade and indeterminate or variable units of analysis confuse the issue, less misleading is the regional picture that emerges in Table 2. Lacunae are many, but for the seven regions for which two or more estimates between 1520–75 are available, some comparative observations can be made. In crude, relative terms, the Northwest appears to have experienced lower population losses than did Verapaz, the Northeast, the Southwest, Totonicapán, and Atitlán. Depopulation seems most pronounced in the Northeast and in Atitlán, the former a lowland region, the latter made up of lands along the southern shores of Lake Atitlán as well as large tracts of the Pacific piedmont lying at intermediate altitudes below the lake. The Atitlán region witnessed the full force of Spanish military conquest and intense economic exploitation thereafter, including enslavement of local populations, the imposition of tribute demands, and involvement in the boom days of cacao (Bergmann 1969; Orellana 1984). The remote Northeast, on the other hand, was spared almost all direct contact with the conquest regime, save for having to contend with the Cortés expedition that passed through the region en route to Honduras in the mid-1520s (Kramer 1990). Two more different physical regions, two more dissimilar colonial encounters, are hard to imagine in the Guatemalan context, yet both shared a fate of early, accelerated, and ruinous decline.

How Indians fared in the Northwest, in the rugged terrain of the Sierra de los Cuchu-

matanes, may be related to the region's mountain isolation and limited economic potential holding the invaders somewhat at bay, but even here there are important exceptions that caution against indiscriminate generalization (Kramer, Lovell, and Lutz 1991). The regional profiles in Table 2 reflect all sorts of deficiencies, but they constitute, demographically, the least hazardous way of either deriving an aggregate contact figure or gaining some idea of what happened in what regions during what periods of time.

Regarding disease, documentary evidence reveals eight outbreaks between 1519–20 and 1632 which, in all likelihood, constitute widespread or pandemic occurrences. Another 25 recorded episodes relate to more local, epidemic flare-ups (Lovell 1992a). As in central Mexico, it is often impossible to determine what specific bouts of sickness might have been, because ambiguous, contradictory, or inadequate descriptions defy accurate diagnosis. This is certainly the case with the first great disease outbreak, recorded in the *Annals of the Cakchiquels* as having arrived in Guatemala sometime between August 1519 and October 1520, four or five years before the wars of conquest waged by Pedro de Alvarado. A well-known passage (Recinos and Goetz 1953, 115–16) runs:

It happened that during the twenty-fifth year the plague began, oh, my sons! First they became ill of a cough. They suffered from nosebleeds and illness of the bladder. It was truly terrible, the number of dead there were in that period. The prince

Vakaki Ahmak died then. Little by little heavy shadows and black night enveloped our fathers and grandfathers and us also, oh, my sons!

It was in truth terrible, the number of dead among the people. The people could not in any way control the sickness.

Great was the stench of the dead. After our fathers and grandfathers succumbed, half of the people fled to the fields. The dogs and the vultures devoured the bodies. The mortality was terrible. Your grandfathers died, and with them died the son of the king and his brothers and kinsmen. So it was that we became orphans, oh, my sons! So we became when we were young. All of us were thus. We were born to die![11]

While we must be grateful that such a poignant and graphic account has survived, difficulties abound, for opinion is divided as to what particular disease or diseases the above passage could have referred to. Dozens of scholars have scrutinized the Cakchiquel description. The balance of commentary favors smallpox, but not unanimously so, for alternative designations suggest influenza, measles, pulmonary plague, and exanthematic typhus. What seems worthy of observation is that medical doctors who analyze the Cakchiquel text are more inclined to diagnose measles than smallpox (Lovell 1992a).

Identification, then, is problematic. Decidedly not, however, is clear reference to high mortality, social disruption, fear, and panic that this sickness brought to the Cakchiquel Maya. The source also distinguishes between a time (August 1519–October 1520) when "the plague raged" and a period thereafter (October 1520 to March 1521) when "the plague spread" (Recinos and Goetz 1953, 115; Lovell 1992a, 60–68; Wright 1992, 54–66). In terms of origin and chronology, Prem (1992) correlates the Guatemalan outbreak with the smallpox that struck central Mexico in 1520 and 1521, but this connection fails to account for a possible appearance of the disease in 1519. The problem disappears, however, if the source of infection is sought in the Yucatán, where smallpox may have made an even earlier American landfall than the commonly accepted date of 1518 (N. D. Cook and Lovell 1992, 218–19). Even if the Cakchiquel were the sole diligent recorders of the sickness in Guatemala, its entry into a "virgin soil" environment must also have affected the neighboring Tzutuhil, Quiché, and Mam. MacLeod (1973, 40–41) refers to the disease outbreaks that preceded Alvarado's intrusion as "the shock troops of the conquest."

The advance guard that cut down the Maya had a similar role to play in the campaign launched by Francisco Pizarro to conquer the Incas of Peru.

"Scattering until They Vanished": The Central Andes, 1524–1635[12]

In terms of aboriginal achievements, comparisons are inevitably made between Mesoamerica and Tawantinsuyu, the latter the name bestowed by the Incas on their Andean empire stretching from southern Colombia through Ecuador, Peru, and Bolivia to northern Chile and northwestern Argentina (Murra 1984). These two vast realms were the ones that attracted Spaniards most, for their resources were varied and abundant. Twentieth-century scholarship has tended to exhibit the same spatial bias, but not quite in equal measure. One reason we know more about Mexico and Guatemala than we do about the Andes is because the Aztecs, Mayas, and other Mesoamerican peoples had developed a strong written tradition by the time of the conquest, which enabled them to record their version of events soon after subjugation. The absence of a similar tradition among the Incas (they kept track of things, as best they could, by means of a knotted string called the *quipu*) meant that much early information was lost, or was put down on paper many years later, with inevitable gaps or lack of detail. This is particularly apparent when it comes to documenting the swath cut by disease, for few native texts exist to illuminate the principal Spanish sources.

The evidence at hand indicates that, as in the case of Guatemala, sickness preceded the physical presence of Spaniards by several years, diffusing ahead of them to weaken military opposition. An outbreak of what could have been hemorrhagic smallpox, whereby a strain of smallpox infects the blood, causing a rash on the skin similar to that produced by measles, entered the Ecuadorian Andes in 1524 (N. D. Cook 1981, 62; Newson 1992, 88–91). There it resulted in heavy mortality. Among its victims was the Inca ruler Huayna Capac, who was then in Quito to consolidate Inca power over northern territories recently brought to heel. The epidemic also claimed the life of Huayna Capac's designated heir, igniting a disastrous civil war between the brothers

Atahualpa and Huascar, rival contenders for the Inca throne (Dobyns 1963, 496). By the time Pizarro followed up his coastal reconnaissance of the late 1520s with a full-fledged campaign in the 1530s, the chaos that sickness and internal dislocations had brought to Tawantinsuyu facilitated Spanish victory, a fact the invaders themselves openly acknowledged (Wright 1992, 72–75).

There is some disagreement as to the origins of smallpox before it reached the Andes. Most scholars consider passage from Central America as the most probable route. Borah (1992, 15), however, suggests a source of contagion among Europeans in the Río de la Plata basin, pointing out that the disease in the mountains was reported to have spread from south to north. Newson (1992, 91) resolves the difficulty by arguing that Inca troops stationed in the north near Túmbez may have fallen sick and carried smallpox south to Cuzco, from where it radiated back towards its source of origin. Newson also contends that other diseases could have struck the Incas before Pizarro's arrival; measles and plague are the most likely candidates, Central America the most probable source.

Andean epidemic history has been examined in seminal contributions by Polo (1913), Lastres (1951), and Dobyns (1963), all three of whose work is synthesized by N. D. Cook (1981, 60–61). After the first outbreak of smallpox, more than twenty different disease episodes took place between 1530–1635, six of them of pandemic dimension. The cumulative effect of these outbreaks, as in central Mexico, was to decrease native population by the early seventeenth century to a fraction of its contact size.

While we lack for Tawantinsuyu the plethora of local studies available for Mesoamerica, we are fortunate to have one comprehensive treatment of Indian depopulation that compensates in quality for the dearth of regional monographs. N. D. Cook (1981) uses the term "demographic collapse" to describe the fate of "Indian Peru" between 1520–1620. In Cook's study, six different methods are either employed or assessed to estimate the size of "Peru's preconquest population." An ecological or carrying capacity model produces a figure of 6.5 million. Archaeological data, reflecting the poorly developed status of the field compared to Mexico, are considered too inadequate for any kind of calculation beyond those that are site-specific. Even at this level of analysis, however, problems abound: excavation at Chan Chan, Cook notes, yields a range of resident occupants from 25,000–200,000. Depopulation ratio models, believed by Cook to be unreliable because of problems of statistical sampling, generate 6 million (Rowe 1946), 10 million (Wachtel 1977), 12 million (Smith 1970), and 37.5 million (Dobyns 1966), all of which are estimates for the central Andes (Ecuador, Peru, Bolivia). Models of political and social structure, an "idealized concept" with "little basis in fact," give a range of 16–32 million (Means 1931, 1932). Census projection models, described as "one of the most promising avenues of approach," deliver a minimum population of 3.9 million and a maximum population of 14.2 million. Cook's enthusiasm for this procedure, however, does not extend to its manipulation by Shea (1976), whose estimate of 2–2.9 million for the central Andes is dismissed on the grounds of insufficient data and the erroneous supposition "that the rate of decline prior to 1581 paralleled the rate following that date" (N. D. Cook 1981, 95, 108–10).

Methodologically, perhaps the most novel of Cook's six different strategies is his deployment of disease mortality models, whereby death rates known to have occurred during certain epidemics are applied, with appropriate modification, outbreak by outbreak to the Peruvian disease chronology. Working from a "calculated base" of 671,505 in 1620, the "maximal population" in 1520 is estimated at 8,090,421 and the "minimal population" at 3,243,985. Cook's reasoning is episode-specific: 30–50 percent mortality during the first outbreak of smallpox; 25–30 percent mortality during the first outbreak of measles; and 30–60 percent mortality when smallpox and measles appear together, as they did in the murderous epidemic of 1585–91, along with mumps, influenza, and typhus. The model overlooks many key variables—differential immunity, age-specific mortality, physiological adaptation—but it does offer a reasonable basis for calculation, provided, of course, that disease identification has been established with some degree of confidence (N. D. Cook 1981, 59–74).

After dealing, point by point, with the strengths and weaknesses of all six procedures, Cook then steps back from the preponderance of numbers to suggest a specific range (4–15 million) and a specific estimate (9 million) for the population of Peru on the eve of Spanish conquest. These figures are advocated "after careful weighing of the evidence, rather than being purely an act of faith" (1981, 114). The estimate of 9 million people alive in 1520 contrasts sharply with the estimate of 600,000 alive about a century later. An overall decline of 93 percent "almost completely wiped out" Indians living along the coast. Those who continued to live in the mountains, despite "disease and outright exploitation," in subsequent centuries recovered demographically to give the Andes of Peru its unmistakable, enduring native complexion.

Besides his pioneering work at the national level of analysis, which inspired Alchon (1991) toward similar goals in Ecuador, N. D. Cook (1982) has published a population history of the Colca valley that serves as a concrete example of the kind of regional investigation urgently needed throughout the Andes. In the opposite direction, Cook is reported as favoring a contact estimate for the entire Inca empire of fourteen million, which means he reckons that some five million people lived under Inca rule in Colombia, Ecuador, Bolivia, Argentina, and Chile (Roberts 1989).

These lands, too, experienced precipitous decline in the size of their native populations because of the onslaught of disease. Nowhere, perhaps, are the consequences of demographic collapse in the Andes more tragically described, nor the upheavals caused by Spanish rule more graphically documented, than in the 1,200-page "Letter to a King" composed and illustrated between 1585–1615 by the remarkable Waman Puma (Adorno 1986). Philip III, far from the scene of human neglect and ecological disaster, is told (Waman Puma 1980, 858, 885):

> The Indians are the natural owners of this realm, just as the Spaniards are the natural owners of Spain . . . [Here] the Inca is king, and so no Spaniard nor any priest has the right to intrude, because the Inca was [both] owner and lawful sovereign.
>
> Consider these poor Indians and their labors . . . that in each town they constructed irrigation canals from rivers or springs, from lakes or reservoirs. In bygone days these were built with so much effort, by hand, and with the greatest skill in the world that it seems every Indian [who lived] raised up a stone. All this was sufficient for the great many people who then were alive.
>
> And so throughout the kingdom all lands produced food, whether crops were planted in the

yungas, or hot lands, or in desert [oases], or in the rugged mountains of this realm. And the Inca kings commanded that no one should damage or remove one stone, and that no livestock should enter the aforementioned canals.

> But now this law no longer applies. And so all the fields are destroyed because of a shortage of water. On account of this the Indians lose their lands, and Your Majesty his royal share, and Holy Mother Church her tithe. For nowadays the Spaniards let loose their animals, their mule trains or their cows, their goats and sheep, and they cause great damage. And they take the water and destroy the irrigation canals so much so that no amount of money could repair them. And the little amount of water that remains, that also is taken from the poor Indians. And so the Indians abandon their towns.[13]

Waman Puma's disclosures triggered no practical response. His voice was silenced and his knowledge lost until early this century, when the manuscript copy of *El primer nueva crónica y buen gobierno* was discovered in the Royal Library in Copenhagen. What Waman Puma has to say has as much relevance to the contemporary situation in Peru as it did four centuries ago.

"How Many Tears?": The Disease Factor in Perspective[14]

The above ports of call were not all made in person by Columbus, but all of them did change dramatically because of what happened after he first landed on an island in the Bahamas 500 years ago. A handful of case studies cannot possibly do justice to every aspect of a complex theme, but they do serve to impart some sense of how disease and depopulation affected the native experience in colonial Spanish America. What bigger picture emerges from these regional vignettes?

The related issue of contact population size and post-conquest demographic collapse continues to engage the interest of hundreds of scholars. Their collective endeavors, for the entire Americas, are systematically treated in the volume of essays edited by Denevan (1976), now updated and revised (1992). Intense debate and marked difference of opinion surface throughout this collection. The reader cannot help but observe that controversy is generated not so much by the numbers themselves as by the divergent views of history that any particular choice of numbers represents. In 1976, Denevan averaged out the figures at his disposal to arrive at a New World population in 1492 of 57.3 million, which he now adjusts to 53.9 million to incorporate the research findings of the past fifteen years. Denevan's hemispheric estimates are notably higher than the 8.4 million of Kroeber (1939), the 13.4 million of Rosenblat (1954), and the 15.5 million of Steward (1949). On the other hand, Denevan's reckoning falls far below that of Borah (1976), who mentions upwards of 100 million, and the 90–113 million favored by Dobyns (1966). His estimates most approximate the 37–48.5 million of Sapper (1924) and the 40–50 million of Spinden (1928). In general, a trend towards acceptance of higher rather than lower contact estimates is apparent, with growing acknowledgement that Native American populations a century or so after European intrusion were roughly one-tenth or less their contact size. The disease factor is crucial in any attempt to explain the massive fall in Indian numbers (N. D. Cook and Lovell 1992).

Progress has been made, but much remains to be done. It would be a mistake, for instance, to think that balanced recognition of the role disease played in depopulating the Spanish Indies is shared by all. This is manifestly not the case, nor is it likely to be. The disease issue is distorted or dodged by all sorts of people for all sorts of reasons, many of them governed more by ideological conviction than by ignorance or lack of interest. In a study of the plague of 1629 in Muzo, a mining community in Colombia, Friede (1967, 341) declares that "when there were epidemics in Spanish America, these were neither general nor of identical consequences throughout the regions affected." We may concede Friede the latter point, but he seems unusually blinkered on the former, perhaps influenced too much by the data for the area he happens to know best. For him, however, there exist "numberless documents which definitely attribute the decrease of the Indian population to excessive work, malnutrition, flight, segregation of the sexes, ill-treatment, cruelty, conscription for expeditions, enslavement [and the labor draft known as] the *mita*" (Friede 1967, 339). Sempat Assadourian (1985) is of a similar disposition. The mindset is perhaps best exemplified by the Peruvian writer Mario Vargas Llosa (1990), who manages to address "questions of conquest" in an extended essay in *Harper's* without once demonstrating awareness that the transfer of

disease had a marked influence on how events unfolded.

At the same time as some intellectuals conveniently ignore or marginalize the disease question, others embrace it far too wholeheartedly. The trait is particularly evident among some Spanish scholars, whose near-exclusive focus on epidemiology and biological inequality serves to deny that which cannot be denied: barbarous heavy-handedness on the part of the conqueror, from which Indians suffered dreadfully and against which individuals like Las Casas fought and lobbied nobly. Thus we may concur with Zamora (1985, 131) that disease must be considered "the fundamental cause" but express reservation at its being designated the "almost single" cause of native disappearance. Similar proclivity to oversimplify the matter may also be found in Guerra (1986, 58), who states with more than a shrug of resignation that "the American Indian was victimized by sickness, not by Spaniards." Historical autopsy should not be performed that surgically, least of all on the countless many who died a conquered death after October 12, 1492.

Acknowledgments

Over the years, conversations with Noble David Cook and Ronald Wright have shaped my understanding of the issues discussed in this paper. Two of my colleagues at Queen's University, Jody Decker and Brian S. Osborne, also listened and responded, encouraging me to pursue the subject further. The sabbatical quiet of South Woodstock, Vermont proved congenial to the process of writing, as did the library and staff of Plumsock Mesoamerican Studies. I especially thank Judy Walker for secretarial assistance. The critical eye of Christopher H. Lutz is always appreciated. Comments and suggestions triggered by the review process proved most helpful, particularly those of Karl W. Butzer, Carville Earle, and Daniel W. Gade. The trace of Woodrow Borah, an inspiration since my days as a graduate student at the University of Alberta, runs throughout.

Notes

1. Las Casas (1957–61, 2:106) states of the island of Hispaniola: "From the year 1494, when their great misfortune began, until the year 1508, which is to say fourteen years, there perished upwards of three million souls, from warfare, from being shipped off as slaves, from work in the mines, and from other labors." It did not serve the Dominican's purpose to mention disease, for the cause he then served called for him to highlight, to the lasting consternation of his fellow Spaniards, the undeniable atrocities referred to. The

good bishop, his gaze wandering far forward, then asked: "Who, among those born in the centuries to come, will believe this? Even to me, who is writing it down, who saw it, and who knows most of it, it now seems to me that it was not possible."

2. Sauer (1966, 37) states that the name Taino, currently in fashion, is "a term introduced in the present century and taken casually from the name for a single social class." He preferred the designation "Island Arawaks" for the native inhabitants of the Greater Antilles (Cuba, Hispaniola, Puerto Rico, and Jamaica), the first New World people to be called, erroneously but enduringly, "Indians." For more on nomenclature, see Berkhofer (1978) and Alcides Reissner (1983).

3. Malaria and yellow fever are usually considered to have arrived in the New World much later than 1493 (Borah 1992, 18–19; N. D. Cook and Lovell 1992, 227–29; Newson 1992, 101–02). The timing of their arrival, however, is still open to debate.

4. Not surprisingly, most Spanish accounts of the conquest of Mexico ring brazenly triumphant, none more so than the soldier's tale narrated by Bernal Díaz del Castillo (1970). The voices of the vanquished, in turn, are brittle and hushed, choked with doom. León-Portilla (1984, 33) quotes a fatalistic Aztec meditation:

"Truly do we live on earth?
Not forever on earth; only a little while here.
Although it be jade, it will be broken.
Although it be gold, it is crushed.
Although it be *quetzal* feather, it is torn asunder.
Not forever on earth; only a little while here."

León-Portilla (1959; 1962) and Anderson and Dibble (1978) explore the Aztec point of view in a series of compelling vignettes.

5. León-Portilla (1959, 154) renders these lines in Spanish, translated from Nahuatl by Angel María Garibay. My English approximation differs from that of Lysander Kemp (León-Portilla 1962, 137–38) and is closer, in texture and voice, to that of Gyles and Sayer (1980, 79).

6. This passage from León-Portilla (1962, 92–93) is translated from Spanish to English by Lysander Kemp. It may also be consulted, in a more literal translation, in Anderson and Dibble (1978, 64). Prem (1992, 24–27) discusses other native texts that describe this outbreak of disease.

7. The computer simulations of Whitmore (1991) indicate that "the large depopulations noted for the sixteenth-century Basin were indeed *possible*, given reasonable assumptions as to cause." This outcome "contradicts those critics who assert that such depopulations were unlikely or even impossible." The latter comment is aimed especially at historical demographers whose work deals exclusively with Europe and whose data for crisis situations indicate less extreme rates of depopulation than the American scenario examined by Whitmore.

8. The descriptive subtitle comes from the account by Long (1987) of the "marvellous adventure" of Alvar Núñez Cabeza de Vaca. Washed ashore more likely near the present site of Galveston in November 1528, following an ill-fated expedition to Florida, Cabeza de Vaca, two fellow Spaniards, and a Moorish slave trekked some 6,000 miles across Texas, New Mexico, Arizona, and northwestern Mexico before reaching Mexico City in July 1536. Cabeza de Vaca's mystical wanderings were recently the subject of a film by the Mexican director Nicolás Echevarría.

9. One section of Sauer's monograph is devoted exclusively to "European Epidemic Diseases." Reff (1991, 9) is of the opinion that, while Sauer may have been aware of the disease factor, he did not feature it prominently enough.

10. The descriptive subtitle comes from the *Annals of the Cakchiquels,* as translated by Recinos and Goetz (1953, 155).

11. See Lovell (1992a) for further discussion.

12. Writing in the early seventeenth century, the native chronicler Santa Cruz Pachacuti (1968, 311) tells us:

"And so, when it came time to eat, there arrived an envoy dressed in a black cloak, who kissed the Inca with great reverence, handing him a *putti*, a small box closed with a key, and the Inca commanded the messenger to open it, but the messenger begged pardon, saying that the Creator had ordained that only the Inca open it. The Inca, seeing the truth of this, opened the little box, and from it flew forth [things] which resembled butterflies or bits of confetti, scattering until they vanished. This was the plague of *sarampión,* and within two days General Mihacnacayna died, along with a good many other captains, their faces covered in scabs. And when the Inca had witnessed this, he ordered that a house of stone be constructed, and afterwards hid himself in it, and there he died."

N. D. Cook (1981, 254) and Wright (1992, 73) note the parallel with the story of Pandora's box, but whether borrowed or embellished, Pachacuti's account imparts a powerful feeling of impending loss, of catastrophe about to happen.

13. I have followed the translation by Wright (1992, 192) closely but not exactly.

14. Writing of the conquest of Guatemala, Las Casas (1957–61: 5, 153) asked: "How many tears were shed, how many groans were uttered, how many people were left to face life on their own?" There is a bust of Las Casas, seldom noticed, in the park beside La Merced church in Antigua, Guatemala. His haunted question hangs in the air each time I walk past.

References

Adorno, R. 1986. *Guaman Poma: Writing and resistance in colonial Peru.* Austin: University of Texas Press.

Alcides Reissner, R. 1983. *El indio en los diccionarios.* México: Instituto Nacional Indigenista.

Alchon, S. A. 1991. *Native society and disease in*

colonial Ecuador. Cambridge: Cambridge University Press.

Amiama, M. A. 1959. La población de Santo Domingo. *Clio* 11:116–34.

Anderson, A. J. O., and Dibble, C. E., trans. 1978. *The war of conquest: How it was waged here in Mexico. The Aztec's own story as given to Fr. Bernardino de Sahagún*. Salt Lake City: University of Utah Press.

Bergmann, J. F. 1969. The distribution of cacao cultivation in pre-Columbian America. *Annals of the Association of American Geographers* 59:85–96.

Berkhofer, R. F. 1978. *The White Man's Indian: Images of the American Indian from Columbus to the present*. New York: Alfred Knopf.

Borah, W. Introduction. 1992. In *"Secret judgments of God": Old world disease in colonial Spanish America*, ed. N. D. Cook and W. G. Lovell, pp. 3–19. Norman: University of Oklahoma Press.

———, **and Cook, S. F.** 1963. *The aboriginal population of central Mexico on the eve of the Spanish conquest*. Ibero-Americana 45. Berkeley: University of California Press.

Brown, R. B. 1985. A summary of late Quaternary pollen records from Mexico west of the isthmus of Tehuantepec. In *Pollen records of late Quaternary North American sediments*, ed. V. W. Bryant and R. G. Holloway, 71–93. Dallas, TX: American Association of Stratigraphic Palynologists Foundation.

Butzer, K. W. Forthcoming. Ethno-agriculture and cultural ecology in Mexico: Historical vistas and modern implications. In *Geographic research on Latin America 1990*, ed. T. Martinson.

Casas, B. de las. 1957–61. *Obras escogidas de Fray Bartolomé de las Casas*, ed. Juan Pérez de Tudela. 5 vols. Madrid: Ediciones Atlas.

Cook, N. D. 1981. *Demographic collapse: Indian Peru, 1520–1620*. Cambridge: Cambridge University Press.

———. 1982. *The people of the Colca valley: A population study*. Boulder, Co: Westview Press.

———, **and Lovell, W. G.,** eds. 1992. *"Secret judgments of God": Old World disease in colonial Spanish America*. Norman: University of Oklahoma Press.

Cook, S. F. 1937. *The extent and significance of disease among the Indians of Baja California, 1697–1773*. Ibero-Americana 12. Berkeley: University of California Press.

———. 1949. *Soil erosion and population in central Mexico*. Ibero-Americana 34. Berkeley: University of California Press.

———, **and Borah, W.** 1968. *The population of the Mixteca Alta*. Ibero-Americana 50. Berkeley: University of California Press.

———, **and** ———. 1971, 1974, 1979. *Essays in*

population history. 3 vols. Berkeley: University of California Press.

———, **and Simpson, L. B.** 1948. *The population of central Mexico in the sixteenth century*. Ibero-Americana 31. Berkeley: University of California Press.

Córdova, E. 1968. La encomienda y la desaparición de los indios en las Antillas mayores. *Caribbean Studies* 8:23–49.

Denevan, W. M., ed. 1976, 1992. *The native population of the Americas in 1492*. Madison: University of Wisconsin Press.

———. Forthcoming. Carl Sauer and native American population size. In *The legacy of intellect: Carl O. Sauer and the Berkeley School of Geography*, ed. M. S. Kenzer. Dordrecht, the Netherlands: Kluwer Academic Publishers.

Díaz del Castillo, B. 1970. *Historia verdadera de la conquista de Nueva España*. México: Editorial Porrúa.

Dobyns, H. F. 1963. An outline of Andean epidemic history to 1720. *Bulletin of the History of Medicine* 37:493–515.

———. 1966. Estimating aboriginal American populations: An appraisal of techniques with a new hemispheric estimate. *Current Anthropology* 7:395–449.

———. 1983. *Their number become thinned: Native American population dynamics in eastern North America*. Knoxville: University of Tennessee Press.

Friede, J. 1967. Demographic changes in the mining community of Muzo after the plague of 1629. *Hispanic American Historical Review* 47:338–43.

Gerhard, P. 1972. *A guide to the historical geography of New Spain*. Cambridge: Cambridge University Press.

———. 1979. *The southeast frontier of New Spain*. Princeton, NJ: Princeton University Press.

———. 1982. *The north frontier of New Spain*. Princeton, NJ: Princeton University Press.

Gibson, C. 1964. *The Aztecs under Spanish rule: A history of the Indians of the Valley of Mexico, 1519–1810*. Stanford, CA: Stanford University Press.

González Quintero, L. and Montúfar López, A. 1980. Interpretación paleoecológica del contenido pólinico de un núcleo cercano a Tula, Hidalgo. In *III Coloquio sobre Paleobotánica y Palinología*, ed. F. Sánchez, pp. 185–94. Colección Científica (Prehistoria) 86. Mexico City: Instituto Nacional de Antropología e Historia.

Guerra, F. 1985. La epidemia americana de influenza en 1493. *Revista de Indias* 45:325–47.

———. 1986. El efecto demográfico de las epidemias trás el descubrimiento de América. *Revista de Indias* 46:41–58.

Gyles, A. B., and Sayer, C. 1980. *Of gods and men:*

The heritage of ancient Mexico. New York: Harper and Row.

Henige, D. 1978. On the contact population of Hispaniola: History as higher mathematics. *Hispanic American Historical Review* 58:217–37.

——. 1986. When did smallpox reach the New World (and why does it matter?) In *Africans in bondage: Studies in slavery and the slave trade,* ed. P. E. Lovejoy, pp. 11–26. Madison: University of Wisconsin Press.

Kramer, W. 1990. The politics of *encomienda* distribution in early Spanish Guatemala, 1524–1544. Ph.D dissertation, University of Warwick, England.

——; **Lovell, W. G.; and Lutz, C. H.** 1991. Fire in the mountains: Juan de Espinar and the Indians of Huehuetenango, 1525–1560. In *Columbian consequences,* vol. 3, ed. D. H. Thomas, pp. 263–82. Washington: Smithsonian Institution.

Kroeber, A. 1934. Native American population. *American Anthropologist* 36:1–25.

——. 1939. *Cultural and natural areas of native North America.* University of California Publications in American Archaeology and Ethnology 38. Berkeley: University of California Press.

Lastres, J. B. 1951. *Historia de la medicina peruana.* 3 vols. Lima: San Marcos.

León-Portilla, M., ed. 1959. *Visión de los vencidos: Relaciones indígenas de la Conquista.* Mexico: Universidad Nacional Autónoma de México.

——. 1962. *The broken spears: The Aztec account of the conquest of Mexico.* Boston: Beacon Press.

——. 1984. Mesoamerica before 1519. In *The Cambridge history of Latin America,* vol. 1, ed. L. Bethell, pp. 3–36. Cambridge: Cambridge University Press.

Lipschutz, A. 1966. La despoblación de los indios después de la conquista. *América Indígena* 26:229–47.

Long, H. 1987. *The marvellous adventure of Cabeza de Vaca.* London: Picador Classics.

López Austin, A. 1988. *The human body and ideology: Concepts of the ancient Nahuas.* 2 vols. Trans. T. Ortiz de Montellano and B. Ortiz de Montellano. Salt Lake City: University of Utah Press.

Lovell, W. G. 1975. Culture and landscape in the Mixteca Alta, Mexico, 1500–1600. M.A. thesis, University of Alberta, Edmonton, Canada.

——. 1990. *Conquista y cambio cultural: La sierra de los Cuchumatanes de Guatemala, 1500–1821.* Antigua, Guatemala and South Woodstock, VT: Centro de Investigaciones Regionales de Mesoamérica and Plumsock Mesoamerican Studies.

——. 1992a. Disease and depopulation in early colonial Guatemala. In *"Secret judgments of God": Old World disease in colonial Spanish America,* ed. N. D. Cook and W. G. Lovell, pp. 49–83. Norman: University of Oklahoma Press.

——. 1992b. *Conquest and survival in colonial Guatemala: A historical geography of the Cuchumatán highlands, 1500–1821,* rev. 2nd ed. Kingston and Montreal: McGill-Queen's University Press.

——, **and Lutz, C. H.** Forthcoming. The historical demography of colonial Central America. In *Geographic research on Latin America 1990* ed. T. Martinson.

——; ——; **and Swezey, W. R.** 1984. The Indian population of southern Guatemala, 1549–1551: An analysis of López de Cerrato's *Tasaciones de tributos. The Americas* 40:459–77.

Lutz, C. H., and Lovell, W. G. 1990. Core and periphery in colonial Guatemala. In *Guatemalan Indians and the state, 1540–1988,* ed. C. A. Smith, pp.35–51. Austin: University of Texas Press.

MacLeod, M. J. 1973. *Spanish Central America: A socioeconomic history, 1520–1720.* Berkeley: University of California Press.

Means, P. A. 1931. *Ancient civilizations of the Andes.* New York: Charles Scribner's Sons.

——. 1932. *Fall of the Inca empire and the Spanish rule in Peru, 1530–1720.* New York: Charles Scribner's Sons.

Moya Pons, F. 1971. *La Española en el siglo XVI, 1493–1522.* Santo Domingo: Universidad Católica Madre y Maestra.

——. 1987. *Después de Colón: Trabajo, sociedad y política en la economía del oro.* Madrid: Alianza Editorial.

Murra, J. 1984. Andean societies before 1532. In *The Cambridge history of Latin America,* vol. 1, ed. L. Bethell, pp. 59–90. Cambridge: Cambridge University Press.

Newson, L. A. 1985. Indian population patterns in colonial Spanish America. *Latin American Research Review* 20:41–74.

——. 1992. Old World epidemics in early colonial Ecuador. In *"Secret judgments of God": Old World disease in colonial Spanish America,* ed. N. D. Cook and W. G. Lovell, pp. 84–112. Norman: University of Oklahoma Press.

Orellana, S. L. 1984. *The Tzutujil Mayas: Continuity and change, 1250–1630.* Norman: University of Oklahoma Press.

Polo, J. T. 1913. Apuntes sobre las edidemias del Perú. *Revista Histórica* 5:50–109.

Prem, H. J. 1992. Disease outbreaks in central Mexico during the sixteenth century. In *"Secret judgments of God": Old World disease in colonial Spanish America,* ed. N. D. Cook and W. G. Lovell, pp. 20–48. Norman: University of Oklahoma Press.

Recinos, A., and Goetz, D., eds. and trans. 1953.

The Annals of the Cakchiquels. Norman: University of Oklahoma Press.

Reff, D. T. 1991. *Disease, depopulation, and culture change in northwestern New Spain, 1518–1764.* Salt Lake City: University of Utah Press.

Roberts, L. 1989. Disease and death in the New World. *Science* 246:1245–47.

Rosenblat, A. 1954. *La población indígena y el mestizaje en América,* 2 vols. Buenos Aires: Editorial Nova.

———. 1976. The population of Hispaniola at the time of Columbus. In *The native population of the Americas in 1492,* ed. W. M. Denevan, pp. 43–66. Madison: University of Wisconsin Press.

Rowe, J. H. 1946. Inca culture at the time of the Spanish conquest. In *Handbook of South American Indians,* vol. 2, ed. J. H. Steward, pp. 183–330. Bulletin 143. Washington: Bureau of American Ethnology.

Sanders, W. T. 1972. Population, agricultural history, and societal evolution in Mesoamerica. In *Population growth: Anthropological implications,* ed. B. Spooner, pp. 101–53. Cambridge: MIT Press.

———. 1976. The population of the central Mexican symbiotic region, the Basin of Mexico, and the Teotihuacán Valley in the sixteenth century. In *The native population of the Americas in 1492,* ed. W. M. Denevan, pp. 85–150. Madison: University of Wisconsin Press.

———, and Murdy, C. 1982. Population and agricultural adaptation in the humid highlands of Guatemala. In *The historical demography of highland Guatemala,* ed. R. M. Carmack, C. H. Lutz, and J. D. Early, pp. 23–34. Institute for Mesoamerican Studies, Publication 6. Albany: State University of New York.

———, and Price, B. 1968. *Mesoamerica: The evolution of a civilization.* New York: Random House.

Santa Cruz Pachacuti, J. de. 1968. *Relación de antigüedades deste reyno del Perú.* In *Crónicas peruanas de interés indígena,* ed. F. Esteve Barba. Madrid: Editorial Atlas.

Sapper, K. 1924. Die Zahl und die Völksdichte der indianischen Bevölkerung in Amerika vor der Conquista und in der Gegenwart. *Proceedings of the Twenty-First International Congress of Americanists.* 1:95–104.

Sauer, C. O. 1935. *Aboriginal population of northwestern Mexico.* Ibero-Americana 10. Berkeley: University of California Press.

———. 1939. *Man and nature: America before the days of the White Man.* New York: Charles Scribner's Sons.

———. 1966. *The early Spanish Main.* Berkeley: University of California Press.

———, and Brand, D. 1932. *Aztatlán: Prehistoric Mexican frontier on the Pacific coast.* Ibero-Americana 1. Berkeley: University of California Press.

Sempat Assadourian, C. 1985. La crisis demográfica del siglo XVI y la transición del Tawantinsuyu al sistema mercantil colonial. In *Población y mano de obra en América Latina,* ed. N. Sánchez Albornóz, pp. 69–93. Madrid: Alianza Editorial.

Shea, D. E. 1976. A defense of small population estimates for the central Andes in 1520. In *The native population of the Americas in 1492,* ed. W. M. Denevan, pp. 157–80. Madison: University of Wisconsin Press.

Simpson, L. B. 1952. *Exploitation of land in central Mexico in the sixteenth century.* Ibero-Americana 36. Berkeley: University of California Press.

Slicher van Bath, B. H. 1978. The calculation of the population of New Spain, especially for the period before 1570. *Boletín de Estudios Latinoamericanos y del Caribe* 24:67–95.

Smith, C. T. 1970. Depopulation of the central Andes in the 16th century. *Current Anthropology* 11:453–64.

Solano, F. de. 1974. *Los mayas del siglo XVIII.* Madrid: Ediciones Cultura Hispánica.

Spinden, H. J. 1928. The population of ancient America. *Geographical Review* 18:641–60.

Steward, J. H. 1949. The native population of South America. In *Handbook of South American Indians,* vol. 5, ed. J. H. Steward, pp. 655–68. Washington: Bureau of Indian Ethnology.

Vargas Llosa, M. 1990. Questions of conquest. *Harper's* 281:45–53.

Verlinden, C. 1968. Le *repartimento* de Rodrigo de Albuquerque á Española en 1514: Aux origenes d'une importante institution économico-sociale de l'empire colonial espagnol. In *Mélanges offerts á G. Jacquemyns,* pp. 633–46. Brussels: Université Libre de Bruxelles.

Wachtel, N. 1977. *Vision of the vanquished: The Spanish conquest of Peru through Indian eyes, 1530–1570.* Hassocks, Sussex: Harvester Press.

Waman Puma [Guaman Poma de Ayala], F. 1980. *El primer nueva crónica y buen gobierno,* ed. and trans. J. Murra, R. Adorno, and J. L. Urioste. Mexico City: Siglo XXI.

Watts, D. 1987. *The West Indies: Patterns of development, culture and environmental change since 1492.* Cambridge: Cambridge University Press.

Whitmore, T. M. 1991. A simulation of the sixteenth-century population collapse in the Basin of Mexico. *Annals of the Association of American Geographers* 81:464–87.

Wright, R. 1992. *Stolen continents: The Americas through Indian eyes since 1492.* Boston: Houghton Mifflin Company.

Zambardino, R. A. 1978. Critique of David Henige's "On the contact population of Hispaniola": History as higher mathematics. *Hispanic American Historical Review* 58:700–08.

———. 1980. Mexico's population in the sixteenth century: Demographic anomaly or mathematical illusion? *Journal of Interdisciplinary History* 11:1–27.

Zamora, E. 1983. Conquista y crisis demográfica: La pobación indígena del occidente de Guatemala en el siglo XVI. *Mesoamérica* 6:291–338.

———. 1985. *Los mayas de las tierras altas en el siglo XVI: Tradición y cambio en Guatemala*. Sevilla: Diputación Provincial de Sevilla.

Spanish Colonization and Indian Property in Central Mexico, 1521–1620*

Hanns J. Prem

Department of Anthropology (Völkerkunde), University of Bonn, 5300 Bonn-3, Germany

FAX (49-228) 735579, bitnetPrem@dbninf5

Abstract. After the conquest of Mexico (1519–21), the Spaniards coopted Indian administrative structures, allowing the King and the new Colonial government to exploit traditional regional revenues. Key participants of the military campaigns were rewarded with rights to the tribute and limited labor conscription (*encomienda*) required of the indigenous population in a particular district. Legally, *encomienda* did not confer property rights, but holders of the privilege also received most of the earliest land grants and had the advantage of conscript labor during the planting and harvest seasons. As the *encomienda* system was gradually reformed and phased out, agriculture and stockraising became the major source of rural income for increasing numbers of Spanish settlers. Public land was overwhelmingly awarded to officials, the military, and the Colonial elite. Following the failure of the Puebla experiment (1531–34), designed to create a new class of farmers with small holdings, agricultural work was relegated to Indian labor. Property became the focus of competition between Spaniard and Indian, ending with partial dispossession of Indian lands by the early 1600s. The granting of lands (*mercedes*) is explicated by three examples: the Basin of Mexico, the district northwest of Puebla, and the Valley of Toluca. Archival documentation of land grants provides a powerful tool to decipher regional settlement histories and to examine the degree to which the Spanish legal system safeguarded Indian property rights. Spanish agricultural expansion was made possible by the Indian demographic collapse, as a result of recurrent epidemics, and was facilitated by Indian settlement amalgamation (*congregación*). While the processes and temporal patterns of property transfer show structural similarities in the heart of Central Mexico, settlement histories in peripheral areas are unique. The means by which Indian communities slowed Spanish expansion are discussed. The pattern of dispossession of the Indian was established during the first hundred years, setting in motion a process that culminated with the powerful haciendas of the nineteenth century.

Key Words: Colonial agriculture, *congregación*, depopulation, *encomienda*, land grants (*mercedes*), hacienda, Indian property, Mexico, Puebla, Toluca.

THE stereotypic view of the rural economy of Latin America is dominated by the *hacendado*, living in a fortress-like estate as lord of vast territories and master over teams of indigenous workers. As timeless as that image may seem, it has lost its general validity through revolutions and reforms. The great estates culminated in the nineteenth century, but they owe their origins to complex processes initiated during the 1520s, soon after the Spanish conquistadors entered Mexico. This paper examines how Colonial policy first experimented with a tribute system, before switching to a settlement policy based on land

*Translated from the German by Karl W. Butzer.

Annals of the Association of American Geographers. 82(3), 1992, pp. 444–459
© Copyright 1992 by Association of American Geographers

grants. The process of awarding public lands to new settlers and its implications for the alienation of traditional Indian landholdings are fundamental to understanding Spanish colonization throughout the Spanish Americas.

Phase One: *Encomienda* and Tribute

Before 1519 the Spaniards had encountered chiefdoms (*cacicazgos*) with limited social organization or centralized authority on the Caribbean islands and along the Isthmus of Panama. Spanish commercial activity, beyond a little barter, had been focused on the exploitation of gold and recruiting of the necessary labor. The state organization of the Aztec empire offered more attractive possibilities, not only to seize its accumulated wealth, but to exploit the apparently unlimited flow of state revenues, to the benefit of all participants in the Conquest, from the king to the common foot-soldier. Such exploitation of tributary revenues marked the first phase of exploitation of the Aztec Empire and, a little later, its Inca counterpart.

Even before Conquest had been completed, the Spaniards had tapped considerable wealth. This included the direct spoils of war and, more important, the "gifts" extorted from the indigenous rulers. The sealed treasury of Moctezuma and the rooms filled with gold that belonged to Atahualpa are the best known examples. Ornaments of inestimable artistic value were hurriedly melted down to gold bars. Treasures lay open for the taking. But before the participants of the military campaigns could claim their reward for the efforts and dangers they had been put to, a fifth of the loot was claimed by the King and another fifth by the expedition leader, who also deducted his expenses as generously as possible. Little remained for the others, so that Bernal Díaz del Castillo (1960, 324) complained of Hernán Cortés's redistribution that "there was so little that many soldiers didn't want to accept it."

At first, the indigenous rulers were allowed to continue as nominal heads of state, while the conquistador-in-chief took control over the flow of tribute mobilized from the economies of the conquered regions. The instructions of the King to Cortés in 1523 state explicitly that

Spain demanded tribute from the indigenous inhabitants: "They will give and pay us for each year as much revenue and tribute as were given and paid until now to their priests and lords" (CDIU 9, 167–72). In order to manage this in organizational terms, it was essential not only to maintain the lower echelons of Indian administration, but also to integrate them into the structures of colonial government.

The two systems interfaced in the *cabeceras*, sometimes recently founded settlements that became centers of administrative districts and the residence of the chief magistrate (*alcalde mayor* or *corregidor*) or his lieutenant, representing the lowest level of authority in the Colonial administration. By keeping the internal, indigenous institutions functional, this hybrid administration of the tribute system was highly advantageous to the conquerors, at least as long as the demographic decline, that began immediately, only reduced widespread population pressure, rather than cutting into productivity. Without further investment, other than the high cost of initial conquest, the new arrangement promised to provide both the crown and the conquerors with an apparently permanent source of revenue.

That income, however, went to the crown or its direct representatives and agents. Consequently another means of recompense and reward had to be found for all those others who had placed their lives and health at stake. The only practicable solution was to award such people rights to *encomienda,* a combination of tribute and service required of the indigenous population to support petty local rulers. This institution, however, had been thoroughly discredited, in the eyes of the King, during the administration initially tested with tragic results in the Antilles. As in Prehispanic times, demand was at first limited to agricultural and craft products, but labor could also be required on a limited scale, as for example, in house construction (Simpson 1966). In return for such an award, the *encomenderos* were supposed to provide for the religious education of their Indian wards. Despite royal interdiction and personal misgivings, Cortés began to award *encomiendas* on a large scale immediately after his subjugation of the Aztec empire (Cortés 1963, 201).

From the beginning, the crown sought to eliminate individual *encomienda* rights, in favor of royal officials (*corregidores*), appointed for a fixed term and with salary to administer a particular district as a crown *encomienda*. According to the King's wish, personal *encomiendas* were only to be used as awards for the first generation of conquistadors, but pressures to extend these privileges were repeatedly supported by the Colonial administration. The clinching argument was that a system of permanent *encomienda* would best guarantee humane treatment of the Indians. In order to eliminate the evident negative impacts of the *encomienda,* the New Laws of 1542 (as well as subsequent legislation) imposed a long list of conditions on the *encomenderos.* Thus they were required to live in the province where they held their *encomienda* (Leyes Nuevas, article 48), yet strictly forbidden to stay for more than one night in the Indian towns they controlled, or to build a house or even a shed there. *Encomenderos* were further prohibited from owning grazing land within their *encomienda* territory, and their rights to raise pigs were also circumscribed (*Recopilación,* book 6, title 9, laws 10–14, 17–20); but ownership of agricultural land was not regulated and hence possible.

Until these restrictions went into effect, the *encomenderos* had at least a decade or two to exploit Indian tribute and the labor conscription that was part of the *encomienda* privileges. At first Spanish economic activity was focused on the lucrative extraction of precious metals. The tax reports known as the *Libros de tasaciones* reveal that many *encomenderos* were already engaged in mining immediately after the Conquest (Miranda 1965, 23). Although efforts were made to stop the use of *encomienda* Indians in mining (Miranda 1965, 12–13; see *Recopilación* 6-9-22), legislation and practice remained difficult to reconcile. Few mining enterprises proved to be really profitable, however, and in general they had little economic success (Haring 1963, 246).

The agricultural activities of the *encomenderos* were far more important as they promptly obtained a large number of royal grants (*reales mercedes*) for agricultural and grazing land. Because only a part of the related documents is preserved, they only provide a selective impression: more than half of the land titles awarded in 1542–43 went to *encomenderos,* a pattern that is even more striking among those grants made by the municipal council of Mexico City from 1525–28 (Miranda 1965, 26–27). At an early stage, the *encomenderos* evidently had little difficulty in acquiring large estates, holdings that were eventually enlarged and consolidated. This led to the conclusion that *encomiendas* were structural analogs of the later haciendas or big estates, although the two institutions were distinct in theory and practice (Lockhart 1969, 418–22).

There indeed were parallels in regard to labor. The *encomenderos* had an advantage over other landowners in that they could use Indian labor, to which the tribute arrangement initially entitled them. But the use of conscript Indian labor was increasingly denied, at least in theory, as tribute payment was progressively standardized and commuted by legislation, limiting it to a sum of money and, for an interim period, delivery of maize. Amounts were fixed on a uniform basis by the authorities, not by the *encomenderos,* and these rates were lower than in Prehispanic times (Leyes Nuevas, articles 49, 51).

The continuing struggle to extend *encomienda* privileges beyond one lifetime may give a contrary impression, but the *encomienda* as such had lost much of its economic importance, and hence its attractiveness, after the mid-sixteenth century. Critical for this development were the increasingly more rigorous legislation and the rapid decline of the Indian population, requiring readjustments every few years to reduce tributary service. As the number of settlers in New Spain continued to increase, and more and more *encomiendas* passed to the crown, the *encomenderos'* share of Indian revenues declined sharply.

A Failed Experiment: Conquistadors as Farmers

Shortly after the conquest of New Spain, it became apparent that *encomiendas* could only provide income for a small part of the Spanish settlers, leading to a search for alternatives (Chevalier 1957, 6; Hirschberg 1979). Based primarily on the suggestions of the Franciscans, who espoused utopian ideas at the time, the colonial government (*Audiencia*) founded the city of Puebla de los Angeles as "a town of Spaniards who are to cultivate the soil and create fields and farms as they do in Spain" (Motolinía 1971, 263). This explicit experiment was expected to serve as a model "that towns be begun in which many Christians who now go about idle and vagrant can be brought together to give an example to the Indians of Christianity and of work as in Spain" (Motolinía 1971). The Spaniards were assigned a little Indian labor to start them off, after which a free labor market was expected to develop (Paso y Troncoso 1939–42, XVI, 11). Exactly what was meant by "as in Spain" is not specified, but the accompanying circumstances imply a society of urban-dwelling small farmers. This was the logical extension of a long-standing royal policy to encourage the emigration of farmers to the New World (Haring 1963, 206–07).

That the foundation of Puebla in 1531 was not some secondary effort, or just another founding of a Spanish town, can be inferred from the plan to make it into the second seat of the Colonial administration of New Spain (Paso y Troncoso 1939–42, XVI, 10). The Bishop's residence for the second diocese of Mexico was indeed moved from Tlaxcala to Puebla (Fig. 1), but none of the offices of secular government were.

The social experiment in Puebla promptly failed. It would be too obvious to attribute this failure only to the opposition of nearby *encomenderos,* who saw this alternative strategy as harmful to their efforts to institute a permanent *encomienda* system. None of the new settlers, who at first included no *encomenderos* (Albi Romero 1970, 79), were willing to get behind a plow. Instead, the small land grants awarded around Puebla and in the fertile adjacent Valley of Atlixco promptly went up for sale. Wealthy and influential people bought them up, one after another, in order to assemble large estates (Prem 1984, 215). Within four years after Puebla had been founded, a handful of landowners had together planted some 10,000 grapevines, showing how quickly large holdings were amalgamated (Albi Romero 1970, 93).

The assumption that a community of small farmers could be installed and maintained in Puebla, in the midst of a sea of large land grants, was a little naive. Cortés and his lieutenant, Diego de Ordáz, already had established large farming operations nearby, a model glaringly incompatible with the idealistic goals set for Puebla. The subsequent evolution of Spanish Colonial agriculture took its inspiration not from Puebla, but from Cortés.

Phase Two: Land Ownership

Hernán Cortés not only aspired to be the conqueror of Mexico, but also its feudal lord and the fulcrum of its economic exploitation. The experience he gained during his campaigns allowed him to select the most promising areas, and his position of power made it possible for him to take them. His claims did require royal approval, which was delayed until 1528 and involved substantial reductions (see García Martínez 1969, 42–48), but this did not impede his pursuit of immediate economic goals. His plans for further voyages of exploration and conquest required time-consuming construction of harbors and ships, but agriculture could realize immediate profits. These efforts were centered in the fertile area he controlled around Cuernavaca, but he also "had wheat planted in Coyoacan, began a sugar plantation . . . in Tuxtla, raised livestock in the Valley of Toluca" (García Martínez 1969, 46), and kept pigs in Huejotzingo, near Puebla (Fig. 1). These agricultural enterprises were begun even before his campaign in Honduras (Prem 1978, 38), and he instructed his representatives accordingly. For example, Hernando de Saavedra in Acapulco was told in 1524 to "set up a good farm with chilis and yucca which, although they are indigenous, will thrive well" (Cortés 1963, 441). At the same time he sought to expand stockraising, as his efforts to introduce livestock from Spain in 1526 show (Cortés 1963, 471).

Cortés's agricultural ambitions reflected an accurate assessment of conditions in the early colony. The increasing demand of Spaniards for their familiar diet—particularly wheat bread, veal, and pork—could only be met by Spanish initiatives to produce them locally. Indian products that reached the Spaniards through trade or as tribute offered little more than maize and turkeys, both of them unfamiliar and unpopular foods. And it was apparent that neither Spanish dietary habits nor Indian agricultural production would change rapidly. Yet no one could have anticipated that five centuries later, the *campesino* of Indian descent would still prefer the higher yields of maize (Chevalier 1963, 51, 59).

The King had already instructed Cortés in 1523 that Spaniards should engage in farming. In Spanish settlements, "farms are to be awarded according to the character and status of the persons and according to their service rendered . . . to reside there for five years in order to obtain the lifelong rights to dispose of [the farm] at will" (Cortés 1963, 590). Such awards were made by Mexico City and Puebla in their vicinity, and also by Cortés, within the areas he claimed; but after 1535, the Colonial administration reserved this right to itself (Gibson 1964, 272–73). Both in principle and practice, awards of land were designed to reward prominent citizens and those who had provided special services, primarily administrative and military. Land was rarely awarded to common immigrants, and the general dependence on Indian labor implied that agriculture required capital. This policy set in train a long process, continuing until 1910, whereby Indian small-holdings were largely displaced by haciendas owned by people of European descent.

The first farming enterprises of Cortés and colonial officials and *encomenderos* accounted for only a minimal part of the available arable land, despite their numbers. Adjacent to Mexico City, these farms were indispensable as a source of familiar provisions for the Spaniards of the capital. Existing Indian property rights were almost meaningless during the administration of the notorious First Audiencia (1528–32) (Gibson 1964, 273). Eventually, during the 1560s, the better lands around the Basin of Mexico began to be transferred to Spanish ownership, so that by 1620 only vestiges of Indian property remained (Gibson 1964, 277–79; Butzer and Butzer 1992).

One of the more significant impacts of the expansion of Spanish landholdings was the intrusion of livestock into Indian maize fields. Stockraising had been introduced on a large scale during the early years of the colony and remained a Spanish monopoly until after the middle of the century, when herds were so large that they undoubtedly posed a significant threat to Indian cultivation. Herds of 12,000–15,000 sheep are reported from the Basin of Mexico by 1560 (Gibson 1964, 280), while almost a thousand tons of wool were shorn in Tlaxcala in 1566 (Albi Romero 1970, 96). The founding of a *mesta*—an association of stockraisers—in Mexico City (1537) and in Puebla (1541) underlines the importance of Spanish livestock operations controlled from the two cities.

Property became the focus of competition between Spaniard and Indian for the remainder of the sixteenth century, until most Indian land in the heartland of Mexico—but not in the peripheral areas—was acquired by the new settlers. Consequently, the methods of how property was gained assume critical importance not only for understanding the history of Colonial settlement but also the partial, but by no means complete, dispossession of Indian lands. Furthermore they are of relevance for Indian-Spanish relationships to Colonial Mexico.

Property was acquired through several procedures, the documentation for which is uneven. At first usurpation was common, reflecting the conquest, the arbitrary rule of the First Audiencia, and the slow implementation of a legal system in the colony. Such usurpation was only gradually replaced by legally sanctioned methods, of which the awarding of a royal land grant was the least ambiguous. Several different forms of land acquisition make the general process difficult to trace. At the same time, over-generalization based on the complex and incomplete documentation can obscure spatial and temporal patterning (e.g., Simpson 1952), while limited studies are liable to distort interpretation of the major trends. Such difficulties notwithstanding, the land grants for understanding regional settlement histories as well as the transfer of land from Indian to Spaniard.

Sketch maps, drawn from Colonial documents and illustrating patterns of property holding, field parcelization, and land use, are reproduced by Wobeser (1983).

The Documentation for Land Grants

The land grants, initially awarded by local authorities, and then exclusively by the viceroy, display a temporal progression as well as changing spatial concentrations. This process took more than a century. Spanish settlers began to receive awards for agricultural and grazing lands by 1525 (K. W. Butzer 1992). After several decades with slowly increasing numbers of awards, a maximum of about 600 grants was awarded in 1591, followed by a slow decrease (see Simpson 1952, 8–9). But the awards made conditionally in Mexico still had to be confirmed later on, requiring examination of titles in addition to payment of relatively mod-

Table 1. Requests (*Acordados*) vs. Grants (*Mercedes*) of Land Titles in the Upper Atoyac Drainage (Puebla), 1587–1620

	Requests and grants		Requests		Neither request nor grant preserved
	Both preserved	Either preserved	Preserved but not granted	Neither granted nor preserved	
Number cases	93	122	103	67*	41*

Source: Data from Prem 1978, 131–32.
*Estimated from binomial distribution.

est and flexible sums of money prior to the granting of patents or permanent titles. This process, known as *composición*, began in earnest in 1631 and was concluded by 1645, except for a few areas (see Chevalier 1963, 266–70; Torales Pacheco 1990, 90–92), and it terminated the distribution of public lands. Subsequently there were many changes in individual ownership, including consolidation and subdivision, but Indian property holdings were no longer reduced. Fundamental structural changes awaited the selling off of tax-exempt lands (*desamortización*) in 1856, which destroyed Indian communal holdings and church properties, with further confiscations after the Mexican Revolution during this century.

Documentation of Colonial land grants involved a register in which the Audiencia officials in Mexico City entered requests for, as well as awards of, titles. These are included in the 86 volumes of the section *Mercedes*, now in the Archivo General de la Nación, Mexico City, which provide a powerful tool. According to Simpson (1952, 7), the 37 volumes up to 1620 include titles for 7553 *caballerías de tierra* (agricultural land, in units of 43 hectares), 1770 *sitios de estancia de ganado mayor* (cattle pastures, in units of 1756 ha), and 2227 *sitios de estancia de ganado menor* (sheep and goat pastures of 780 ha each). Just how complete this registry is remains unclear. About a third of the 40 years between 1541–80 are not included in the available registry lists, while most of the subsequent years are represented in two or three parallel volumes, with partial overlap. An explanation for this is the use of several registry books at once, to deal with the large number of title entries. In any case, the records are incomplete and in part fragmentary, and it is difficult if not impossible to ascertain to what degree.

I have attempted to estimate how complete

the records are for the period 1587–1620, based on a detailed study of both the title requests and actual grants in the upper Río Atoyac drainage, northwest of Puebla (Prem 1978). Requests or applications for titles (referred to as a *mandamiento acordado*) and successful title awards (a *merced*) are mixed throughout the extant volumes, so that loss of individual volumes would affect both categories. The high number of requests for which there is no corresponding title must therefore include requests that were never granted, as well as ones for which the confirmatory deed has been lost. Similarly, the record of titles awarded includes those with preserved requests and those without. These either/or categories can be arranged as a binomial distribution, from which it can be estimated that 256 titles were actually awarded in the area. The probability that a title is preserved is only 60 percent for this period of good documentation. For 41 (16 percent) of these, neither an application nor a title is preserved, and for 93 (36 percent) both documents are preserved. Further, about two out of every five requests were denied (Prem 1978, 131–32; see Table 1).

For the period before 1587, the probability of preservation for titles in about 25 percent, assuming that all years without any records represent lost registers. This careful examination for a limited region shows that evaluation of the available documentation is liable to distortion by poor as well as uneven preservation.

Another limitation is that more land may have been awarded in the hinterland of the larger cities—in the Basin of Mexico, the Puebla district, and the Valley of Toluca (Fig. 1)—than there actually was. In the upper Atoyac drainage, title was given for 808 km^2 of land according to the *mercedes* and other sources. Yet the productive surface, including the high mountains and small tracts of barren

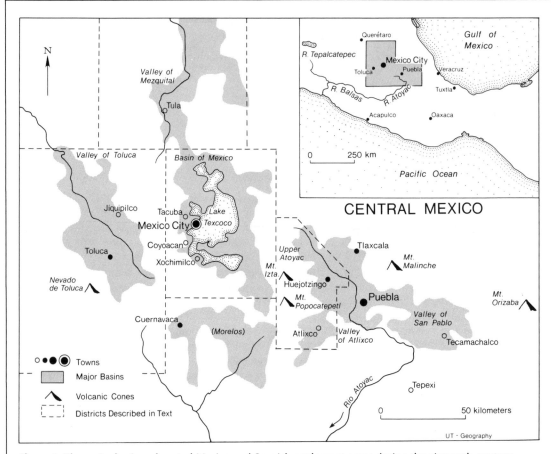

Figure 1. The major basins of central Mexico and Spanish settlement areas during the sixteenth century.

land, is little larger than 1000 km². Allowing for missing land titles, the total may even have exceeded the available area. It may well be that livestock estancias, especially those within the forested uplands, were never properly measured. In addition, their owners may have deliberately requested land segments that were known to overlap, simply to avoid the possibility that an interloper might claim land somewhere in between. Another problem for this evident discrepancy is that it is not known to what elevation the mountains were utilized for sheep grazing, or whether the upland forests would even have been awarded to private owners. Detailed study of these issues is needed.

Despite the lack of evaluation of the land grant records for large parts of New Spain, and the impossibility of a complete quantitative analysis because of the incomplete records, the broad lines of the granting process can be discerned. The timing, rate, and completeness of Spanish land acquisition depended on local circumstances. Key factors were the number of Spaniards resident in the area, proximity to market centers and expected profitability, and the density of Indian land use (Lockhart 1976, 5). These criteria distinguish the central Basin of Mexico from its hinterland, around Puebla and Toluca, and outlying, peripheral areas.

The Center: The Basin of Mexico

Spanish land holdings in the Basin of Mexico first expanded from the capital along the margins of the old lake. A total of 2112 farm units (90,400 ha) and 416 sheep estancias (3245 km²) were awarded here (Butzer and Butzer 1992; but see the much lower totals given by Gibson [1964, 277] or Simpson [1952, 55]). Measured against 233,100 ha of cultivable land (Sanders, et al. 1979, 378) and 5000 km² of land surface overall, this implies that 83 percent of the total was awarded. No grants were given in the Indian territory around Xochimilco, however, while the land to the southwest of Mexico City was controlled by Cortés and his descendents. Titles there were given out independent of the viceroy, and consequently do not show up in the Audiencia records. This means that, even without allowing for incomplete preservation, more grants were given than there was available land. However the excess of titles for grazing may be explained, most of the arable land outside of the Xochimilco district was taken over by Spaniards no later than the 1620s. The pressures on Indian holdings implied by this process are easy to imagine. The government rule that land grants had to be at least 500 *varas* or yards away from the center or outskirts of Indian settlements illustrates the degree to which such villages were crowded in.

Apart from the small numbers of grants distributed west of Mexico City in 1525–32, a pattern of systematic awards was delayed until the early 1560s, when accelerating numbers of titles began to be granted around ten key centers in the northwestern, eastern, and southeastern sectors of the basin (Butzer and Butzer 1992). In these areas, some 85 percent of the grants had been awarded by the 1590s, but grants for smaller centers in between, and in the area northeast of the lake, were delayed by about twenty-five years. The process becomes more transparent by analyzing the composite data: all but fifteen of 146 documented cases of purchase of or encroachment on Indian lands or water rights date from 1581–1617, and the 27 titles to "abandoned" lands (*tierras eriazas*) were given out between 1584–1620 (K. W. Butzer, personal communication). These circumstances show that the centers of traditional Indian landholdings remained relatively intact until after severe population loss from the pandemic of 1576.

Gibson (1964, 323–25) has estimated the size of areas with wheat cultivation on the basis of allocations of Indian workers. If his assumptions are valid, then in 1563, 44 percent of the wheat farms had less than 50 *fanegas* (31 or 178 ha, depending on which type of *fanega*) of cultivated land, while in 1602 some 92 percent would have been larger than 100 *fanegas,* and 51 percent larger than 200 *fanegas*. Regardless of whether his samples are representative and which type of *fanega* is implied, it is evident that arable holdings, originally awarded in units of 43 ha, were being consolidated into very large farms, through purchase or other manipulations. At the same time, since the number of holdings increased roughly fourfold during these forty years, the area of wheat cultivation must have increased tenfold.

The expansion of Spanish land ownership was predicated upon or interrelated with several other processes. It was the dramatic decline of the Indian population that opened up such a large area to Spanish acquisition. Although reconstructions for that decline after 1519 continue to diverge (see Cook and Borah 1971–79 vs. Prem 1991, Prem et al. n.d.), its importance is beyond doubt. The demographic consequences of actual warfare during the conquest were not inconsequential, but they were not the primary cause of decline. Far more incisive was the high mortality associated with the pandemics that swept Mexico at short intervals after 1520. A mortality of 50 percent can be estimated for the smallpox epidemic of 1520, while the pandemics of 1545 and 1576 with mortalities of 50 percent locally, up to 90 percent must have had even greater demographic impact. The many minor epidemics in between affected each district differently, but were also important (Prem 1991). During the period 1560–1600, which includes only one of these pandemics, the population of central Mexico declined by two-thirds, so that a substantial part of the Indian lands must have been uncultivated by 1600, opening them to Spanish acquisition. This is consonant with the evidence cited above.

A second factor, often overestimated as to its importance for the shift from Indian to Spanish ownership, was the process of Indian settlement amalgamation (*congregación*). This began during the mid-1500s but was concentrated between 1590–1605 (Gerhard 1977; Licate 1981, 88–98). The purpose of amalgamation was to nucleate Indian populations that had been dispersed in small hamlets into new, planned towns that were easier to administer and located at more accessible sites. The missionaries had repeatedly complained that the wide dispersal of the Indian population amid complex topography made it very difficult for them to administer and oversee the numerous small communities. The colonial authorities responded in 1551 and at later dates by ordering nucleation in central sites (*Recopilación* 6-3-1), which also facilitated administration.

While the process of resettlement associated with *congregación* was explicitly not intended to affect Indian property holdings, Indians from more distant locations could only use and tend their traditional fields with difficulty, and many milpas thus remained unused. This secondary effect benefitted Spaniards trying to obtain land. But many of the amalgamation projects were evidently not implemented, and even successful efforts at nucleation could not prevent substantial numbers of Indians from only nominal compliance, as they either remained in their traditional settlements or returned there promptly, or fled (see Gibson 1964, 282–83; Lovell 1992). Nonetheless the *congregación* process did lead to abandonment of marginal lands that, according to Spanish law, could then be awarded to others.

Much of the land of central Mexico was unsuitable for maize cultivation but adequate for pasture, so that the introduction of livestock led to a substantial expansion of permanent land use. Forest grazing was possible in parts of the mountain country that did not allow maize harvests because of elevation and frost hazards. Sheep and goats could also find food in other areas where steep slopes, soil erosion, salinization, or lack of adequate moisture inhibited agriculture. Furthermore, Spanish irrigation was introduced to some areas or expanded in others.

Another factor that contributed directly to the reduction of land cultivated by Indians was work conscription on Spanish holdings (*repartimiento*): as part of the tributary obligations of their communities, Indians were required to provide labor at a rate specified by the Colonial authorities (Chevalier 1963, 66–68), and they were allocated accordingly by a Spanish official. Although the number of absent Indians engaged in conscript labor at any one time was small, the effect was that a percentage of the Indian work input was shifted to Spanish holdings. Such work was limited to the planting and harvest seasons and, by the end of the 1500s, such obligations were increasingly switched to wage labor (*gañanes*) that was no longer assigned to particular

Spaniards. This development favored long-term employment on Spanish farms, with the result that more and more families moved out of their traditional communities to take up permanent residence on the growing estates.

During the early period, repeated mention is made of lands whose production, prior to the Conquest, had been assigned to support Indian institutions such as temples, temple schools, the army, and government officials (Chevalier 1963, 52). The extent of such lands cannot be estimated but, in comparison to the other factors discussed above, they were unimportant, if only because they were directly transferred to the ownership of the last persons to legally farm them at the time of conquest.

Although the basic circumstances for property transfer to Spaniards were similar in the broad valleys surrounding the Basin of Mexico, that process unraveled differently in each, particularly in regard to timing. But since study and interpretation of the available documentation remains uneven, comparisons can only be made with caution.

A Secondary Center: The Puebla District

All authors are in agreement that the second center of Spanish agriculture was located between the volcanic ranges of Popocatepetl in the west and Mt. Orizaba in the east. The transfer of property to Spanish settlers in the piedmont of the upper Río Atoyac drainage, northwest of the city of Puebla, has been exhaustively studied (Prem 1978). This area belonged to the independent state of Huejotzingo in Aztec times. Cortés began raising pigs here before 1525, and in 1530 the *encomendero* of Huejotzingo, Diego de Ordáz, introduced cattle raising and began wheat cultivation in the adjacent Valley of Atlixco (Fig. 1). Shortly thereafter, the first settlers of Puebla (see above) received farmlands here amounting to 1840 ha in the first year alone. Just how attractive Atlixco was can be judged by the slow settlement of Huejotzingo proper, where only 10 agricultural grants are documented before 1578.

Indian settlement amalgamation in Huejotzingo during the mid-1500s was not very successful (Dyckerhoff 1990b, 44–45) and did not benefit the expansion of Spanish holdings. But

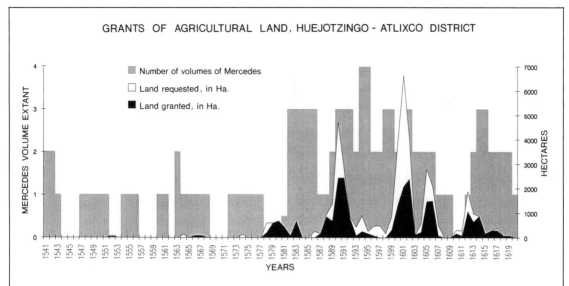

Figure 2. Awards of agricultural lands (*caballerías de tierra*) in the Huejotzingo-Atlixco district (Puebla), 1541–1620, in ha.

the pandemic of 1576 probably reduced the Indian population by close to a half, with the result that land awards began to accelerate in 1579 (Fig. 2). The linkage is clear, although the exceptional preservation of large numbers of titles in some years distorts the pattern. After an interruption in 1585, not related to the quality of documentation, the number of requests for land increased dramatically until 1592, followed shortly thereafter by a first peak in titles awarded. Two years later both the applications and titles declined sharply, terminating altogether in 1598.

A fresh increase began in the following year, first of applications, then of title deeds, but both the number and the size of the awards were less than half of what was requested. Two more waves of granting are apparent before 1620, although their amplitude was decreasing. These oscillations are difficult to explain. Several further epidemics between 1587–97 did not cause significant population losses and played no important role. The answer may lie in the mechanics of the application process itself. A rapid increase in the number of requests would quickly dispose of the lands momentarily available, so that the ratio of unsuccessful bids would discourage further applicants, thus the number of requests would decline until no new requests were made. During

interruption of the granting process, only a few new requests would be made, most of them unsuccessful.

The accelerating half-cycle may be linked to a new phenomenon of the late sixteenth century. Most of the land in several parts of the area was in Spanish hands by then, but not all of it had clear title. This led to efforts by the owners in question or by potential interlopers, or the front men for either group, to apply for grants to land already held but incompletely or inadequately covered by titles (*en demasías*). After each wave of new grants, remaining questions of title or possible gaps in the property cover would only become apparent as time elapsed.

Each wave of grants represented an advance of Spanish property holdings into the core areas of Indian settlement. After 1600, title requests concentrated on areas with semi-continuous Indian agriculture, but, for more than half of the land applied for, appear to have been denied, suggesting increasingly effective Indian resistance.

The last wave of applications, from 1613–16, was directed at the last gaps of cultivation within the Indian core area. By then the peripheral belt was solidly in Spanish hands, and larger estates were actively engaged in consolidating their holdings. An example for this is

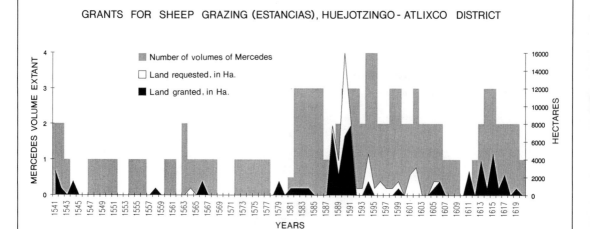

Figure 3. Awards of estancias for sheep grazing (*sitios de ganado menor*) in the Huejotzingo-Atlixco district (Puebla), 1541–1620, in ha. Two grants for cattle grazing (*sitios de ganado mayor*) are included in the diagram.

provided by the Apapasco hacienda, belonging to the Augustinians of Puebla; in 1610 it controlled almost 3000 ha, mostly arable.

A similar evolution can be noted for the acquisition of grazing rights in the region, almost exclusively for sheep and goats, but the details vary from one sector to another. Sheep estancias were awarded to Spaniards on a large scale even before they were able to acquire cultivable lands. Most but not all of these were on the forested slopes of the high mountain range (to above 3000 m elevation), in areas too cool for maize but in proximity to the two mountain roads from Puebla to Mexico City (Fig. 3). Grants for sheep estancias followed at a steady pace, reaching a first maximum in 1588–92, more or less simultaneous with the early peak in agricultural titles. The end of this wave was abrupt, and a detailed mapping of the locations of the sheep estancias (Prem 1978, 235–60) shows that essentially all areas of lowland marsh and steep forest had already been awarded. The remaining areas, on even less desirable tracts, were given out in a last wave from 1611–19.

For both processes the end result was the same. By 1620 most of the productive land was in the hands of people of European descent. This is verified by the *composición* or complete inventory of confirmed titles for the district of Huejotzingo-Atlixco in 1643. Although

lacking in detail here, the *composición* confirms the fragmentary record of successive grants, while local property owners declared that there was no more free land available. Complete details are included in the *composición* for the Valley of Atlixco, which documents that 18,915 ha out of a total of about 23,000 (including settlements and some unproductive tracts) belonged to persons of European descent. Some 44 percent of this surface was irrigated, allowing two harvests per year on the unusually fertile vertisols (Albi Romero 1970, 93; Prem 1984, 212, 215).

The Valley of Toluca and the Peripheries

Equally fertile and attractive for agricultural expansion was the Valley of Toluca, west of the Basin of Mexico (Fig. 1). The sequence of land acquisition here was similar to that around Puebla, beginning with Cortés's early involvement with local cattle raising. More than 150,000 head of cattle were reported in the early 1550s (García Martínez 1969, 140), and the first peak of title awards in 1560–70 came two decades earlier than around Huejotzingo, while the climax of several waves of awards came a little later (Quezada Ramírez 1972, 102).

A spatial breakdown of the grants shows that

the northern part of the valley around Jiquipilco was settled first, the southern and southwestern mountainous peripheries last; 34,150 ha of agricultural land were awarded and 325,600 ha of grazing for cattle (52 percent), sheep (46 percent), and horses (2.7 percent) (Butzer and Butzer 1992). This represents only 28.5 percent of the larger region, and even allowing for missing records for Cortés's cattle estates and for large tracts of mountain topography, this shows that large parts of the Toluca district remained in Indian hands. There were small, scattered Spanish wheat farms around Toluca itself (Lockhart 1975, 438–47), but most of the Spanish farm land was concentrated around the periphery rather than in the center of the basin (Butzer and Butzer 1992). The spatial pattern and social context was then quite different from that of the Huejotzingo district, in that core Indian settlement was not overwhelmed.

Moving out from the heartland of central Mexico (Fig. 1), the structural similarities weaken and each regional settlement history became more or less unique. In the Valley of Mezquital, the region to the north of the Basin of Mexico, Spaniards acquired 60 percent of the land for sheep grazing, but only 4 percent for agriculture; the rest remained in Indian hands (Melville 1990). In the smaller fertile Valley of San Pablo, 50 km east of Puebla, Spanish wheat farms were important (Licate 1981, 116). As in Toluca, the Spanish acquisition of land in the peripheral zone was less complete, and stockraising dominated over grain farming. Two other examples, from areas outside of the region emphasized here, serve to broaden the perspective.

In the Valley of Oaxaca, the properties of Hernán Cortés again provided the first nucleus of European agriculture. Stockraising remained dominant during the 1500s (Taylor 1972, 113–21), but Spanish acquisition was slow and incomplete until the early 1600s.

The preponderance of stockraising is much more striking in the Valley of Tepalcatepec, a major tributary river of the Río Balsas in western Michoacan. Until the late 1500s, land titles were almost exclusively awarded for cattle pastures, and any agricultural land was designed to supply grain for consumption by the labor employed on the estates. Located in an area of sparse Indian settlement, there was little direct interethnic competition. During the early 1600s, Spanish agriculture expanded with the benefit of irrigation, to grow cacao and sugar cane (Barrett 1973, 82–84). Nonetheless, 95 percent of the area remained in pasturage.

The Indian Response

The expansion of Spanish landholdings did not inevitably lead to conflict with the Indian population. It is true that the expansion of stockraising, even in the early years, invariably was detrimental to the Indians. Complaints about livestock breaking into maize fields and destroying them are legion (Gibson 1964, map 8; Taylor 1972, map 3), as are viceregal attempts to regulate the problems; the numbers alone argue that efforts at control were unsuccessful. Equally clear is that, in their purchase and lease of land, as well as in their quest for land titles, the Spaniards enjoyed close connections with the Colonial authorities and used them to their full advantage vis à vis the Indians.

But on the other hand, the Indians were not simply victims. They themselves engaged in the sale of their properties, effectively supporting the growth and consolidation of Spanish estates (Prem 1978, 285–92; Barrett 1974, 86). Hurdles placed by the Colonial administration to limit the sell-out of Indian lands to Spaniards were circumvented jointly, by both parties. However, the Indian government of Huejotzingo prohibited land sales by Indians in 1579, apparently on account of many illegalities during such transactions, but the viceroy failed to approve this resolution because it contradicted official procedures. The motivation of the Spaniards is evident, but it is difficult to understand why so many Indians were eager to sell their properties, almost always at very low prices. Even the requisite affidavits, that the Indians offering land for sale did not need such properties and held sufficient other land to feed their families, do not seem to have made them aware of the consequences of such actions. A justification that they needed cash to pay their tribute was almost always added to two or three other reasons offered to convince the authorities. There was in fact no reasonable relationship between the regular tribute payment of a peso per year to the much higher value of a land sale (Prem 1978, 285–92).

During the second half of the sixteenth century, Indian communities as well as individuals began to protect their land by obtaining land titles of their own, even though such traditional ownership was secured by Spanish law. However great the pressures of Spanish land owners may have been, this procedure seems absurd: the condition for granting a title was that the land be unclaimed, so that an Indian technically had to give up his rights in order to then obtain a title for the land. This option was not commonly used in most areas, but it deserves mention because one might otherwise assume that the Indians retained only that land to which they had acquired formal titles.

In Morelos, favorably located in proximity to Mexico City, Indians do not appear to have requested titles (Martin 1985, 28–32). The same is true in peripheral Tepexi (Jäcklein 1978, 178). In Hueyotzingo the grants given to Indians amounted to only four percent of the total awards, most of these given in one town. The proportion in the Valley of Toluca appears to have been similar (Quezada Ramírez 1972), but in Tepalcatepec the Indians received 16 percent of the awarded lands (see Barrett 1973, 1974). Yet in Tecamachalco, a third of the titles went to individual Indians or to their communities (Licate 1981, 115), while in the Valley of Mezquital, the Indians acquired titles to almost all the 36 percent of the land they retained (Melville 1990).

Even more striking is that only 32 percent of the land represented in formal titles for the Valley of Oaxaca went to Spaniards. The remaining land went to Indians, approximately half to communities, the other part to individuals, many of whom probably represented their communities. This situation appears to be unique, but a convincing explanation is lacking. The small number of resident Spaniards probably played a role (Taylor 1972, 198); in addition, limited local demand for wheat and the great distance to Mexico City probably reduced incentives to grow this Spanish crop.

Other strategies also served to halt the alienation of Indian holdings, such as the inspection of the often flawed Spanish land titles during *composición*. Numerous cases of litigation sustained Indian rights vs. haciendas, and sometimes land was bought back by Indians. By such means the Indian communities were repeatedly able to stabilize the situation and to slow the advance of Spanish property seekers, as for example, in Metztitlán (Osborn 1973).

The Spanish Land Owners

It has already been emphasized that the *encomienda* did not inaugurate Spanish acquisition of land, either legally or in fact. But the *encomenderos,* as the most influential persons of the early colony and as the beneficiaries of tribute, were the first to get land and to practice agriculture (Lockhart 1969, 418). It was not their role as *encomenderos* but their interdigitation with the Spanish Colonial elite that made this possible. Colonial officials such as local magistrates also were among the first to obtain land titles. Both the *encomenderos* and officials selected their properties in adjacent districts, because ownership within one's own jurisdiction was illegal. Small wonder that the Audiencia officials, who controlled the award of titles, had little difficulty acquiring property themselves (Chevalier 1963, 123–27). Not all were as skilled as Gaspar Rodríguez de Castro, the private secretary of Viceroy Montesclaros, who acquired an incredible number of land titles, including the permission to sell them immediately, during the viceroy's last months in office in 1607 (Prem 1978, 203–04). Relatives and retainers of officials showed no compunction to serve as surrogates for title applications when the real owner did not wish to be identified (Chevalier 1952, 136). By contrast, Viceroy Velasco (1550–64) stood out by his undisputed integrity, but at the price of going heavily into debt.

Legalistic historians are prone to believe that church institutions were excluded from obtaining land. While it is true that every grant deed specified that the land in question could not be transferred to clergymen or to religious institutions, this rule as well as that interdicting sales of titles was ignored for many years. Time and again, persons obtaining a title or permission to sell one showed up in front of a notary only days later to declare that they had acted in proxy for the Augustinian monastery of Puebla; the transfer would then be sanctioned without difficulty and without comment (Prem 1978, 188). Another effective device was to obtain a permit to plant crops (*licencia para sembrar*) on estancias granted for stock raising, thus converting to cultivation an area equivalent to twenty-seven *caballerías*. This strategem, used not only by monasteries, was one of many ways to acquire land legally. In such ways the Augustinian hacienda Apapasco acquired 1926 ha of cultivable land, while another 800 ha of pasture were cultivated without a record for permission (Prem 1978, 190). Other religious orders, with the notable exception of the Franciscans, also strove diligently and successfully to amass property.

Study of the royal land titles obviously does not provide a complete picture of land acquisition. Not every Spaniard sought to obtain land through the proper but somewhat cumbersome legal procedures. Since Indian ownership was legal and undisputed in theory, sale of land to a Spaniard carried some legal weight. Most of the available deeds of purchase are indirectly linked to grants of title. One of the most common difficulties and impediments to secure title in areas of denser Indian settlement was a requirement to demonstrate that the land in question was neither owned nor claimed by someone; this was to be investigated by the resident Spanish magistrate in front of an assembly of the Indians, and commonly led to protestations. The simplest way to avoid such a procedure was to buy the land from the rightful Indian owners well in advance. This was both a common and widespread practice (Prem 1978, 285–92; Cline 1986, 155–56).

Another approach, to obtain property by marriage, is rarely documented and is all too commonly overlooked. Younger Spaniards with little prospect of economic advancement not infrequently married into the families of the Indian elite. They and their children (their daughters commonly marrying Spaniards as well) aspired to inherit the offices of Indian nobility (*caciques*), together with their often substantial properties or the lands held by the mid-level community elite.

Land acquisition and agriculture required capital that could be gained through other economic activities. One such opportunity was to operate textile workshops (*obrajes*) that produced wool and cotton cloth or clothing for local or distant markets (Lewis 1976, 129; Szewczyk 1976, 145–47). Trade offered another possibility. Many Spaniards owned small shops in the city centers (Szewczyk 1976, 140–42; Lewis 1976, 131), selling goods locally, while buying their wares from distant source areas, via agents or directly from itinerant tradesmen.

Gristmills and Irrigation as Indices

Although maize, the traditional Indian staple, was always ground to meal at home immediately before use, wheat was purchased in the form of milled flour. Gristmills were therefore set up at the same time that wheat cultivation was introduced to an area. Such mills were already set up in the environs of Mexico City at Tacuba and Tacubaya during the First Audiencia, implying that many of the small irrigated tracts awarded nearby (*suertes de huerta*) were used to grow wheat. Some of the highest officials of the Audiencia were so engaged (Paso y Troncoso 1939–42, XIV, 178).

Gristmills therefore serve as an indirect indicator for wheat production. Between 1542–1640, at least twenty-three mill sites were applied for or granted in the Atlixco or Huejotzingo areas. Not all requests were honored, but others can be documented for which no titles are preserved. The latter include the gristmill of the Indian community in Huejotzingo, which has an inscription dated 1559. It was, however, never operated by the Indians but was leased to Spaniards instead (Prem 1975, 31). Awards for gristmills were most common around 1594, at the time of the first maximum of awards of agricultural lands to Spaniards. In the Basin of Mexico, 41 of 66 documented licenses to build gristmills were granted between 1581–1607, approximately coeval with the majority of the titles awarded for agricultural land (K. W. Butzer, personal communication).

A second feature that elucidates Spanish land acquisition was the introduction of irrigation. Although irrigation was probably used in the Valley of Atlixco in Prehispanic times, it was only introduced in the northern part of the Valley in Colonial times (Dyckerhoff 1990a, 23). The last land awards, given for the level terrain northwest of Huejotzingo during the first decade of the 1600s, terminated the process of acquisition. Subsequently, increases of production could only be achieved here by intensification. It therefore comes as no surprise that thirty-six of forty-two applications for or awards of title for irrigation waters date to the decade 1610–20.

Conclusions

The process of land transfer from Indian to Spanish hands in the heartland of Mexico took about one hundred years. Traditional Indian lands were protected under Spanish law, but only as long as they were cultivated. Land abandonment was primarily a result of the Indian demographic collapse, reinforced by Indian resettlement in nucleated new towns and by migration of workers from traditional communities to Spanish estates. Alienation of Indian landholdings began on a large scale after 1580, and by 1620 most Indian properties in the Basin of Mexico and around Puebla had been awarded as land grants to Spaniards. The Spanish farms, owned by absentee landlords and worked by Indian wage labor, were steadily expanded through purchase and consolidated into large estates. In areas peripheral to Mexico City, Spanish acquisition of Indian property was incomplete and, with increasing distance, stockraising became more important than farming. Each regional settlement history differed in detail, depending on the size of the resident Indian population, the quality of land, and the proximity of larger Spanish towns and major roads.

The processes and patterns identified by this study are far more complex than those envisioned in Chevalier's (1963) general overview for all of Mexico. Further, detailed local studies are needed to explicate the pattern of regional divergence and to link the process of estate consolidation to the emergence of the great haciendas of the eighteenth and nineteenth centuries.

References

Albi Romero, Guadalupe. 1970. La sociedad de Puebla de los Angeles en el siglo XVI. *Jahrbuch für Geschichte von Staat Wirtschaft und Gesellschaft Lateinamerikas* 7:76–145.

Barrett, Elinore M. 1973. *Encomiendas, mercedes and haciendas in the tierra caliente of Michoacan. Jahrbuch für Geschichte von Staat Wirtschaft und Gesellschaft Lateinamerikas* 10:71–107.

———. 1974. Indian community lands in the tierra caliente of Michoacan. *Jahrbuch für Geschichte*

von Staat Wirtschaft und Gesellschaft Lateinamerikas* 11:78–120.

Butzer, Karl W. 1992. Personal communication.

——— **and Butzer, Elisabeth K.** 1992. Transfer of the Mediterranean livestock economy to New Spain: Adaptation and consequences. In *Legacies of the Columbian Encounter*, B. L. Turner II, ed., forthcoming. Madrid: Consejo Superior de Investigaciones Científicas.

Chevalier, François. 1957. *Significación social de la fundación de la Puebla de los Angeles.* Puebla: Centro de Estudios Historicos.

———. 1963. *Land and society in colonial Mexico: The great hacienda.* Trans. Lesley Byrd Simpson. Berkeley: University of California Press. (Lacks the documentation of the original 1952 French ed.)

Cline, S. L. 1986. *Colonial Culhuacan, 1580–1600: A social history of an Aztec town.* Albuquerque: University of New Mexico Press.

Colección de documentos inéditos, relativos al descrubrimiento, conquista y organización de las antiguas posesiones españolas de ultramar (CDIU). 1885–1932. 25 vols. Madrid: Rivadeneyra.

Cook, Sherburne F., and Borah, Woodrow. 1971–1979. *Essays in population history.* 3 vols. Berkeley: University of California Press.

Cortés, Hernan. 1963. *Cartas y documentos.* Ed. M. Hernández Sánchez-Barba. Mexico City: Porrúa.

Díaz del Castillo, Bernal. 1960. *Historia verdadera de la conquista de la Nueva España.* 2 vols. Mexico City: Porrúa.

Dyckerhoff, Ursula. 1990a. Control hidráulico en el Huejotzingo prehispánico. *Papeles de la Casa Chata* 5(7):19–27.

———. 1990b. Colonial Indian corporate landholding: A glimpse from the Valley of Puebla. In *The Indian community of Colonial Mexico*, Arij Ouweneel and Simon Miller, eds., 40–59. Amsterdam: CEDLA.

García Martínez, Bernardo. 1969. *El Marquesado del Valle.* Mexico City: El Colegio de México.

Gerhard, Peter. 1977. Congregaciones de indios en la Nueva España antes de 1570. *Historia Mexicana* 26:347–95.

Gibson, Charles. 1964. *The Aztecs under Spanish rule: A history of the Indians of the Valley of Mexico.* Stanford, CA: Stanford University Press.

Haring, C. H. 1963. *The Spanish empire in America.* New York: Harcourt, Brace.

Hirschberg, Julia. 1979. Social experiments in New Spain: A prosopographical study of the early settlement at Puebla de los Angeles, 1531–1534. *Hispanic American Historical Review* 59:1–33.

Jäcklein, Klaus. 1978. *Los Popolocas de Tepexi (Puebla): Un estudio etnohistórico.* Wiesbaden: Steiner, Mexiko-Projekt der Deutschen Forschungsgemeinschaft, 15.

Lewis, Leslie. 1976. In Mexico City's shadow: Some aspects of economic activity and social process in Texcoco, 1570–1620. In *Provinces of early Mexico: Variants of Spanish American regional evolution,* Ida Altman and James Lockhart, eds., 125–36. Los Angeles: UCLA Latin American Center Publications.

Licate, Jack A. 1981. *Creation of a Mexican landscape: Territorial organization and settlement in the eastern Puebla Basin, 1520–1605.* Department of Geography Research Paper 201. Chicago: University of Chicago.

Lockhart, James. 1969. *Encomienda* and *hacienda:* The evolution of the great estate in the Spanish Indies. *Hispanic American Historical Review* 49:411–29.

————. 1975. Españoles entre indios: Toluca a fines del siglo XVI. In *Estudios sobre la ciudad iberoamericana,* Francisco de Solano, ed., 435–91. Madrid: Consejo Superior de Investigaciones Científicas.

————. 1976. Introduction. In *Provinces of early Mexico: Variants of Spanish American regional evolution,* Ida Altman and James Lockhart, eds., pp. 3–28. Los Angeles: UCLA latin American Center Publications.

Lovell, W. George. 1992. The real country and the legal country: Spanish ideals and Mayan realities in Colonial Guatemala. *GeoJournal* 26:181–85.

Martin, Cheryl English. 1985. *Rural society in Colonial Morelos.* Albuquerque: University of New Mexico Press.

Melville, Elinore G. 1990. Environmental and social change in the Valle de Mezquital, Mexico, 1521–1600. *Comparative Studies in Society and History* 32:24–53.

Miranda, José. 1965. *La función económica del encomendero en los orígenes del régimen colonial (Nueva España 1525–1531).* Mexico City: Universidad Nacional Autónoma de México.

Motolónia (or Benavente), Toribio de. 1971. *Memoriales o libro de la Nueva España y de los naturales della.* Ed. Edmundo O'Gorman. Mexico City: Universidad Nacional Autónoma de México.

Osborn, Wayne S. 1973. Indian land retention in Colonial Metztitlan. *Hispanic American Historical Review* 53:217–38.

Paso y Troncoso, Francisco, ed. 1939–42. 16 vols. *Epistolario de Nueva España.* Mexico City: Robredo.

Prem, Hanns J. 1975. Los afluentes del Río Xopanac: Estudio histórico de un sistema de riego. *Comunicaciones Proyecto Puebla-Tlaxcala* 12:27–40.

————. 1978. *Milpa y Hacienda: Tenencia de la tierra indígena y española en la Cuenca del Alto Atoyac, Puebla, México (1520–1650).* Wiesbaden: Steiner. Mexiko-Projekt der Deutschen Forschungsgemeinschaft, 13. (Second printing: Mexico City: Fondo de Cultura Económica 1988.)

————. 1984. Early Spanish colonization and Indians in the Valley of Atlixco. In *Explorations in ethnohistory,* H. R. Harvey and Hanns J. Prem, eds., 205–28. Albuquerque: University of New Mexico Press.

————. 1991. Disease outbreaks in central Mexico during the sixteenth century. In *Secret judgments of God: Old World disease in Colonial Spanish America,* ed. Noble David Cook and W. George Lovell, pp. 20–48. Norman: University of Oklahoma Press.

————; **Dyckerhoff, Ursula; and Feldweg, Helmut.** n.d. Reconstructing Central Mexico's population. Manuscript.

Quezada Ramírez, Maria. 1972. *Los Matlatzincas: Epoca prehispánica y época colonial hasta 1650.* Mexico City: Instituto Nacional de Antropología e Historia, Investigaciones, 22.

Recopilación de leyes de los Reynos de las Indios. 1973 [1681]. 4 vols. Madrid: Ed. Cultura Hispánica.

Sanders, William T.; Parsons, Jeffrey R.; and Santley, Robert S. 1979. *The Basin of Mexico: Ecological processes in the evolution of a civilization.* New York: Academic Press.

Simpson, Lesley Byrd. 1952. *Exploitation of land in central Mexico in the sixteenth century.* Ibero-Americana 36. Berkeley: University of California Press.

————. 1966. *The encomienda in New Spain.* Berkeley: University of California Press.

Szewczyk, David M. 1976. New elements in the society of Tlaxcala, 1519–1618. In *Provinces of early Mexico: Variants of Spanish American regional evolution,* ed. Ida Altman and James Lockhart, pp. 137–54. Los Angeles: UCLA Latin American Center Publications.

Taylor, William B. 1972. *Landlord and peasant in Colonial Oaxaca.* Stanford, CA: Stanford University Press.

Torales Pacheco, Maria C. 1990. A note on the *composiciones de tierra* in the jurisdiction of Cholula, Puebla (1591–1757). In *The Indian community of Colonial Mexico,* ed. Arij Ouweneel and Simon Miller, pp. 87–102. Amsterdam: CEDLA.

Wobeser, Gisela von. 1983. *La formación de la hacienda en la época colonial. El uso de la tierra y el agua.* Mexico City: Universidad Nacional Autónoma de México.

Landscape, System, and Identity in the Post-Conquest Andes

Daniel W. Gade

Department of Geography, University of Vermont, Burlington, VT 05405-0114,
FAX 802/656-8429.

Abstract. This article synthesizes the broad impact of Spanish introductions in the New World for the Central Andes (Peru, Ecuador, and Bolivia). Beginning in 1531, the Spaniards brought, from Iberia and Middle America, material elements of their culture which in time were acquired by native people through both imposition and free choice. Plants, animals, and tools were selectively integrated into native agropastoral systems and architectural elements into settlement patterns. Of the screens that filtered the array of Old World rural traits, keeping some out, permitting others to successfully pass and be adopted, the most significant were conditions that the highland environment imposed and competition from existing elements of the already well-developed Andean agricultural complex. Depopulation disrupted the native agroecosystem, and in the restructuring that followed, European goods and practices were adopted along with the indigenous. About a dozen crop introductions became important among peasants out of a total list three times that long, but European domesticated animals contributed most saliently to peasant livelihoods. These Old World biotic contributions juxtaposed with the native elements into a complex that crystallized between 1550–1650. With house types, building materials, and settlement pattern, the two traditions melded. Much of the Central Andes since then has changed relatively little.

Key Words: cultural ecology, cultural landscape, agropastoralism, crops, animals, tools, house types, settlement, Andes, Peru, Bolivia, Ecuador.

FROM the time Spaniards unleashed their brand of European civilization on the lands across the sea, the native peoples of the Western Hemisphere had to deal with a jarring array of new realities. Only those pieces of Spanish cultural baggage that were adaptable to New World conditions survived their passage through the screen of time, distance, and competition. To varying degrees, the rural landscapes of the Americas are juxtapositions of selected elements of the Old World tradition and those indigenous to the hemisphere. In some places the introduced has largely displaced the native American components. In still other regions, the material bases of everyday life manifest a felicitous convergence in which the two are merged as one.

These folkways are the stuff of a particularistic geography in touch with visible landscapes as complex compositions of multiple influences. They evoke reflections on both the origin and spread of contrasting forms, as well as on the integration of elements into a cultural-ecological system that attests to the adaptive choices of a group. Form and function of these elements are intertwined concerns of a geographical approach to the outcome of the cultural encounter that started with Columbus five hundred years ago. The availability of Spanish material culture in the New World depended on either its physical transfer or replication in place (Foster 1960; Arguedas 1968; Alcina Franch 1986). Successful diffusion required both adaptability to new environments and human receptivity (Denevan 1983).

The manifold geographical diversity of Hispanic America almost requires that a discussion

Annals of the Association of American Geographers. 82(3), 1992, pp. 460–477
© Copyright 1992 by Association of American Geographers

of impacts on landscape and system be confined to one specific setting. The Central Andean Highlands are chosen to examine the process and outcome of Spanish introductions to rural life in the New World. In this region, pre-Columbian land use had evolved into a sustainable sedentary existence that was no less stable than the farming-herding complex across the Atlantic. Unlike most of the lands of tropical latitudes, European elements flourished in this mountain redoubt that bore certain broad resemblances to the homeland. Spaniards were, in all cases, the initial agents of diffusion, largely to meet their own needs and desires, but the focus here is on the transfer of these introduced elements of material culture to the native people of the Andes.

An Andean focus also places contemporary agropastoralism and settlement there as a double heritage. Peasant life and livelihood in the Andes have often been viewed as a straight and pure line from the Incas. Exaltation of the indigenous tended to place Western influence as a negative force or, at best, an epiphenomenon. The notion of a continuity with the indigenous past holds a compelling fascination for many members of postindustrial societies who are, moreover, able to marshall broad sympathy outside the realm for a folk often viewed as oppressed. Dispossession and death were grim chapters in post-Conquest Andean history, and European subjugation brought with it the ruin of some of the intricate adjustments that people had made with their montane environment. But the inhabitants of upland South America also profited from this impingement, however rude it was, to sustain themselves by learning new techniques of increased efficiency; accepting new crops that added new textures, flavors, and nutrition to their diets; and adopting domesticated animals that, in addition to their uses, greatly increased the energy flow to humans from non cultivated lands. Indians were never as culturally hermetic as some of the ethnographic and travel literature purport them to have been.[1]

The Central Andean Stage

Highland Ecuador, Peru, and Bolivia form a supranational unit whose coherence is more than the physiographic outcome of the Cenozoic collision of tectonic plates. Cultural groups in that part of the tropical Andes reached a higher level of sophistication than in other mountain regions of the world before the modern era. More than five thousand years of sedentary living gave rise to a series of regional polities of whom the Inca are best known. An elaborate state ideology, official religion, policy of cultural transplantation, and a road system with Cuzco at its center consolidated an exceptionally fractured territory. Regional continuity persisted after the Spanish Conquest for almost two hundred years, when the Viceroyalty of Peru with its capital in Lima placed the Central Andes under one administrative unit. Since then, the politically regionalized highlands have continued to share a cultural configuration of locally organized societies of conservative peasants long noted for their frugality, poverty, and often passive resistance to the modernizing assumptions emanating from their capital cities.

Andean land use has been marked by the extravagant verticality which telescopes climates and compresses ecological belts like few other places on earth (Troll 1931). Such diversity in short distances has encouraged a single group to manage several zones. Tuber cultivation and camelid herding above 3700 m contrasted with the temperate valleys and basins where the staple crop, maize, was grown on irrigated and regularly fertilized land. Warm depressions etched below ca. 2500 m produced tender crops such as capsicum pepper, cherimoya and lucma; below ca. 1800 m, coca grew. Periodic movement of a single community among different production zones promoted economic self-sufficiency, though trade between different groups also occurred.

Andean people were proficient in manipulating their mountain habitat for sustainable food production. Earthworks, whose construction was plausibly prompted by population increase that started long before the Inca, had water management as their raison d'être (Donkin 1979; Guillet 1987). More than a million hectares in the Central Andes were fashioned into irrigated agricultural terraces, most of them in Peru (Masson 1984). Stone-faced bench terraces found in valleys at elevations suitable for maize cultivation were the most elaborate of these cascading structures (Denevan 1987). Aside from terraces, hillsides also underwent ridging and furrowing in places whose mark on the land lingers even after they have been long since abandoned (Schjellerup 1985). Raised fields, identified by scientists only in the 1960s, were built on flat land in various places from Northern Highland Ecuador and Central Peru to the Lake Titicaca Basin and beyond (Smith, et al. 1968; Knapp and Denevan 1985; Knapp 1988). Recent experiments to reconstruct their ancient use highlight their considerable food productivity. The ridges improved drainage, and the standing water between them may have fixed nutrients and moderated temperatures for the crops grown there; organic matter that accumulated in the ditches was periodically spread over the mounds as fertilizer.

Pathways of Hispanic Diffusion

Francisco Pizarro and his men arrived on the coast of Peru in 1531 and conquered the Incas within a year. More than any other part of South America, the Central Andes with their mineral wealth, valleys of dense populations, and high productive capacity appealed to sixteenth-century Spaniards. Four decades intervened between Columbus's landfall and the first European incursions into this zone, and during that time the Spaniards had become self-confident in their ability to dominate whomever and whatever they encountered in the New World. This aplomb of the hidalgo mentality, combined with firearms and horses, resulted in one of the most sudden and traumatic conquests of any high civilization recorded in world history. The acculturation to European ways, however, lagged far behind the political hegemony imposed on the land and native people.

Most of those Spaniards who came directly to the broadly defined land called Peru in the first years after the Conquest were from Andalusia, Castile, and Extremadura (Pérez de Barradas 1941). Emigrants from eastern and northern Spain were far fewer, and fewest of all were Catalans. In 1535, of the 56 people who embarked for Peru from Seville, 65 percent of them were plateau dwellers from Old and New Castile and Extremadura (Bermúdez Plata 1942). The eightfold increase in movement to Peru a quarter of a century later did not notably change the provenance. Of the 444 people listed as going to Peru in 1560, most came originally from the Meseta (Romera Iruela and Galbis Diez 1980). Spaniards from the plateau may have had a special affinity for the Andes

as a colonial destination, especially if they had knowledge of the contrast between the cool, malaria-free highlands as compared to the general unhealthiness of the lowlands. Those colonists already present in the New World when Pizarro conquered Peru had sounder information on which to make a decision to go to the Andes. The Spanish settlements on the Pacific coast from Mexico to Panama contributed many migrants in the first decade after the Conquest.

Reaching the Andes from Spain necessitated much more time and effort than going to the Antilles. The journey from Seville to Callao commonly took five months or more and required crossing the Isthmus of Panama (Fig. 1). The trip across this strip of land from the Caribbean port at Nombre de Dios (and after 1597 at Portobelo) to the Pacific side required from four to fourteen days. Once in Panama City, delays often occurred, for the minimum sixty-day trip to Callao could only be undertaken during the six months of the year when winds favored the southward sail along the west coast of South America. Little of the precious space on board the smallish ships was available to bring the paraphernalia of rural life from Spain directly to Peru. Bulky tools, millstones, plant cuttings, domesticated animals, and the necessary food and water for their transfer were low-value cargo. As much as the segmented sea voyages, the Panama Isthmus hindered the direct flow of European artifacts to western South America. The high cost of moving anything across those ten leagues of forest and swamp could only be justified by its high monetary or exceptional sentimental value. The difficult traverse also took its pathogenic toll on people, beasts, and plants.

Not surprisingly, most material introductions of Spanish culture to the Andes did not come directly from Spain. Western Nicaragua and Mexico were the major early sources of cows, pigs, goats, horses, donkeys, sheep, and chickens, and of most plants that had earlier been taken from Hispaniola and Jamaica (Borah 1954, 84, 86). In spite of long distances, however, from whatever source, by 1540 the bulk of Spanish material culture had landed in Western South America, and by 1555 this dominion was reproducing most of its own plants, animals, and farming implements. That relative rapidity suggests how a limited number of introductions, even just one, was all that was required to launch a diffusionary spiral with historic con-

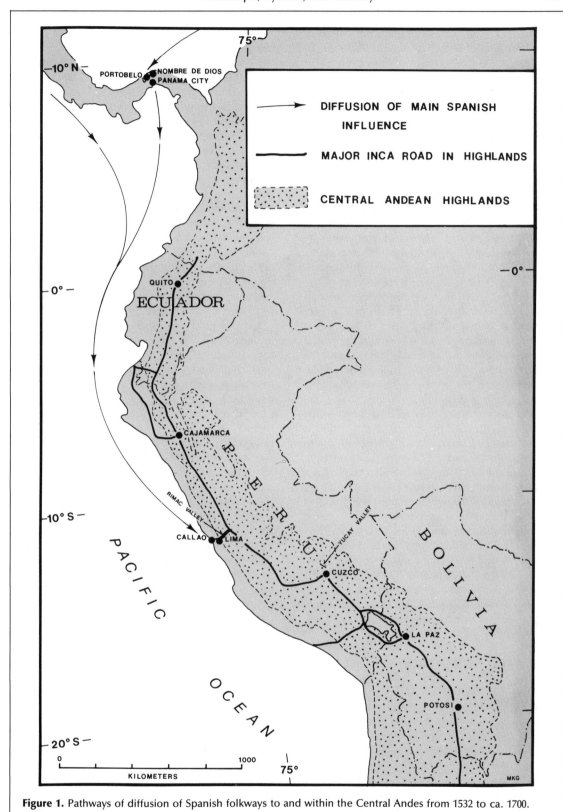

Figure 1. Pathways of diffusion of Spanish folkways to and within the Central Andes from 1532 to ca. 1700.

sequences. Callao was the main port of entry for introductions that eventually diffused to the entire Central Andean region, both north and south over the Inca road system.

Agricultural innovations first reached the irrigated farms established by Spaniards in the Rimac Valley around Lima, and from there spread to nearby valleys. Beginning in 1535, this one small coastal oasis became the seat of Spanish administration in western South America and a major focus of Spanish colonization. Though the coastal region was rainless and lay only 10° from the equator, its anomalous coolness (19°C yearly average) and water for irrigation permitted the successful cultivation of many temperate crops and most tropical plants as well. In that setting, seeds and cuttings multiplied, as did offspring of the denizens of the Iberian barnyard; they did not farther north in the hot, wet Guayas Basin. Transportation access also explained why the coastal valleys around Lima served as the critical staging area for subsequent diffusion of Spanish material culture to the highlands that loomed only a few kilometers to the east over an existing Inca road.

Spaniards moving to the Sierra were much more likely to have picked up seeds, cuttings, and animals in Lima than to have brought them from Spain as part of their personal effects. Once in the highlands, many Spaniards could fashion from local materials tools and building styles they had known in Spain. Over the next several decades, these introductions spread throughout a large part of the highlands. They comprised a combination of particularly useful elements that tended to be accepted together. By the 1590s, this bundle of Spanish rural traits had evolved into an established complex which remained in place, due to custom, isolation, and inertia, for the next four centuries.

Contact, Acceptance, and Refusal

Reconstruction of the elusive process of entrance, rejection or acceptance, and spread of European traits into Andean life cannot be sketched in detail.[2] Even an intensive historical analysis of one limited highland zone near Lima does not pinpoint these changes (Spalding 1984). Spaniards originally brought their material culture for themselves and their compatriots, who in 1570 numbered between

10,000–15,000 in the highlands outside the mining areas (López de Velasco 1971). Subsequent deployment of Old World elements to Indians, who, at that time, numbered about 1,000,000 in the region, depended on three sets of agents: clerics, headmen, and colonists. Virtually all missionaries were Spaniards who belonged to religious orders with designated territories. In the Indian communities they served, their uncontested moral authority carried over to the mundane content of rural life. Priestly directives, blandishments, and threats bent the normally submissive native population to their will. Indians of high rank called *curacas* served as intermediaries for the Spanish authorities to collect tribute and enforce compliance. In addition to his civil authority, the *curaca* was an innovatory exemplar, for he was the native person schooled in Spanish ways and most likely to first receive European introductions.

Spanish colonists, disdaining manual labor, depended on a docile supply of native workers for agricultural tasks. In the *encomienda* system, the Crown obligated the Indians to work for the conquerors; later, as land was taken over as private property, peons farmed and herded for the estate owners as well as for themselves in a system of servitude that continued in force past the mid-twentieth century.

In those nonvolitional settings, Indians rapidly learned to use the tools, grow the crops, eat the foods, and raise the animals brought by their European overlords. Embracing these strange things was another matter: like many peasants everywhere, native Andean people initially were distrustful of innovations. Gradually they experimented with the available European elements while maintaining their own. In the 1570s–80s, Indians had accepted without coercion a series of Old World items in locales closest to Spanish towns. Only later did native communities in isolated districts integrate pieces of the new order into their agroecosystem and living patterns. By the early seventeenth century, enough had been accepted to modify, though not transform, the cultural landscape of the Andes outside the grassy heights called the *puna* and its more humid facies known as the *páramo*.

This particular schedule might not have been achieved as it was if Indian populations had not dropped so precipitously after the Conquest. From the estimated 12–14,000,000 people in the coast and highlands of Peru, Bolivia, and Ecuador in 1520, disease caused the population to decline by 90 percent by 1620 (Cook 1981). This, combined with dislocations due to forced mine work, led to less intensive land use. The fact that indigenous people of the Andes suffered egregiously at the hands of the Europeans has become a dominant theme of the Old World-New World encounter. Scholarly discussion of Spanish impact has often focused on its disadvantages, disharmony, or disorganization (Dollfus 1982; Usselmann 1987). Their status as putative victims has overshadowed the ingenious ability of Andean peasants to manipulate elements of Spanish culture and incorporate them into their livelihoods.

Post-Conquest Crop Accretions

Broad thermal similarities made it environmentally feasible to transfer much of the content of Iberian agriculture, which followed a Mediterranean rhythm of winter cropping of annuals, to an Andean setting most suitable for high-sun cultivation. Altitudes mitigated the heat of a tropical latitude to the extent that seasonal frost occurrence above 2500 m truncated the growing season as it did in most of Spain at sea level. Furthermore, a sharply defined rainfall regime, which set a cyclical rhythm for plowing, planting, and harvest, also occurred in the Central Andes. Although the warmest parts of the year in the two areas were calendrically reversed, the rainy months and the vegetative cycle of the staple annual crops occurred in the same months in both Iberia and the Andean Highlands. Harvest festivals to honor St. Isidore, patron saint of farmers in Spain and the Andes, took place in the month of May in both of these disparate regions far removed from each other.

The Old World crops that passed into the agroecosystems of the native peasantry in the early colonial period met the tests of usefulness, environmental fit, and niche competition. Within a century after the Conquest, Andean peasants had effectively integrated a dozen plants and peripherally accepted a dozen others, together comprising less than half of the total number of plants brought by the Spaniards (Gade 1975). Spanish colonists had a list of accepted crops about twice that of the native peasantry's introductions. Some plants—saffron, endive, artichoke, and hazel-

nut among others—grown in Spain may not have reached the Andes at all (Herrera 1970; Oliveros de Castro 1968).

Among the grain crops, only wheat and barley became widely accepted in the Andes. From the time of their arrival, Spaniards were determined to have wheat. By the 1540s, they were growing it in the highlands, and in the 1550s, it was abundant enough for the price to fall to that of other staples. To Spaniards, wheat bread was essential to a civilized existence. Its cultural importance as much as its nutritional value caused the Iberians to include wheat among the tribute items required from Indians (Cook 1975). Perhaps because of this imposition, native people in some locales were growing it as one of their own food staples by the late sixteenth century ("Reparto de tierras en 1595" 1957). Indians parched and triturated wheat kernels to make a gruel as they did with their native grains, but almost everywhere they learned to prefer bread when they could get it. Wheat straw and stubble were fed to the growing number of Indian-owned livestock (Fig. 2). In terms of land use, hillsides of closely sown wheat were less vulnerable to soil erosion than were those planted with row crops. Normally planted and harvested at least a month after maize, wheat cultivation did not directly conflict with other labor commitments in the

Figure 2. Wheat harvest using a sickle, with animals grazing on the stubble, near Sangarará, Peru (3600 m).

agricultural schedule.

Indians adopted barley for its grain, straw, and stubble. Cut green, it was sold to Spaniards as high-quality fodder for horses and mules. Barley's main advantage over wheat was its ability to grow in drier zones, somewhat salty soils, and lower temperatures. As with wheat, the introduction and acceptance of barley by Indian communities expanded nonirrigated agriculture. Both crops fit well into sectorial fallowing on communal lands, a pre-Conquest practice that survived through the Colonial period. After a variable period (four, seven, or ten years) of fallow, the cropping cycle of a sector started with the potato. Either during the second, third, or fourth year of the cycle, that same plot was used for wheat and/or barley (Orlove and Godoy 1986). Neither oats, rye, millet, or rice emerged as even minor crops among Spanish colonists or Indian peasants in the highlands. In Iberia oats and rye were typically planted where wheat would not yield well, whether in cool rainy zones or on poor or exhausted soils. The Andes had quinoa and its even hardier relative known as cañihua for the marginally productive lands.

Mediterranean perennials adapted to summer drought did not bear much, if any, fruit in the Andes with its high-sun rainfall. Almond, carob, pistachio, jujube, or the olive did not yield satisfactorily enough under Andean conditions to become accepted tree crops. If the olive had successfully fructified, its adoption still would have been unlikely: Indians had no agricultural tradition of oil crops or culinary tradition that included frying. The grapevine was in a somewhat different category among Mediterranean crops. Spaniards in the Andes grew it with mixed success; among Indians, grapes were rarely grown and, in any case, not for making wine, though they were fond of its Dionysian effects. To Spaniards wine enhanced sociability; to Indians it offered inebriation until supplanted in the nineteenth century by brandy and then rum. Though chicha making from maize persisted without interruption, a craving for stronger alcoholic beverages emboldened native people to enter the money economy controlled by Spaniards and mestizos. A technological barrier also explained an early Spanish monopoly on growing sugarcane. Although sugarcane was taken to the warm valleys of the Sierra from the Coast by the 1540s, only Europeans had the technology needed to process the juice into white sugar and distilled spirits. Indians later grew sugarcane for its sweet stalk and juice to make a fermented beverage and hardened molasses. Artisanal wooden presses moved by oxen or by hand were replicated from a Spanish design to extract the juice, but the sugarcane product they valued most was beyond their means to fabricate.

Several Andean domesticated plants declined in the face of competition from Old World introductions; for example, wheat expansion brought the contraction of quinoa, the latter a crop that required multiple washings to remove a bitter principle. Still quinoa and cañihua continued to dominate at high elevations where European small grains failed to mature their seeds. Broad bean (*haba*), in Spain a crop of the cool Mediterranean winter, adapted well to the zone between 3300–3800 m, much the same niche as that of tarwi, a native lupine. Though high yielding and disease resistant, the advantages of this native domesticate did not compensate for the multiple washings needed to remove the toxic substances in its seeds.

Turnips, leeks, parsnips, salsify, and beets did not catch on among highland Indians. Yet several native root crops nevertheless declined: oca, ullucu, añu (mashua), and maca eventually lost agronomic space to another native, the potato, especially at elevations below 3500 m. Greater food choice and security as a result of Old World introductions marginalized the small tubers, but the main beneficiary was the more efficient potato that was also regarded by Andean people as better tasting.

Vegetables, condiments, and fruits of Old World origin added to the food possibilities of the post-Conquest Andes. Native potherbs were quinoa and amaranth leaves, and those of certain field weeds collectively called *yuyo;* their use has persisted. Of the many European greens, only cabbage gained marginal Indian approval, whereas lettuce, eggplant, celery, cardoon, and orach scarcely were known or appreciated.[3] Onions, garlic, coriander, basil, and other herbs were embraced by native people, but did not replace capsicum pepper, which remains the most appreciated condiment to this day. Anise, a Mediterranean herb with a strong flavoring in its seed-like fruits, has been cultivated sparingly but continuously since its sixteenth-century introduction.

Almost a dozen sweet fruits of the warm valleys were domesticated in or near the Andes, but none of them could compare with the food value of the banana or the refreshing acidity of the orange. In the temperate valleys, trees of apple, medlar, quince, pear, plum, and peach that the Spaniards brought gained some currency among Indians, who were enjoined to plant them where the local climate permitted (Saravia Viejo 1989, II:258). But these rosaceous fruit trees produced rather poorly in their transplanted Andean setting, compared to the capuli cherry, which the Spaniards brought to the Andes from Middle America in the sixteenth century.

Assimilation of European Livestock

The sharp population decline in the Central Andes in the first century after the Conquest may have hastened native adoption of European livestock. In the production of food calories, animal husbandry normally requires less human labor than does crop growing. It was more feasible to pasture animals on the weeds of abandoned terraced or ridged fields than to cultivate and repair them (Caillavet 1989, 122–24). Small children enlisted to watch grazing animals freed elders for other tasks.

The Spanish animal inventory offered Andean folk several advantages and had a greater overall impact than did the corresponding plant list. The range of useful beasts increased subsistence security by providing a form of living capital that could be kept in reserve until butchered, traded or sold, at which time quadrupeds could move under their own power to local markets. Livestock also served as a food reservoir in case drought, flood, or frost destroyed standing crops. Andean acceptance of Old World herbivores was encouraged by the institution of common lands that continued after the Conquest (Godoy 1991). Spaniards were accustomed to this shared resource surrounding most villages in Iberia (Vassberg 1984); they viewed collective land use in the New World Indies as appropriate for herds of privately-owned animals. Unlike its fine-tuned seasonality in late Medieval Spain, transhumance never broadly emerged in the Andes, although localized movements of animals are not unknown (Stewart et al. 1976). Livestock of Eurasian origin also provided the main organic

fertilizers after the Conquest when the regular transport of guano from the coastal islands to highland maize plots stopped with the decline of llama trains. In Spain at the time of the Conquest, fields were typically manured by livestock grazing on the stubble, which became one of the ways in which livestock raising was part of a larger agricultural system (Butzer 1988).

European beasts of burden were generally superior to the llama. Though cheaper to maintain, capable of surviving on dry native grasses and brackish water, and more sure-footed in rugged terrain than a mule, the llama carried only one fourth the weight, had less stamina, and was harder to drive. Mules became important in the Andes because they had no real competition from oxcarts. The rugged terrain, absence of suitable bridges, and the strong tendency for native people to porter their belongings did not favor cart transport of the kind used in medieval Castile (Ringrose 1970). In the early Colonial period, most mule breeding and selling was in the hands of Spaniards and mestizos, although Indians were engaged as muledrivers. For most of the sixteenth century, Indians were forbidden to ride horses, as riding was a prerogative of Spaniards, though they did use them as pack animals. Donkeys better fit the needs of a hardscrabble peasantry. Hardy and economical to keep, they carried harvested crops, firewood, and fertilizer over irregular terrain. By the end of the Colonial period, equines had largely supplanted llamas as pack animals in Ecuador, northern Peru, and southernmost Bolivia, as well as elsewhere at elevations below 3000 m.

The sheep was the single European introduction most valuable to native people. First kept on Spanish estates, by the 1590s they formed large flocks (Egaña 1966). At least as early as 1560, Indians were keeping sheep; by the seventeenth century, they had well integrated sheep into the native economy and land use. Softer yet greasier than llama fiber, sheep's wool was woven for the warm homespun clothing needed in the frigid Andean nights. Greasiness is an advantage for water-resistant garments. Ovines yielded mutton, tallow, dung, and in a few places, milk. Sheep, with no set lambing period in these tropical latitudes, had lower mortality and higher fertility than did the alpaca. Below 3500 m, sheep displaced the camelids, but they also prevailed above that elevation and elsewhere if Spanish influence was strong enough (Fig. 3). For example, on the *puna* of Tarma in the eighteenth century, camelids were no longer mentioned as livestock on either haciendas or in native communities (Arellano Hoffmann 1988).

Cattle proved to be less suitable for Indian needs than were sheep, especially at high elevations and on steep terrain. Satisfactory fodder during the dry season was often in short supply. A cow or bull represented a major investment whose loss through accident, disease, or theft created economic hardship. Milk, one of the major reasons for keeping cows elsewhere in the world, was not originally part of the Andean diet, though some Indians did learn to make cheese. When butchered, cattle provided meat, and cow dung had use as a fuel and fertilizer. Where peasants adopted the plow, oxen were the only draft animals, for unlike in Spain, cows, horses, mules, or donkeys were not used for this purpose in the Andes.

Innate resourcefulness of the goat and pig stood these creatures in good stead. The goat's Andean niche was in warm dry valleys where a market developed for wineskins (*odres*) used to carry liquids, especially alcohol. In these

Figure 3. Sheep and llama grazing together near Huancané, Peru (3820 m).

places, the goat's browsing habits made creative use of land that was not feasible to irrigate. Introduced with Pizarro in 1531, the pig became a component of Andean rural life for the twin rewards of meat and lard (Gade 1986). The key to its ready acceptance was the foraging ability of the long-legged, narrow-snouted Iberian breed. Lacking the acorns that they fed on in Spain, the Iberian pig in the Andes became a village forager of garbage, gleanings, and—in the absence of a latrine tradition—excrement.

Live chickens and eggs were sixteenth-century tribute items, so that their initial adoption may not have involved free choice. Ability to forage weed seeds and dooryard insects was critical in their acceptance into the household economy. But live hens and eggs, when sold, provided market income for peasant women. The meat, characteristically tough and therefore stewed, was eaten on special occasions, and the fat had medicinal uses. The chicken partially displaced the Muscovy duck, a native Andean domesticate that is a less efficient egg or meat producer. Other fowl introductions were generally unsuccessful. Old World species of ducks and geese, and the turkey brought to the Central Andes from Mesoamerica after the Conquest, seldom became part of the barnyard menagerie. Iberians also brought domestic pigeons to the Andes to be used for food and fertilizer, but only in a few places of Spanish influence did peasants take to raising them.

The Old World rabbit and the New World guinea pig occupied similar niches: small but prolific, both herbivores yield valuable protein. Rabbits (*conejos de Castilla*) were the more efficient meat producers, but Indians stuck to their guinea pigs (*conejillos de Indias*), which had the ability to thrive with little care in the dark recesses of the dwelling (Gade 1967). Andean affinity for their squeaking rodents went deeply into Andean tradition as a featured food at events marking one's life cycle and in folk curing rites.

Old World livestock contributed heavily to native livelihood, but they also had their negative effects. The livestock trampled and obliterated many abandoned ridged fields and weakened the facing of agricultural terraces. Their sharp hooves and heavy weight damaged the traditional bridges woven of plant fibers (Gade 1972). Roving flocks pulverized the soil surface

Figure 4. Work teams near Yauyos, Peru in 1942, plowing bench terraces for maize cultivation with the *chaquitaclla* as women sow on prepared land. (A. Guillén, photographer. Abraham Guillén collection, Latin American Library, Tulane University. Reproduced with permission.)

on slopes, provoking gully and sheet erosion during the torrential downpours of the rainy season. Need for additional pasture accelerated removal of some of the few woodlands still remaining after the Conquest. Livestock intrusion into fields of standing crops was a frequent cause of social discontent and violence within and between communities.

Rural Technology

Indian agriculturalists accepted the European plow without giving up their native spade-like equivalent, the *chaquitaclla*, a curved piece of wood with a bronze blade or a fire-hardened wooden point, and a footrest to provide leverage (Gade and Rios 1972) (Fig. 4). Beginning in the latter half of the sixteenth

century, the oxen-pulled plow gave an alternative to the *chaquitaclla* on valley floors, first where Spaniards took over the land and later in indigenous communities. Native acceptance was arguably accelerated by Viceroy Toledo's edict of 1575 mandating a plow and oxen for each Indian agglomeration. Acceptance of the ard brought with it a radically new idea in Andean agriculture: the collective cultivation of certain crops as a field unit rather than individual attention imparted to each plant by the work of a mattock.

Of the four basic kinds of plows used in sixteenth-century Spain, only the Mediterranean scratch plow (*arado dental*) spread to the Andes. Since the Roman period, this lightweight wooden tool was the instrument used in Extremadura and Western Andalusia to prepare the ground before planting (Caro Baroja

Figure 5. A scratch plow constructed of eucalyptus wood but with no metal plowshare, near Sucre, Bolivia (2900 m).

1949). The ard's New World success can be attributed to the simplicity of its design and perhaps the small amount of iron needed in the plowshare; even that could be dispensed with in light soils (Fig. 5). No document shows that a prototype of the scratch plow was unloaded in Peru from either Seville, Central America, or the Antilles. Shipping a bulky tool such as a plow halfway around the world was hardly necessary, since many Spanish peasants who disembarked in South America could have constructed them from memory using the wood of native trees.

The *chaquitaclla* was relegated to slopelands too steep for oxen to maneuver. It also remained useful for working heavy soils, boulder-strewn flatlands, and narrow agricultural terraces and for specific tasks such as drilling seed holes, harvesting tubers, preparing mud for making adobes, removing rocks, digging ditches, and making furrows. Likewise the mattock, a short-handled and sharp-angled tool used for weeding maize and harvesting tubers, was not abandoned when the long-handled hoe was introduced. Instead, the mattock was fitted with a metal piece the width of a shovel and called a *lampa*. But the sickle, closely associated with wheat and barley harvesting, had no native counterpart. Ripe chenopod plants are still often pulled up by their roots. The scythe, a later improvement on the sickle, was not used in the Andes.

Small seeds in the pre-Conquest Andes were threshed with sticks or poles. The flail, one of several threshing devices in Spain, was an improvement over a simple pole, but rarely seen in the colonial Andes. What did catch on was having animals, preferably equines but never llamas, trample wheat and barley on a circular floor (Fig. 6). In Spain the hooves of livestock were largely superseded by the tribulum or *trillo* (Sanz Moreno 1985). This flint or iron-studded sled pulled by a draft animal removed grain kernels from their glumes and cut the straw into small pieces for use as fodder. It was a relatively efficient device, but the absence of flint and scarcity of iron in the early decades may explain why the Spaniards did not build and use it in the Andes.

Bread-making came to the Andes in the sixteenth century. Spanish artisans brought the concept of the arch and built water-driven grist mills of that design. Sixteenth-century Spain had both the horizontal waterwheel (*molino de rodezno*) and the more efficient vertical waterwheel (*aceña*), which dominated milling in or near cities. The more primitive technology continued to operate on streams close to small settlements in rural Iberia (Escalera Reyes and Villegas Santaella 1983). Only the horizontal wheel, whose gearless simplicity required minimal skill to operate or repair, was successfully implanted in the Andes (Gade 1971). Although used and operated by Indians, the mills long remained in the hands of Spaniards or mestizos. The bread oven also was of Spanish origin;

Figure 6. Donkeys threshing barley near Layo, Peru (3900 m).

Indians had baked in earthen pits. As with mills, oven design scarcely changed over the next four centuries (Urribari de González 1967).

Hispanic Influences on Settlement

The Folk Dwelling

The possibilities for melding rather than simply juxtaposing traditions were greater with settlement features than with agropastoral elements. The basic rural Andean dwelling of rectangular form and gabled roof goes back to the Inca period. Other forms coexisted with it both before and after the Conquest, as different ethnic groups maintained their own pre-Inca construction styles that included round form, more than one room and/or story, and flat roofs. Europeans, like the Incas before them, favored rectangularity, although circular construction was not unknown in Spain. Viceroy Toledo's decree of 1570 mandated a squarish dwelling form in the Indian villages. Straight walls best accommodated the two pieces of furniture that Spaniards regarded as necessary to a civilized existence: tables to eat from and beds to sleep on (Vargas Ugarte 1951, I:373–74). In contrast to the importance the Spaniards placed on those domestic accoutrements—perhaps a cultural reaction against Moorish custom, which had neither—Andean Indians did not use furniture and even today often see no need to partition their one-story dwellings in which cooking, eating, sleeping, and crop storage occur within a single room. In Southern Spain, most rural houses were one story (Giese 1951, 588), and although two-story dwellings were known to both Incas and Spaniards, those constructed in the Colonial period reflect Spanish design.

Adobe, sod, fieldstone, and cut stone were Andean building materials before the arrival of the Spaniards. The exquisitely fashioned ashlars associated with Inca civilization were not used for vernacular buildings. Fieldstone with mud mortar continues to serve for wall construction up to the present, but in the Colonial period adobe became the most widespread building material. In both pre- and post-Conquest times, adobes were made by puddling soil of at least 15 percent clay content with wild grass as the binding agent and drying in the

Figure 7. Adobe dwellings with thatch roofs at Capacmarca, Peru (3400 m).

sun (Sutter Esquenet 1985). A Spanish introduction, the wooden mold to shape the mud, substantially improved the uniformity of the block over the irregular Inca adobes (Fig. 7). Spaniards from some parts of Spain were experienced in adobe construction, which the Moors may have taught them; the word is derived from the Arabic, *attub*, meaning brick.

Another earthen wall construction of independent invention was the tapial method, which saves time and labor over adobes. Used in pre-Conquest Peru (Cobo 1956, 241), this type of wall was also known in Moorish Spain. The Spanish method of constructing the wall by using a box-like wooden frame in which to pack the earth diffused in the Andes at the expense of the indigenous method in which earth was molded around straight bamboo-like canes (Muelle 1978). Whether tapia or adobe, the Spaniards brought and sometimes imposed on the indigenous population whitewashing for protection and appearance. Fired bricks also came from the Iberian Peninsula, where they date from the Roman period, but were not much used in the rural Andes. Before the nineteenth-century arrival of eucalyptus, fuelwood in the Andes was much scarcer than it is now (Johannessen and Hastorf 1990).

The highland cottage has had a pitched roof whose steepness varied regionally. In rural zones, the indigenous method of lashing roofing timbers long prevailed over the use of jointed beams, which was a Spanish introduction. Roofing materials also showed cultural differences. Thatch of locally available grasses was the only real roofing material before the Spaniards came. Baked tiles made of clay, used first by Spaniards on their own buildings, gradually spread to the countryside in the late Colonial period. Grass thatch, though free for the taking, requires some skill to install properly, normally lasts less than ten years, and shelters vermin. The conquerors tried to impose the concept of a proper lockable door on native dwellings for security and privacy (Jiménez de la Espada 1965, I:97). At least the wooden door set in a wooden frame was more successfully implanted than were windows. Inca dwellings sometimes had a small gable opening to let in light, whereas Spanish design favored windows below the roof line. The interior wall niche, another design detail of the Inca vernacular house, does not appear in native dwellings of the Colonial period or later.

Nucleation and Dispersion

At the time of the Spanish Conquest and for four decades thereafter, most Andean people lived near their fields. In 1570 the Spanish viceroy, Francisco de Toledo, ordered native people to group in compact agricultural villages (reducciones) to facilitate catechization, tribute collection, and work assignments (mita). Reordering the Andean settlement pattern rested on a fundamental cultural assumption of the Iberian conquerors that agglomeration was another of the elements essential for civilized living. In New Castile, Extremadura, and Andalusia of the fifteenth and sixteenth centuries, peasants lived in nucleated settlements. Towns, not the countrysides, controlled and directed agriculture, which placed the rural focus in Spain on urbanitas not rusticitas (Blok and Driessen 1984). The daily interactions in this arrangement fostered an urban way of life, not by functional diversity, which was nonexistent in these villages, but by providing the opportunities to acquire the civilized virtues that have been the mark of Mediterranean existence for more than two millenia.

The Spanish attempt to implant the values of polis and civitas in the isolated valleys and plateaus of the High Andes evoked the agrotowns of the Iberian Peninsula. Nucleation was perceived as a fundamental prerequisite for learning European values of cleanliness and order, as well as the more subtle human qualities of finesse, vivacity, and the art of pleasing. A sixteenth-century Spanish jurist in Peru, Juan de Matienzo (1967, 48), expressed that attitude when he wrote of native people that "they cannot be Christianized nor even men without being together in towns . . . ." The gridiron layout of these tight clusters of farmers around an open square paralleled the accepted design for Spanish colonists. The inspiration for right-angled settlements is uncertain, for most Spanish towns or cities had no such layout. A notable exception and possibly the model for Spanish America was Santafé, near Granada. Founded by Queen Isabella in 1491 with a gridiron regularity of streets, Santafé was the headquarters for the siege of the last redoubt of Moorish control in Europe.

In the Andes, the Mediterranean concept of nucleation failed to achieve its goals, for the agro-village did not retain the indigenous farming population (Gade and Escobar 1982). A farmer could commute not much more than four kilometers between his/her village and fields. Even before the end of the sixteenth century, Indians departed reducción villages and reestablished themselves near farm plots. They also dispersed to remote, inhospitable puna zones to escape their oppressors or to avoid social conflict with other families (Favre 1975; Houdart 1980). Nucleation made working the land more difficult and exacerbated tensions of living near strangers that contradicted their kin-based concepts of proper social organization.

A 1604 decree from Madrid commanding Indians to live in the reducción was rescinded only fourteen years later when the Spaniards realized the agglomerated ideal had disintegrated and could not be reconstituted (Recopilación de leyes 1841). Diffuse settlements of pre-Conquest pattern from isolated or semi-dispersed dwellings to loose hamlets reemerged, but without legal titles to the lands they occupied. To legitimize the claims of these reconstituted communities, Hispanic, not Inca, concepts were used: a chapel was constructed, a patron saint selected, a fiesta sponsored and, at a later time, a school was built. While the rural population of the Central Andes has partly reverted to the pre-Conquest dispersed pattern, most sixteenth-century reducciones survive, not as *pueblos de índios,* but as mestizo villages (Gade and Escobar 1982).

Spanish Impact in Space and Time

European ideas and materials were combined in uneven spatial patterns with those already in the Andes. In the more accessible temperate valleys and basins between 2500–3500 m elevation, the two cultures had converged by the late eighteenth century. Attracted by the abundant native population, alluvial soils, and amenable climate, Spaniards established their haciendas on the valley floors. Many elements of Old World material culture were preadapted to this elevational range much better than above or below it. To the agropastoral mélange was added the miscegenation (*mestizaje*) that gradually reformulated the ethnic composition of most temperate valleys. A notable example from Peru is the Yucay Valley (that portion of the Urubamba or Vilcanota depression between 2800–2900 m above sea level), which Spaniards repeatedly compared to the Tagus Valley around Aranjuez (Gade 1968). The benign climate, absence of malaria, and dense Indian population prompted Spaniards to appropriate it for themselves, which gradually shifted the racial and ethnic character of the rural peasantry from Indian to mestizo. Between 2500–1000 m, the European influence was even more prevalent due to the sparse indigenous populations at these generally insalubrious elevations. Spaniards, lured to the warm valleys by the possibilities of commercial sugar and coca production, used seasonal migrants and black slaves who themselves had little stake in the land (Gade 1973). Indigenous land use and settlement patterns persisted most tenaciously at elevations above 3600 m, where European crops were undependable in the freeze-prone climate of these altitudes. Though sheep were present, llamas and alpacas, because of their superior physiological adaptation to the altitude and natural forage, continued from central Peru to southern Bolivia to have an importance they had lost in the valleys below. Spaniards shunned these cold, hypoxic zones of *puna* and its wetter variant, the *páramo,* leaving them as refuges for Indians retreating from Spanish domination. Rudimentary dwellings dispersed in the pre-Conquest pattern reflected the pastoral emphasis in these lofty *punas* and *páramos.* Later the Spaniards and mestizos coveted the land for grazing, but even then not for residence.

The successful introductions of many Spanish rural elements to the Central Andes occurred rather early in the Colonial period. Some of these adoptions swept through the highlands not simply because they were available, but because they filled a need at a critical time. Catastrophic depopulation swept Andean communities after the Conquest and forced a shift from intensive cultivation to extensive agropastoralism. From the array of goods and ideas that the Spaniards brought, the native people selected those that enhanced family security in the face of the breakdown of the Inca system of food redistribution and the demographic decimation. Those Old World elements that were perceived to meet the exigencies of the period gained an entrée into the cultural-ecological system. The livestock additions fit into the gaps left in the changed agricultural situation that resulted after a community's labor force had been greatly diminished. They also enabled the peasantry to better survive the uncertainties of crop production due to drought, hail, and unseasonal freezes that periodically scourged the highlands. New crops helped to reduce the risk of food failure, but the two pre-Conquest staples, maize and potatoes, have remained the outstanding sources of food and nutrition in the region up to the present. Both provide high caloric content, adapt to a range of environmental conditions, and carry emotional, even religious, associations.

The Andean peasantry acquired a simplified version of the Spanish inventory of rural material life. Many elements were eliminated. Moreover, the Old World introductions to the Central Andes did not overwhelm the native elements as they did in the Argentine Pampa, Middle Chile, or Northern Mexico. The Spanish inventory did not displace the well-developed agricultural achievements in crop raising, pastoralism, technology, and settlement left by the Inca. Instead the two traditions, each having been altered—the Spanish, simplified, the Inca, disrupted—merged into one hybrid cultural complex. This expanded agropastoral complex, though it did not lead to well-being

Figure 8. Andean rural life juxtaposes different cultural forms and functions that themselves do not necessarily belong to different time periods. Pack llamas transport potatoes to a village of twentieth-century origin [Hector Tejada, Department of Cuzco, Peru] having buildings with colonial-style doors and balconies that, at the same time, incorporate the much more modern notion of the sheet-metal roof.

or escape from poverty, has lasted 400 years, evidence of its environmental adaptation and integration into Andean life. Andean peasants consider their Old World plants and animals to be autochthonous ("*criollo*"), so well are these heirloom varieties and antique breeds integrated into their system. Field preparation, rotation schemes, intertillage, mixed grazing, vernacular architecture, and settlement patterns continue to show features of both traditions (Fig. 8). European elements have also interlaced with the Andean in clothing, diet, folk medicine, religion, and language. These elements, introduced by 1550 and widely accepted by 1650, tended to crystallize into an established pattern that did not allow much subsequent variation. This concept of cultural crystallization that froze in time the wherewithal of peasant existence explains in part the archaic cast of contemporary Andean livelihood (Foster 1960, 227–34).

Conclusion

The Andean cultural landscape is above all a syncretism. In spite of their hermetic reputation, Andean people have always been pervious to outside influences when nonnative elements demonstrated superiority or when they filled an apparent vacuum if the risk of adoption was not too high. European introductions created new possibilities for enhancing rural livelihood. Those elements of Western material culture preadapted to Andean conditions that were of value to Andean people were incorporated into their folkways in the first half of the Colonial period without much later variation.

In this century and especially since the 1940s, the Andean peasant view of the world has been much broadened beyond the local community. Pendular migration to adjacent lowlands, military service, contact with development agencies, easier communications that include more vehicle roads as well as radio and telegraph, and growing politicization at several scales, have accelerated acceptance of parts of the national cultures emanating from the large cities.

Given the more than four centuries of Hispanic domination, it is quite remarkable that this irreparable cultural amalgam still characterizes the Central Andean realm. Only some of the diffused elements from Spain were successfully implanted into peasant usage; others lingered with a peripheral status, and a few never gained assent at all. But those European crops, animals, tools, and dwellings that did gain acceptance enriched Andean livelihoods by stretching the range of possibilities to better spread the risks imposed by nature and by offering nutritional combinations unknown before. The Central Andean cultural landscape of the late twentieth century, which owes much to both traditions, is still a time warp. Poverty and isolation have played a role in greatly slowing the pace of modernization into the Andes. But technological décalage should not obscure the fundamental accommodations that gradually emerged from the Encounter of these two earthly segments. Moreover, it should not deceive one into thinking that people themselves are artifacts of some earlier era. The Columbian Quincentennial holds a special charge to geographers to explore without deterministic preconceptions the adaptational dimension of intercontinental transfers around the world in the context of time, space, and real places.

Notes

1. Particularly influential in presenting the distorted view of contemporary Andean culture as indige-

nous was the study by Mishkin (1946), whose generalizations about Andean subsistence and social organization were largely based on ethnographic descriptions gathered in 1937–38 in the isolated high-altitude village of Kauri in the Department of Cuzco. Another author, Castro Pozo (1946), wrote a highly glossed essay that misrepresented the social structure of the rural Andean community as a kind of Inca socialism. Both the above works, published in the same volume, have influenced the formulation of research projects over the past four decades. The notion of continuity from the pre-Inca and Inca past into the present has been a compelling interest in Andean studies (e.g. Isbell 1977; Rasnake 1988). That romanticization of the native extends to a recent volume on the agricultural botany of lesser Andean crops, some of whose virtues are overrated (National Research Council 1989). "Andeanism" refers to the false notion, held by an array of scholarly, artistic, and popular observers, of a highland peasantry "outside the flow of modern history" (Starn 1991, 64).

2. Major lacunae in the documentary record make reconstruction of the rural folkways and land use in historic times, whether of Spain or the Andes, an approximation. Several published sources form the bulk of what we know. For the Iberian Peninsula, the work of Gabriel Alonso de Herrera (1970) describes the state of Castilian farming in the late fifteenth and early sixteenth centuries. For the Central Andes of the early Colonial period, the observations of chroniclers José de Acosta (1962), Pedro Cieza de Leon (1986), Bernabé Cobo (1956), Felipe Guaman Poma de Ayala (1980), and Antonio Vázquez de Espinosa (1948) provide accessible and generally reliable data. El Inca Garcilaso de la Vega (1960) has much to say on this theme, but his facts are not always accurate and must be used with reserve. The *Relaciones geográficas,* a collection of essentially local reports in response to a Crown request, is a rich source on late sixteenth-century rural life in the Andes (Jiménez de la Espada 1965).

3. Among the fifteenth-century crops in Seville were several that may have been originally brought to the Andes as cultivated plants, but which later spread mainly as weeds: purslane (*Portulaca oleracea*), sow thistle (*Sonchus* spp.), rocket (*Eruca vesicaria*), radish (*Raphanus sativus*), and turnip (*Brassica campestris*) (Aviñon 1885).

References

Acosta, Joseph de. 1962 [1590]. *Historia natural y moral de las Indias.* Mexico City: Fondo de Cultura económica.

Alcina Franch, J. 1986. *La cultura de Castilla y León en América: La cultura material.* In *Etnología y folklore en Castilla y León,* ed. L. Díaz Viana, pp. 357–69. Salamanca: Junta de Castilla y León.

Aviñon, J. 1885 [1418–19]. *Sevillana medicina.* Sevilla: Sociedad de Bibliófilos andaluces.

Arellano Hoffmann, C. 1988. Anotaciones del clima, ganado y tenencia de pastos en la puna de Tarma, siglo XVIII. In *Llamichos y paqocheros: pastores de llamas y alpacas,* ed. J. A. Flores Ochoa, pp. 77–84. Cuzco: CONCYTEC-CEAC-Editorial UNSAAC.

Arguedas, J. M. 1968. *Las comunidades de España y del Perú.* Lima: Universidad Nacional Mayor de San Marcos.

Bermúdez Plata, C. 1942. *Catálogo de pasajeros de Indias.* Sevilla: Consejo Superior de Investigaciones científicas.

Blok, A., and Driessen, H. 1984. Mediterranean agro-towns as a form of cultural dominance with special reference to Sicily and Andalusia. *Ethnologia Europaea* 14:111–24.

Borah, W. 1954. *Early colonial trade and navigation between Mexico and Peru.* Ibero-Americana 38. Berkeley: University of California Press.

Butzer, K. 1988. Cattle and sheep from old to New Spain: Historical antecedents. *Annals of the Association of American Geographers* 78:29–56.

Caillavet, C. 1989. Las técnicas agrarias autóctonas y la remodelación colonial del paisaje en los Andes septentrionales (siglo XVI). In *Ciencia, vida y espacio en Iberoamérica,* ed. J. L. Peset, pp. 109–26. Madrid: Consejo Superior de Investigaciones científicas.

Caro Baroja, J. 1949. Los arados españoles (sus tipos y reparticiones). *Revista de Dialectología y Tradiciones populares* 5:3–96.

Castro Pozo, H. 1946. Social and economico-political evolution of the communities of central Peru. In *Handbook of South American Indians,* vol. 2, ed. J. Steward, pp. 483–500. Bureau of American Ethnology Bulletin 143. Washington: Smithsonian Institution.

Cieza de León, P. 1986. *Crónica del Perú.* 3 vols. Lima: Fondo Editorial P. Universidad Católica del Perú.

Cobo, B. 1956 [1653]. *Obras de Bernabé Cobo.* Madrid: Biblioteca de Autores Españoles.

Cook, N., ed. 1975. *Tasa de la visita general de Francisco de Toledo.* Lima: Universidad Mayor de San Marcos.

———. 1981. *Demographic collapse: Indian Peru, 1520–1620.* New York: Cambridge University Press.

Denevan, W. 1983. Adaptation, variation and cultural geography. *The Professional Geographer* 35:399–407.

———. 1987. Terrace abandonment in the Colca Valley, Peru. In *Pre-Hispanic agricultural fields in the Andean region* (part 1), ed. W. Denevan, K. Mathewson, and G. Knapp, pp. 1–43. International Series 359 (i). Oxford: British Archaeological Reports.

Dollfus, O. 1982. Development of land-use patterns in the Central Andes. *Mountain Research and Development* 2:39–48.

Donkin, R. 1979. *Agricultural terracing in the ab-*

original New World. Tucson: University of Arizona Press.

Egaña, A., ed. 1966. *Monumenta peruviana (1586–1591),* vol. 4. Rome: Apud "Monumenta Historica Soc. Iesu."

Escalera Reyes, J., and Villegas Santaella, A. 1983. *Molinos y panaderías tradicionales.* Madrid: Editora Nacional.

Favre, H. 1975. Le peuplement et la colonisation agricole de la steppe dans le Pérou central. *Annales de Géographie* 84:415–40.

Foster, G. 1960. *Culture and conquest: America's Spanish heritage.* Chicago: Quadrangle Books.

Gade, D. 1967. The guinea pig in Andean folk culture. *Geographical Review* 57:213–24.

———. 1968. Aranjuez of the New World. *Américas* 20:12–19.

———. 1971. Grist milling with the horizontal waterwheel in the Central Andes. *Technology and Culture* 12:43–51.

———. 1972. Bridge types in the Central Andes. *Annals of the Association of American Geographers* 62:94–109.

———. 1973. Environment and disease in the land use and settlement of Apurimac Department, Peru. *Geoforum* 16:37–45.

———. 1975. *Plants, man and the land in the Vilcanota Valley of Peru.* Biogeographica 6. The Hague: W. Junk B. V. Publishers.

———. 1986. The Iberian pig in the Central Andes. *Journal of Cultural Geography* 7:35–50.

——— and Escobar, M. 1982. Village settlement and the colonial legacy in southern Peru. *Geographical Review* 72:430–49.

——— and Rios, R. 1972. Chaquitaclla: The native footplough and its persistence in central Andean agriculture. *Tools and Tillage* 2:3–15.

Garcilaso de la Vega, I. 1960. *Comentarios reales de los Incas.* Cuzco: Ediciones de la Universidad Nacional del Cuzco.

Giese, W. 1951. Los tipos de casa de la Península Ibérica. *Revista de Dialectología y Tradiciones populares* 7:563–601.

Godoy, R. 1991. The evolution of common-field agriculture in the Andes: A hypothesis. *Comparative Studies in Society and History* 33:395–414.

Guaman Poma de Ayala, F. 1980. *El primer nueva corónica y buen gobierno,* ed. J. Murra and R. Adorno. 3 vols. Mexico City: Siglo Veintiuno.

Guillet, D. 1987. Terracing and irrigation in the Peruvian highlands. *Current Anthropology* 25:409–30.

Herrera, G. de Alonso. 1970 [1512]. *Obra de agricultura.* Madrid: Biblioteca de Autores Españoles.

Houdart, M. 1980. Un exemple de scissiparité de village dans les Andes: Le cas de Pilchaca. *Bulletin de l'Institut Français d'Etudes andines* 9:35–58.

Isbell, B. 1977. *To defend ourselves: Ecology and ritual in an Andean village.* Austin: University of Texas Press.

Jimenez de la Espada, M., ed. 1965 [1580]. *Relaciones geográficas de Indias,* 3 vols. Madrid: Biblioteca de Autores Españoles

Johannessen, S., and Hastorf, C. 1990. A history of fuel management (A.D. 500 to the present) in the Mantaro Valley, Peru. *Journal of Ethnobiology* 10:61–90.

Knapp, G. 1988. *Ecología cultural prehispánica del Ecuador.* Quito: Ediciones del Banco Central del Ecuador.

——— and Denevan, W. 1985. The use of wetlands in the prehistoric economy of the northern Ecuadorian Highlands. In *Prehistoric intensive agriculture in the tropics,* ed. I. Farrington, pp. 185–207. International Series 232. Oxford: British Archaeological Reports.

López de Velasco, J. 1971 [1574]. *Geografía y descripción universal de las Indias.* Madrid: Biblioteca de Autores Españoles.

Masson, L. 1984. *Las terrazas agrícolas: Una tecnología olvidada.* Lima: Banco Continental.

Matienzo, J. 1967 [1567]. *Gobierno del Perú,* ed. G. Villena Lohmann. Paris-Lima: Institut français d'Études andines.

Mishkin, B. 1946. The contemporary Quechua. In *Handbook of South American Indians,* vol. 2, ed. J. Steward, pp. 411–70. Bureau of American Ethnology Bulletin 143. Washington: Smithsonian Institution.

Muelle, J. 1978. Tecnología del barro en el Perú precolombino. In *Tecnología andina,* ed. R. Ravines, pp. 573–79. Lima: Instituto de Estudios Peruanos.

National Research Council. 1989. *Lost crops of the Incas.* Washington: National Academy Press.

Oliveros de Castro, M., and Jordana de Pozas, J. 1968. *La agricultura en tiempo de los reyes católicos.* Madrid: Instituto Nacional de Investigaciones Agronómicas.

Orlove, B., and Godoy, R. 1986. Sectorial fallowing systems in the Central Andes. *Journal of Ethnobiology* 6:169–204.

Pérez de Barradas, C. 1941. Las regiones españolas y la población de América (1509–1534). *Revista de Indias* 6:81–120.

Rasnake, R. 1988. *Domination and cultural resistance: Authority and power among an Andean people.* Durham, NC: Duke University Press.

Recopilación de leyes de los reinos de las Indias (Carlos II), 5th ed. 1841. Madrid: Boix.

Reparto de tierras en 1595. 1957. *Revista del Archivo Histórico* (Cuzco) 8:428–32.

Ringrose, D. 1970. Carting in the Hispanic world: An example of divergent development. *Hispanic American Historical Review* 50:30–51.

Romera Iruela, L., and Galbis Diez, M. 1980.

Catálogo de pasajeros a Indias, vol. 4 (1560–1566). Sevilla: Ministerio de Cultura.

Sanz Moreno, M. 1985. Una artesanía del pasado: Los trillos de Cantalejo (Segovia). *Estudios Geográficos* 46:496–502.

Sarabia Viejo, J. 1989. *Francisco de Toledo: Disposiciones gubernativas para el Virreinato del Perú 1575–1580.* 2 vols. Sevilla: Escuela de Estudios Hispano-Americanos.

Schjellerup, I. 1985. Observations on ridged fields and terracing systems in the northern highlands of Peru. *Tools and Tillage* 15:100–21.

Smith, C.; Denevan, W.; and Hamilton, P. 1968. Ancient ridged fields in the region of Lake Titicaca. *Geographical Journal* 134:353–67.

Spalding, K. 1984. *Haurochirí: An Andean society under Inca and Spanish Rule.* Stanford, CA: Stanford University Press.

Starn, O. 1991. Missing the revolution: Anthropologists and the war in Peru. *Cultural Anthropology* 6:63–91.

Stewart, N.; Belote, J.; and Belote, L. 1976. Trans-

humance in the Central Andes. *Annals of the Association of American Geographers* 66:377–97.

Sutter Esquenet, P. 1985. Arquitectura andina tradicional y sus problemas. *Cultura* (Quito) 7:145–214.

Troll, C. 1931. Die geographische Grundlagen der andinen Kulturen und des Inca Reiches. *Ibero-Amerikanisches Archiv* 5:258–94.

Uribarri de González, V. 1967. El pan en Ayacucho (Perú). *Revista de Dialectología y Tradiciones populares* 23:347–66.

Usselmann, P. 1987. Un acercamiento a las modificaciones del medio físico latinoamericano durante la colonización. *Bulletin de l'Institut français d'Études andines* 16:127–35.

Vargas Ugarte, R., ed. 1951. *Concilios limenses* (1551–1772). Lima: privately printed.

Vassberg, D. 1984. *Land and society in Golden Age Castile.* New York: Cambridge University Press.

Vázquez de Espinosa, A. 1948 [1613]. *Compendio y descripción de las Indias.* Smithsonian Miscellaneous Collections, vol. 109. Washington: Smithsonian Institution.

Pioneers of Providence: The Anglo-American Experience, 1492–1792

Carville Earle

Department of Geography and Anthropology, Louisiana State University, Baton Rouge, LA 70803

FAX 504/388-2912, e-mail gaearl@lsu.vm.bitnet.

Abstract. The English colonization of North America has always seemed providential for the legatees of that process, and for good reason. Awakened at last to the potentialities of the New World by the profits of privateering and emboldened by the daring actions of Elizabeth and Francis Drake, the English shook off their profound disinterest in the Americas and embarked on a colonial venture of immense and improbable proportion. During the ensuing two centuries, they entered into the imperial scramble for the New World; established hegemony over the Atlantic Seaboard of North America; implanted (not always wittingly) a profuse variety of sturdy regional societies and economies committed more or less to ethnocultural pluralism, capitalist institutions, and exponential demographic and economic growth; and, in the end, capitulated to the colonies' revolutionary insistence on independence from the Crown. When, soon after, the new nation was propelled forward by an industrial revolution, her citizens were prepared to believe that indeed they were pioneers of providence—all of which has been of small comfort to their less fortunate co-colonials around the globe.

Key Words: agrarian innovation, American Revolution, British North America, colonization, frontier, long waves, migration, pluralism, settlement, slavery, staple economies, urbanization.

ALTHOUGH, one hundred years after Columbus's landfall, the English had little to show for their collective efforts in the New World, they rapidly made up for lost ground. Their several colonies on the Atlantic Seaboard numbered more than a quarter of a million persons by 1700 and some 2.75 million, not to mention some of the largest cities in the New World, by the time of the American Revolution. The increases were astonishing, population and economy averaging more than three percent per annum and settled area more than two percent. Small wonder, then, that after the achievement of independence in 1783, Americans regarded themselves as pioneers of providence, that Malthus used them as his exemplar of unconstrained demographic growth, and that Tocqueville forecast their inevitable rise to global power.

This essay recounts these remarkable achievements, assesses the structures and contingencies that permitted them, and points up the ambiguity in their meaning for Americans and their co-colonials around the globe. The English colonization of North America, I submit, bestowed good fortune upon a reluctant, insecure, and insular people, thrusting them from a marginal corner of Columbus's New World into the cockpit of an expanding world system. These pragmatic provincials found a way of muddling through the paradoxes that bedeviled them—of slavery and freedom, of poverty and plenty, of enlightenment and intolerance—toward a global hegemony that was, in the end, no less perplexed. Acknowledging the Anglo-American experience's imperviousness to rational forms of explanation, the Founding Fathers and their legatees concluded, rather too agreeably, that their achievements were nothing less than the gift of a wonder-working providence. All of which, of course, has been of small comfort for dependent peoples elsewhere.

Annals of the Association of American Geographers. 82(3), 1992, pp. 478–499
© Copyright 1992 by Association of American Geographers

A Profound Disinterest

When Columbus died in Valladolid in 1506, his passing did not warrant an obituary in the city's paper. Nor did his achievements gain much notoriety outside of Iberia. "The European reading public," it seems, "displayed no overwhelming interest in the newly-discovered world of America" (Elliott 1970, 12). In France, for example, four times as many geographical books published between 1480 and 1690 were devoted to the Turks and Asia as to America (Elliott 1970, 10–12; Scammell 1969). The impact of the Admiral and his "discovery" was greeted, on the whole, with profound disinterest. And for good reason. Europeans in general and the English in particular were preoccupied with a medley of problems that commanded their attention: building nation-states, steering the course of a religious reformation unleashed by Luther, coping with unprecedented population growth, rising prices, and European economic differentiation, and managing the internal strife and the international friction that accompanied the recentering of the European economy from Italy to the northwest of Europe.

To these sound reasons for ignoring Columbus and the New World may be added one other: the ambivalence of an age poised precariously between ancient and modern, between medieval fears of discord and decay and modernity's faith in progress, between an older pessimism and a newer optimism. It is hard to imagine a world view so full of dread, so frightened by the genuine conviction that the earth was "rusting" away, decaying from senescence (to mix the familiar Elizabethan metaphors). "This is Nature's Nest of Boxes," wrote John Donne, "the Heavens Contain the Earth, the Earth, Cities and Men. All of these are Concentrique; the common center to them all is decay, ruine" (Hodgen 1964, 264). In this predicament, compounded by the memory of lives too often abbreviated by grisly contagions of pox and plague, the best one could do was to hold the line, to maintain stability in the social order, to preserve nature's great chain of being. "Loosing the strings" of society invited discord and, worse, descent in the hierarchy stretching from God and the angels at one end to the animals, the plants, and the metals at the other. So too did the colonization of foreign lands. Europeans who settled abroad, they feared, would be seduced into a way of life that was unsettled, licentious, and barbaric. These fears were hardly idle, particularly for the English who had witnessed firsthand this process of cultural declension as it unfolded in their colonization of Ireland. Had not English people there abandoned the civility of life in villages and towns in favor of a nativist seminomadism? Had they not as well surrendered their language and their faith? "One would not beleeve," William Camden observed, "in how short a time some English among them degenerate and grow out of kind" (quoted in Hodgen 1964, 365–66). Overseas colonization, in other words, was hardly a conventional process; it cut rather to the heart of the precious sense of English culture amid what was, for many, a world in an advanced state of decay. Even Puritan optimists, it seems, made ready their preparations for the millennium (Glacken 1973).

Born in Piracy

Of course not all English people were so frightened by this backcloth of medieval pessimism. Many made forays out into the Atlantic, sailed onto the Mediterranean, or ventured boldly down the west coast of Africa. But these voyages were merely prelude for the burst of English maritime activity after 1560 (Parry 1961). As huge quantities of bullion began to flow back from New Spain, English fears of the New World suddenly gave way to the promise of enormous profits from privateering (as it was known in polite circles) or legalized piracy (as it was known in fact). The greatest of the English privateers, and rightly so, was Francis Drake. On his return to England in 1580 following nearly three years plundering the Spanish in the New World, the English were astonished by the value of his prizes—variously estimated as 25 million dollars or more by today's standards (Andrews 1967). His achievement at once galvanized an industry into action and a country into a nationalist frenzy (Cawley 1966, 285–86). In the two decades after Drake's return, English by the thousands followed suit, entering into this new industry as privateers proper or investors who assumed the considerable risks of a "venture" (Andrews 1964).

The English turn toward privateering and toward America was not an easy one for the Crown. To be sure Elizabeth had been in power some nineteen years by the time of Drake's voyage, but her position was hardly secure either at home or abroad. She could ill afford a frontal challenge to Catholic Spain abroad as she doused the flames of sectarian hatred, fed by puritans, Catholics, and Anglicans, at home, unless of course the rewards were great or the costs of inaction were high. And, as it turns out, they were indeed.

To understand Elizabeth's willingness to risk everything in offering her support for Drake and for the privateering industry is to come to grips with the perilous state of the English economy, ca. 1575. Population had grown at a spectacular pace; prices had risen to unprecedented levels; grains, for example, increased by as much as 500 percent during the century and raw wool commanded high prices from Flemish weavers (Brown and Hopkins 1957, 298), all of which "loosed" the strings of English society. For some, these changes translated into astounding prosperity; for others, a miserable poverty. In a time when "sheep ate men," to use Marx's apt expression, enclosing landlords evicted the unfortunate peasants and cottagers whose tenures in land were insecure. For these poor, the new economy dictated a term of unemployment (seasonal or year-round) which they served out as squatters in the country forest or adrift among London's teeming masses (the city was approaching 120,000 by 1575) (Coleman 1956; Stone 1966). Conversely, those blessed with secure tenures in land, that is, owners or even tenants with long leases at fixed rates, soon acquired great wealth and hurriedly expended it in a gluttony of conspicuous consumption. This included rebuilding their homes (and the English landscape), decorating them with the finest silks and tapestries, and tabling them with exotic foods, including fine wines and spices, currants and citrus, sugar and the like, imported from Venice, the Levant, and Morocco, and which, by 1590, constituted 65 percent of English imports (Stone 1949–50).

That was not the worst of it, however. The impact of unrestrained consumption was soon reflected in a deteriorating balance of trade. By the last quarter of the sixteenth century, the value of England's imports fast approached the value of her exports. On the eve of Drake's voyage, the spectacular growth of English population, agrarian prices, and consumption had driven the nation to the edge of a fiscal crisis. Elizabeth's options were few (currency deflation and taxation, for example), and all but one, privateering, was politically unpalatable. Privateering constituted the quickest and least painful fix, provided that its conduct was discreetly distanced from the Crown and that Elizabeth's charms could subdue the anger of Phillip II of Spain. Elizabeth thus gambled that English privateers would balance the nation's trade while she preoccupied the Spanish with her dalliances. The strategy, in retrospect, proved an enormous success. English privateers lived up to their end of the bargain, generating an income of £100,000–£200,000 per year—nearly a fifth of all English exports (Andrews 1964, 128–29; Stone 1949–50). Elizabeth held up her side as well, deferring a hostile Spanish response until the Armada of 1588 and the war for Holland's independence in the 1590s. By then, the crisis had been met and passed.

English privateers, though plundering on a global scale, secured the bulk of their prizes from captures in the western Atlantic, and this reality initiated a reorientation in the geography of English strategy abroad.[1] Preferment subtly but steadfastly shifted from the "northern men" such as Humphrey Gilbert and their search for a northwest passage to a more southerly location. Walter Raleigh, Gilbert's half-brother, underlined the significance of this privateering theater when, in the mid-1580s, he secured a charter for a New World colony which he founded in 1585 on the Outer Banks of North Carolina, a colony that was ideal for, and designed from the outset as, a privateering base. Roanoke, on the Outer Banks, admirably served Raleigh's purposes. Perched on the edge of the sealanes running from Mexico back to Spain, Roanoke offered easy and direct access to the gold- and silver-laden caravels; moreover, the base offered fleeing privateers a secure refuge, protected as it was from Spanish pursuers by the treacherous currents around Cape Hatteras and the shoals inside the island barrier. Raleigh's initial expedition arrived there in 1584, and after a couple of false starts, John White established a fort and left an armed contingent to secure the base in 1587, much as Columbus did at Navidad in January 1493 (and with the same sad results). The plan for a return expedition in 1588 was disrupted by the general mobilization for the Spanish Armada, and relief was delayed until 1590. When the expedition finally arrived at Roanoke, they discovered that the colonists had disappeared without a trace. After a futile search for the "lost" colonists and some reconnoitering in the surrounding region (including the Chesapeake Bay), the expedition returned to England, thus closing the first abortive chapter in the history of English overseas colonization (Quinn 1955; Andrews 1964; De Vorsey 1987).

The Hakluyts and Their Model of English Colonization

Even as Roanoke languished, the English geographers (and cousins) Richard Hakluyt the Elder and the Younger were circulating a more ambitious colonial plan. Drawing upon their extensive compilation of overseas voyages of exploration and discovery, the Hakluyts presented a plan that rested on four propositions: American colonization promised, first, a dependable source of colonial staple commodities in exchange for people and goods from the mother country (the roots of mercantilism, I believe); second, and more specifically, exotic staples which complemented the English economy and eliminated the need for costly importations of silk, spices, wine, and sugar from foreign powers, provided of course that the colonies were located in the latitudes of the Mediterranean; third, a "vent for the glut of population" that had resulted in so much misery and unemployment in England; and fourth, a challenge, albeit oblique, to Catholic hegemony in the New World. One does not have to read between the lines in order to realize that the Hakluyts' propositions inexorably targeted a single location for the English colonization of the New World: on the Atlantic Seaboard of North America and, more precisely, in the "Mediterranean latitudes" of what is today Virginia and North Carolina (Taylor 1935, II; 1930; Parks 1928).

What the Hakluyts did not say, however, is of equal significance. On the matter of bullion, they were unusually restrained, noting merely that gold and silver might eventually be found in the interior mountains. Similarly their plan pretty much ignored a role for the "native inhabitants," perhaps because previous expeditions had confirmed the "meanness" of the

sedentary peoples along the Atlantic Seaboard of North America. These silences are pregnant. For bullion-chasing or native conversion, the Hakluyts had little time; their ruthlessly singular intent was the establishment of enduring English settlements and economies in North America. In seeking after the nation's glory rather than American gold, after permanence rather than ephemerality, these geographers brought a distinctively modern cast to their colonial plan (Taylor 1935, II; Pennington 1979).

Their purity of motive notwithstanding, the Hakluyts' plan did not win immediate acceptance. The Crown, preoccupied by the continuing flow of privateering profits and the Anglo-Dutch alliance against the Spanish during the 1590s, temporarily shelved further plans for American colonization. But matters had changed substantially by 1604. The profits from privateering had dried up, and an Anglo-Spanish treaty had been concluded by James I, shortly after his ascendance to the Crown following the death of Elizabeth in 1603. In this context, English merchants and gentry seeking new investment opportunities dusted off the Hakluyts' plan. Their opportunity arrived in 1606 when the Crown chartered the Virginia Company of London, a joint stock company modeled after the English trading companies working the Mediterranean, the Levant, and the Baltic. But this was not a company in the usual sense; the Virginia venture symbolized all of the hopes and aspirations of a restless nation. It would also, in short order, serve as England's template for New World colonization in the ensuing century (Rowse 1955; Rabb 1967; Brenner 1972).

Colonization in Practice

But that would get us ahead of our melancholy story, which properly begins in the spring of 1607 with the dispatch of the first Virginia expedition (Fig. 1). Following their instructions to the letter, the expedition entered the Chesapeake Bay, chose one of its largest arms, reconnoitered upstream, and, when they encountered "clean, well-made naturals," dropped downstream to the security of an island site which they named Jamestown, in honor of their King. All went well at first, as the expedition of highly-skilled artisans set about building a fort and a town on the island and laying the groundwork for an exotic economy based on silkworms, grapes and wine, and citrus. The vision turned nightmarish, however, by mid-July when the 104 settlers were racked with diseases bearing the ghoulish names of the "bloudie flixe" and "the burning fever" (most likely, dysentery and typhoid). Deaths mounted steadily, and by summer's end, the toll stood at nearly half of the 104 men. Autumn brought an end to the carnage. But after a respite of eight months, the nightmare resumed. Disease and mortality returned in the summer of 1608 and every summer thereafter (save for 1613–1616) until the Crown, in exasperation, dissolved the Company in 1624 (Earle 1979).

I have recounted this tragicomic scene elsewhere, and suffice it to say that the root cause traces to the Company's pigheaded insistence on remaining in Jamestown, one of the most dynamic and deadly ecological niches on the Atlantic Seaboard—in the fresh-salt transition (the oligohaline zone) of the James River estuary. In this zone, "our drink [in summer] was cold water taken out of the River, which was at floud [tide] very salt, at low tide full of slime and filth [including *Salmonella typhi* and *Endameoba histolytica*], which was the destruction of many of our men . . . ." (Percy 1907, 21–22). The combination of a riverine water supply, the entrapment of pollutants by the landward summer migration of estuarine salinity/sediment traps, and the ongoing concentration of settlement at Jamestown proved deadly indeed, costing the lives of perhaps three thousand of the 5,000 settlers who came to Virginia between 1607 and 1624. Ironically, most of them died needlessly, for on at least two occasions, Virginians understood the nexus between site and mortality. Captain John Smith in 1608 and Sir Thomas Dale in 1613–16 understood the causal links between water supply and mortality, and they eliminated that link through the preventative medicine of settlement dispersal only to have their costly insights overturned by company agents freshly arrived in Virginia (Earle 1979).

The Virginia Colony never quite lived up to the nation's expectations, yet certain key elements in that experience would serve as a template for subsequent English colonization. The template delineated a series of distinct policies on matters of location, agent, extent, evaluation and allocation, and dissolution of English

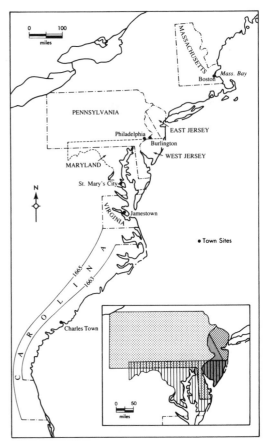

Figure 1. The English colonies of North America chartered prior to settlement, 1607–90. The inset shows in more detail the charter boundaries of the Middle Atlantic colonies and the extent of overlapping territorial claims. Source: Earle 1992.

colonies (Fig. 1). A word on each is in order. The template first targeted locations at the hem rather than the center of Iberian spheres of influence, that is, along the Atlantic Seaboard of North America; second, in acknowledgment of a penurious English Crown, shifted the risks of colonial ventures from royal agents to the monopoly colonization of private franchises—companies in Virginia and Massachusetts Bay and proprietors in Maryland, Carolina, and Pennsylvania; third, restricted the extent of territorial grants (Virginia after all was initially bounded in a square with a side of just one hundred miles), thus affording ample opportunities for future royal benefices; fourth, privileged grants located in the Mediterranean latitudes, thus ensuring the production of complementary staples for the mother country (Dunbar 1958; Merrens 1969); and fifth, when colonies failed, defined a mechanism for dissolving their franchises and incorporating them as royal colonies (Earle 1977; Shammas 1979).

This template for English colonization in the New World, constrained as it was by practical geopolitics, royal finance, climatic theory, and hard reality, defined nonetheless the critical parameters of the Anglo-American experience, an experience predicated on geopolitical *decentralization* in its creation of several colonies of modest size and relative autonomy; *ethnocultural pluralism* in its allocation of the best lands to royal friends and coreligionists and the worst lands (those that replicated England, that is, New England) to religious dissenters such as the Puritans and later the Quakers; and a *reluctant imperium* in its inexorable absorption of failed franchises into the royal domain. In this fashion, the English colonized the Atlantic Seaboard, ensuring as they went a variegated strand of decentralized colonial administrations, a multiplicity of religious faiths and ethnicities, of, in a word, ethnocultural pluralism, and an Empire endlessly in need of royal salve (Fig. 2, Panel I).[2]

The pluralist geography inherent in English colonization yielded an exquisite variety of regional societies and economies in all particulars save one, the founders' unanimity on the imperative of establishing towns as bastions of English culture. On this point, colonizers from New England to Carolina were agreed. No business was more important than establishing cities and towns. The Carolina Proprietors spoke for them all:

> We must assure you that it is your and our concern very much to have some good towns in your plantations for otherwise you will not long continue civilized or ever be considerable or secure, there being no place in the world either of these without them (Saunders 1886–90, I, 229).

The medieval fear of cultural declension thus endured well into the seventeenth century.

The first task for corporate as well as proprietary officials involved the location and establishment of a town, a chief settlement serving the triple role of administrative center, cultural refuge, and economic entrepôt. With respect to location, these monopoly colonizers unani-

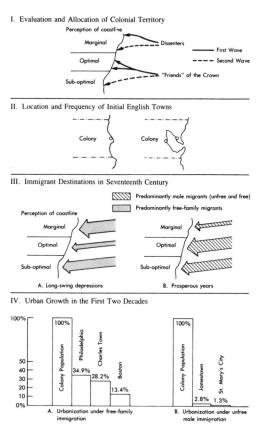

Figure 2. The English model of monopoly colonization: evaluation, allocation, city location, immigration, and urbanization. Source: Earle 1992.

mously located the chief town near the central point of the colony's coastal boundary or of a navigable bounding estuary (Fig. 2, Panel II). Their unanimity on this point is remarkable, the location of none of these towns erring by more than 25 percent and most falling within 10 to 15 percent of the central site (Earle 1977).

Establishing a town did not guarantee urban viability, however. Indeed, the urban successes and failures of seventeenth-century colonization seemed decidedly perverse to the English mind. The most successful colonial towns resided in the worst lands from the English point of view: New England and Pennsylvania; the failures, in turn, occurred in the optimal lands located in Mediterranean latitudes. These perverse patterns of urban success and failure, as it turns out, had more to do with timing than with English environmental perceptions. Boston in the 1630s and Philadelphia, and to some extent Charles Town, in the 1680s were founded in the midst of protracted depressions in the Atlantic economy, depressions that initiated vast flows of dissenting Puritans, Quakers, and, in the case of Charles Town, French Huguenots in search of religious refuges in the New World. Numbering in the hundreds and thousands, these family migrants poured through their receiving port cities and triggered a steady demand for provisions, tools, livestock, and the like (Fig. 2, Panels III and IV). Prices rose; urban merchants did a brisk business; tiny nuclei grew overnight into palpable places. Boston in 1650, for example, numbered more than 2,000 persons; Philadelphia and Charles Town in 1690 numbered more than 4,000 and 1200 respectively, an initial advantage that they never entirely relinquished (Bridenbaugh 1938; Rutman 1965).

Towns located in Mediterranean latitudes were, by contrast, of little consequence. Jamestown in Virginia and St. Mary's City in Maryland both ceased to exist in the 1690s, and were replaced by newly-established capitals in Williamsburg and Annapolis, respectively. Their demise and the failure of others is principally attributable to the immigration of single males rather than families. Families simply avoided the Chesapeake; it received instead an abundance of men and boys seeking their fortune in staple production or indenturing their labor in exchange for the costs of transportation. Neither motivation translated into economic demands for the goods and services of Chesapeake towns (Fig. 2). In the absence of an economic base of immigrant families, these capital cities languished until Governor Francis Nicholson administered their coup de grace in the 1690s (Reps 1972).

It may be useful to summarize the English model of monopoly colonization by contrasting it with models deployed elsewhere in the New World (Fig. 3). The English model constituted a mixed system, a hybrid of centralized and decentralized administration. As such, it lay between the extremes of the highly-decentralized capitalism of the Dutch (Vance's mercantile model) and the highly-centralized bureaucratic model of the Spanish and, to a lesser extent, the French. The decentralized free-trade model of the Dutch fostered a proliferation of multiple scattered ports, each repre-

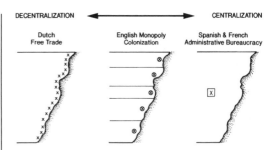

Figure 3. Schematic models of colonization under varying degrees of administrative centralization.

senting one of the multiple companies that competed under the rubric of the Dutch West India Company (the model used by Taaffe et al. [1963] and Vance [1970]). The centralized model concentrated urban settlement in one overwhelmingly primate city flanked in due course by a hierarchical structure of subsidiary administrative towns (Christaller's central place model, if you will).

The English hybrid combined elements of both models—decentralizing colonization through a limited number of modestly-sized territorial franchises (monopoly colonies), yet centralizing it through charter provisions that committed substantial authority (administrative, executive, and juridical) to enfranchised monopolists—the English companies and proprietors (Earle 1977). In place of the profusion of trading towns characteristic of Dutch colonization or the primate cities characteristic of Spanish and French colonies, English policy gave birth to a series of highly varied colonial cities arrayed among several equally varied colonies. The enduring success of some few of these cities attests perhaps to the virtues of admixing administrative styles in the process of colonization. A purely decentralized policy of capitalist trade (such as practiced by the Dutch) left few marks on the colonial landscape.

The principal exception to the rule is Dutch New Amsterdam. The settlement initially flourished on the basis of an extensive Indian trade deep into the Hudson Valley, but just as New Amsterdam's superior location was advancing that city beyond its competitors, the Dutch found themselves surrounded by the swarming of new English colonies and by the tactical superiority of the English Navy, all of which resulted in the colony's surrender in 1664 (Bachman 1969; DeJong 1975, 1–27). Henceforth, the English controlled the entire length of the Atlantic Seaboard from central Maine to the Carolinas. With that strand secured, American provincials set their sights westward toward what they called the Piedmont and Appalachian backcountry. A century hence, these too would be theirs.

A Gathering of Peoples

Once established, the English colonies attracted an outpouring of immigrants that was unique among European colonies in the New World. By 1700, the English colonies numbered more than 250,000 persons, mostly in New England and the Chesapeake (Bailyn 1986). New France, by contrast, received fewer than 11,000 immigrants during the entire span of its occupation (1608–1763) (Harris and Warkentin 1974).[3] And thanks to the English policy of monopoly colonization, their colonies displayed remarkable ethnocultural variety when compared to the homogeneity of immigrants to New France or the ethnocultural mixing characteristic of New Spain. Although mostly English in origin, these pre-1700 colonists represented diverse sociogeographic regions, distinctive folkways, and a variety of religious beliefs. At the risk of oversimplifying a sometimes mottled pattern in favor of typicality, it is fair to say that New Englanders came mainly from Puritan strongholds in East Anglia, Chesapeake planters from the south and southwest, Pennsylvanians from Quaker hearths in the north and northwest (Fischer 1989). To this pluralist ensemble must be added a smattering of Scots, Irish, Swedes and Finns on the Delaware, and contingents of Dutch in New York and Delaware and French Huguenots in Carolina, as well as a small but growing number of African slaves. England's decentralized policy of monopoly colonization and her precedent of establishing dissenting ethnocultural groups in English North America, albeit on what were perceived as the poorest lands, had yielded the most diverse colonies in the New World.

The Crown's penurious policy thus paid huge dividends for the English. Their decentralized American population, abetted by immigration and disproportionate numbers of women of reproductive age, grew at rates of nearly three percent per annum between 1650–1700; the economy grew even faster, pushing over three percent. Much of this growth was channeled into unbounded frontier expansion. Between 1650–75 alone, the settled region (areas with two persons or more per square mile) expanded at the astonishing rate of three percent per year (Earle and Cao forthcoming; Craven 1971, 14–17). The rapid pace of growth—demographic, economic, and frontier—soon exceeded the capacities of immature provincial administrations. Native Americans, pushed back by breakneck frontier expansion, turned hostile. In New England, the eruption of King Philip's War broke the uneasy peace that had prevailed. Similarly, in Virginia, frontier settlers rebelled when their complaints of repeated Indian attack were neglected by the royal governor. Although Nathaniel Bacon's rebellion of 1676 was abortive, it shook Virginia's royal establishment to the very core (Washburn 1957; Cronon 1983).

War and rebellion initiated a rethinking of British policy in the 1680s and 1690s. Buoyed by recent victories over the Dutch, English officials tightened the screws on growth in New England and the Chesapeake and effected what I have called elsewhere "the Great Compaction." Their policies slowed the pace of frontier expansion by raising land prices (through the abolition of the headrights systems and the vigorous collection of quit-rents), encouraging the establishment of towns and cities, and shifting the burden of defense to the colonists themselves. These actions, in combination with a protracted depression, simultaneously reduced the rate of expansion (from three percent per annum to one percent) and increased the density of colonial population (from just three persons per square mile to nearly ten persons) between 1675–1700 (Earle and Cao forthcoming).

The Hakluyts would have been pleased by these results. Much of their visionary plan for permanent English settlement along the Atlantic Seaboard of North America had been realized by 1700. While they did not anticipate the pluralism of the Seaboard's economic and social geographies, they would have been delighted by England's achievements at the very backdoor of New Spain and by a colonial population that arguably had provided a "vent for [England's] surplus." The emigration of more than 375,000 English to the American colonies by 1700 certainly eased the worst problems of unemployment, particularly in times of protracted depression such as the 1630s and 1680s when migrant totals rose to between 10,000–20,000 (Gemery 1980). At other times, migrant numbers were small but steady in their flow; servants to Virginia alone arrived at an average pace of more than 1,000 per year after 1650 (Craven 1971, 14–17). It is noteworthy that as the pace of American colonization increased, the population of England and Wales slowed down and then leveled off at about 6,000,000 between 1650–1720. Had these American migrants remained instead in England, they might have increased English unemployment by six percent (not allowing, of course, an addition for their children). If incremental unemployment of that amount is added to depression normals, it is not hard to imagine a social crisis of frightening dimensions.

A Pluralist Human Geography

For their insights into the nexus between colonization, geopolitics, and demography, the Hakluyts are deserving of the nation's glory; they are less worthy when our assessment turns to the geographic particulars in their colonial plan. Relying upon a Greek model of global climate, they believed that latitude was the prime determinant of a region's climate and, ergo, its economic potentiality. They reasoned by analogy that the optimal lands on the Atlantic Seaboard of North America would occupy Mediterranean latitudes and would produce valued commodities such as citrus, sugar, mulberries for silkworms and silk, and grapes for wine; and that the poorest lands would be located in the latitudes of England and would produce redundant commodities of little use to the nation (hence the epithet "New England") (Dunbar 1958; Earle 1977; Kupperman 1982). All of this was wrongheaded of course, since it ignored, among other things, the roles of oceanic and atmospheric circulation systems, the disposition of land and water, and precipitation. Continental North America was, to recall Sauer's felicitous expression, a "more robust and lustier land," brimming with seasonal extremes, remarkably wide interannual variabilities, and innumerable acts of God—floods, drought, violent storms, hail, tornadoes, and hurricanes to mention only a few (Sauer 1941; Meinig 1958).

Contrary to received opinion, the Seaboard was not the temperate, maritime analogue of Europe; yet that in fact was what many English colonizers believed as late as 1700. On this fallacious theory was premised an uproarious comedy which unfolded during the course of the seventeenth century. The early Virginians, for example, planted grapes that made insipid wine; they imported silkworms to feed upon the abundant mulberries, only to discover that the hard leaves of the American variety were inedible for silkworms imported from France; and they brought in Polish woodcutters who searched in vain for large stands of identical species sufficient for making potash (Earle 1979). The colonists (though not the English) soon abandoned these foolish strategies and sought instead an economy attuned with the American environs. Virginians switched to tobacco, which they grew even in the streets of Jamestown by 1616. Similarly, when the poor soils and the dank climate of New England produced meager yields of English grains, Bostonians in the 1640s–50s shifted their attention from agricultural staples to foreland trade and commerce. By the 1680s, the Hakluyts' latitudinal theory of climate and resources was suspect; Carolinians and Pennsylvanians, accordingly, sought an economic base more attuned to environmental realities. Within a decade or two of initial settlement, they established agrarian economies (wet rice and grains, respectively) that were more suited to their environmental regimes.

Setting aside flawed climatic theories, the English colonists created a remarkably varied series of regional economies along the Atlantic Seaboard of English North America (Fig. 4). The product of pluralist colonization, environmental variability, and empirical experimentation, these economies evolved into four distinct systems of settlement—systems that graded conveniently from north to south (Sheridan 1984). To the north was the split personality of New England, a more or less self-sufficient Puritan interior and a commercial Yankee coast; to the south, the primate city of Charles Town, South Carolina, and its envelope of rich rice plantations worked by scores of African slaves. Between these extremes were the Chesapeake's tobacco coast with its cellular landscape of small communities, each linked directly with London and British outports and, just north, the grain belts of the Bread colonies, crowned by the entrepôts of Philadelphia and New York

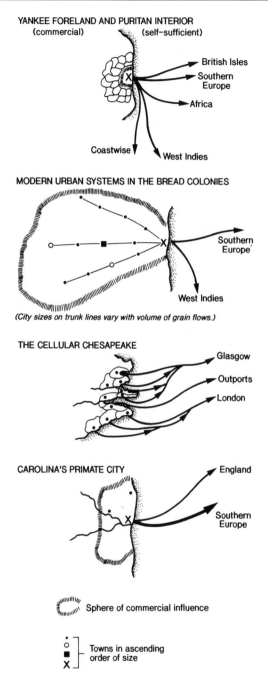

YANKEE FORELAND AND PURITAN INTERIOR
(commercial)   (self-sufficient)

→ British Isles
→ Southern Europe
→ Africa
Coastwise ↓
→ West Indies

MODERN URBAN SYSTEMS IN THE BREAD COLONIES

→ Southern Europe
→ West Indies

(City sizes on trunk lines vary with volume of grain flows.)

THE CELLULAR CHESAPEAKE

→ Glasgow
→ Outports
→ London

CAROLINA'S PRIMATE CITY

→ England
→ Southern Europe

⟜ Sphere of commercial influence

· ⎫
o ⎬ Towns in ascending
■ ⎭ order of size
X

Figure 4. Settlement systems in the British colonies of North America.

City and ornamented by the lesser towns that serviced the city's vital grain trade as it moved to market along tributary rivers and highways and, at a later date, by auxiliary central places

(McCusker and Menard 1985; Meinig 1986; Lemon 1972).

These distinctive regional economies had one feature in common, an active and enduring engagement with the Atlantic economy following a decade or two of initial settlement and economic experimentation (Price 1984). Virginians led the way, abandoning Mediterranean exotics in favor of the "stinking weed," tobacco, by 1620. And for good reason. With prices running at three shillings per pound, profits were enormous and a single planter's annual earnings exceeded those of an English laborer by sevenfold (Morgan 1975). Land of course was cheap, and in any event, tobacco required only two or three acres per worker, while labor was supplied by indentured servants, who provided four to seven years of labor in exchange for their costs of transportation and a small parcel of land and a tiny grubstake of clothes, tools, and provisions at the end of their terms. Abandoning the Company's fixation on Jamestown, the "planters" (so-called because they tended a planted rather than a broadcast crop) dispersed their plantations along the estuaries and in the "necks" that divided them. Not coincidentally, a curious healthiness spread over the face of the countryside as the system of settlement decentralized, a fact that was not lost on Virginia planters. Indeed it was not until the rise of the French snuff trade in the early 1700s that Chesapeake urbanization experienced a significant recovery; but even then these fledgling tobacco ports cut a small figure: eight to ten merchants collecting the tobacco from a hinterland of a hundred square miles or less, with an artisan or two and an inn thrown in for good measure. Most "urban services" were in fact performed in the countryside, among increasingly self-sufficient planters and their neighbors (Earle and Hoffman 1976; Menard 1980; Price 1973).

New Englanders followed a different path, creating perhaps the most unusual and certainly the most distinctive regional system in Anglo-America. Like the Virginians, Bostonians sought an agrarian staple on which to base their economy once the flow of immigrants began to run dry in the late 1640s–50s. Their efforts to commercialize the interior were blunted, however, by the infertility of the region's soils and its millennial Puritanism (Bailyn 1955). Thereafter, New England's personality split in two as Boston and the interior went their separate ways until reengaged, however modestly, a century hence on the eve of the American Revolution. During that century, rural Puritans in the interior cultivated souls rather than markets. As a peasant-like mentality of self-sufficiency, family, and land settled upon rural New England's villages and open-country communities, Yankee Bostonians looked elsewhere for a dependable staple (Daniels 1979; Lockridge 1970; Henretta 1978; Wood 1982). Lacking a productive hinterland, the city's merchants carved out an extensive overseas foreland for trade and commerce. Ferrying the goods of others throughout the Atlantic economy, Boston's merchants conducted the triangular trade in textbook fashion. Her vessels served markets where other mariners would not go, into out-of-the-way estuaries in the Chesapeake, the tricky shoals of Pamlico Sound, and the smaller islands of the West Indies. Her foreland economy eventually encompassed an array of destinations, with ports-of-call in the coastwise trade, whence came most of the city's provisions, the West Indies, Africa, and Europe. The profits from ship and commercial services as well as molasses for rum, in turn, were deposited back in Boston. On this basis, Boston rose to the rank of the largest city in British North America, some 16,000 persons by 1740, a rank that it held until the 1750s. For a hinterland-less city, Boston's achievement was not inconsiderable (Bailyn and Bailyn 1959; Pares 1956).

Although Carolina and Pennsylvania shared a common date of settlement and a staple economy based on grains, their histories otherwise have little in common. Carolina had been chartered in 1663 to members of the Royalist nobility, and after a series of false starts, the proprietors finally established a colony that appealed to people of their liking, people with wealth and status, viz., Barbadian sugar planters fleeing the desperately depressed West Indies or French Huguenots seeking a refuge from the Counter-Reformation signaled by the revocation of the Edict of Nantes. Initially, these Carolinians engaged in a variety of economies, including the Indian trade in deerskins and the provisions trade of the the West Indies, but, during the 1690s, they envisioned new possibilities with the introduction of Carolina rice. Wet-rice agriculture was well-suited for Carolina since only planters of considerable wealth could afford it. With its maze of irrigated fields, canals, and sluiceways and its subtle deployment of estuarine hydraulics for raising and lowering water levels in the fields, this agrarian system required hundreds of acres of prime freshwater back swamp for the rice and fifty slaves or more for preparing, planting, harvesting, and maintaining the operation (Clowse 1971; Coclanis 1989).

In Carolina, wealth begat wealth, and it was reputed that some of the world's wealthiest men resided in the unalluring backswamps of the Carolina Low Country by the time of the American Revolution. But not for long, since they came and went with the seasons, which were, as one observer remarked, in the spring a paradise, in the summer a hell, and in the autumn a hospital. As paradise descended into hell, rich planters and their families wisely evacuated the swamp for the safety of their town houses in Charles Town or the pleasures of Newport, Rhode Island.

Their minions, however, were less fortunate. The thousands of African slaves who remained in the swamps, managed by a handful of white overseers, constituted a resoundingly black majority. Left virtually alone to toil and suffer, these slaves fashioned a way of life that preserved and nurtured African languages, religion, and folkways (Wood 1974). Indeed, in the endless scholarly debate over the Old World's acculturation in the New, it may be that the Carolina slaves constitute the archetypal case of, and the best argument for, culture transfer. Slaves in the Chesapeake, also introduced in large numbers during the 1680s–90s, retained a much smaller fraction of their African or West Indian origins, perhaps owing to their scattering in groups of one to ten among the more numerous tobacco plantations (Berlin 1980).[4]

At the center of Carolina's "black majority" stood the anachronistic splendors of Charles Town. Resembling nothing so much as the primate cities of the Third World, Charles Town's elite maintained an active social calendar and sustained an exotic array of dance instructors, divines, architects, makers of fine furniture and cabinetry, and silversmiths, along with an assortment of merchants, draymen, and stevedores in the rice trade. There was, in truth, no city like it in British North America (Earle and Hoffman 1976).

Pennsylvania stood a world apart from the Carolina dandies. It was, in contrast, a sober society formed by the intersections of the meeting house and the counting house, of liberal conscience and the bottom line. Pennsylvania Quakers deftly orchestrated the development of a liberal society, a society that was ethnically diverse yet economically homogeneous. Opening the colony to all faiths and ethnicities, including numerous German pietists, Philadelphians soon engaged them all in a diversified commercial economy predicated on grains and livestock, especially corn and wheat (and flour) for export to burgeoning markets abroad. In short order, family farmers and a growing pool of seasonal farm laborers in Pennsylvania and flanking regions won a deserved if prosaic reputation as "bread colonies" (Nash 1968; Lemon 1972). Although New Yorkers and Baltimoreans adopted slightly different developmental styles, they too were the beneficiaries of a cascading series of food demands emanating from the Atlantic economy, initially in the West Indies in the early 1700s, in southern Europe after 1730, and in Ireland and England itself in the 1760s–70s. American grain, though it did not fully satisfy the dietary requirements of these markets, constituted the critical margin between dearth and sufficiency (Earle and Hoffman 1976; Lemon 1984).

The vast quantities of grain that flowed through Philadelphia, New York, and, after 1750, Baltimore generated a pattern of settlement with all the earmarks of modern urban systems—a large coastal entrepôt; radial tributaries linking interior farmers with the entrepôt; transport service centers located at wagon-journey intervals of a quarter, a half, and a full day (roughly 30 miles), among which were the first sizable interior towns in English North America, smaller centers serving the dispersed rural settlers, and a systematic structure in which a city's size was an inverse function of its rank. All of this was made possible by the volume of grain flows and the sizable marketing margins that accrued to the handlers of these bulky, weighty, sometimes explosive, and always perishable commodities. The farm-entrepôt margin on wheat, for example, averaged more than thirty percent of the Philadelphia wholesale price as compared to less than ten percent in the case of tobacco. And it was this threefold differential in commodity margins that accounts for most of urbanization's success in the bread colonies and its failure along the tobacco coast (Price 1974; Lemon 1972; Mitchell and Groves 1987; Earle 1992).

The Periodic Rhythms of Anglo-American Macrohistorical Geography

The economic achievements of the Anglo-American colonies, and they were considerable, trace their origins to what Max Weber once referred to as "the great problem": western Europe's sixteenth-century transformation from feudalism to capitalism. This transformation, among other things, reworked the rhythms of macrohistory, displacing what Ladurie has called "motionless history" with a relentless rhythm of a half-century, more or less. In the seemingly motionless histories of pre-sixteenth century Europe, time seemed to stand still. The languid rhythms of population growth and economic expansion in the Eurasian rimland flowed in *longue durée* draped loosely over centuries, two-and-a-half to three on average. In any one lifetime, very little seemed to change (Ladurie 1977). All of that began to change in the sixteenth century as the tempo of daily life experienced a dramatic acceleration. By the 1580s and perhaps as early as the 1530s, the capitalist transformation was installing its characteristic half-century rhythm and its recurrent novelty. These cycles, though clearly capitalist in origin, were not merely economic; to the contrary, they involved a periodic conjuncturing of reinforcing cycles: in policy, domestic and foreign; religious revitalizations and awakenings; frontier expansion; the economy's long-waves; and the innovation and diffusion of fundamental agrarian technologies, all of which are neatly compressed in the holistic periodizations of a traditional narrative history (Braudel 1979–84; McLoughlin 1978; Murrin 1984; Dodgshon 1978; Baechler et al. 1988; Earle 1992).

These rhythmic divisions of modern history may be further divided for heuristic purposes into a natural history consisting of six distinct phases (Fig. 5), marked off at either end by a *Crisis* of protracted economic depression and deepening social malaise and in between by the sequential phases of: *Creativity*, with its multiplicity of experimentations aimed at resolving Crisis; *Conflict*, with its invariable international wars (albeit of highly variable ranges and magnitudes); *Diffusion*, with its installation of fundamental innovations (especially agrarian ones) and the rapid economic growth they set

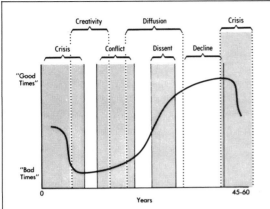

Figure 5. The periodic structure of American macrohistory and its six phases. Source: Earle 1992.

in motion; *Dissent,* with its internal conflicts over civil issues (state, section, individual) amid moments of remarkable prosperity; and *Decline,* with its recession in economic growth and employment, elevation of Malthusian rhetoric, and decline toward the Crisis that initiated the next cycle. Behavior within this natural history waxed intermittently determinant and contingent, determinant in the sense that the generic conditions of any one phase were repeated across all periods; contingent in the sense that human behavior within phases, Creativity and Dissent for example, was full of novelty and unpredictability, as we shall see (Earle 1992; Schlesinger 1986).

The virtues of a macrohistorical interpretation of Anglo-American history, its periodic structure, and its phased natural history have been recounted in full elsewhere. The exposition here, owing to the limitation on space, focuses exclusively on the generative sources of that structure, viz., the institutionalized, recurrent, and dialectic processes of agrarian innovation and logistic diffusion in multiregional space.

Elizabethan England offers our first hints of periodic innovations and their logistic diffusion. The hints in this case appear in the dramatic increases in grain yields per worker and per acre that began during the crisis of the 1570s–80s, when the Hakluyts lamented the "glut of population" and the abundance of unemployment, and concluded in the 1630s (Overton 1984). Simultaneous innovations in privateering and corporate organization (regulated and joint-stock companies) further bolstered the economy's recovery (North and Thomas 1973). A second cycle of innovation between the 1630s–70s extended the process to the several regions of English North America. In Virginia, planters offset the free fall of tobacco prices in the 1620s by introducing two critical innovations, tobacco topping, which tripled or quadrupled yields, and "house" curing which ensured high-quality leaf, and diffusing them in the ensuing half-century (Menard 1980). While these innovations salvaged the tobacco economy in Virginia, tobacco planters in Barbados responded quite differently. When tobacco prices fell, they quickly abandoned the "stinking weed" in favor of sugar cane. Sugar production subsequently diffused in logistic fashion, as did the procurement of slaves for the plant's cultivation (Dunn 1972, 46–116). And in Boston, merchants responded to the crisis in the Atlantic economy with equally creative solutions. Following a futile search for a reliable staple commodity from the city's hinterland, they cultivated instead a foreland economy predicated on shipping and mercantile services in the long-distance overseas trade (Bailyn 1955).

These processes were repeated in the 1680s–90s, when a long and protracted depression initiated the third cycle in the Anglo-American economy. Between 1680–1740, agrarian innovation and diffusion unfolded on both sides of the Atlantic (Fig. 6). In England, East Anglian farmers introduced the soil-building innovations of clover and turnips and diffused them in a half-century logistic (Overton 1985). Simul-

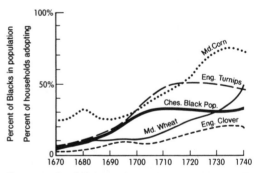

Figure 6. The diffusion of agrarian innovations in England and the Chesapeake, 1670–1740: East Anglian clover and turnips, Chesapeake slavery, and the following crops of wheat and corn. Source: Earle 1988, used by permission of Cambridge University Press.

taneously, Chesapeake planters rescued once again a beleaguered tobacco economy, this time installing a suite of innovations—shifting cultivation (or long fallow), following crops of corn and wheat, and massive importations of slave labor—and diffusing it between 1680–1740 (Earle 1988). Pennsylvanians and Carolinians meanwhile introduced the staples of wheat and corn and wet rice, respectively. And in this fashion did they extend the reach of a liberal ideology of the market until it embraced, eventually and more or less, the whole of the colonies from Massachusetts to Georgia (Ellis 1979).

These examples make the case that fundamental agrarian innovations and logistic diffusion constituted a periodic and multiregional process in England and her colonies in North America. It is pointless to extend this litany of innovation down to the present; suffice it to say that these processes have recurred periodically across intervals of a half-century, more or less in the 1740s, 1790s, 1830s–40s, 1880s, and 1930s and simultaneously across macroregional space. For our purposes, the more critical issue concerns the subtextual dialectic responsible for this periodic rhythm (Earle 1992).

Innovation is a contentious process, and rightly so since a great deal is at stake—nothing less than the economic and environmental welfare of their host regions. From the standpoint of regional economic welfare, agrarian innovations invariably entail class bias, that is, their impacts are nonneutral (Yapa 1983). From an egalitarian perspective, low-cost innovations are preferable because they offer access to the majority of agrarian households, rich or poor, elite or folk. The Chesapeake during the 1630s offers a case in point. Innovations of modest cost, tobacco topping and house curing, fostered an economically mobile, egalitarian society in which ex-servants rose into the ranks of the planter and, in some cases, the gentry (Menard 1973; Carr et al. 1991).

High-cost innovations, by contrast, favor the elite. They engender societies that are more stratified, inegalitarian, and class-based. Consider again the Chesapeake, this time in the cycle between 1680–1740. The outcomes of innovation in this cycle were quite different from those in the preceding cycle. Among other effects, the diffusion of high-cost slave labor (and shifting cultivation) produced a simultaneous increase in the level of white tenancy; both rose from about five percent of the population in 1680 to about thirty percent by 1740.

Class-biased agrarian innovation thus constituted the economic basis for the emergence of a Chesapeake elite by 1740, an elite which included not a few of the Founding Fathers' fathers and mothers (Main 1982; Kulikoff 1986; Isaac 1982).

These case studies in Chesapeake agrarian history nicely illustrate the workings of the elite-folk dialectic. The first cycle's folk innovations (1630–70s) and their egalitarian consequences gave way to elite critique and innovation (high-cost slavery) in the 1680s–90s. Subsequent cycles re-enacted this dialectical alternation. The egalitarian diversification of Chesapeake agrarian systems between the 1740s–80s (in response to new markets for grain) succumbed to elite "high farming reforms" between 1790–1840. Similarly in the cotton south: the cotton gin's introduction in the 1790s and the attendant revitalization of slavery favored elites; their successor, the innovation of a cotton-corn-cowpeas rotation devised during the Crisis of the 1840s, benefited all planters, with slaves or without (Earle 1988).

The American experience thus suggests that Marx was right about the power of dialectics; his error was in the application of Hegel's method. Marx's dire prediction of a secular trend in capitalist hyperaccumulation and class hypertension has been repeatedly blunted by the "safety valve," if you will, of dialectical alternations in elite and folk innovations (what contentious contemporaries veiled thinly under the euphemisms of "science versus practice"). Periods thus have alternated between egalitarian and inegalitarian, elite and folk and, generally speaking, long and short. The Anglo-American dialectic persists because it has become almost a set piece, a highly-stylized, institutional response to recurrent Crisis, passed on from one generation to another (Earle 1992).

Its periodic half-century rhythm persists for quite different reasons. First, and perhaps foremost, is the logistic dynamics of an innovation's diffusion. In the case of fundamental innovations, a half-century more or less is required before they are thoroughly diffused (saturated, as diffusionists would say), before productivity gains are fully wrung out, and before supply consistently overshoots demand, at which point, of course, Decline and Crisis ensue and prepare the way for their opposite number (Rostow and Kennedy 1979; Goldstein 1988; Berry 1991). Second is the belated appearance of an innovation's environmental im-

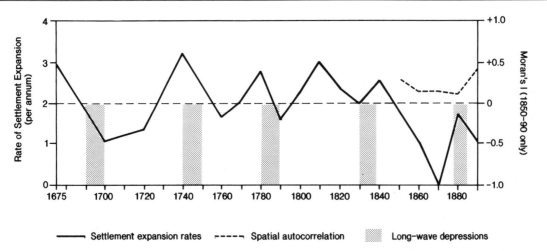

Figure 7. Annual rates of settlement expansion, 1650–1890, and spatial concentration, 1850–90. Spatial concentration after 1840, as measured by the spatial autocorrelation statistic Moran's I, is the mirror image of frontier expansion between 1650–1840. Concentration is highest in long-wave depressions (1890) or immediately thereafter (1850) and lowest in the intervening times of prosperity (1860, 1870, 1880). Source: Earle and Cao, forthcoming.

pacts, impacts which are occasionally destructive and almost always unanticipated. The adverse effects on productivity, which are rarely known until three or four decades into the cycle, serve to hasten the economy's Decline and to deepen its Crisis. A case in point is the dramatic acceleration of soil erosion and exhaustion which accompanied post-Revolutionary elite reforms (including plows and clean tillage) between 1790–1840. Folk innovations in the ensuing cycle (e.g., the cotton-corn-cowpeas crop rotation) were ecologically wise and environmentally benign by comparison (Earle 1988).

If the welfare effects of recurrent innovations varied dialectically, their effects on economic and social revitalization were remarkably uniform. The trajectory of prices, the general health of the economy, the revitalizations of religion and policy, and the expansion of settlement all moved in recurrent long waves (McLoughlin 1978; Earle 1992). The steady rhythm of frontier expansion between 1650–1890 offers perhaps our best evidence of this structural consistency (Fig. 7). Rates of settlement expansion (the area having two persons or more per square mile) slavishly followed the long wave in the colonial economy, increasing to three percent per annum or more in times of prosperity and falling below two percent in the phase of Crisis. This sequence

was repeated in four cycles between 1650–1840; thereafter, however, the cycling of settlement expansion ceased as rates dropped below two and then one percent per annum. With the closing of the frontier in 1840, a half-century earlier than Turner imagined, spatial concentration replaced spatial extension as the prevailing dynamic in the American settlement system, albeit retaining a familiar half-century rhythm of concentration in long-wave depressions and dispersal in the interludes of prosperity (Earle and Cao forthcoming).

Regions also varied cyclically in their rates of frontier expansion, but in a somewhat curious fashion. During bad times (Crisis) in the colonial economy, regional rates declined with remarkable unanimity; but in good times, they behaved erratically (increasing in about half the cases, and decreasing in the rest). All of which testifies to the enormous power of capitalist crises and to the unpredictable contingencies associated with regional and local solutions to them (Earle and Cao forthcoming).

Geopolitics, Policy Cycles, and Revolution

In 1776, New Englanders initiated a revolution that defied credulity. First, the revolt pitted thirteen disparate colonies against the most powerful nation in the world. Second, it erupted in a time of enormous prosperity and affluence (what has been called the "golden age of colonial culture"). Third, it constituted a paranoiac colonial overreaction to judicious policies of taxation, or so it seemed to the rational minds of British administrators as well as Whiggish historians. Perhaps. The perspective of macrohistorical geography offers, however, an alternative explanation of the coming of the Revolution, one that accents the dialectical alternation of policy cycles, the invariable eruption of civil dissent in times of long-wave prosperity, the unwitting spatial biases of British policy following the French and Indian War, and the rationality of Bostonians, the vanguards of Revolution.

The story begins with British colonial policies and their three periodic alternations: (1) 1630s–70s, the rise of mercantilism, especially under Cromwell; (2) 1680s–1740s, the era of "salutary neglect" in which mercantilist strictures were dismantled or more often ignored; and (3) 1740s–1780s, the neo-mercantilist revival in the "Age of Empire." These alternations between mercantilist protectionism and relatively unconstrained free trade serve as the backdrop for colonial dissent and Boston's curious role as vanguard of revolution (Earle 1992; Bushman 1985; Kammen 1974).

The liberalism of "salutary neglect" worked wonders for Boston's distinctive foreland economy. In these times of relatively unfettered trade, the city's population grew to 16,000 in 1740, ranking it first among Britain's American colonies and second or third in the Empire as a whole. Thereafter, however, ill winds began to blow. Boston's population stagnated for the next 30 years, and during the 1750s–60s, it was surpassed by its rivals, New York and Philadelphia. Boston's fall from grace had several causes, not the least of which was the restructuring of the Atlantic economy, viz., the rise of the European direct grain trade, which benefited entrepôts in the Bread Colonies; the increased competition of these ports as well as Norfolk for the West Indies trade; and the scarcity of money arising in part from the Crown's exclusionary denial of currency emissions from Massachusetts. Experiencing the first pangs of spatial relative deprivation, Boston merchants adapted to the realities of the Atlantic economy by establishing a new line of trade—the wholesaling and reexporting of up-market European goods for the burgeon-ing markets in the Middle and Southern colonies (Nash 1979; Price 1974; McCusker and Menard 1985, 108–10, 198–99).

Their adroit response to the Atlantic economy was largely nullified by neomercantilist policy initiatives following the French and Indian War. British taxes on trade and commerce fell disproportionately upon Boston's foreland economy and its wholesaling of up-market goods. The Stamp Act of 1765 offers a case in point. When British Customs officials issued stamped paper, they unwittingly assumed that tax receipts would be nearly identical in the colonies of Massachusetts, Pennsylvania, and New York; in fact, Massachusetts paid as much as 40 percent of the tax as compared to 15–18 percent each in Pennsylvania and New York. The location of Customs Office headquarters in Boston further exacerbated the city's problems. Smuggling and commercial underreporting ended instantly. The situation had not improved by 1772, when Boston's taxes and associated fees amounted to some £16,000 or about 2 percent of New England's earnings from overseas and coastal trades. In a mercantile world in which rates of commission, interest, and return on capital ranged between 2 and 10 percent, Boston's tax burden was large indeed (Dickerson 1951, 172–207; Morgan 1953; Harper 1939).

Bostonians were rightly outraged by the unfairness of policies that struck at the heart of their foreland economy, while leaving others unscathed. As early as 1764, they had assembled a repertoire for expressing their dissent, consisting of rhetoric (taxation without representation), organization (committees of correspondence), and action (both reasoned and violent). Action begat reaction and counterreaction in an endless spiral. Dissent reached a climax with the mass uprising that greeted word of Parliament's simultaneous enactment of the Massachusetts Government Act and the Quebec Act in 1774. These acts, by extending punitive actions from Boston to the colony as a whole, accomplished what Boston had repeatedly failed to do: galvanize an alliance of the Puritan interior and Yankee Boston. "The people," wrote British General Gage to his superiors in 1774, were "numerous, worked up to a Fury and not just a Boston Rabble, but the Freeholders and Farmers of the Country," many of whom had entered only recently and somewhat reluctantly into a courtship with the market. The unimaginable was at hand (Bushman 1976, 81–82; Brown 1970, 178–209; Rothenberg 1981).

The momentary coalition of spatial opposites, of Yankee Boston and the Puritan interior, shook the Empire and in short order "turned the world upside down." What had been unthinkable in 1773 had become a reality with the coalition of the thirteen colonies into the United States and their defeat of Cornwallis at Yorktown in 1781 (Egnal 1988). One wonders, in retrospect, if the whole thing might have been averted had the British understood Boston's unusual geography, based as it was on foreland trade and commerce.

Meaning

Two centuries after the first stirrings of the English in America, the colonists had secured their independence by defeating the world's most powerful nation; acquired title to over a million square miles of land; mushroomed to nearly three million persons; displayed an ethnocultural and economic variety unmatched in the Euroamerican New World; acknowledged these sectional pluralisms in federal and republican governance; secured their niche within the Atlantic economy; and, in response to capitalism's periodic crises, devised recurrent, dialectical, and institutionalized processes of creative experimentation, innovation, and logistic diffusion. Moreover, most Americans believed that their one outstanding contradiction, slavery, was on the road to extinction, or at least to confinement in the rice swamps of the Carolina Low Country.

Small wonder then that the Founding Fathers regarded themselves as pioneers of providence, blessed by divine intercession in behalf of a destiny made manifest. This deist conceit notwithstanding, the story of British settlement in North America owes a great deal more to determinism and contingency, to capitalism's relentless periodic rhythms and sheer luck (Bonomi 1986). In an odd way, the Americans were lucky that the English came late to the New World and thus were consigned the leftovers in North America; that they were seduced by the Hakluyts' ill-conceived climatic model which targeted colonization in the Mediterranean latitudes on the Atlantic Seaboard; and that a penurious Crown, unable to afford the costs of colonization, opened the door to monopoly colonization and to ethnocultural and economic pluralism.

Although contingency and luck played continuing roles in the British colonization of North America, these roles were increasingly subsumed by the periodic rhythm of Anglo-American macrohistory. Economic and social crises and the institutionalized responses to them—creative experimentation, fundamental agrarian innovations (as well as in the polity and society), and logistic diffusion in the ensuing half-century—recurred at regular intervals. These prosaic processes periodically revitalized the structure of American macrohistory; dialectical alternation maintained its equilibrium. Crisis delegitimated the elite innovations of one cycle and prepared the way for the folk innovations of the next. These cyclical alternations, in turn, fostered societies that were increasingly stratified (class-based) or increasingly egalitarian. They also rang out the old. Innovations that had ceased to stimulate economic growth and had accelerated environmental degradation were, in Schumpeter's deft phrase, readied for "creative destruction" (1939). These processes and the periodic structures they created were fixed and invariant; the particulars, however, were contingent upon human agency, contention, and, at critical times, luck. The stirrings of the industrial revolution offer an apt case.

Insofar as the geography of Anglo-American history is a story of endless beginnings, it seems a fitting conclusion for this essay to say a few words about the commencement of U.S. history proper and that period's crowning geographical achievement—the industrial revolution, circa 1790–1840. Much of this great transformation from a rural to an urban society, from an agrarian to an industrial way of life, and from artisanal to mechanical modes of production, is unremarkably predictable. Given what we know about the timing of recurrent innovations, it is hardly surprising that this first chapter in the American Industrial Revolution unfolded between the 1790s–1840s. Nor, given our knowledge of the disposition of cheap, unskilled labor—the grain belt's seasonally underemployed farm laborers and New England's demographic surplus of young, unmarried women—is industry's location in these regions. What is surprising (and, I suspect, unpredictable) is the appearance of these industrial innovations in the first place. The principal problem, as Hamilton understood, was in securing an American market for coarse, machine-made goods and protecting it from foreign competition. In normal times, this problem would have been intractable, given the Revolution's rejection of "oppressive" neomercantile policies and the dialectical alternation of policy cycles. But the times were hardly normal. The ineluctables of free trade were denied by an Age of Revolution which at once sheltered infant American industries from foreign competition, reinforced Hamiltonian protectionism, and, for perhaps the only time in our past, reversed the dialectic of American macrohistory (Earle and Hoffman 1980; Earle 1991).

These were extraordinary times indeed. An Age of Revolution, lasting from 1776 through the Latin American revolutions of the 1820s, disrupted the lanes of international commerce and trade and provided unintended protection for infant industries throughout the Atlantic economy. In the case of the U.S., this meant the commencement of an industrial revolution a half-century ahead of schedule.

And thus in the end as in the beginning, Anglo-Americans have been blessed with unusual good luck at the most critical moments, being among the last to arrive in the New World and the first to leave the womb of colonial dependency, just in time to take advantage of the revolutions that their example had set in motion elsewhere.

The American Revolution and the ensuing economic miracle, by serving at once as the model for the unshackling of colonial dependency and as the benchmark for measuring the success of that achievement, have invited unkind comparisons with the rest of the world where political revolution has more often entrained poverty than progress, torment than freedom. Conversely, among Americans, our exceptionalism has fostered an unfortunate sense of the providential, of manifest destiny, of inherent Anglo-American superiority.

The truth, I believe, is rather different. This was a land founded by a reluctant and insecure culture that flourished as often in spite of, as because of, itself. In time, the profits derived from piracy, native expulsion, labor compulsion, socioeconomic pluralism, and the institutionalization of periodic, logistic, and dialectical innovation buoyed the confidence of its creole descendants into the kind of provincial arrogance required of those who would con-

spire to bring down the greatest empire of its day. That they succeeded was beyond belief; that they did so in time to enter ahead of schedule into the industrial revolution is all the more astonishing. One need not deny the genius and the effort, nor the folly and the pain, that went into these accomplishments in making the point that the American achievement owed a great deal to sheer luck.

A half-century later, however, when Latin Americans attempted to duplicate the American feat, the luck of the revolutionaries unfortunately had run out. The industrial revolution was well underway; Napoleon had been put to bed and the protectionism that his wars had offered had melted away into a ruthlessly enforced doctrine of free trade and laissez-faire (always a problem for poor peoples and nations). Perhaps they would have failed to measure up in any event owing to the absence of pluralist, decentralized, and periodically-revitalizing institutional geographies. Perhaps, but we do not know for sure. In the interim, comparisons that point toward improvidence or the frailties of persons or cultures are unkind indeed for those on a roll (however momentary).

Notes

1. Late Elizabethan privateers were especially successful in American waters, where they captured thirty percent of their prizes and, more critically, seventy percent of prize value (Andrews 1964).

2. Geographers have made much ado over culture transfer, or the lack thereof, in the various regions of British North America (Zelinsky 1973; Harris 1977; Meinig 1986; Jordan and Kaups 1989). The debate has unfortunately displaced the larger, anterior question: why the Crown allowed, indeed encouraged, the immigration of such varied ethnocultural groups in the first place? These sociogeographic enclaves, in fact, would not have existed at all were it not for the peculiar circumstances that were shaping the English colonial policy of monopoly colonization: first, the Crown's penury, which favored granting charters to a series of decentralized colonial monopolists over the alternative of a centralized royal administration; second, the Stuarts' relaxation of Elizabethan trade restrictions, which encouraged the "commercialization of colonization" as well as novelty in colonial organizational forms—colonies run, for example, by joint-stock companies or by single or multiple proprietors; and third, the curiously tolerant perspective of the Stuart monarchs with respect to religious dissent, owing perhaps to the marginality of their own preferences for high Anglicanism and their pro-Catholic sympathies, which lent itself to the establishment of religious

havens in English North America, albeit on lands regarded as of marginal economic utility (Shammas 1979). Our pluralist tradition thus owes a great deal to the liberalism of the Stuarts; all of which is ironic indeed for a monarchical house accused more than once of tyranny and twice deposed.

3. Although figures on European migration to the New World are little more than rough estimates, they are sufficiently useful for comparison of Spanish, English, and French colonial strategies. In the first century of Spanish colonization (1492–1600), some 175,000 Spaniards emigrated to Spanish America. The first century of English and French colonization (1607–1700) meanwhile dispatched some 375,000 British to the mainland of North America and the Caribbean and some 45,000 French to the Caribbean and Canada (very few to the latter, in fact, as only 11,000 went there between 1608–1763). Note that in their first century of colonization, British migrants exceeded Spanish by fifty percent; moreover, the rather more homogeneous ethnocultural enclaves of the English on the North American mainland contrasted sharply with the ethnic admixturing of Spanish America, where each settlement contained a medly of settlers from Old Castille and New, from Andalusia and Extremadura (Borah 1976; Gemery 1980; Mörner 1976, 769).

4. It is a well-known principle in social theory that cultural persistence is a function of the mass and homogeneity of a cultural group; contra for assimilation and cultural change. Hence the establishment of sizable, homogeneous ethnocultural enclaves (colonies) in New England and South Carolina (including Afro-Americans) ensured trans-Atlantic cultural persistence, while the ethnocultural mixing in the Chesapeake and Pennsylvania, the first the result of economics, the second of conscious policy, facilitated cultural change (Wolf 1982; Earle 1974).

References

Andrews, K. R. 1964. *Elizabethan privateering: English privateering during the Spanish War, 1585–1603.* Cambridge: Cambridge University Press.

———. 1967. *Drake's voyages: A reassessment of their place in Elizabethan maritime expansion.* New York: Charles Scribner's Sons.

Bachman, V. C. 1969. *Peltries or planatations: The economic policies of the Dutch West India Company in New Netherland.* Baltimore: Johns Hopkins University Press.

Baechler, J.; Hall, J. A.; and Mann, M. 1988. *Europe and the rise of capitalism.* Oxford: Basil Blackwell.

Bailyn, B. 1955. *The New England merchants in the seventeenth century.* Cambridge: Harvard University Press.

———. 1986. *The peopling of America.* New York: Knopf.

———, and Bailyn, L. 1959. *Massachusetts's ship-ping, 1697–1714: A statistical study.* Cambridge: Harvard University Press.

Berlin, I. 1980. Time, space, and the evolution of Afro-American society on British mainland North America. *American Historical Review* 85:44–78.

Berry, B. J. L. 1991. *Long-wave rhythms in economic development and political behavior.* Baltimore: Johns Hopkins University Press.

Bonomi, P. U. 1986. *Under the cope of heaven: Religion, society, and politics in Colonial America.* New York: Oxford University Press.

Borah, W. 1976. The mixing of populations. In *First images of America: The impact of the New World on the Old,* ed. Fredi Chiappelli, vol. 2, pp. 707–22. Berkeley: University of California Press.

Braudel, F. 1979–84. *The structures of everyday life: Civilization and capitalism, 15th–18th century,* 3 vols. Trans. Sian Reynolds. New York: Harper and Row.

Brenner, R. P. 1972. The social basis of English commercial expansion, 1550–1650. *Journal of Economic History* 32:361–84.

Bridenbaugh, C. 1938. *Cities in the wilderness: Urban life in America, 1625–1742.* New York: Ronald Press.

Brown, E. H. P., and Hopkins, S. V. 1957. Wage-rates and prices: Evidence for population pressure in the sixteenth century. *Economica,* 2nd. ser., 24:289–309.

Brown, R. D. 1970. *Revolutionary politics in Massachusetts: The Boston committee of correspondence and the towns, 1772–1774.* Cambridge: Harvard University Press.

Bushman, R. L. 1976. Massachusetts's farmers and the revolution. In *Society, freedom, and conscience: The American Revolution in Virginia, Massachusetts, and New York,* ed. R. M. Jellison, pp. 77–124. New York: W. W. Norton.

———. 1985. *King and people in provincial Massachusetts.* Chapel Hill: University of North Carolina Press.

Carr, L. G.; Menard, R. R.; Walsh, L. S. 1991. *Robert Cole's world: Agriculture and society in early Maryland.* Chapel Hill: University of North Carolina Press.

Cawley, R. R. 1966. *The voyages and Elizabethan drama.* Modern Language Association of America, Monograph Series. New York: Kraus Reprint.

Clowse, C. D. 1971. *Economic beginnings in colonial South Carolina, 1670–1730.* Columbia: University of South Carolina Press.

Coclanis, P. A. 1989. *The shadow of a dream: Economic life and death in the South Carolina Low Country, 1670–1920.* New York: Oxford University Press.

Coleman, D. C. 1956. Labour in the English economy of the seventeenth century. *Economic History Review,* 2nd. ser., 8:280–95.

Craven, W. F. 1971. *White, red, and black: The seventeenth-century Virginian.* Charlottesville: University Press of Virginia.

Cronon, W. 1983. *Changes in the land: Indians, colonists, and the ecology of New England.* New York: Hill and Wang.

Daniels, B. C. 1979. *The Connecticut town: Growth and development, 1635–1790.* Middletown, CT: Wesleyan University Press.

DeJong, G. F. 1975. *The Dutch in America, 1609–1674.* Boston: Twayne.

De Vorsey, Louis. 1987. The new land: The discovery and exploration of eastern North America. In *North America: The historical geography of a changing continent,* ed. R. D. Mitchell and P. A. Groves. Totowa, NJ: Rowman and Littlefield, 25–47.

Dickerson, O. M. 1951. *The Navigation Acts and the American Revolution.* Philadelphia: University of Pennsylvania Press.

Dodghson, R. A. 1987. *The European past: Social evolution and spatial order.* Houndmills, U.K.: Macmillan Education.

Dunbar, G. 1958. Some curious analogies in explorers' preconceptions of Virginia. *Virginia Journal of Science,* n.s., 3:323–26.

Dunn, R. S. 1972. *Sugar and slaves: The rise of the planter class in the English West Indies, 1624–1713.* New York: W. W. Norton.

Earle, C. V. 1974. Reflections on the colonial city. *Historical Geography Newsletter* 4:1–17.

———. 1977. The first English towns of North America. *Geographical Review* 67:34–50.

———. 1979. Environment, disease, and mortality in early Virginia. *Journal of Historical Geography* 5:365–90.

———. 1988. The myth of the southern soil miner: Macrohistory, agricultural innovation, and environmental change. In *The ends of the earth: perspectives on modern environmental history,* ed. D. Worster, pp. 175–210. Cambridge: Cambridge University Press.

———. 1992. *Geographical inquiry and American historical problems.* Stanford, CA: Stanford University Press.

———, and Cao, C. Forthcoming. The rate of frontier expansion in American history, 1650–1890. In *GIS and the social sciences: A handbook,* ed. C. Earle, L. Hochberg, and D. Miller. New York: Basil Blackwell.

———, and Hoffman, R. 1976. Staple crops and urban development in the eighteenth-century South. *Perspectives in American History* 10:5–78.

———. 1980. The foundation of the modern economy: Agriculture and the costs of labor in the United States and England, 1800–1860. *American Historical Review* 85:1055–94.

Egnal, M. 1988. *A mighty empire: The origins of the American Revolution.* Ithaca, NY: Cornell University Press.

Elliott, J. H. 1970. *The Old World and the New, 1492–1650.* Cambridge: Cambridge University Press.

Ellis, J. J. 1979. Culture and capitalism in pre-Revolutionary America. *American Quarterly* 31:169–86.

Fischer, D. H. 1989. *Albion's seed: Four British folkways in America.* New York: Oxford University Press.

Gemery, H. A. 1980. Emigration from the British Isles to the New World, 1630–1700: Inferences from colonial populations. *Research in Economic History* 5:179–231.

Glacken, C. J. 1973. *Traces on the Rhodian shore: Nature and culture in western thought from ancient times to the end of the eighteenth century.* Berkeley: University of California Press.

Goldstein, J. 1988. *Long cycles: Prosperity and war in the modern age.* New Haven, CT: Yale University Press.

Harper, L. A. 1939. The effect of the Navigation Acts on the thirteen colonies. In *The era of the American Revolution,* ed. R. B. Morris, pp. 3–39. New York: Columbia University Press.

Harris, R. C. 1977. The simplification of Europe overseas. *Annals of the Association of American Geographers* 67:469–83.

———, and Warkentin, J. 1974. *Canada before Confederation: A study in historical geography.* New York: Oxford University Press.

Henretta, J. A. 1978. Families and farms: *Mentalité* in preindustrial America. *William and Mary Quarterly,* 3rd ser., 35:3–32.

Hodgen, M. T. 1964. *Early anthropology in the sixteenth and seventeenth centuries.* Philadelphia: University of Pennsylvania Press.

Isaac, R. 1982. *The transformation of Virginia, 1740–1790.* Chapel Hill: University of North Carolina Press.

Jordan, T. J., and Kaups, M. 1989. *The American backwoods frontier: An ethnic and ecological interpretation.* Baltimore: Johns Hopkins University Press.

Kammen, M. 1974. *A rope of sand: The colonial agents, British policies, and the American Revolution.* New York: Vintage Books.

Kulikoff, A. 1986. *Tobacco and slaves: The development of southern cultures in the Chesapeake, 1680–1800.* Chapel Hill: University of North Carolina Press.

Kupperman, K. O. 1982. The puzzle of American climate in the early colonial period. *American Historical Review* 87:1262–89.

Ladurie, E. L. 1977. Motionless history. *Social Science History* 1:115–36.

Lemon, J. T. 1972. *The best poor man's country: A geographical study of early southeastern Penn-

sylvania. Baltimore: Johns Hopkins University Press.

———. 1984. Spatial order: Households in local communities and regions. In *Colonial British America: Essays in the new history of the early American era*, ed. J. P. Greene and J. R. Pole, pp. 86–122. Baltimore: Johns Hopkins University Press.

Lockridge, K. A. 1970. *A New England town: The first hundred years*. New York: W. W. Norton.

McCusker, J. J., and Menard, R. R. 1985. *The economy of British North America, 1607–1789*. Chapel Hill: University of North Carolina Press.

McLoughlin, W. G. 1978. *Revivals, awakenings, and reform: An essay on religion and social change, 1607–1977*. Chicago: University of Chicago Press.

Main, G. L. 1982. *Tobacco colony: Life in early Maryland, 1650–1720*. Princeton, NJ: Princeton University Press.

Meinig, D. W. 1958. The American colonia era: A geographic commentary. *Proceedings, Royal Geographical Society of Australia, South Australian Branch* 59:1–22.

———. 1986. *The shaping of America: A geographical perspective on 500 years of history*, vol. 1, *Atlantic America, 1492–1800*. New Haven, CT: Yale University Press.

Menard, R. R. 1973. From servant to freeholder: Status mobility and property accumulation in seventeenth-century Maryland. *William and Mary Quarterly*, 3rd ser., 30:37–64.

———. 1980. The tobacco industry in the Chesapeake colonies, 1617–1730: An interpretation. *Research in Economic History* 5:109–77.

Merrens, H. R. 1969. The physical environment of early America: Images and image makers in colonial South Carolina. *Geographical Review* 59:530–56.

Mitchell, R. D., and Groves, P. A. 1987. *North America: The historical geography of a changing continent*. Totowa, NJ: Rowman and Littlefield.

Morgan, E. S. 1953. *The Stamp Act crisis: Prologue to revolution*. Chapel Hill: University of North Carolina Press.

———. 1975. *American slavery, American freedom: The ordeal of colonial Virginia*. New York: W. W. Norton.

Mörner, M. 1976. Spanish migration to the New World prior to 1800: A report on the state of research. In *First images of America: The impact of the New World on the Old*, ed. Fredi Chiappelli, vol. 2, pp. 737–82. Berkeley: University of California Press.

Murrin, J. M. 1984. Political development. In *Colonial British America: Essays in the new history of the early modern era*, ed. J. P. Greene and J. R. Pole, pp. 408–56. Baltimore: Johns Hopkins University Press.

Nash, G. B. 1968. *Quakers and politics: Pennsylvania, 1681–1726*. Princeton, NJ: Princeton University Press.

———. 1979. *The urban crucible: The northern seaports and the origins of the American Revolution*. Cambridge: Harvard University Press.

North, D. C., and Thomas, R. P. 1973. *The rise of the Western World: A new economic history*. Cambridge: Cambridge University Press.

Overton, M. 1984. Agricultural revolution? Development of the agrarian economy in early modern England. In *Explorations in historical geography: Interpretative essays*, ed. A. R. H. Baker and D. Gregory, pp. 119–39. Cambridge: Cambridge University Press.

———. 1985. The diffusion of agricultural innovations in early modern England: Turnips and clover in Norfolk and Suffolk, 1580–1740. *Institute of British Geographers, Transactions*, n.s. 10:205–21.

Pares, R. 1956. *Yankees and creoles: The trade between North America and the West Indies before the American Revolution*. Cambridge: Harvard University Press.

Parks, G. B. 1928. *Richard Hakluyt and the English voyages*. American Geographical Society Serial Publication 10. New York: American Geographical Society.

Parry, J. H. 1961. *The establishment of the European hegemony, 1415–1715*. New York: Harper and Row.

Pennington, L. E. 1979. The Amerindian in English promotional literature, 1575–1625. In *The westward expansion: English activities in Ireland, the Atlantic, and America 1480–1650*, ed. K. R. Andrews, N. P. Canny, and P. E. H. Hair, pp. 175–94. Detroit: Wayne State University Press.

Percy, G. 1907. Observations of Master George Percy, 1607. In *Narratives of early Virginia, 1606–1625*, ed. L. G. Tyler, pp. 5–23. New York: Charles Scribner's Sons.

Price, J. M. 1973. *France and the Chesapeake: A history of the French tobacco monopoly, 1674–1791, and of its relationship to the British and American tobacco trades*. 2 vols. Ann Arbor: University of Michigan Press.

———. 1974. Economic function and the growth of American port towns in the eighteenth century. *Perspectives in American History* 8:123–86.

———. 1984. The transatlantic economy. In *Colonial British America: Essays in the new history of the modern era*, ed. J. P. Greene and J. R. Pole, pp. 18–42. Baltimore: Johns Hopkins University Press.

Quinn, D. B. 1955. *The Roanoke voyages, 1584–1590*. 2 vols. London: The Hakluyt Society.

Rabb, T. K. 1967. *Enterprise and empire: Merchant and gentry investment in the expansion of En-*

gland, 1575–1630. Cambridge: Harvard University Press.

Reps, J. W. 1972. *Tidewater towns: City planning in colonial Virginia and Maryland.* Williamsburg, VA: Colonial Williamsburg Foundation.

Rostow, W. W., and Kennedy, M., with the assistance of Nasr, F. 1979. A simple model of the Kondratieff Cycle. *Research in Economic History* 4:1–36.

Rothenberg, W. B. 1981. The market and Massachusetts's farmers, 1750–1855. *Journal of Economic History* 41:283–314.

Rowse, A. L. 1955. *The expansion of Elizabethan England.* New York: St. Martin's Press.

Rutman, D. B. 1965. *Winthrop's Boston: Portrait of a Puritan town, 1630–1649.* Chapel Hill: University of North Carolina Press.

Sauer, C. O. 1941. The settlement of the humid east. In *Climate and man, Yearbook of agriculture, 1941,* pp. 157–66. Washington: Goverment Printing Office.

Saunders, W. L. 1886–90. *The colonial records of North Carolina,* 10 vols. Raleigh, NC: P. M. Hale.

Scammell, G. V. 1969. The New World and Europe in the sixteenth century. *The Historical Journal* 12:389–412.

Schlesinger, Jr., A. 1986. *The cycles of American history.* Boston: Houghton Mifflin.

Schumpeter, J. 1939. *Business cycles.* 2 vols. New York: McGraw-Hill.

Shammas, C. 1979. English commercial development and American colonization, 1560–1620. In *The westward expansion: English activities in Ireland, the Atlantic, and America 1480–1650,* ed. K. R. Andrews, N. P. Canny, and P. E. H. Hair, pp. 151–74. Detroit: Wayne State University Press.

Sheridan, R. B. 1984. The domestic economy. In *Colonial British America: Essays in the new history of the early modern era,* ed. J. P. Greene and J. R. Pole, pp. 43–85. Baltimore: Johns Hopkins University Press.

Stone, L. 1949–50. Elizabethan overseas trade. *Economic History Review* 2nd ser., 2:30–57.

———. 1966. Social mobility in England, 1500–1700. *Past and present* 33:16–55.

Taaffe, E.; Morrill, R. L.; and Gould, P. R. 1963. Transport expansion in underdeveloped countries: A comparative analysis. *Geographical Review* 53:503–29.

Taylor, E. G. R. 1930. *Tudor geography 1485–1583.* London: Methuen.

———, ed. 1935. *The original writings & correspondence of the two Richard Hakluyts,* no. 76. 2 vols. London: The Hakluyt Society.

Vance, Jr., J. E. 1970. *The merchant's world: The geography of wholesaling.* Englewood Cliffs, NJ: Prentice-Hall.

Washburn, W. E. 1957. *The governor and the rebel: A history of Bacon's rebellion in Virginia.* Chapel Hill: University of North Carolina Press.

Wolf, E. R. 1982. *Europe and the people without history.* Berkeley: University of California Press.

Wood, J. 1982. Village and community in early colonial New England. *Journal of Historical Geography* 8:333–46.

Wood, P. H. 1974. *Black majority: Negroes in colonial South Carolina from 1670 through the Stono Rebellion.* New York: Knopf.

Yapa, L. 1983. Innovation bias, appropriate technology, and basic goods. *Journal of African and Asian Studies* 17:32–44.

Zelinsky, W. 1973. *The cultural geography of the United States.* Englewood Cliffs, NJ: Prentice-Hall.

From Cabot to Cartier: The Early Exploration of Eastern North America, 1497–1543

John L. Allen

Department of Geography, University of Connecticut, Storrs, CT 06269-2148

Abstract. Initial European responses to the Co-lumbian discovery included an exploratory process that, in the space of a half-century, delineated the basic geographical features of North America's Atlantic coast. This explor-atory process was conditioned by pre-Colum-bian European "geosophy" or images of lands in the western Atlantic and by the desire to locate a water route to Asia. The first European explorers to make contact with North America did so far to the north of the area contacted by Columbus, and their voyages would almost certainly have taken place regardless of the success or failure of Columbus. John Cabot and the Corte-Real brothers explored the Lab-rador-Newfoundland region as early as 1497, searching for a sea-level strait through what they believed was an island archipelago off Asia's eastern shores. Subsequent explorations by Giovanni da Verrazzano and Jacques Cartier added to the growing store of geographical information and developing geographical im-ages about North America. Verrazzano's coastal voyage from Florida to Canada and Cartier's entry into the St. Lawrence helped define the key features of the Atlantic coast of the continent. Information derived from both voyages also helped perpetuate the belief in a sea-level route to Asia. Although the first half-century of European exploration of eastern North America resulted in a relatively accurate depiction of that region, the exploratory pro-cess also contributed to a growing body of theoretical and speculative geography of the Northwest Passage upon which much Euro-pean exploration up to the mid-seventeenth century would be based.

Key Words: North American exploration, geo-sophy, geographical images, John Cabot, Giovanni da Verrazzano, Jacques Cartier.

> Explorers have seldom gone forth merely to probe about for whatever they may discover. They have gone in quest of definite objectives believed to exist on the basis of such information as could be gathered from the geographical lore of their own and earlier times.
>
> —John Kirtland Wright, 1943

B EGINNING late in the fifteenth century, the European world burst outward in what has been termed "the First Great Age of Discovery" (Goetzmann 1986), a period of approximately two centuries during which Europeans came to know much more than they had previously known about the basic geo-graphical configuration of the entire world. In its incipient stage, that having to do with the "discovery"[1] of the New World by Columbus and the subsequent establishment of contact between two great culture regions long sepa-rated, this European outburst flowed from the twin impulses of cupidity and curiosity, aug-mented somewhat by religious caprice. The na-ture of these impulses has not gone unrecog-nized in this quincentenary year of the Columbian discovery, a year that has occa-sioned articles, books, symposia, conferences, and colloquia on Columbus, his motives for discovery, the location of his first landfall in the New World, and the consequences of that landfall for the disintegration of Native Ameri-can cultures. As great an achievement as Columbus's discovery was, however, it can be argued that it has been overemphasized, not as an event of huge cultural significance but as an act of exploration. This is particularly true in

Annals of the Association of American Geographers. 82(3), 1992, pp. 500–521
© Copyright 1992 by Association of American Geographers

relation to the early voyages to North America, voyages which had a "certain unity of purpose and of geography" that were largely independent of the Columbian cycle (Morison 1971, 3). It is a virtual certainty that, even had Columbus never left the small port of Palos in search of a water route to the Orient and thereby discovered a New World, other European voyagers of the late fifteenth century would soon have touched upon American shores. Basques, Bretons, and Bristolmen were as motivated by greed and geographical inquisitiveness as Columbus and were active in westward voyagings even before 1492. While their voyages before and after that cardinal date cannot be viewed in isolation from the Columbian discovery, it must be noted that the news of Columbus's landfall created relatively little stir in the western and northern ports of Europe. Here the combination of ancient and Medieval geographical lore and current events had already created a mindset well-prepared to deal both conceptually and operationally with the eventuality of the discovery of lands in the northern and western Atlantic (Glacken 1967; Elliott 1970). The reports of the Columbian discovery added, it is true, a measure of political incentive to the existing economic imperative of the discovery of a short route to the riches of the Orient. Other European nations, deeply absorbed in the creation of nation-states and the shifting of the European economic center from the Mediterranean to the Atlantic and the North Sea, could not afford to let Spain control what, at first glance, might have been the Passage to India. Spain, led by the Genoese navigator, was the first player in the game of exploration and incipient empire. But England, Portugal, and France entered the game shortly after 1492, basing their exploratory strategy on what was already known or believed to be known about the lands westward into the Ocean Sea; in other words, the explorers of European nations predicated their goals and objectives upon both "empirical" geographical lore obtained through direct observation and experience, and "nonempirical" geographical lore derived from myth, legend, and rumor (Allen 1972).

Scholars of "geosophy" or the study of geographical knowledge have come to an understanding that this combination of empirical and nonempirical geographical lore, of experience and imagination, is how people have always developed their images or patterns of belief about the world or any of its regions (Wright 1947; Allen 1975a). The Greek geographer Strabo, one of the first thinkers to inquire into the process of how geographical images are formed, wrote that man is informed of the nature and content of his world "through perception and experience alike." But even for Strabo and his contemporaries, "perception and experience" was necessarily combined with theory and imagination. Strabo's world view was not confined to his recognized *oikoumene* or "known world," but included images of unexplored regions which, for Strabo at least, were similar to places well-known and carefully studied. Hence both imagination and experience played a role in the creation of the Greek world view. For those who attempt to merge the study of geosophy with the history of exploration, the combination of experience (the process of developing understanding through experience and the direct perception of geographic reality) and imagination (the system of developing man's understanding of his world through the application of theoretical reasoning and creativity) has been particularly important for interpreting that process called exploration. For in the exploratory process, theory and reality often merge to condition the objectives of exploration, to determine the nature of exploratory behavior during the course of an expedition, and to modulate the consequences of an exploration for geographical knowledge (Allen 1975a). Such was certainly the case with the exploratory cycle which began with the first European contacts with the North America continent, just a few short years after 1492. The first Europeans to penetrate the mists of the Ocean Sea in search of lands in the northwestern Atlantic predicated their exploratory goals upon existing geographical lore. This preexisting geographical lore, combined with the empirical observations obtained during exploratory voyages, shaped the course of initial and subsequent voyages westward. And the entire complex of lore, both that which predated European expansion in the late fifteenth century and that which was accrued as a result of the first half-century of exploration, was fundamental in the development of the patterns of belief or geographical images that developed about North America by the middle of the sixteenth century.[2] The aim of this essay is to articulate that process of imagination and exploration, the anvil upon which the first consensual empirical views of North America were forged.

Geographical Lore of North America before 1492: Apocrypha and Actuality

Prior to the initial Columbian voyage of 1492, there were six primary sources for European geographical knowledge bearing upon the northern and western Atlantic. Arranged chronologically these included: rumors of ancient and classical voyagers northwestward from Europe, legends of Celtic exploration west from Ireland in the sixth or seventh centuries, empirical and nonempirical lore derived from the Norse explorations of the tenth through the twelfth centuries, Medieval tales of Atlantic isles, apocryphal voyages supposedly occurring between the Norse discoveries and Columbus, and speculative-but-possible explorations by Portuguese and English in the years immediately preceding the first Columbian voyage. Nowhere were these sources gathered into a single collection; rather they were scattered throughout the bits and pieces of classical literature left to late Medieval Europe, tucked away in reports and correspondence of the Church, available in manuscript collections or printed "histories," marginally accessible as fragmentary government documents or official correspondence, or present only as oral tradition among certain segments of the European community. Even more important, no single individual or institution in immediate pre-Columbian Europe possessed anything approaching complete awareness of all these source materials. Nevertheless, the reservoir of geographical knowledge existed and portions of it were accessible to those Europeans who sought information on the wider world west of European shores.

The remnants of classical geography that Medieval Europe had inherited provided definite knowledge of the earth's sphericity and of a land-water distribution that included the World Island of Europe-Asia-Africa, surrounded by an all-encircling Ocean Sea and thus providing the theoretical basis for reaching the Orient by sailing west from Europe (Bunbury 1957). Classical geographical lore

also bequeathed to pre-Renaissance Europeans some firm basis for a belief in lands (islands) to the north and west of Europe that were not properly part of Asia but lay off that continent's eastern shore. Tales of the *Insulae Fortunatae* or Fortunate Isles (also called the Elysian Fields, the Happy Isles, the Hesperides, the Isles of the Blessed, and other names in nearly every European vernacular) were abundant in the literature of antiquity and many Europeans equated these inventions of Hesiod and other classical writers with lands supposedly discovered west of Europe by Phoenician and Greek voyagers. The most common tales of ancient and classical voyagers centered around Phoenicians from Sidon and Tyre and Carthage who almost certainly discovered the Canary Islands, confused in most classical texts with the purely mythical *Insulae Fortunatae*. Herodotus, the Greek geographer-historian who served as the major source of information on Phoenician voyages, concluded that ships attached to the fleet of Hanno, a sixth-century B.C. Carthaginian who circumnavigated Africa, were blown westward across the "Ocean Sea" or Atlantic and made landfall on large islands or mainland thousands of leagues northwest of the Pillars of Hercules or Straits of Gibraltar (Boland 1961). Almost as prevalent were the narratives of Pytheas, a navigator sailing from the Greek colony of Massillia (Marseilles) in the third century B.C., who voyaged northwest from the Mediterranean to Thule or, as described by Seneca and Pliny, *Ultima Thule*, the earth's utmost verge (Tillinghast 1889). Some modern scholars accept these voyages as fact and claim proof of trans-Atlantic discoveries even before the Norse, although there is virtually no verifiable evidence to support such claims (Cortesão 1953). Nevertheless, it is the presence of such fables in the literature existent in late Medieval Europe that is important; whether such voyages took place or not, their inclusion in geographical lore made them a part of the data available to geographers and would-be explorers of the Columbian age.

Even more common in the European literature than the legends of Mediterranean voyagers were the stories of Celtic explorations into the Atlantic. The primary sources of data on these explorations were two well-known pre-Columbian Latin texts, the *Vita Sancti Brendani* and the *Navigatio Sancti Brendani Abbatis*, manuscript copies of which were located in libraries throughout Europe and with both prose and metrical translations in English and French widely available in late Medieval Europe. The central figure in these texts was the early Irish saint, Abbot Brendan of Ardfert, who supposedly discovered North America in the sixth century A.D. (Ashe 1962). Sailing with companion monks in skin boats or *curraughs*, Brendan's tale is a Christian version of the Odyssey (Macpherson forthcoming), involving seven years of journeying in the Atlantic, visiting numerous wonderful islands before, finally, discovering "a land wide, and full of grass and fruit . . . [with] no plants that had not flowers, nor trees that had no fruit. The stones of that land are precious stones" (O'Meara 1976). Brendan and his companions traveled westward through this great land for fifteen days before reaching a huge river which flowed from east to west. Here they were turned back by an angel who told them that "after many years this land will be made manifest to those who come after you." Beginning as early as 1580 with the Elizabethan advisor and cosmographer John Dee, scholars have attempted to claim England's prior right to discovery to North America upon the Brendan legend (even though the *Navigatio* itself makes it clear that Brendan's discovery of a mainland west of Europe was really a "rediscovery" of a land already contacted by an earlier Irish cleric named Mernoc!). Brendan was an actual historical figure who may have made western voyages, perhaps as far as Iceland, known to have had an Irish monastic colony at the time of Norse colonization in the ninth century (Oleson 1964). Although, as with the purported journeys of Phoenicians and Greeks, there is no evidence to suggest a North American landfall for Brendan or other Irish clerical explorers, the Brendani literary cycle was a significant part of late Medieval geographical lore.

The records of the Norse discoveries of the tenth and eleventh centuries stand in sharp contrast to those of earlier periods, at least insofar as the Norse discoveries can be documented while the voyages of Brendan and his classical predecessors cannot. Based upon historical records (particularly the Icelandic-Greenlandic *saga* literature) and upon archaeological evidence (the l'Anse aux Meadows site in northern Newfoundland), the argument for Norse discovery of North America is incontrovertible (Ingstad 1985; Jones 1986). Working

their way across the north Atlantic from Norway to northern Britain to the Faeroes, the Norse colonized Iceland in the ninth century A.D. and Greenland in the tenth. During the period between 1000 A.D. and 1015 A.D., there were several voyages by Bjarni Herjfolfsson and Leif Eiríksson from Greenland to North America (Vinland), including at least one attempt at planting a permanent colony in what is now Newfoundland. For the next two and a half centuries, North America or Vinland drifted in and out of the European literature and consciousness (Macpherson forthcoming), and the Greenland colony maintained tenuous ties with the European community until nearly 1400. Despite the reliability of the historical record of Norse voyaging westward to North America, there is still considerable debate as to the extent to which geographical literature and knowledge emanating from the Norse experience was widely available to Europe during the years immediately before 1492 (Skelton, et al. 1965). It is more than probable that these actual discoveries were viewed by late Medieval European scholars as no more important than those of Pytheas or Brendan or other even more apocryphal explorers. Indeed, it may well be that many Europeans had access to information regarding the mythical earlier voyages but lacked any significant data on the Norse experience. A number of important late Medieval works such as Adam of Bremen's *Descriptio Insularum Aquilonis*, the *Inventio Fortunatae* by an English Minorite friar (probably Nicholas of Lynn), and Pierre d'Ailly's *Imago Mundi* contained geographical accounts and descriptions of lands west of Europe that were almost certainly based upon Norse geographical information, but the specifics of the Norse discovery of North America were probably not explicitly a part of mainstream European lore. The most concrete illustration of the paucity of Norse data in European lore is that those Medieval *mappaemundi* that portrayed the pre-Columbian explortory experiences in the Atlantic Ocean only rarely displayed Iceland, even more rarely Greenland and, with the exception of the still-controversial Vinland map, showed Vinland not at all.

Unlike the Norse voyages, which have a definite basis in historical fact but which may have had little significant impact on European lore, many other purported journeys of exploration during the Medieval period—nearly all of them apocryphal—did become an integral and specific part of the fund of knowledge available at the time of Columbus. Among the false voyages, two were the most durable and persistent in the literature and oral tradition of pre-Columbian Europe: the voyages of the Welsh prince Madoc ap Gwynedd, who supposedly fled internecine warfare in Wales by escaping across the Atlantic, where he discovered a "Great Land," and then returned to Wales to gather his followers and colonize North America in the twelfth century (Armstrong 1950; Deacon 1967); and the journey of the Venetian "Zenii," or the brothers Niccolo and Antonio Zeno, who reportedly visited the large and populated islands of Estotiland, Frisland, Drogeo, and others located south and west of Iceland and Greenland in the fourteenth century (Pohl 1961; Taylor 1964). Also a part of European lore of the late fifteenth century, and probably the only actual voyages in the dozen or so explorations reported in late Medieval literature between 1100–1492, were the two or three Portuguese voyages which, between 1432–53, discovered and colonized the Azores (Morison 1940). The persistence of tales of Madoc and the Zenii to this very day argues for a very long tradition in European geographical lore. With the exception of the Azorean discovery, however, few of these explorations received much print in manuscripts or published works until after the Columbian landfall, when all manner of European scholars began attempting to make the case for the prior discovery of the New World by their own countrymen. Similarly, late Medieval maps almost never illustrated the results of these voyages of exploration, although post-Columbian maps showing Madoc's "Great Land" and the island creations of the Zenii are not uncommon.

Although late Medieval maps did not often contain representations of the great actual voyages of Herjolfsson, Eiríksson, and other Norse explorers, or the apocryphal journeys of Madoc and the Zenii and others, they did portray much of the fictional geography that was part of the European world view of the fourteenth and fifteenth centuries. The northern Atlantic, in particular, was "filled by the imaginations of the coast-dwelling peoples of the Old World with fabulous and fantastic isles" (Wright 1965, 350). These "flyaway islands," often appearing on late Medieval maps, included the Fortunate Isles of antiquity (often

labeled as the "Hesperides"), the land of "Perdita" or the Lost Island which may have symbolized the great land reportedly discovered by Brendan, and the Isle of Satanazes, for which no one has yet found a satisfactory explanatory legend to justify its existence (Fig. 1). In addition to these mythical islands, two other Atlantic isles or island groups were often notably displayed on late Medieval maps; both of the these, the Isles of Antilia and the Isle of Hy-Brasil, also figured prominently in establishing the goals of Columbian and post-Columbian explorations. Some modern scholars have tried to make a case for Antilia and Hy-Brasil on the Medieval maps as representations of real geographical locations in the New World, proving pre-Columbian discoveries of North and South America (Cortesão 1953; Babcock 1922). This is most unlikely. In all probability, the Isles of Antilia were based upon the legend of the Portuguese archbishop who, with seven bishops and their followers, fled the Moorish invasions of Iberia by sailing westward into the Atlantic, where they built seven cities of gold and pearl and alabaster. Antilia appeared not only on maps but on the important Martin Behaim globe, which was probably the best representation of Europe's pre-Columbian world view. According to Morison, Columbus planned on using the Isles of Antilia as a "convenient staging point for the ocean route to the Indies" (Morison 1971, 101) and laid out his course across the Atlantic accordingly. The Isle of Hy-Brasil was almost certainly an Irish invention that predated even the Brendan legend; the name itself means Isle of the Blest in Gaelic. No one has yet located a literary source for this island, which was normally depicted on maps as a round island with an east-west strait running through its center, and was located on the Angelino Dulcert chart of 1325 (and many later fourteenth and fifteenth-century maps) westward off the Irish coast. An ancient oral tradition in Irish folklore claims that Hy-Brasil appears off the western Irish coast every seven years, a tradition highly similar to the legendary Isle of Avalon of the Arthurian cycle (also in the Celtic tradition). Both Antilia and Hy-Brasil were described late in the fifteenth century as goals of the first and second voyages of John Cabot or Giovanni Caboto, like Columbus a Genoese by birth, a naturalized Venetian citizen in English employ, who was the first European to touch North American shores since the Norse (Ruddock 1966). Both islands (but partic-

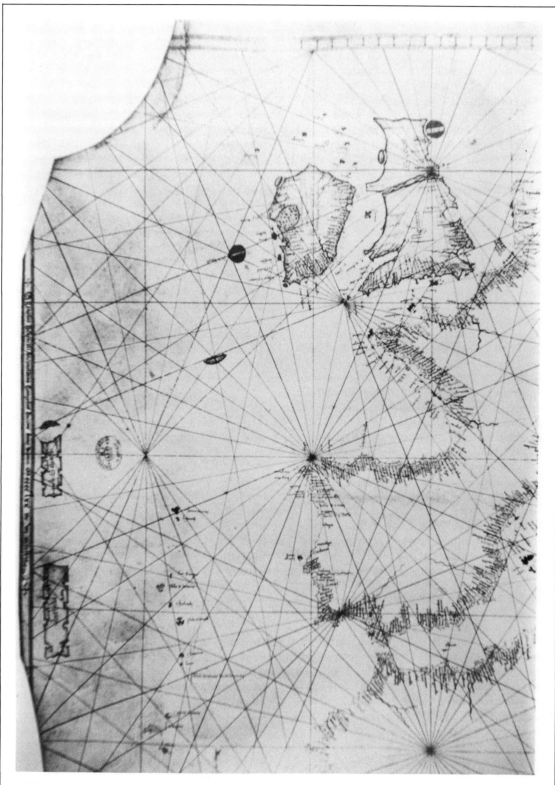

Figure 1. Islands of the Western Ocean; chart drawn by Andrea Benincasa, 1470. Courtesy of the British Museum, London.

ularly Hy-Brasil) were also exploratory objectives of Bristol voyagers who, some have argued, discovered North America not only before Cabot's landfall of 1497 but before Columbus as well (Quinn 1974).

According to a letter written in 1498 by an
English wine merchant calling himself "John
Day" (apparently an alias for Hugh Say; see
Ruddock [1966]) to a Spanish "Almirante
Mayor" (almost certainly Christopher Columbus), in 1497 an unnamed explorer sponsored
by England discovered a land in the western
Atlantic that Day identified with "the Island of
the Seven Cities" (Vigneras 1956; Williamson
1962; Quinn 1979). The explorer was John
Cabot, and the letter is an important historical
confirmation of the first verifiable North American landfall by a European since the Norse.
But the letter also presents evidence that an
English discovery of North America may have
preceded both Cabot and Columbus. In his
letter, Day wrote that the land (Newfoundland)
in the western Atlantic discovered by Cabot
"was found and discovered in other times by
the men of Bristol who found 'Brasil' as your
Lordship knows. It was called the Ysle of Brasil
and it is assumed and believed to be the mainland that the Bristol men found" (Quinn 1974,
6). Since the author of this letter seems to have
been a well-educated and knowledgeable person, and the letter itself is rational and nondog-
matic, two important conclusions may be
drawn from the portion of the Day letter in
which the writer refers to a Bristolian discovery: (1) Bristol sailors had, for some time, been
interested in pursuing westward exploration;
and (2) knowledge of a Bristol discovery of
North America sometime around 1480 may
have been, if not common, at least available to
certain interested parties (the phrase "as your
Lordship knows" in reference to a Bristolian
discovery is telling in this respect). Scholars
disagree over this latter conclusion, although
not over the authenticity of the letter itself.
David Beers Quinn (1961, 277–85; 1974, 17–23)
suggests that the letter may refer to an actual
exploratory event that preceded Columbus
and Cabot; Samuel Eliot Morison (1971, 208–
09) rejects Quinn's suggestion out-of-hand. I
am inclined to follow Quinn, that is, to keep
an open mind. The fact remains that in the
absence of additional supporting evidence[3] regarding the "men of Bristol" and an alleged
pre-Columbian and pre-Cabotian discovery of

North America, to John Cabot belongs the
honor of the first post-Norse North American
discovery. For the purposes of this essay, there
may be other and more relevant conclusions to
be drawn from the John Day letter: (1) knowledge of legendary Atlantic isles and other elements of imaginary geography, along with the
empirical geography of experience, played an
important role in the European world view of
the late fifteenth century; and (2) Europeans
interested in western discoveries communi-
cated with one another regarding the latest developments in the exploratory process, and
there was at least one important link between
Mediterranean and northern Europe. If these
conclusions are correct, then the basic assumption of John K. Wright that explorers go forth
"in quest of definite objectives believed to exist
on the basis of such information as could be
gathered from the geographical lore of their
own and earlier times" (Wright 1943, 20) is also
correct. It is that assumption upon which the
following discussion of early North American
discovery is based.

The English Discovery of North America: The Voyages of John and Sebastion Cabot

While there is evidence, in the form of the
John Day letter and other materials, that links
the Columbian enterprise with the first docu-
mentable English voyages by John Cabot and
his sons Sebastian, Lewis, and Sancius in 1495–
97, it would be a mistake to make too much of
this connection. As pointed out above, the
news of the initial Columbian landfall was met
with relative disinterest in England; the motives
of Cabot and his contemporaries were more
firmly based on what they already knew or
thought they knew of the western Atlantic, than
they were a "response" to Columbus's discoveries much farther south than the lands that
formed Cabot's goals. The Day letter and other
contemporary sources are conclusive in determining Cabot's goals as the "Isle of Brasil,"
well-established as lying due west of Ireland,
while the exploratory objectives of Columbus
were along a latitudinal line that would allow
taking advantage of the trade winds in an Atlantic voyage (Fuson forthcoming). On the
other hand, the letters of patent granted by
King Henry VII of England simply gave Cabot

full authority to "sail to all parts, regions and coasts of the eastern, western and northern sea . . . to find, discover and investigate whatsoever islands, countries, regions or provinces" (Williamson 1962, 204). Henry certainly did not suggest that Cabot avoid a southerly route across the Atlantic and, indeed, seemingly left such a route open to inquiry; but no evidence, documentary or otherwise, suggests that Cabot ever thought of sailing in any direction other than due west from Ireland. As nearly as his intent can be reconstructed from fragmentary records, it would seem that Cabot planned to sail west from Bristol, round Ireland to its west coast, and then sail toward the northwest by way of the Isle of Hy-Brasil where he "would come to India by a shorter route," probably by running southeast down the coast to make a landfall at Cipangu (Japan) and from thence to Cathay (China) and India (Ramusio 1563). This course would have him sailing the traditional northern European route used by Irish, Norse, and other real and imaginary voyagers to the islands of the Ocean Sea; in other words, he would follow the old Vinland course of the Greenlanders to the northwestern islands (Hy-Brasil or others), which presumably lay off the Asian coast.

The Day letter speculated that Cabot may have made a voyage in 1495 or 1496, prior to his 1497 voyage on which he discovered North America. Virtually nothing is known of this first voyage other than what Day reported: "He went with one ship, his crew confused him, he was short of supplies and ran into bad weather, and he decided to turn back" (Quinn 1979, 99). More information exists for Cabot's 1497 expedition in the small vessel *Matthew*, which left Bristol in May of that year. Day's letter offers some details of Cabot's 1497 journey, noting that the landfall was made on June 24, "1800 miles west of Dursey Head which is in Ireland" and that Cabot and his Bristolmen "landed at only one spot of the mainland [*terra firme*], near the place where land was first sighted . . . and they found tall trees of the kind masts are made, and other smaller trees, and the country is very rich in grass" (Quinn 1979, 98–99). The exact location of Cabot's landfall cannot be determined, but it was almost certainly in Newfoundland; Morison (1971) claims that it was near the l'Anse aux Meadows site of the short-lived Norse Newfoundland colony of nearly five centuries earlier, very unlikely given the

fact that the Norse colony was located in a treeless environment quite different from the land covered by "tall trees" described by Cabot. After more than a month of coasting without discovering a way through what Cabot probably viewed as an island archipelago to Asian shores beyond, he and his men returned to England. A letter from Raimondo de Soncino, an agent of the Duke of Milan resident in England, written to his master in late 1497 (after Cabot's return), supplies particulars on the conceptual geography arising from Cabot's discovery and on Cabot's plans for further exploration:

> Messer Zoane [Caboto] has his mind set upon even greater things, because he proposes to keep along the coast from the place at which he touched, more and more towards the east,[4] until he reaches an island which he calls Cipango, situated in the equinoctial region, where he believes that all the spices of the world have their origin as well as the jewels . . . By means of this they hope to make London a more important mart for spices than Alexandria. The leading men in this enterprise are from Bristol, and great seamen, and now they know where to go, say that the voyages will not take more than a fortnight, if they have good fortune after leaving Ireland (Quinn 1979, 97).

While the Day letter stipulated that the land Cabot discovered was "called the Island of Brasil, and it is assumed and believed to be the mainland that the men of Bristol found [in 1480?]," Soncino's letter makes it clear that Cabot's own geographical imagination had extended beyond the discovery of Hy-Brasil to "even greater things," viz., the discovery of a water route from Bristol to the Orient. Indeed, the reward granted Cabot by Henry VII was "to hym that founde the new Isle" (Quinn 1979, 95), suggesting that the English believed Cabot's discovery was *new* land rather than the illusory Isle of Brasil or even the old Isle of the Seven Cities (Antilia). In 1498, Cabot was given a second letter of patent by King Henry to further explore this new land and, with a fleet of five ships, departed Bristol for the northwest. Virtually nothing is known of this third westward voyage, except that, according to the words of a contemporary chronicler, Cabot was "believed to have found the new lands nowhere but on the very bottom of the ocean, to which he is thought to have descended together with his boat, the victim himself of that self-same ocean; since after that voyage he was never seen again anywhere" (Hay 1950, 117).

John Cabot's death did not destroy English

interest in pursuing the tantalizing glimpse of a route to Asia his first voyage had offered. Between 1501 and 1509, a series of Bristol voyages to "the new found island" were made, although little is known of these ventures other than that they represent the inauguration of English trade with indigenous peoples of North America and the initiation of the Newfoundland fishery (Ruddock 1974). Several letters of patent for Bristol merchants, allied with Portuguese Azoreans (most notably João Fernandes, who had rediscovered Greenland on a northwestern voyage in 1499 or 1500), give these western voyagers of "the Company of Adventurers into the New Found Lands" the rights to "have, enjoy and receive of the goods and wares to be brought from the said islands, mainlands and countries into this our realm of England," after the Crown had taken its share of half the proceeds (Quinn 1979, 104–05).[5] It is apparent that John Cabot's son Sebastian was active in this burgeoning trade with North America since he was granted a pension for "the good and gracious service . . . about the discovery of the new Land [circa invencionem nove terre]" (Ruddock 1974, 97). Whatever those services may have been, they paled in significance beside the second of the great Cabot voyages to North America, undertaken in 1508–09.

Little is known about Sebastian Cabot's voyage; the first recorded reference to it did not appear in the literature until 1516, when Peter Martyr (Pietro Martire d'Anghiera), dean of the Granada cathedral, published his De orbe novo decades (Decades of the New World), in which he related the latest information on the exciting discoveries that were being made in the western Atlantic (Arber 1971). Some authorities have even suggested that Cabot's 1508–09 voyage falls into the "supposed" class; Morison, for example, refers to Sebastian as "a genial and cheerful liar" (1971, 222). As with other such debatable excursions, whether Sebastian actually contacted North American shores on a 1508–09 journey is much less important than the presence, in the European geographical and exploratory literature upon which learned Europeans based their developing views of the newly discovered lands of the western Atlantic, of detailed and plausible reports of his voyage. According to Martyr, Sebastian followed his father's route across the Atlantic to around 55° N[6] and then turned southwest along the coast and past the "land

of the Bacallaos [codfish]" or Newfoundland. Not finding any opening through an unbroken coastline, Sebastian "extended his course furthermore to the southward owing to the curve of the coastline, so that his latitude was almost that of the Straits of Gibraltar and he penetrated so far to the west that he had the island of Cuba on his left hand almost in the same longitude with himself" (Williamson 1929, 71). If this account is true, then Sebastian was the first European to coast the Atlantic Seaboard from Canada to the Caribbean. Much more consequential was the report Cabot gave Martyr and other chroniclers of "the same flow of the waters to the west, although mild in force, as the Spaniards find in their passage to their southern possessions" (Williamson 1929, 71). Spanish explorers from Columbus on had reported a current bearing west, and Cabot had noted the same phenomenon. For learned men such as Peter Martyr and Giovanni Battista Ramusio (whose Navigationi et Viaggi rivaled Martyr's work as an accepted geographical authority), the conclusions were inescapable: Sebastian had discovered that another great continent lay to the north of the mainland of South America discovered by Columbus; through that continent or between the northern and southern continents, there were straits that penetrated to the sea that washed Cathay's shores. As Martyr put it, "it is not only probable but necessary to conclude that between those two lands hitherto unknown lie great straits which provide a passage for the waters flowing from east to west, which I judge to be drawn round by the attraction of the heavens in their rotation round the earth" (Quinn 1979, 124). If the inception of a specific geographical idea can ever be firmly pinpointed, the concept of the Northwest Passage upon which more than three centuries of North American exploration were to be predicated began with Sebastian Cabot's voyage and the publication of Martyr's De Orbe Nove Decades.

Portuguese Explorations in the Northwestern Atlantic

While the English were making their first contacts with North American shores, their chief competitors in the game of incipient empire were also active. Spain continued to concentrate her efforts to the south, from Cuba and Hispaniola to northern South America, although at least one Spanish letter of patent granted to the Spanish explorer Alonso de Ojeda "six leagues of land" in the island of Hispaniola "on account of what you shall discover on the coast of *Tierra Firme* for the stopping of the English" (Quinn 1979, 140). As far as is known, nothing came of Ojeda's patent. The Portuguese, on the other hand, were nearly as active as were the English in northwestern discoveries, in spite of their increasing economic emphasis on the circum-African trade route to India. Chief among the concerns of the Portuguese was forestalling English exploitation of lands that might have lain east of the line of the Treaty of Tordesillas and thus were considered to be in Portuguese territory. The Portuguese were also concerned, quite naturally, that this new western route might prove to be a shorter (and therefore more profitable) avenue to the Spice Islands than the newly-opened route around the Cape of Good Hope and should be kept in Portuguese control rather than falling to the English. It is also possible that Portuguese fishing was already active off the Grand Banks; hence the Portuguese might have had a commercial reason to limit the availability of their geographical information to others, particularly the English (Barkham 1982). For their part, the English do not seem to have ever been overly concerned with the treaty line of 1494 and letters of patent granted to English sailors only forewarned them about claiming lands "first discovered by the subjects of our very dear brother and cousin the king of Portugal" (Quinn 1979, 111).

There are some hints that Portuguese discoveries in the northwestern Atlantic may have taken place before 1500. The Azorean Portuguese João Fernandes and Pedro de Barcelos, who became associated with the Bristol merchants around 1501, indicated to their new partners in westward enterprises that they had discovered land in a high latitude east of John Cabot's landfall (Quinn 1979, 145); in all probability, this land was Greenland, but no documentary evidence of a Fernandes voyage thither has been found.[7] More solid evidence exists for a northern voyage by another Azorean Portuguese, Gaspar Corte Real, before 1500. The letter of patent issued by King Manoel I to Corte Real on May 12, 1500 notes that the Portuguese navigator had "made efforts in the past, on his own account and at his own expense, with ships and men, to search out, discover and find by dint of much labour

and expenditure of his wealth and at the risk of his life, some islands and a mainland" (Quinn 1979, 146). This suggests that a previous attempt by Corte Real had been undertaken; again no documentary evidence in the form of journals or ship's logs exists. In 1501, however, Corte Real made a documented voyage of discovery to North America. Sailing from Lisbon in May, the three ships of Corte Real's fleet traveled northwest until reaching pack ice and then steered west, where they caught site of

a very large country which they approached with very great delight. And since throughout this region numerous large rivers flowed into the sea, by one of these they made their way about a league inland, where on landing they found abundance of most luscious and varied fruits, and trees and pines of such measureless height and girth, that they would be too big as a mast for the largest ship that sails the sea (Quinn 1979, 148–49).

Like Cabot, Corte Real had probably reached Newfoundland; this is substantiated by the fact that the two ships of his fleet that returned to Lisbon (the other ship, with Corte Real on board, having suffered the same fate as John Cabot on his third voyage) carried with them approximately fifty Beothuk Indians from the Newfoundland coast who had been "forcibly kidnapped . . . [and] brought to the king" (Quinn 1979, 149). In the following year, 1502, Gaspar Corte Real's older brother Miguel was granted a letter of patent by Manoel I to go in search of the lands his brother had discovered and, hopefully, to learn something of Gaspar's fate. Unfortunately, like his brother, Miguel Corte Real did not return from his westward explorations; a third Corte Real expedition, led by Vasco Annes [Vaasqueanes], the eldest Corte Real brother and sole survivor of his generation of the family, was dispatched in 1503 but returned without having learned anything of the fates of either Gaspar or Miguel. With this failure, official Portuguese exploration in northwestern Atlantic waters ended, although the development of the Newfoundland fishery proceeded extremely rapidly throughout the following decades, and the Portuguese continued to refer to the Corte Real discoveries as *Terra do Corte Reals*.

The Early English Search for the Northwest Passage

By the end of the first decade of the sixteenth century, two apparently contradictory notions

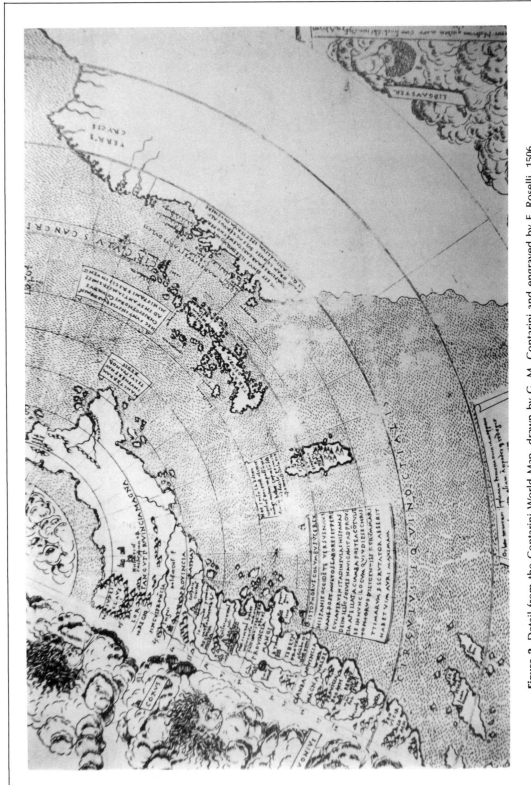

Figure 2. Detail from the Contarini World Map, drawn by G. M. Contarini and engraved by F. Roselli, 1506. Courtesy of the British Museum, London.

had developed relative to the lands discovered by the English and Portuguese in the northwestern Atlantic. It may well be that the English assumed that John Cabot's first landfall was a promontory of Asia; certainly the Portuguese understood that to be the case, and early cartographic representations of the English and Portuguese voyages to North America portrayed such a belief. The Alberto Cantino map, drawn in Lisbon in 1502, carried the following legend near what was probably Greenland: "This land . . . is believed to be the Point of Asia. Those who discovered it did not disembark, but saw on it jagged mountains. This is the reason, in the opinion of cosmographers, it is believed to be the point of Asia" (Harrisse 1900, 30; Quinn 1979, 149). And another legend, near what was probably Newfoundland, noted that "This land was discovered . . . by Gaspar de Corte Real, a gentleman of the king's household. He sent thence [to Lisbon] a ship with certain men and women which lived in this land and remained with his other ship and has not since returned. It is believed he perished. Here there are plenty of masts" (Harrisse 1900, 31; Quinn 1979, 149). The great Contarini world map of 1506, the first printed map to show any part of North America, also portrayed the lands discovered by Cabot and the Corte Reals as a promontory of Asia, part of the province of Tangut mentioned by Marco Polo (Cumming, et al. 1972, 53) (Fig. 2). At the same time as the Cantino and Contarini maps were depicting Greenland and Newfoundland as part of Asia, there was an increasing awareness of North America as *terra firma* or a mainland separate and distinct from Asia, probably as a result of the reports of Sebastian Cabot's voyage of 1508–09. Whether the northwestern Atlantic lands were part of Asia or an entirely new and previously-unknown continent, they posed a barrier to the easy passage of European merchants to the silk and spices of the Orient. The English, in particular, began a focused effort to find a way around or through that barrier.

Notwithstanding the flurry of Crown-sanctioned northwestern enterprises encompassing the Cabot explorations and those of the Bristol-Azorean Company of Adventurers and the promise that the Cabot discoveries held forth, there was a decline in official English concern in the northwestern Atlantic after the accession of Henry VIII to the English throne, as internal clerical politics began to assume dominance over external economic interests. But the unofficial (that is to say, private and commercial) desire for the discovery of a passage around or through Sebastian Cabot's apparently unbroken continental barrier continued as the locus of sponsorship of exploration shifted from Bristol to London. As early as 1517, there was an abortive attempt at northwestern exploration and even colonization (the first such attempt by England), led by a lawyer-printer-publisher named John Rastell. Rastell's venture never got beyond Waterford, Ireland and thus provided no new geographical data on the northwestern Atlantic lands or the passage to the "South Sea" (as the Pacific came to be known after Balboa's crossing of the Isthmus). But Rastell wrote an elaborate justification for English colonization of the newly discovered lands and contained within that argument was a stated belief in "certeyn poyntes of cosmography . . . of the cause of the ebbe and flode of the see" (Coleman 1971; Quinn 1979, 169). Rastell's treatise illuminates the early sixteenth-century English view of the Northwest Passage, which suggests, at least, an English belief in the "indrawing sea" configuration described in more detail by Peter Martyr in his description of Sebastian Cabot's voyage of 1508–09. That Martyr's conception of a continental landmass divided by sea-level straits connecting the Atlantic and Pacific (as derived from Sebastian Cabot) was current in England at this time can be substantiated by the fact that Cabot visited England in 1521 and attempted, with others, to obtain support from English merchants to finance a Northwest Passage voyage (Lyell 1936; Quinn 1979, 172–79). The effort failed, largely because the London merchants were unwilling to risk ships and funds on the strength of Sebastian Cabot's word that the northern continent and straits existed (Quinn 1979, 176).

The English necessity of a voyage in search of the Northwest Passage, however, derived further impetus from the knowledge, obtained in 1522, of Magellan's passage of Cape Horn and entry into the Pacific in 1519. The English believed Magellan's voyage conferred considerable trading advantages upon Spain, and the hope of a passage by sea through or to the north of the northern continent, a passage that would be easier than Magellan's tortured passing of the Cape, was renewed; in 1527 John Rut left England "to make a certaine exploration toward the north, between Labrador and Newfoundland, in the belief that in that region there was a strait through which to pass to Tartary" (Quinn 1974, 178–79). Rut's voyage in order "to go and discover the land of the Great Kahn" carried him to Labrador, Newfoundland, and down the Atlantic coast to the West Indies, and would seem to have been based upon the indrawing-seas concept of Martyr and Cabot (Quinn 1979, 192). But the passage by the northwest was not found; one of Rut's ships was lost near 53°N and, after proceeding some ten more futile degrees northward, Rut broke off the attempt and returned to England. By the time of Rut's exploration, some thirty years of English exploratory experience had accumulated without any valid or objective sighting of the indrawing sea or Northwest Passage. This fact had not diminished the strength of imaginary geography, and in the same year as Rut's voyage, an English merchant named Robert Thorne produced an elaborate theoretical justification for the continued belief in a passage to the Spice Islands around the northern end of North America (Taylor 1968; Quinn 1979). Addressing his theoretical statement to King Henry VIII, Thorne wrote: "There is left one way to discover, which is into the North; for that of the foure partes of the worlde, it seemeth three parts are discovered by other Princes"[8] (Quinn 1979, 180). In addition to waxing enthusiastic over the riches to be obtained by the English discovery of such a northern route, Thorne laid out his belief that the strait leading to Asia could best be found by sailing directly over the North Pole—this would be the shortest distance and, in Thorne's opinion, there was "no sea unnavigable" (Wright 1953, 339). Establishing by geometry that the shortest route to the "Spiceries" lay "over or across the Pole," Thorne concluded that "if from the sayd New found lands the Sea be navigable there is no doubt, but sayling Northward and passing the Pole, descending to the Equinoctial line, we shall hit these Islands, and it should be a much shorter way, than either the Spaniards or the Portingals have" (Quinn 1979, 187). Thorne's theoretical geography was supported by Roger Barlowe, an Englishman living in Spain who had accompanied Sebastian Cabot on a voyage to South America in 1526–28. In his "Briefe summe of geographie" (Taylor 1968; Quinn 1979) Barlowe repeated Thorne's sailing directions for an English route via the strait or indrawing sea which would lead to and across

the Pole, and climaxed his argument with the following: "And beside all this yet, the comoditie of this navigation by this waie is of so grete advantage over the other navigations in shorting of half the waie, for the other must saile by grete circuites and compasses and thes shal saile by streit wais and lines" (Quinn 1979, 216). Thorne's cosmography may have prompted a mysterious and obscure voyage by Captain Richard Hore of London, described as "a man of goodly stature and great courage, and given to the studie of cosmographie . . . who encouraged divers Gentlemen and others to accompany him in a voyage of discoverie upon the Northwest parts of America" (Burrage 1906, 106–10). With two ships, Hore left England in 1536 and sailed to Cape Breton and then to Newfoundland in search of the passage. In latitudes so high that "they sawe mightie Islands of yce in the sommer season," his company's food supply ran low, and the expedition was forced to return to England without having discovered the indrawing sea or strait to Asia (Quinn 1979, 208). This voyage marked the end, for several decades, of serious English attempts to locate the indrawing sea and the passage to Cathay. The first round of English efforts to define and circumvent the North American continent had died out in the icefields and the English gave up, for a time, the discovery of the short route to Asia by the northwest, having an image of the geography of eastern North America that was not much more accurate than that possessed by John and Sebastian Cabot (Wright 1953).

The French Intrusion: Verrazzano and Cartier

France was the last of the four great European maritime powers to take an active role in North American exploration, and its late entry[9] into the game may be attributed to a number of factors: it was less a seafaring nation than either England or Portugal; it had internal politics and boundaries to worry about, with the House of Hapsburg nibbling at French territory; and a series of wars with Spain and the Holy Roman Empire had caused military affairs to take precedence over maritime ones. In spite of the relative lateness of French involvement in the northwestern Atlantic, in many ways the French contributions in the third and fourth decades of the sixteenth century were the most productive in developing a reasonable base of geographical knowledge of eastern North America. Part of the reason for this lies in the fact that France was less encumbered by the baggage of mythical Atlantic isles in the northern ocean than was England. In addition, France's orientation to both the Mediterranean and the Atlantic gave it more access to both the information contributed by the Cabots and the Portuguese and that tendered by Spanish explorers in the Caribbean and along the southeastern coast of North America. Hence, for nearly four decades following Sebastian Cabot's seminal discoveries, most of the important exploration of the western borderlands of the North Atlantic were carried out by France, rather than by the English (to whom credit must be given for the initial exploration of North America) or the Spanish (who continued to be more occupied with their new empire of the south).

The Spanish, early in the sixteenth century, had sought a passage through the Caribbean, recognizing that the great current that flows into that sea along the north coast of South America had a westerly set and was identified by Columbus himself as a possible passage to the Pacific (Jameson 1905). This current encouraged a belief that North and South America were separate land masses on the grounds that such a volume of water must have an outlet. By the 1520s, however, Spanish and Portuguese exploration to the south had proven the existence of two major continental landmasses—North and South America—joined by a narrow isthmus which Balboa had crossed in 1513 and climbed a peak "from which he myght se the other sea so longe looked for, and never seen before by any man comynge owte of owre worlde" (Skelton, et al. 1965, 62). The discoveries of Balboa and others had shown the true position and form of the Atlantic coasts of Central and South America and of the Gulf coast of North America. The explorations of Ponce de Leon and of Pineda (1513–21) had proven that the Gulf of Mexico contained "no strait there by which ships could reach Asia" (Winsor 1889, 237). Knowledge of the northern continent in the opening years of the 1520s, on the other hand, was still inexact and speculative, as was any additional information regarding the "indrawing seas" of higher latitudes. Among the Spanish explorers, only Lucas Vas-

ques de Ayllón in 1521 had made any contact with the North American coast north of the Florida peninsula, and the reports of his voyages were inconclusive as to the details of coastal geography and the presence or absence of a sea-level strait through what was gradually taking shape on European maps as a continental land mass.

The initiative for North American exploration after Ayllón's journey fell, finally, to the French. The first major North American expedition, and the first serious attempt on the Northwest Passage north of the Caribbean since Sebastian Cabot, began in 1523 when Francis I officially entered the race toward Asia and dispatched an exploring expedition under the leadership of the Florentine navigator, Giovanni da Verrazzano (Wroth 1970; Bacchiani 1910). Verrazzano's stated intention in this voyage was:

> to reach Cathay and the extreme east of Asia, not expecting to find such an obstacle of new land as I found; and if for some reason I expected to find it, I thought it not to be without some strait to penetrate to the Eastern Ocean. And this has been the opinion of all the ancients, believing certainly our Western Ocean to be one with the Eastern Ocean of India without interposition of land. This Aristotle affirms, arguing by many similitudes, which opinion is very contrary to the moderns and according to experience untrue (Quinn 1979, 288).

More explicitly than many explorers, Verrazzano declared his unequivocal objective to be the Northwest Passage.

Sailing from the Normandy port of Dieppe (the later center of French geographical learning and of some of the most spectacular cartographic work the world has ever known) to the Madeiras, Verrazzano stayed somewhat north of the by-now-traditional Spanish trans-Atlantic route, made his landfall on the American coast in 34°N, and coasted first south and then north of that landfall "with the continual hope of finding some strait or true promontory at which the land would end toward the north in order to be able to penetrate to those blessed shores of Cathay" (Bacchiani 1910, 200). The actual extent of his coastal voyage is difficult to reconstruct from his records (no ship's log has survived), but it is a virtual certainty that the Florentine navigator saw a good deal of the Atlantic coast from the Carolina Low Country to northern New England and provided Europe, via his letter to Francis I describing his voyage, with its first detailed description of North America.

His landscape descriptions were lyric, evoking memories of the *Insulae Fortunatae:*

> We could see a stretch of country much higher than the sandy shore, with many beautiful fields and plains full of great forests, some sparse and some dense; and the trees have so many colors, and are so beautiful that they defy description . . . .And these trees emit a sweet fragrance over a large area . . . .We think that they belong to the Orient by virtue of the surroundings, and that they are not without some kind of narcotic or aromatic liquor . . . .The air is salubrious and pure, and free from the extremes of heat and cold; gentle winds blow in these regions, and the . . . .sea is calm and unruffled, its waves gentle (Quinn 1979, 282).

Verrazzano was also the first European explorer of North America to interact significantly with the indigenous people, although the extent to which they may have provided him geographical information is not evident from his letter (Lewis forthcoming). Nevertheless, inhabiting the blissful landscape that Verrazzano depicted were peoples patterned after the Happy Hyperboreans of classical lore: "When sowing they observe the influence of the moon, the rising of the Pleiades, and many other customs derived from the ancients . . . .They live a long time, and rarely fall sick; if they are wounded, they cure themselves with fire without medicine; their end comes with old age. We consider them very compassionate and charitable toward their relatives" (Quinn 1979, 286). Not all the vast land Verrazzano coasted, of course, was so blissful. Toward the north the coasts grew more rocky and barren (although still frequently described as "beautiful") and the people "full of crudity and vices, and were so barbarous that we could never make any communications with them" (Quinn 1979, 287). But, on balance, it was a happy land and many later European images of the Garden of the World and of the precontact "golden age" of indigenous populations in North America may be traced, directly or indirectly, to Verrazzano.

Although Verrazzano failed in his objective to find a passage through the northern continent, and missed many important geographical features (such as Chesapeake and Delaware bays) on his coastal voyage, his exploration made significant contributions to geographical knowledge in that he filled the gap, more or less, between the Spanish ventures to the south and the English and Portuguese enterprises to the north (Hoffman 1964). The configuration of North America as a promon-

tory of Asia would continue to appear on maps for the next two centuries, but Verrazzano's letter to the King of France was firm on this point and bolstered the growing conviction among the best French and English geographers that North America was a separate continent: "All this land or New World which we have described above is joined together, but is not linked with Asia or Africa (we know this for certain)" (Quinn 1979, 288). In Verrazzano's geography, the fact that North America was known "for certain" to be a continent did not mean that it could not be broached and that his initial objective of "those blessed shores of Cathay" could not eventually be attained in a later voyage. It is one of the unfortunate ironies of exploratory history that much of Verrazzano's excellent and detailed description of the North American continental margins has been overshadowed by his one great geographical mistake. While coasting along the outer banks of North Carolina, the Florentine navigator (who was, after all, searching for a route to the South Sea) looked across the sandy bars toward Pamlico Sound and, not seeing the mainland beyond, believed he was gazing on the Pacific. The conjectural geography that emerged from this view included a narrow isthmus of land around the 34th parallel, beyond which lay the South Sea or Pacific. This isthmus mirrored the one discovered by Balboa farther south and suggested that, if a sea-level strait could be found through it, the passage through to the Pacific would be a short one. Verrazzano's "isthmus" played a major role in the subsequent geographical interpretations of North America by English and French geographers.[10] And even though the voyage of Estevão Gomes, sailing along the North American Atlantic coast for Spain in 1525 and having "no other thing in charge than to search out whether any passage to the great Chan, from out the diuers windings and vast compassings of this our Ocean were to be founde" (Martyr 1612, fol. 246), proved there was no strait south of the forty-fifth parallel, Verrazzano's geographical data, including representations of great straits through the North American continent, would haunt theoretical geography and cartography for a century and more (Cumming, et al. 1972) (Fig. 3).

Verrazzano's failure to discover a strait through the continent between Florida and New England (even though his "isthmus" hinted at its possibility) caused the second

Figure 3. Detail from the Planisphere made by Juan Vespucci, 1526. Courtesy of the Hispanic Society, New York.

significant French explorations in search of the passage, and the last French efforts for many years, to be directed farther north, beyond his furthest advance. Thus did France miss the ripe opportunity, given the English unwillingness or inability to mount significant explorations during this period, to exploit the vast riches of the Atlantic Seaboard of what became the U.S. But these next French explorations, led by Jacques Cartier, a St. Malo pilot and perhaps France's most competent explorer-navigator-cartographer, and Jean-François de la Roque, sieur de Roberval (Protestant, aristocrat, and considerably less proficient than Cartier), from 1534–43, were responsible for the creation of France's overseas American empire which, if not as rich as the lands they overlooked, still brought great wealth to France until the middle of the eighteenth century. The Cartier-Roberval explorations were also the first continental penetrations of North America and brought about a major restructuring in the cartography of the continent.

The first Cartier voyage of 1534 was designed to follow up on the lead Verrazzano had provided regarding a passage to the Pacific and "to discover certain islands and lands where it is said a great quantity of gold and other precious things are to be found" (Biggar 1930, 42). Departing St. Malo with two ships, Cartier followed both Cabot's sailing directions and those of the Breton fisherman who were by then actively exploiting the Newfoundland codfishery. He reached the eastern Newfoundland coast only twenty days out from France, near where both John Cabot and the Norse voyagers had made their landfalls. From his landfall, he turned northwest, passed through the Straits of Belle Isle between Newfoundland and Labrador and, over the summer months of 1534, made a great clockwise reconnaissance around the Gulf of St. Lawrence. Like Verrazzano, he found much to be enthusiastic about in the character of the land he explored, describing territories adjacent to the Gulf as "the finest land one can see, and full of beautiful trees and meadows" (Quinn 1979, 298) with "fields of wild corn and peas in bloom as thick and fair as any you can see in Brittany" (Cumming, et al. 1972, 73). "By reason of the great depth and breadth of the gulfe," Cartier commented, "we conceived hope that we should finde a passage [to the Pacific]" (Burrage 1906, 18); such was not to be, however,

and in August 1534, Cartier and his ships returned to France. Henceforth, French explorations would be focused on the area in and around the Gulf of St. Lawrence and up the great river which offered a key to the geography of the interior.

On his second voyage of 1535, Cartier sailed with a larger fleet of three ships and with the injunction of his French Majesty to improve geographical knowledge of the region beyond Newfoundland "and on this voyage to endeavor to do and accomplish that which it has pleased the said Lord King to command and order you to do," that is, to find both riches and a passage to the Sea of the South (Morison 1971, 388). Entering the Gulf of St. Lawrence via his earlier route of the Strait of Belle Isle, Cartier sailed along the northern coast of the Gulf and into the St. Lawrence proper "because he would know if between the lands any passage [to the Pacific] might be discovered" (Burrage 1906, 42). He sailed up the river as far as the Indian town called "Hochelega" on the site of present-day Montreal, before determining that the river was not a sea-level strait. But he did learn that the river "went so farre upwards, that they never heard of any man who had gone to the end therof" (Burrage 1906, 42) and learned of a huge lake of "illy-smelling water" (by which he took to mean salt-water) which lay many days' journey to the west and another great river "which commeth from the West" (Burrage 1906, 63). Cartier's second voyage was the first noteworthy continental penetration of North America north of Mexico, and it set the feet of French explorers on a different path from those of other European nations. After Cartier, French exploration in search of both the Northwest Passage and exploitable riches would focus on the river and lake systems of the continental interior, thereby providing both a theoretical and an experiential basis for much of North American exploration well into the nineteenth century (Allen 1975b).

The continental basis of further French interest was evidenced by the goal of Cartier's third North American voyage. Having learned from a Huron chief named Donnaconna of an immensely rich (but purely mythical) kingdom of Saguenay which lay north of the Indian town of Stadacone (present Québec City), Cartier and his sponsors determined that a subsequent expedition should undertake the search for Saguenay, where there were "many mines of gold and silver in great abundance, and men who dress and wear shoes like we do; and that there is abundance of clove, nutmeg and pepper" (Quinn 1979, 329). That Saguenay just happened to lie on the same route toward the west where "would be found a passage to the other southern ocean" only sharpened the French exploratory appetite and, after what must have been a frustrating delay of five years, Cartier's third North American expedition departed France in May, 1541, bound for the discovery of Saguenay and the establishment of a French colony to exploit the promised riches of what France hoped would be their equivalent of Mexico or Peru. This third expedition was, ostensibly, a joint venture with the Sieur de Roberval, who would also lead a force to the St. Lawrence region and would be, at least in name, the supreme commander of this first French enterprise to attempt colonization in North America.

Roberval did not leave France until nearly a year after Cartier's 1541 departure, by which time Cartier's searches for Saguenay and the Passage and his attempts to establish a colony on the St. Lawrence had failed miserably. Arriving in North America in August 1541, Cartier and his fleet sailed up the St. Lawrence to Stadacone (Québec City), where they built a rude fort that would serve as the center of the first (albeit temporary) settlement of New France. Leaving most of his command at Québec, Cartier penetrated inland via the Saguenay River in search of the mythical kingdom. It did not take more than a month to realize that Saguenay was a geographical will-o'-the-wisp, and he returned to the colony. Although detailed records of the winter at Québec have not survived, it was apparently miserable, with attacks by the Huron and the onset of scurvy. Roberval, who was supposed to join Cartier at this site, had not showed up by spring; short of supplies, having lost many settlers during the winter, and concerned over the failure of Roberval to meet him, Cartier and his colonists abandoned their settlement in 1542. Sailing down the St. Lawrence, they met Roberval and his three ships, laden with supplies, at the harbor of St. John's, Newfoundland. Cartier attempted to convince Roberval to give up any attempt at colonization and return to France; when Roberval refused, Cartier and his fleet left the New World for good. Roberval, after his own abortive year-long attempt at finding Saguenay and a passage to the Pacific and establishing a colony, followed Cartier's lead in abandoning Canada in 1543. The early French efforts to explore and settle North America had ended in failure.

The expeditions of Cartier and Roberval, although not resulting in tangible immediate benefits for Francis I, were extremely significant for European geographical knowledge of North America. They reinforced much existing geographical information which continued to support the geographical proximity of North America and Asia and the theory of a passage from Atlantic to Pacific waters around or through the northern end of the new-found lands. A Portuguese report on Cartier's third voyage of 1541–42 noted that the great river entered by Cartier "is very long . . . and that on the other side it empties itself into a great sea" (Quinn 1979, 135), while the report of Jean Allfonce, Roberval's pilot, noted that the Saguenay River, shortly above its mouth at the St. Lawrence, "widens after two or three leagues, and begin to take on the character of an arm of the sea, for which reason I estimate that this sea leads to the Pacific Ocean or even to *la mer du Cattay*" (Morison 1971, 451). And another Portuguese report of the Cartier-Roberval venture repeated, in spite of French failure, the tales of mythical Saguenay and the passage to the Pacific:

> Greatly praising the rich novelty of the land and telling these and other tales; and that there are men who fly, having wings on their arms like bats, although they fly but little, from the ground to a tree, and from tree to tree to the ground. And the said Jacques brought to the King a sample of gold, ten or twelve stones shaped like small goose quills, and he says it is fine gold and comes from the said city of Sagana. And he believed that by this river would be found a passage to the other southern ocean (Quinn 1979, 329).

Conclusion: A Continent Defined

The Cartier-Roberval experiences represent an ending to the first phase of exploration in North America. Beginning with the first discoveries of John Cabot, motivated more by Medieval fancies than by accurate geographical lore, European exploration of eastern North America had, in less than half a century, provided a wealth of geographical detail on a New World. Geographical misconceptions and myths still were present—the continuing belief in the

Indian "kingdoms" in the interior up to the eighteenth century are witness to that fact. The coastal outlines on period maps were still vague and less than accurate and some major geographical features, such as Chesapeake Bay and the Cabot Straits, had yet to be discovered. The names the early Europeans gave to geographical features were transitory, and few have remained to the present to remind us of that brilliant early period from 1497–1543. The English, Portuguese, and French who explored North America did not establish permanent settlements to rival those of Spain in the Caribbean and Central America. And the hopes and dreams of those who left European ports for North American landfalls were most often unattained. Yet, in spite of failures and frustra-

tions, the period from Cabot to Cartier was one of remarkable achievement. Exploratory accounts were printed in numerous contemporary works such as those of Ramusio and Hakluyt and illustrated in the maps drawn by Gerhardus Mercator and others (Fig. 4). Even into the seventeenth century, much of what was known or believed to be known about eastern North America derived from this earliest exploratory period. Finally, the period from Cabot to Cartier produced an evolution of European cartographic representation of lands west of Europe, from the first primitive depictions of islands off the Asian coast or North America as a promontory of Asia in the early sixteeth century to the brilliant and detailed maps of the Dieppe school of French cartogra-

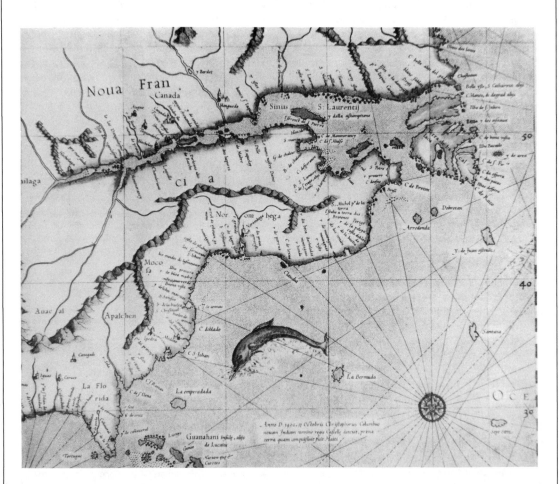

Figure 4. Detail from the Mercator World Map, drawn by G. Mercator in 1569. Courtesy of the Prins Hendrik Maritiem Museum, Rotterdam.

in the minds of those who read them, a continent was defined. And if for no other reason, this early period of exploratory endeavor was one of the most remarkable in the annals of the world. After Cartier, European interest in North America in general or the Northwest Passage in particular waned temporarily, largely as the result of the internal dynamics of a European society beset by economic and political upheaval and by religious warfare. But when European interest in North American exploration was reawakened by men such as John Dee, Sir Humphrey Gilbert, and Sir Walter Raleigh of Elizabethan England, the contributions to geographical lore made by the European explorers from Cabot to Cartier were fundamental in a new period of northern European involvement in North American affairs—an involvement that culminated in the planting of the colonies that would come to occupy a center stage in the development of the world system of our own time.

Notes

1. Columbus, of course, "discovered" a world that was hardly "new" to its millions of inhabitants whose ancestors made the initial "discovery" of North America via the land bridge across Beringia during the waning centuries of the Pleistocene. Nevertheless, from the standpoint of European geographical knowledge (the perspective of this paper), the Columbian contact of 1492 truly represented a discovery in that the "New World" was indeed unknown to European science.
2. Most of this paper relies on documentary evidence and primary materials from the period before Columbus up through the mid-sixteenth century. Fortunately for scholars pursuing studies of early North American exploration, a remarkable five-volume collection of documentary materials pulls together formerly widely scattered published and manuscript sources and offers, in many instances, new translations from older and less accurate renderings into English from the Spanish, French, Portuguese, Dutch, and other European languages: *New American World: A Documentary History of North America to 1612* (Quinn 1979).
3. There is some sketchy supporting evidence. In the civil records of Bristol is a document indicating that one Thomas Croft, a customs official of the port city, sent two ships in 1480 "to serch & fynde a certain Isle called the Isle of Brasile." There is no corroborating ship's journal or log, however (Quinn 1934, 283).
4. Writers of the time used the phraseology "towards the east" when they meant "in the direction of the Orient." Thus Soncino's comment on Cabot's future plans does not suggest an easterly course but a westerly one toward Japan or "Cipango."
5. Samuel Eliot Morison claims (1971, 218) that these letters of patent specifically instruct the "Adventurers" to ignore the claims of other European maritime powers to western lands and locate a strait to Asia. They do nothing of the sort; rather, Henry's patent to Hugh Eliot, Thomas Ashehurst, and others instructs them to "in no wise occupy themselves with nor enter the lands, countries, regions or provinces . . . first discovered by the subjects of our very dear brother and cousin the king of Portugal, or by the subjects of any other princes soever, our friends and confederates." And there is absolutely no mention of a "strait" or Northwest Passage; that geographical idea does not take shape until after the voyage of Sebastian Cabot in 1508–09.
6. A later sixteenth-century account (Ramusio 1563) puts Cabot's northernmost course at $67^1/2°$N. This would seem to be way too far north.
7. The name "Labrador" was stuck on Greenland by some period cartographers. Morison and other authorities believe the name came from João Fernandes' Portuguese title of *lavrador* or "landholder." In any event, "lavrador" soon became "Labrador" and migrated westward to the North American main where, regionally, residents still refer not to "Labrador" but "the Labrador" as the appellation for that part of Canada.
8. Sixteenth-century geographers followed the classical Cartesian division of the habitable world into four quarters; it is this division that Thorne refers to as "the foure partes of the worlde." His reference to "three parts" having been discovered would seem to refer to the three known routes from Europe to the Orient: around the Cape of Good Hope to India, west across the Atlantic to the Isthmus and thence across to the Pacific, and southwest around Cape Horn and into the Pacific.
9. There was at least one French voyage to North America early in the sixteenth century, probably in 1504. A report from one Eusebius of Caesarea (1512) noted that a Breton ship had returned from "Terre-Neuve" with "seven savage men." Some other chronicles refer to periodic Breton fishing voyages between 1500–25 to Newfoundland. But these were far from official exploring voyages and did not have the sanction of the government (indeed, they probably went unnoticed for the most part).
10. As late as 1650, an important English map of the Virginia colony (drawn by John Farrar and published in Edward Williams's *Virgo Triumphans; or, Virginia richly and truly valued*) showed "The Sea of China and the Indies" only a short distance west of the Atlantic coast—just beyond the Blue Ridge Mountains.

References

Allen, J. L. 1972. An analysis of the exploratory process. *Geographical Review* 62:13–39.

———. 1975a. Lands of myth, waters of wonder.

In *Geographies of the mind,* ed. M. J. Bowden and D. Lowenthal, pp. 41–62. New York: Oxford University Press.

———. 1975b. *Passage through the garden.* Urbana and London: University of Illinois Press.

Arber, E., ed. 1971. *The first three English books on America.* New York: Krause Reprint Co.

Armstrong, Z. 1950. *Who discovered America?* Chattanooga, TN: Lookout Press.

Ashe, G. 1962. *Land to the west.* New York: Viking Press.

Babcock, W. A. 1922. *Legendary islands of the Atlantic.* New York: American Geographical Society.

Bacchiani, A. 1910. Giovanni da Verrazana and his discoveries in North America made in 1524. In *15th annual report of the American Scenic and Historic Preservation Society,* trans. E. H. Hall, app. A, pp. 135–226.

Barkham, Selma. 1982. Documentary evidence for 16th-century Basque whaling ships in the Strait of Belle Isle. In *Early European settlement and exploration in Atlantic Canada,* ed. G. M. Story, pp. 53–96. St. John's, NFD: Memorial University.

Biggar, H. P. 1930. *A collection of documents relating to Jacques Cartier and the Sieur de Roberville.* Publication 14. Ottawa: Canadian National Archives.

Boland, C. M. 1961. *They all discovered America.* New York: Doubleday.

Bunbury, E. H. 1957. *A history of ancient geography.* 2 vols. New York: Dover Publications.

Burrage, H. S. 1906. *Early English and French voyages, 1534–1608.* New York: American Historical Society.

Coleman, R. 1971. *The four elements.* Cambridge: Cambridge University Press.

Cortesão, A. J. 1953. The nautical chart of 1424. *Imago Mundi* 10:1–13.

Cumming, W. P.; Skelton, R. A.; and Quinn, D. B. 1972. *The discovery of North America.* New York: American Heritage Press.

Deacon, R. 1967. *Madoc and the discovery of America.* London: G. Braziller.

Elliott, J. H. 1970. *The Old World and the New, 1492–1650.* Cambridge: Cambridge University Press.

Fuson, R. H. Forthcoming. The Columbian voyages. In *North American Exploration,* vol. 1, ed. J. L. Allen. Lincoln: University of Nebraska Press.

Glacken, Clarence. 1967. *Traces on the Rhodian shore.* Berkeley: University of California Press.

Goetzmann, W. H. 1986. *New lands, new men: America and the second great age of discovery.* New York: Viking Penguin.

Harrisse, H. A. 1900. *Découverte et évolution cartographique de Terre-Neuve.* Paris: E. Leroux.

Hay, D. 1950. *The Anglia Historia of Polydore Vergil.* London: Longmans.

Hoffman, G. 1964. *From Cabot to Cartier.* Toronto: University of Toronto Press.

Ingstad, A. S. 1985. *The Norse discovery of America.* Oslo, Norway: Norwegian University Press.

Jameson, J. F. 1905. *The northmen, Columbus, and Cabot.* New York: American Historical Society.

Jones, G. 1986. *The Norse Atlantic saga.* New York: Oxford University Press.

Lewis, G. Malcolm. Forthcoming. Native North Americans' cosmological ideas and geographical awareness: Their representation and influence on early European exploration and geographical knowledge. In *North American exploration,* vol. 1, ed. J. L. Allen. Lincoln: University of Nebraska Press.

Lyell, L., ed. 1936. *Acts of Court of the Mercers' Company, 1453–1527.* Cambridge: Cambridge University Press.

MacPherson, A. J. Forthcoming. Pre-Columbian discoveries and exploration of North America. In *North American exploration,* vol. 1, ed. J. L. Allen. Lincoln: University of Nebraska Press.

Martyr, Peter. 1612. *Decades of the New World.* Trans. M. Lok. London: T. Adams.

Morison, S. E. 1940. *Portuguese voyages to America in the fifteenth century.* Cambridge: Harvard University Press.

———. 1971. *The European discovery of America: The northern voyages, A.D. 500–1600.* New York: Oxford University Press.

Oleson, T. J. 1964. *Early voyages and northern approaches.* London: Oxford University Press.

O'Meara, J. J. 1976. *The voyages of St. Brandan.* Dublin: Dolmen Press.

Pohl, F. J. 1961. *Atlantic crossings before Columbus.* New York: T. Y. Crowell.

Quinn, D. B. 1961. The argument for the English discovery of America between 1480 and 1494. *Geographical Journal* 127:277–85.

———. 1934. Edward IV and exploration. *Mariner's Mirror* 21:275–84.

———. 1974. *England and the discovery of America.* London: George Allen & Unwin, Ltd.

———. 1979. *New American world: A documentary history of North America to 1612,* vol. 1. New York: Arno Press.

Ramusio, G. B. 1563. *Navigationi et Viaggi.* Venice.

Ruddock, A. A. 1966. John Day of Bristol and the English voyages across the Atlantic before 1497. *Geographical Journal* 132:225–33.

———. 1974. The reputation of Sebastian Cabot. *Bulletin of the Institute of Historical Research* 67:97.

Skelton, R. A.; Marston, T.; and Painter, G. 1965. *The Vinland Map and Tartar relation.* New Haven, CT: Yale University Press.

Taylor, E. G. R. 1968. *Tudor geography, 1485–1583.* New York: Octagon Books.

———. 1964. A fourteenth century riddle and its solution. *Geographical Review* 54:573–76.

Tillinghast, W. H. 1889. The geographical knowledge of the ancients. In *Narrative and critical history of America,* ed. Justin Winsor, vol. 1, pp. 1–59. Boston: Houghton-Mifflin.

Vigneras, L. A. 1956. New light on the 1497 Cabot voyage. *Hispanic-American Historical Review* 36:507–09.

Williamson, J. A. 1962. *The Cabot voyages and Bristol discovery under Henry VII.* Cambridge: Cambridge University Press.

———. 1929. *The Cabot voyages.* London: Argonaut Press.

Winsor, J. 1889. *Narrative and critical history of America,* vol. 2. Boston: Houghton-Mifflin.

Wright, J. K. 1943. Where history and geography meet: Recent American studies in the history of exploration. *Proceedings of the Eighth American Scientific Congress* 9:17–23.

———. 1947. Terrae incognitae: The place of the imagination in geography. *Annals of the Association of American Geographers* 37:1–15.

———. 1953. The open Polar Sea. *Geographical Review* 43:338–65.

———. 1965. *Geographical lore of the time of the Crusades.* New York: Dover Publications.

Wroth, L. C. 1970. *The voyages of Giovanni da Verrazzano, 1524–1528.* New Haven, CT: Yale University Press.

Rereading the Maps of the Columbian Encounter

J. Brian Harley*

Department of Geography, University of Wisconsin, Milwaukee, WI 53201

Abstract. Maps of the Encounter have been judged by the agenda of a positivist geographical history seeking to reconstruct the pathways, landing places, and settlements of European explorers and discoverers. They were studied largely for their practical use as tools of navigation, as aids to wayfinding on land, as plans for new colonial fortifications and towns, or as public propaganda images to attract new settlers to America. This paper argues that Native American mapping belongs in the cartographic record of the Encounter, and that European maps of the period can be viewed as statements of territorial appropriation, cultural reproduction, or as devices by which a Native American presence could be silenced. Recent studies in anthropology, art history, and ethnohistory identify a corpus of indigenous maps that represent valid "alternative" cartographies, different from European maps, yet important in the history of spatial representation. In Mesoamerica, further decoding of cartographic elements in the pre-Conquest genealogical and historical manuscripts may well require revision of ideas about the cradles of cartographic innovation. Even in North America, where such artifacts are more fragmentary, there is a growing sense of the universal presence of mapping in a wide range of cultures. In Colonial America, Indian maps not only helped to guide the invaders, but Indian geographies were incorporated into the fabric of European maps that would become standard images of America for much of the sixteenth and seventeenth centuries. There also appears to be an ideological transformation in the indigenous use of maps as native peoples sought to resist Colonial power with the maps that were once part of their traditional culture.

Key Words: European imperialism, indigenous cartographies, colonial policy, religious iconography, place-names and naming, anticipatory geography.

> . . . [in Europe] wee have the right of Lawes, the dignity of the Christian Religion, the force of Armes . . . Moreover, Europe manageth all Arts and Sciences with such dexterity, that for the invention of manie things shee may be truely called a Mother . . . shee hath . . . all manner of learning, whereas other countries are all of them, overspread with Barbarisme.
>
> —Gerardus Mercator (1968 [1595])

THE geographical explorations of Europeans in the fifteenth and sixteenth centuries—together with the new cartography that was linked to these events—go to the heart of the Columbian Encounter. Yet in 1992, as we observe the 500th anniversary of Columbus's First Voyage to America, the mood has changed from the Euro-centered celebrations that were a hallmark of 1892, to one of critical reflection. For Europeans, their earliest printed and manuscript maps of the New World had become "super-icons" by the nineteenth century, visible witnesses to the success of their predecessors in extending their just civilization and political dominion beyond the geographical limits of the Ancient and Medieval world. Indeed, in many cases, the earliest maps that show the Americas have acquired a canonical status (Fite and Freeman 1926; Nebenzahl 1990). Such maps have become reified signs that tend always to say the same thing about the heroes of the great voyages (Morison 1971,

*Deceased 20 December, 1991. Text edited by Karl W. Butzer and William M. Denevan.

Annals of the Association of American Geographers. 82(3), 1992, pp. 522–542
© Copyright 1992 by Association of American Geographers

1974) or the achievements of the European colonization in the New World.

In attempting to reread these maps as an act of geographical decolonization (Huggan 1989), I take my directions from two current debates. The first is about the significance of 1492 and its meaning in American history. The second is a debate about the nature of maps and their historical claims to truth as representations of the world. After introducing the scope of these two debates, I will show how they can intersect to contribute to a rereading of the maps of the Columbian Encounter.[1] Next I will introduce an ethnohistorical perspective on sixteenth- and seventeenth-century mapping of the Americas, and finally return to the European maps of the encounter to reveal something of their ideological underpinnings, both as overt symbols of European imperialism and also as a record of the political unconscious.

1492 History and 1992 Maps: Two Contemporary Debates

Of the two debates that frame this discussion, the first—about the meaning of 1492, its consequences, and its relevance to the modern world—is the more strident. The voices of revision are presently loudest in seeking to unmask what they perceive to be the false consciousness of historiography centered on the European experience. Everyone is in agreement that 1492 was a turning point in history (McNeill 1985), yet the consequences are perceived to be contentious. In the case of Spain, we remember 1492 as the year when Jews and Moors were so cruelly expelled, instead of the end of the glorious *reconquista*. For Mexico, we are reminded not of its "discovery" but of its "invention" (O'Gorman 1961). Instead of a history of Europeans in America, we are now concerned with an ethnohistory (Axtell 1981, 1985; Hoxie 1988). Instead of a benign colonization of America, we are now invited to perceive a European invasion or conquest, with different cultures engaged in a struggle of imposition and appropriation (Jennings 1975; Mignolo 1989; Todorov 1984). Instead of Columbus the heroic figure, we now read about the Columbian legacy of environmental destructiveness (Sale 1990). Instead of the peopling of the New World by Europeans, we now confront the seeds of racism and the enslavement and genocide of the Indian and African peoples (Carew 1988). As Mario Vargas Llosa puts it in a recent issue of *Harper's*: "Was the discovery and conquest of America by Europeans the greatest feat of the Christian West or one of history's monumental crimes?" (1990, 46).[2]

The second debate is about the nature of maps. Though at first sight it may seem to have little bearing on the events of 1492, this debate also has the power to radicalize the past. Since the 1970s the teleological notion of cartography as a scientific discipline, with a progressive trajectory from the Renaissance to the late twentieth century, has been challenged. This challenge has come not only from a more humanistic turn in cartography (Wood and Fels 1986; Szegö 1987), but also from other disciplines, such as art history (Edgerton 1987) and comparative literature, as scholars have turned to maps among other "texts" and forms of representation (Boelhower 1984, 41–53; 1988; Helgerson 1986; Clarke 1988).

Under attack is a standard scientific model of knowledge and cognition for cartography (Harley 1989). In place of this assessment of cartography is one in which all maps, like all other historically constructed images, do not provide a transparent window on the world. Rather they are signs that present "a deceptive appearance of naturalness and transparence concealing an opaque, distorting, arbitrary mechanism of representation, a process of ideological mystification" (Mitchell 1986, 8).

It is the thrust of this second debate, coupled with the critique of traditional "discovery" history, that can come together in a rereading of the maps of the Columbian Encounter. The point of intersection is one of historical conjunction: when Europeans were mapping America for the first time, a new paradigm in cartography was simultaneously being diffused. The series of innovations—in surveying, instruments, map projections, printing (Wallis and Robinson 1987)—that characterize the Renaissance and the scientific revolution would later lead to cartographic modernity. They also established an ideological shift in ways of viewing the world.

For the nation states of early modern Europe, the consequences of the new cartography were empowering (Hale 1971, 52–53). Similarly, were it not for the new maps, America would hardly have entered the European consciousness and could not have been colonized in the way it was. We have only to compare some of the *mappaemundi* of the fifteenth century (Woodward 1987) with the rediscovered world maps of Ptolemy, complete with their graticule of latitude and longitude, to see how radically the rules of cartographic vision had changed. This new "scopic regime" with its "privileging of the visual" (Jay 1988) was undoubtedly an increment to the technology of the European power in its first great age of expansion into the overseas world. It offered opportunities for the visualization of the land not only in an intellectual sense but also for its conquest, appropriation, subdivision, commodification, and surveillance. As David Harvey puts it, "it seemed as if space, though infinite, was conquerable and containable for purposes of human occupancy and action. It could be appropriated in imagination according to mathematical principles" (1989, 246).

Cultural Exchange in Indian and European Cartographies

The history of the mapping of America after 1492 has been written largely from a European perspective. It has been insufficiently recognized that geographies were made and remade by "a process of transformation in which members of both the colonized as well as the colonizing cultures" entered into an interactive dialogue (Mignolo 1989, 94). Such an ongoing exchange, shaping both Indian and European cultures after 1492, has left few traces in scholarly histories of mapping in the "discovery" period (Cumming 1962),[3] still less in works written for wider readerships (Klemp 1976; Schwartz and Ehrenberg 1980). Even a work as distinguished as Fredi Chiappelli's *First Images of America* contains no hint that the geographical lore of Native American peoples may have contributed to the early European cartography of America, let alone that maps were being drawn by the Indians themselves (Thrower 1976).

To help us redress this "denial of coevalness" (Fabian 1983, 31) and to inject an ethnohistorical perspective into the cartographic history of the Encounter period, I will outline three areas where current research promises to enhance our understanding of the cultural exchange between the first Americans and the newcomers from Europe. The first concerns the evidence for mapmaking within those indigenous cultures during the period of early contact. The second relates to the identification of the hidden stratus of Indian geographical knowledge in the European maps of the period. The third illustrates how, in some cultures, Indian groups were able to adopt European uses for maps and to reappropriate them as tools of resistance in a colonial struggle.

Indigenous Cartographies

Gregory Waselkov (1989, 292) wrote that "drawing maps was within the competence of every adult southeastern Indian of the early colonial period," but his contention is difficult to document for many parts of North America. Contact with many Native American cultures— such as the Inuit—who were in due course discovered to have made maps, would not be made until after the early Colonial period. Moreover, such was the nature of Indian mapping—with geometries and conventions unfamiliar to Europeans of the "scientific" Renaissance (Lewis forthcoming)—that on many occasions, instances of what we might define as a map today went unrecorded. The evidence we have is thus tantalizingly fragmentary.

Only a handful of maps survive from before 1700, the earliest (1602) relating to parts of eastern Texas (Lewis forthcoming). Our knowledge of Indian mapmaking is thus largely of a textual rather than a graphic nature. It is found in the reports of explorers such as Captain John Smith, Jacques Cartier, Samuel Champlain, and Henry Norwood when they were interrogating Native American peoples for geographical intelligence about the areas where the explorers intended to penetrate (Lewis forthcoming). Such maps seem to have been generally ephemeral productions, "scratched in the sand or in the cold ashes of an abandoned camp fire, sketched with charcoal on bark, or painted on deerskin" (Waselkov 1989, 292).

More extensive evidence of another cradle of cartography independent from that of the Old Word is found in Mesoamerica. What has survived for this region is not only literary evidence for mapmaking from the time of the Spanish conquest but also (and despite the systematic destruction of many documents) a number of pre- and post-Conquest manuscripts identified as maps. As an example of the first category, we can cite Cortés's decision that his encounter with native mapmaking was of sufficient moment to be mentioned in two of the letters he wrote to Emperor Charles V in 1519–20. In the second he relates how Moctezuma had drawn for him "a cloth with all the coast painted on it" (Pagden 1971, 344). We cannot doubt that Cortés was dealing with a culture in which there were well-established traditions of map making.

A distinctive corpus of surviving maps in native style reinforces this inference. The origin of Mesoamerican cartography in paintings such as the murals from Tetitla in Teotihuacan (Classic period, 500–700 A.D.) remains obscure (Miller 1973, 151–52). To judge, however, from manuscripts from both central Mexico (Robertson 1959) and the Mixtec area of south central Mexico (Smith 1973), an art of picture mapping had been formalized by post-Classic times. This survived into the Conquest period.

Specialist linguistic and art-historical skills are required for reading the maps. Because of this, the primary tasks of making an inventory of the manuscripts (Glass 1975; Glass and Robertson 1972; Robertson 1972) and of interpreting them have been initiated in disciplines other than geography, such as art history (Robertson 1959; Smith 1973), anthropology, and literature (Caso 1949; León-Portilla and Aguilera 1986; Brotherson 1979; Mignolo 1989). More difficult to resolve is the tardy assimilation, in part an issue of cultural hierarchy. Maps identified by art historians did not fit the notion of a "scientific" map as understood by cartographers and geographers trained in Western traditions.

But to read the maps from Mesoamerica, we also have to learn a new set of cartographic rules. The physical form of such maps—whether as *lienzos*, *tiras*, or screenfolds—is very different from the sheet, book, wall, or atlas maps of early modern Europe. Similarly the pictographic conventions for signifying places, lacking any separate identifying toponyms, let alone a label in a recognizable language, could not qualify for membership within the canonical club of Renaissance European cartography.

Even so, a recent study of the Mixtec codices (Pohl and Byland 1990, 115) notes that despite being a "significantly different form of information," they are "applicable to spatial analysis."

Colonial manuscripts such as the *Historia Tolteca-Chichimeca* (Robertson 1959), the lienzo of Tlapiltepec (Parmenter 1982), or the Codex Xolotl (Dibble 1951; McGowan and Van Nice 1979), have for some time been described in terms of their cartographic characteristics. For the place of cartography in ancient Mesoamerican culture, however, it is especially significant that a similar form of mapping has been identified in parts of eighteen pre-Conquest codices.

Formerly these documents were described largely in terms of their genealogical and historical content. Recently, a combination of archaeologically recovered settlement patterns, an understanding of locational terminology acquired through interviews with local Mixtec speakers, and insight into the meaning of place signs and genealogy derived from the Mixtec historical codices and other pictorial sources (Pohl and Byland 1990, 116), has led to the reconstruction of the geographical content of these manuscripts and its relationship to the landscape. Such Mixtec mapping may be defined as producing "spatial histories,"[4] where time and space are projected onto the same two-dimensional plane, and in which records of geographical perceptions, ancestral migration, and dynastic history are combined into single documents. Comparative study of parts of the various codices reveal recurrent spatial patternings of identifiable place signs. These reappear in the same sequences, either within the same landscape frame of hills and mountains, or the same position as defined by the cardinal points. They are also found to be comparably spaced according to travel time (Pohl and Byland 1990). They are essentially strip maps representing the pathways of an ancient migration through the Valley of Mexico.

In Mesoamerica, as in other cultures in the Old World and North America, the mapping impulse extended also to representations of the cosmos. To give but one example from a complex subject, the opening page of the pre-Conquest Fejérváry screenfold presents an image that would undoubtedly have been rejected as a map, by both the sixteenth-century Spanish conquerors of Mexico and the modern cartographic historians of the nineteenth and twentieth centuries. Although social concepts rather than Euclidean space are represented, the mapping of cosmic principles and rituals nevertheless embodied rational ordering and careful measurement and often geometrically precise execution. A recent description of the map notes that

> In the center is the old god of fire presiding over the whole *imago mundi*. Each of the cosmic regions has its corresponding color—red, yellow, greenish blue, and bluish green—and also its own gods, trees, birds, and other related attributes. . . . The four cosmic regions are the stage on which time, destinies, and life interact (León-Portilla 1991, 507–08).

In other words, the artist of the Fejérváry screenfold has miniaturized the world to set its gods in their appointed place in time and space.

It becomes clear, then, that in 1492 mapping was by no means alien to the cultures of either Middle or North America. Since such indigenous forms of mapping had developed in situ and away from any possible influence from the Old World, we may need to revise our ideas about the levels of geographical awareness and representation in American Indian cultures as a whole. And, although the links may be more tenuous, we are also simultaneously alerted to the capacity of the Indians to play a sometimes decisive role in choreographing the early pathways of European exploration.

Hidden Geographies

Recognition of the existence of native mapping traditions in the Americas helps us to address the second research question, that of an Indian contribution to the European maps of the New World, another neglected aspect.[5] The basic question is the extent to which one can trace the existence in European maps of knowledge transmitted by Indian informants to European explorers and mapmakers (Lewis 1986, 1987). A good a priori case can be made for asserting that most European maps, manuscript or printed, from Juan de la Cosa's world map of 1500 onward, disguise a hidden stratum of Indian geographical knowledge. James Axtell (1987) once reflected on the nature of Colonial America without the Indians: adapting his question, it is interesting to speculate on what European sixteenth- and seventeenth-century maps of America might have looked like had the navigators and explorers arrived in an unpopulated land. Undoubtedly the details on the maps would have been much sparser beyond the thin trace of coastal contact. Without Indian contributions to the cartography of

the interior, maps of continental scale would have unrolled far more slowly in front of European eyes.

To document in detail the Indian contribution is a more difficult task. Three sets of clues are available as to the presence of Indian knowledge in European cartography. The first is the most ambiguous. It relates to the presence—assumed to be universal—of Indian guides and interpreters in situations where Europeans were likely to have been making maps. From the first landfall on 12 October 1492, the degree of dependence of Columbus and the other navigators and explorers on Indian knowledge would have been considerable (De Vorsey 1978). As early as 13 October 1492, Columbus was reporting that he was taking directions from Indian guides, a practice that became an almost daily routine. Indeed, Indian men were taken prisoner for the purpose. On other occasions Indians were kidnapped and taken back to Europe—by Spanish, English, and French alike—for longer periods of debriefing (Jaenen 1976, 12–15). But a specifically Indian contribution to the maps eventually published in Europe is usually impossible to disentagle.

A more explicit source relates to those documented occasions when Indians made maps at the request of Europeans. As already noted, this normally took place at the immediate site of exploration in the Americas, but sometimes captive Indians were interrogated in Europe. In his *History of the Indies,* Las Casas relates how João II of Portugal, speaking with Columbus,

> ordered that a bowl of beans be brought and put on the table. Using signs, He asked one of the Indians to make a map with them, showing the many islands in the sea where he came from, which the Admiral claimed to have discovered. The Indian very naturally and readily showed the islands of Hispaniola, Cuba, the Lucayas, and others that he knew of, the King . . . undoing it . . . asked another Indian to use the beans and to depict the lands he knew to lie in that sea from which Columbus had brought then. This Indian diligently and as one who chanced to show the same islands as the other Indian, also added many more islands and lands, explaining in his own language (although no one understood it) all that he had set forth (Parry and Keith 1984, 65).

Similarly, in the Northeast, Jacques Cartier along the St. Lawrence in 1541 (Quinn and Skelton 1965, 2:723; Ganong 1964, 264–70), Captain Bartholemew Gosnold during his voyage to the Maine coast in 1602 (Purchas 1965, 18:304), and Samuel Champlain along the coast of Maine and New Hampshire in 1605 (Biggar 1922–26, I, 335–36), all had maps drawn for them on one occasion or another. The Powhatan Indians in the early seventeenth century "spontaneously produced maps on at least three occasions" (Waselkov 1989, 292). In Mexico, Montezuma provided Cortés with a map. In the Southwest, we know that Hernando Alarcón, traversing the lower Colorado River in 1540, had once asked an elderly Indian to "set . . . downe in a chart as much as he knew concerning that river . . ." which he did willingly (Hakluyt 1904, 315). Native competence in drawing maps must have been a potentially significant element in the maps we usually classify as "European."

A third source of evidence for such a contribution can be found in the European maps themselves. Sources are rarely listed on sixteenth- and seventeenth-century maps, but just occasionally an Indian authority is acknowledged. The best known example is John Smith's map of Virginia (1612), where the readers are instructed "that as far as you see the little Crosses on rivers, mountaines, or other places have been discovered; the rest was had by information of the *savages,* and are set downe according to their instructions" (Smith's italics; Barbour 1986, I, 140–41). Likewise, on the map of northeast North America sent in 1611 to Spain by don Alonso de Velasco (the Spanish ambassador in London), the map user is informed, in relation to the details in the interior, that "all the blue is done by the relations of the Indians" (Cumming, et al. 1971, 264–67).

In the absence of such explicit testimony, we have to proceed through an analysis of map content. This consists of identifying "diagnostic characteristics," configurations that suggest an Indian informant rather than solely field reconnaissance by European explorers (Lewis 1986). Thus in the maps of America of the sixteenth and seventeenth centuries, we can look for recurrent features such as artificially straightened rivers or circular lakes, symmetrical river networks, topography that is duplicated, or fabulous cities such as Cibola, El Dorado, and Norumbega. By identifying in this way delineations that incorporate Indian concepts of distance and topography, and by establishing their cultural and ecological priorities within the landscape of the contact zone, something can be reconstructed not only of the Indians' contribution to the cartographic

image of America, but also of the assumption of European mapmakers when confronted with this type of knowledge.

Representation as Resistance

There is a danger, when attempting to write cartographic history from an ethnographical perspective, of treating the Indian contribution as passive compliance with European requests for information, or believing that the Indians were the unresponding victims of the map. By assuming that the effects of mapping are unidirectional, we risk the charge of an a priori ideological determinism (Greenblatt 1991, 4) in which native voices are quickly silenced and their maps replaced by the "technologically superior" territorial representations of the politically dominant culture of the invaders. However, this is only part of the story. In this section, I will argue that in some Indian cultures, maps were part of the intellectual apparatus by which the imposition of colonial rule was resisted. In general terms, it is well documented that the Indian guides pressed into service by Europeans were often "reluctant informants when strangers came to their lands requesting vital geographic information such as the location of lakes, rivers, mountains, and other marking points in the landscape" (Prins forthcoming).

Especially relevant in this context is the evidence for the preparation by Indians of maps in support of their claims to land from which they had been dispossessed. Like writing in other colonial situations (Adorno 1986), making a map became a conscious strategy of resistance. From Mesoamerica, where pre-Conquest cartography was a well-established tradition, come numerous instances of maps being used in this way.

A change of context from territorial control by the pre-Conquest aristocracy to territorial resistance on their part did not fundamentally change the format and style of mapping. Yet the purpose of such mapping had been transformed to become quintessentially Colonial to serve the needs of a conquered people. Manuscripts such as the Codex Columbino and the Codex Xolotl (Smith 1973) can be read as examples of how these changed relations of domination and subordination became enshrined in cartography. For example, we can trace in the Codex Xolotl the work of an Indian aristocracy seeking to restore its legitimacy in the Valley of Mexico. This seems to have been a dynastic history that is also a cartography, linking genealogy and territory and serving as proof of ancient nobility.

Reassertions of both native territorial claims and ways of representation are also found at local community level. Among the maps of the *relaciones geográficas,* we can also see the survival of pre-Conquest cartographic traditions.[6] One explanation could be a shortage of mapmakers trained in European techniques. Once they were made, however, these "alternative cartographies" acquired an independence and authority divorced from the circumstances of their creation. While the Spanish authorities became suspicious of the legitimacy of these maps (Smith 1973, 170), for Indian peoples they *were* their territory, standing as a record of past ownership and as a challenge to appropriation by the colonists.

Such is the *relación geográfica* map of Teozacoalco, a Mixtec town west of Oaxaca in the diocese of Antequera (1580). Drawn by a native hand, it shows how an instrument of colonial power could be reappropriated by a colonized people. The map is composed of two distinct parts (Caso 1949; Smith 1973, 55–58, 162–71). To the left, columns of figures, based on an earlier genealogical manuscript, record the history of the native ruling dynasty Tilantongo. To the right, the main map of the town is painted in circular form with east at the top. Since circular maps had pre-Conquest origins, even in this we see a reassertion of native concepts of space. The circle defines the jurisdictional boundary of Teozacoalco. The semicircular appendage at the top represents the town of Elotepec, once under the jurisdiction of Teozacoalco. While the map also shows signs of adjustment and acculturation to Spanish influence—as in the representation of estancias and churches—it nevertheless captures the coexistence and dialectic of native and European cartography.[7]

European Ideologies in the Early Maps of America

It will now be clear that the early Native American maps and the European maps of America have each been interpreted in the past from very different angles. Native American maps have been interrogated from the perspectives of anthropology, art history, genealogy, and history. European maps of the Americas have been studied mainly from a traditional geographical and historical standpoint: questions posed have tended to concern the way maps may have underpinned the conceptions of the "discoverers" and explorers of America; how cartographic evidence might help us to reconstruct the routes and tracks of the European explorers; at the antiquarian intersection of geography and map history, it has been asked how they might assist in locating the landing places of the navigators.[8] What has been missing is sufficient common ground between such geographical work on European maps and that of art historians and anthropologists on indigenous American mapping. In this last section, I shall suggest that a meeting place for the two directions of research may be found in a study of the ideologies that permeate the maps of both cultures (Harley 1988b, 1989). Something of the ideological nature of Native American mapping, seen as engaged in a struggle of resistance, has already been described,[9] so the argument here concentrates on the ideological features of European maps and their role in the construction of a geographical space in which colonial societies could take root.

As a form of knowledge through which power could be exercised, cartography in the sixteenth and seventeenth centuries was simultaneously a practical instrument of colonial policy, a visual rhetoric fashioning European attitudes toward the Americas and its peoples, and "an analogue for the acquisition, management and reinforcement of colonial power" as a whole (Huggan 1989, 115). Yet neither the signs of ideology nor their social effects are simple. I will draw a distinction here between the visible emblems of cartographic ideology, which lend themselves to straightforward iconographic analysis, and their "hidden transcripts" (Scott 1990), comprising the more generalized and abstract signs and consequences of that ideology and which form the political unconscious of the map.

Geopolitical and Religious Emblems

Early European maps of America usually are stridently geopolitical documents. Above all they bear the traces of the territorial moves by which the colonial powers of early modern Europe sought to delimit, divide, and assert control over their overseas territories. Lines of demarcation drawn on the maps became symbols as well as records of the division of the world into different national spheres of influence. The prominence of the line of the 1494 Treaty of Tordesillas on some maps from the early 1500s reflects the importance that Spain and Portugal attached to its provisions. Some maps of the period suggest that the line was moved or even falsified to favor the claims of the respective countries (Cortesão and Teixeira da Mota 1960, 1:96, 100, 104).

The entire context in which the Cantino map (1502) was made supports the contention that forces of imperial ideology and political advantage were at work. Alberto Cantino, the Duke of Ferraro's agent, had illicitly obtained a copy from Lisbon of the official *padrão* (standard map of the world). Breaching all policies of secrecy, his own map made the information concerning the "discoveries" widely available among nations interested in geographical intelligence about the Americas (Cortesão and Teixeira da Mota 1960, 1:7).

Nor was the territory claimed on maps only demarcated by boundary lines. "Decoration," inscriptions recording discovery, and commemorative portraits are all an integral part of cartographic discourse. The Cantino map is planted with national flags—Spanish and Portuguese—as if claiming ownership of the new territories and marking out spheres of political influence. Coats of arms of the ruling families of Europe are also a hallmark of Colonial cartography. Both flags and coats of arms may be seen as commemorations of the elaborate ceremonies by which new land was claimed by explorers (Stewart 1982, 13). Also helping to validate national claims to the new territories are names of discoverers inscribed on maps. On the Cantino map, we read of Brazil that it was "found by Pedro Alvares Cabral, a nobleman of the King of Portugal," while on the West Indies were the "Antilles of the King of Castille" (*Has antilhas Rey de castella*), "discovered by Columbus, who is Admiral of them" (Cortesão and Teixeira da Mota 1960, 1:11).

Later, as on De Bry's map of 1595, allegorical portraits of the discoverers were also placed in the corners of the American hemisphere, as if adding authority to European colonization (Berger 1985, 50). Only occasionally were car-

tographers explicit about these practices. Martin Waldseemüller's large wall map of the world of 1507 also contains a celebration of European overseas power, explained in the accompanying booklet *Cosmographiae Introductio* (published in the same year), which states that the purpose of the flags and shields on his map was to act as a territorial sign: "As farmers usually mark off and divide their farms by boundary lines, so it has been our endeavor to mark the chief countries of the world by the emblems of their rulers" (Waldseemüller 1507, 67 verso).

In such ways, the map had enabled the world to be visualized as a series of royal or imperial properties. Old World "emblems" included representations of the papal keys, the Islamic crescent, the Habsburg imperial double eagle, and the anchor of the Great Khan. On the part of the map relating to the Americas, the "fourth division of the earth, discovered by the kings of Castile and Portugal," there were placed, as Waldseemüller (1507, 67 verso) wrote, "the emblems of those sovereigns." Discovery was possession.

The cartographic discourse of the sixteenth and seventeenth centuries was never solely secular. Many of the early European maps of the Americas also proclaim a religious imperialism as well as a political conquest. The world view of Columbus and his European contemporaries had been greatly influenced by earlier images of Medieval Christian geography. If the real shape of a fourth continent was now emerging, it nevertheless represented the working out of a divine purpose. The words of the Psalm 2:6–8, "I will make the nations your inheritance and the ends of the earth your possessions," were now being written into the maps of America. On the Juan de la Cosa map, a compass rose astride the Tropic of Cancer portrays the Holy Family, while a vignette of Columbus shows him carrying the Christ Child on his shoulders. This is an adaptation of the ancient image of the converted pagan giant, St. Christopher, as a portrayal of Christoferens, the bearer of Christ across not a swift river but the ocean to the unknown shores of America (Watts 1985, 99–107).

Place-names on this and many other maps commemorate shrines of the Virgin in Castile, Catalonia, or Italy. Located thus on the new land, they also became emblems of religious possession. In his Journal for Friday 16 November 1492, Columbus relates how "in all the places, islands, and lands that he entered he always left a cross set up" (Dunn and Kelley 1987, 157). Each name on the map is a written record of an act of territorial consecration. Similar acts of toponymic possession convey the same sense of appropriation legitimized by religion. On maps such as Johannes Ruysch's world map of 1508 (Fite and Freeman 1926, 28–31), South America was named in the Portuguese fashion not only "The New World" (*Mundus novus*) but also "The Land of the Holy Cross" (*Terra sancte crucis*). The frontispiece of Sebastian Lopes's manuscript atlas (c. 1566, Cortesão and Teixeira da Mota 1960, IV, 9–14; Harley 1990, 109–111), is a drawing of the Crucifixion. In the same atlas, much of the interior of Brazil is filled with a picture of an Indian family seemingly designed to suggest that the biblical allegory of the Garden of Eden had been transplanted into the Americas. On some Portuguese charts, such as Jorge Reinel's chart of the South Atlantic (c. 1534), yet other emblems are used to convey biblical meanings. The letters "IHUS" inscribed on the neck of the parchment are the initial letters for the name of Christ. The five black dots in the flag of Portugal are the wounds of Christ. On each of the compass roses, a cross on the outer circumference points to the east (Cortesão and Teixeira da Mota 1960, I, 45–46, plate 15; Harley 1990, 103–05).

It is on the maps of the Americas produced in the Catholic countries of Europe—notably Spain, Portugal, Italy, and France—that religious iconography is most evident. But it is by no means absent from the maps of the Protestant north. In the so-called "Christian Knight" map (c. 1596–94), published in Calvinist Amsterdam and designed as a piece of anti-Catholic propaganda, we see depicted at the foot of a world map, drawn on Mercator's projection, an allegory not only for the struggle between good and evil at a cosmic scale but, more particularly, between Catholic and Protestant countries for the domination of the riches of the overseas world (Barber 1990). Despite the impact on cartography of the geometrical and printing revolutions, religious persuasion was still a central part of the mapmakers' agenda. Through the rhetoric of such maps, we can glimpse the process by which Europe was imposing "its own image, its own aspirations, and its own values, on a newly-discovered world" (Elliott 1970, 7).

The Political Unconscious of the Map

Yet more elusive and abstract configurations of power can be read from the map in addition to the more obvious emblems of royal power or religion. Such configurations may be defined as the political unconscious of the map, in the sense that we are recovering from cartography and its context processes that are usually hidden, taken for granted, and seldom made explicit in cartographic histories. They help us to understand more of the ways in which colonial power has been reinforced and made legitimate through cartography. By considering and noticing details that are normally unconsidered and unnoticed, I am aiming to identify a further dimension of cartographic power, one that involves an intellectual rather than a solely practical process of colonial domination.

The first example relates to the giving of names by Europeans to the lands they encountered in the Americas, but what, in particular, about those cases where the Indian names were retained by the conquerors and entered on a map? Surely these denote a cultural exchange and provide an index of Indian contribution to mapping? This might be true at one level as already suggested. Equally, however, it can be argued that the very adoption of native toponyms by the colonists was initially an act of appropriation and control. An archetypal example of place-naming—taken from Columbus's first letter to the Sovereigns of February-March 1493 and from the map accompanying it—serves to make the point. In this, a founding document of the European colonization of America, we read:

> To the first island which I found I gave the name *San Salvador*, in remembrance of the Divine Majesty, Who has marvelously bestowed all this; the Indians call it "Guanahani." To the second, I gave the name *Isla de Santa Maria de Concepción*; to the third *Fernandina*; to the fourth, *Isabella*; to the fifth, *Isla Juana*; and so to each one I gave a new name (Parry and Keith 1984, 59).

The ideological message is a dual one. From a European perspective, the names reproduce the divine hierarchy relocated in the New World. The order is significant: His Heavenly Majesty, Santa Maria, Fernandina, Isabella, and Juana. It was second nature for Columbus to honor first God, and then the Virgin Mary, and only then the King of Spain, the Queen, and the Royal Prince in turn.

We can also interpret the one Indian place name contained in Columbus's letter, "The Indians call it Guanahani." Here, from an Indian perspective, is another act of possession but one in a different sense. This sentence preserves an exchange of language, a trace of a dialogue once held between a European and an Indian. What is encapsulated in the letter, however, is the uneven record of the dialogue, one between colonizer and colonized. It is Columbus who is determining the terms of the exchange. He gives authority to the name but only by embedding it in a European letter whose purpose was to confirm the political and religious possession of the land and by giving "Guanahani" the status only of a quotation. Thus the name was "preserved out of context in a linguistic environment quite foreign to it, a stuffed bird in a museum case, it scarcely mattered whether the aboriginal name was the 'real' one or not" (Carter 1988, 1–33).

The second example concerns the way mapmaking created an artificial image that gave America a European identity. In this sense, cartography helped to invent America in the European consciousness. Jean Baudrillard (1983, 11–13), writing about the "successive phases of the image," saw the simulacrum as a product of the twentieth-century technology, but it has always existed in cartography. Sixteenth- and seventeenth-century European maps of America contain many features of the simulacrum. So when Baudrillard (1983, 2) observed that the map "precedes the territory . . . it is the map that engenders the territory," he could well have had an atlas by Mercator or Ortelius in front of him, open at the pages depicting the Americas.

The very metaphors used by European cartographers to name their productions heighten the sense of unreality: Mercator's world map represents the earth as a "Theater" for human activity, implying America is a stage for its first European colonists. In Ortelius's "New Description of America or the New World" (1570), the scenario is also European: what catches our eye are Latinized names and Dutch conventional signs. Through the artifacts of the engraver, the American landscape has been made to look European. Spotlighting Peru in Ortelius's map, we see the extent to which the engraving style of Frans Hogenberg and his

Dutch assistants, with standard signs for towns with church towers and spires—a wholly Christian landscape—had confirmed the Spanish possession of the Americas, even though (in this case) many of the place names are still of Indian origin. Or again, looking at John Smith's map of Virginia (1612), what strikes the reader is not the wilderness but the gentility of the landscape: an open parkland is portrayed, dotted with round trees like the familiar oaks and elms of southern England or lowland France. By creating an illusion of sameness, by defining identity in terms of "home," the map made America easier to assimilate into the European consciousness.

Another feature of the simulacrum is that we have to read it for a geography of absences. The "cast" of the "cartographic theater" in terms of signs and names becomes increasingly representative of only one culture (Harley 1988b). Scanning some of the European maps of seventeenth-century America, we could be forgiven for believing that the Indians no longer existed. In the words of Karen Kupperman (1980, 1), "It is as if America were a stage tableau, with the arrival of the Europeans as the raising of the curtain and the beginning of the action." Cartography has thus served to dispossess the Indians by engulfing them with blank spaces. Of course, there are regional and national differences in the extent to which an Indian geography is silenced in the maps of America. The silencing was later most thorough in maps of some of the English colonies, reflecting up to a point the decimation of the Indian population by disease, but also a function of the cultural values of a Puritan colonization.

The third and final process of empowerment picks up Baudrillard's notion of map preceding territory. There are many instances of this tendency in colonial cartography. The division of the world by a Pope—on a map—*preceded* the arrival of most European peoples, yet it endangered political demarcations that were and were meant to be enduring. The names New England, New France, or New Spain were placed on maps long *before* the settlement frontiers of New England, New France, or New Spain became active zones of European settlement (Meinig 1986). John Smith's well-known map of New England of 1614, with its carefully fabricated English names, *preceded* the arrival of Puritan settlers. For a time, the map was the only "territory" as far as the majority of English were concerned. It certainly helped to create what followed. Likewise, with the Colonial boundaries that were drawn on maps: these provide perhaps the most spectacular illustrations of how an anticipatory geography served to frame colonial territories in the minds of statesmen and territorial speculators back in Europe. Maps were the first step in the appropriation of territory. Such visualizations from a distance became critical in choreographing the Colonial expansion of early modern Europe. In the word of Edmundo O'Gorman (1961), America first had to be "invented" and integrated into the European consciousness before it could be owned, colonized, and merchandised, and before it could become a player in the rise of capitalism.

Conclusion

The way in which Indian and European maps were used interactively in colonial situations underlines our understanding of the cultural exchange in geographical knowledge. It also reinforces the claim of cartography to historical importance. Strengthening our appreciation of their role in the shaping of America, maps can be shown to operate not only within material and practical processes but also as reified symbols of power, part of the political unconsciousness of European society. Through a simulacrum, maps gave a geographical "reality" to new worlds in a way that no other document could offer. Whether we call the process invention or visualization, maps were critical agents in the graphic inscription by which the space of America was filled with some of the placenames, signs, emblems, and memories of the Old World. Yet, in these contexts—of cultural transfer and identity formation—we are confronted with the ultimate cartographic paradox. The map is *not* the territory: yet it *is* the territory. In America, cartography is part of the process by which territory becomes. The paper dispositions and anticipations of the map often preceded the "real" geography which we seek so earnestly to triangulate.

Acknowledgments

This essay was first presented as a paper at the Annual Conference of the American Historical Association at San Francisco in December 1989 and in modified form as lectures in 1991 at Clark University and The Pennsylvania State University. I am indebted for helpful comments from Catherine Delano Smith, David Woodward, and Carlos Rincón-Mautner. I also wish to acknowledge the help given by Ellen Hanlon and Pellervo Kokkonen in preparing the text for publication. The research for this paper was undertaken with the assistance of a grant for a public exhibition on the theme "Maps and the Columbian Encounter" from the Division of Public Programs of the National Endowment for the Humanities, an independent federal agency.

Editorial Note

The manuscript was essentially complete but in the process of revision when Brian Harley passed away. The abstract was constructed from the author's original summary, which has now been omitted from the conclusion. Deletions indicated by the author on a working draft were honored, except where such omissions seemed to cut substantive detail. The bibliographic citations and references were completed with the assistance of Ellen Hanlon, and the final manuscript was checked by David Woodward (University of Wisconsin-Madison) and Paul Laxton (University of Liverpool).

No reproductions of maps had been prepared or even selected by Harley to complement the text, an omission particularly unfortunate in regard to the indigenous cartographies discussed. Consequently, three indigenous maps were selected from the holdings of the Benson Latin American Collection, the University of Texas at Austin. These are illustrated and explicated in the attached Addendum. We are particularly grateful to the director of the Collection, Laura Gutierrez-Witt, and to her staff, for expediting reproduction and generously granting the necessary permissions. An obituary essay on J. Brian Harley (1932–91), written by Paul Laxton, can be consulted in the gazette of The Independent (London), Friday, 27 December 1991. We thank George Lovell for drawing this to our attention.

Notes

1. I shall not attempt to offer technical discussions of any of the European maps, which already have an extensive literature, nor yet to describe their often perplexing geographical content, which has been a focus of cartographic history since at least the nineteenth century (Winsor 1884–89, vol. 2; Nordenskiöld 1973; Cumming, et al. 1971). (A selection of indigenous maps is discussed in the Addendum.)
2. Even at a popular level, there is a merging of historical and political discourses. Newspapers and magazines have caught on to the alternative view of the historical significance of 1492. We read headlines such as "Exploding the Columbus Myth! De-celebration in the News" (1991); "Public Enemy No. 1492" (Bremner 1991); "Settling the Score with Columbus" (Harding 1991); "Scourge of America" (Koning 1991); and "The Trouble with

Columbus" (Gray 1991). Or again churches, once enlisted in the armies of colonization, have recently begun to ask whether 1492 should be regarded as a "symbol of freedom or oppression," with the governing board of the National Council of the Churches of Christ in the U.S. declaring that 1992 should be a year of "reflection and repentance" (General Secretariat, Organization of American States 1990).

3. In a discussion of "Primary Cartography: The Discovery," Cumming's work makes no mention whatsoever of an Indian contribution to the various European manuscript and printed maps that are described.

4. There are, of course, other occurrences of this phenomenon in other ancient mapmaking cultures. In this respect, the medieval European *mappaemundi* (Woodward 1985) provide a comparable example of a spatial representation of geographical features and historical events.

5. For example, if we examine the descriptions of individual maps in Nebenzahl (1990) and Levenson (1991), there is no allusion to possible Indian contributions to the configuration of the American continent and its parts.

6. Robertson (1972) enumerates ninety-one *pinturas* accompanying the *relaciones geográficas* of 1579–86 relating to Mesoamerica. Of these, seventeen were drawn and painted in native styles, a further thirty-eight show a mixture of native and European styles, and the remainder are European.

7. The evidence of maps being used along with written documents as a form of colonial resistance is not confined to Mesoamerica. A Peruvian example is found in the 1615 "Mapa Mundi of the Indies" by Felipe Guaman Poma de Ayala; see Adorno 1979a, 1986; and Brotherston 1979.

8. Washburn (1992, 2, 405), sums up the futility of some of this research when he writes: "It might be assumed that the geographical location of the landfall island could be most easily determined from the cartographic evidence. But the maps on which the landfall island and surrounding islands are recorded form an unreliable guide." Notwithstanding these difficulties, there has been a revival of interest in early European maps that might provide evidence for the first landfall of Columbus (De Vorsey and Parker 1985; Gainer 1988).

9. For an assertion of the ideological foundations of the pictorial mapping of Mesoamerica, see Pohl and Byland (1990).

References

Acuña, René. 1985a. *Relaciones geográficas del siglo XVI: México*, vol. 1. Mexico City: Universidad Nacional Autónoma de México, Instituto de Investigaciones Antropológicas.

———. 1985b. *Relaciones geográficas del siglo SVI: Tlaxcala*, vol. 2. Mexico City: Universidad Nacional Autónoma de México, Instituto de Investigaciones Antropológicas.

Adorno, Rolena. 1979a. Paradigms lost: A Peruvian Indian surveys Spanish colonial society. *Studies in the Anthropology of Visual Communication* 5:78–96.

———. 1979b. Icon and idea: A symbolic reading of pictures in a Peruvian Indian chronicle. *Indian Historian* 12(3):27–50.

———. 1986. *Guamán Poma. Writing and resistance in Colonial Peru*. Austin: University of Texas Press.

Axtell, James. 1981. *The European and the Indian: Essays in the ethnohistory of Colonial North America*. Oxford: Oxford University Press.

———. 1985. *The invasion within: The contest of cultures in Colonial North America*. New York: Oxford University Press.

———. 1987. Colonial America without the Indians: Counterfactual reflections. *Journal of American History* 73:981–96.

Barber, Peter. 1990. The Christian knight, the most Christian king and the rulers of darkness. *The Map Collector* 52:8–13.

Barbour, Philip L., ed. 1986. *The complete works of Captain John Smith (1580–1631)*, 3 vols. Chapel Hill: University of North Carolina Press and Institute of Early American History and Culture.

Baudrillard, Jean. 1983. *Simulations*. Trans. Paul Foss, Paul Patton, and Philip Beitchman. New York: Semiotext.

Berger, M. Yves, ed. 1985. *The discovery of the world. Maps of the earth and the cosmos*. Chicago: University of Chicago Press for the David H. Steward Museum.

Biggar, H. P., ed. 1922–26. *The works of Samuel de Champlain*. Toronto: The Champlain Society.

Boelhower, William. 1984. *Through a glass darkly: Ethnic semiosis in American literature*. Venice: Edizioni Helvetia.

———. 1988. Inventing America: A model of cartographic semiosis. *World and Image* 4:475–97.

Bremner, Charles. 1991. Public enemy no. 1492. *The Times Saturday Review* [London], 15 June, p. 4.

Brotherston, Gordon, ed. 1979. *Image of the New World: The American continent portrayed in native texts*. Translations prepared in collaboration with Ed Dorn. London: Thames and Hudson.

Burland, C. A. 1967. The map as a vehicle of Mexican history. *Imago Mundi* 15:11–18.

Carew, Jan. 1988. Columbus and the origins of racism in the Americas. *Race and Class* 29(4):1–19; and 30(1):33–59.

Carter, Paul. 1988. *The road to Botany Bay: An exploration of landscape and history*. New York: Knopf.

Caso, Alfonso. 1949. La mapa de Teozacoalco. *Cuadernos Americanas* 47:145–181.

Clarke, C. N. G. 1988. Taking possession: The cartouche as cultural text in eighteenth-century American maps. *Word and Image* 4:455–74.

Cortesão, Armando, and Teixeira da Mota, Avelino. 1960–62. *Portugaliae monumenta cartographica*, 6 vols. Lisbon: Comissão do V Centenario da Morte do Infante D. Henrique.

Cumming, William P. 1962. *The Southeast in early maps. With an annotated check list of printed and manuscript regional and local maps of southeastern North America during the Colonial period.* Chapel Hill: University of North Carolina Press.

——; Skelton, R. A.; and Quinn, D. B. 1971. *The discovery of North America.* New York: American Heritage Press.

De Vorsey, Louis. 1978. Amerindian contributions to the mapping of North America: A preliminary view. *Imago Mundi* 30:71–78.

—— and Parker, John, eds. 1985. *In the wake of Columbus: Islands and controversy.* Detroit: Wayne State University Press.

Dibble, Charles E. 1951. *Códice Xolotl.* Mexico City: Universidades de Utah y de México, Instituto de Historia, Prima Serie 22.

Dunn, Oliver, and Kelley, James E., Jr. 1989. *The Diario of Christopher Columbus's first voyage to America 1492–1493.* Norman: University of Oklahoma Press.

Edgerton, Samuel Y., Jr. 1987. From mental matrix to *mappamundi* to Christian empire: The heritage of Ptolemaic cartography in the Renaissance. In *Art and Cartography,* ed. David Woodward, pp. 10–50. Chicago: University of Chicago Press.

Elliott, John H. 1970. *The Old World and the New, 1492–1650.* Cambridge: Cambridge University Press.

Exploding the Columbus myth! De-celebration in the news. 1991. *Indigenous Thought. A Working Newsletter to Link Counter-Columbus Quincentenary Activities* 1(1):1–3.

Fabian, Johannes. 1983. *Time and the other: How anthropology makes its object.* New York: Columbia University Press.

——. 1986. *Language and colonial power: The appropriation of Swahili in the former Belgian Congo 1880–1938.* New York: Cambridge University Press.

Fite, Emerson D., and Freeman, Archibald. 1926. *A book of old maps delineating American history from the earliest days down to the close of the Revolutionary War.* Cambridge, MA: Harvard University Press; reprinted New York: Dover, 1969.

Gainer, Kim Dian. 1988. Evidence for the Columbus landfall. *Terrae Incognitae* 20:43–68.

Ganong, W. F. 1964. *Crucial maps in the early cartography and place-nomenclature of the At-* lantic Coast of Canada. Toronto: University of Toronto Press.

General Secretariat, Organization of American States. 1990. *Quincentennial of the Discovery of America: Encounter of the Two Worlds* 24:1.

Glass, John B. 1975. A survey of native Middle American pictorial manuscripts. In *Guide to ethnohistorical sources,* part 2, ed. Howard F. Cline, pp. 3–80. *Handbook of Middle American Indians* 14. Austin: University of Texas Press.

—— and Robertson, Donald. 1972. A census of native Middle American pictorial manuscripts. In *Guide to ethnohistorical sources,* part 3, ed. Howard F. Cline, pp. 81–252. *Handbook of Middle American Indians* 14. Austin: University of Texas Press.

Gray, Paul. 1991. The trouble with Columbus. *Time,* 7 October, pp. 52–56.

Greenblatt, Stephen. 1991. *Marvelous possessions: The wonder of the New World.* Chicago: University of Chicago Press.

Hakluyt, Richard. 1904. *The principal navigations and voyages,* vol. 9. Glasgow: James MacLehose.

Hale, J. R. 1971. *Renaissance Europe: Individual and society, 1480–1520.* New York: Random House.

Harding, Colin. 1991. Settling the score with Columbus. *The Independent* [London], 11 July, p. 13.

Harley, J. Brian. 1988a. Maps, knowledge, and power. In *The iconography of landscape: Essays on the symbolic representation, design, and use of past environments,* ed. Denis Cosgrove and Stephen Daniels, pp. 227–312. New York: Cambridge University Press.

——. 1988b. Silences and secrecy: The hidden agenda of cartography in early modern Europe. *Imago Mundi* 40:57–76.

——. 1989. Deconstructing the map. *Cartographica* 26(2):1–20.

——. 1990. *Maps of the Columbian Encounter: An interpretive guide to the traveling exhibition.* Milwaukee: University of Wisconsin, Golda Meir Library.

Harvey, David. 1989. *The condition of postmodernity. An enquiry into the origins of cultural change.* Oxford: Basil Blackwell.

Helgerson, R. 1986. The land speaks: Cartography, chorography, and subversion in Renaissance England. *Representations* 16:51–85.

Hoxie, Frederick E., ed. 1988. *Indians in American history: An introduction.* Arlington Heights, IL: Harlan Davidson.

Huggan, Graham. 1989. Decolonizing the map: Post-colonialism, post-structuralism and the cartographic connection. *Ariel* 20(4):115–31.

Jaenen, Cornelius J. 1976. *Friend and foe: Aspects of French-Amerindian cultural contact in the six-*

teenth and seventeenth centuries. New York: Columbia University Press.

Jay, Martin. 1988. Scopic regimes of modernity. In *Vision and visuality*, ed. Hal Foster, pp. 3–23. Seattle: Bay Press.

Jennings, Francis. 1975. *The invasion of America: Indians, colonialism, and the cant of conquest*. Chapel Hill: University of North Carolina Press.

Klemp, Egon, ed. 1976. *America in maps dating from 1500 to 1856*. Trans. Margaret Stone and Jeffrey C. Stone. New York: Holmes and Meier.

Koning, Hans. 1991. Scourge of America. *Guardian Weekly*, 28 July, p. 22.

Kupperman, Karen O. 1980. *Settling with the Indians. The meeting of English and Indian cultures in America, 1580–1640*. Totowa, NJ: Littlefield.

León-Portilla, Miguel. 1991. Codex Fejérváry-Mayer. In *Circa 1492: Art in the Age of Exploration*, ed. Jay A. Levenson, pp. 507–08. Washington: National Gallery of Art.

────── **and Aguilera, Carmen.** 1986. *Mapa de México-Tenochtitlan hacia 1550*. Mexico City: Celanese Mexicana.

Levenson, Jay A., ed. 1991. *Circa 1492: Art in the Age of Exploration*. Washington: National Gallery of Art.

Lewis, G. Malcolm. 1986. Indicators of unacknowledged assimilations from Amerindian *maps* on Euro-American maps of North America: Some general principles arising from a study of La Vérendrye's composite map, 1728–29. *Imago Mundi* 38:9–34.

──────. 1987. Misinterpretation of Amerindian information as a source of error on Euro-American maps. *Annals of the Association of American Geographers* 77:542–63.

──────. 1992. Native North Americans' cosmological ideas and geographical awareness: Their representation and influences on early European exploration and geographical knowledge. In *North American Exploration*, ed. John L. Allen, forthcoming. Lincoln: University of Nebraska Press.

McGowan, Charlotte, and Van Nice, Patricia. 1979. *The identification and interpretation of name and place glyphs of the Xolotl Codex*. Greeley: University of Northern Colorado, Department of Anthropology.

McNeill, William H. 1985. How Columbus remade the world. *Humanities* 6:3–7.

Meinig, D. W. 1986. *The shaping of America. A geographical perspective on 500 years of history*, vol. 1: *Atlantic America, 1492–1800*. New Haven, CT: Yale University Press.

Mercator, Gerard, with Hondius, Henry. 1968 [1636]. *Atlas or geographicke description of the regions, countries of the world, through Europe, Asia, Africa, and America, represented by new*

and exact maps. Reprinted Amsterdam: Theatrum Orbis Tarrarum.

Mignolo, Walter D. 1989. Colonial situations, geographical discourses, and territorial representations: Towards a diatopical understanding of colonial semiosis. *Dispositio* 36–38:93–141.

Miller, Arthur G. 1973. *The mural painting of Teotihuacan*. Washington: Dumbarton Oaks.

Mitchell, W. J. T. 1986. *Iconology. Image, text, ideology*. Chicago: University of Chicago Press.

Morison, Samuel Eliot, ed. 1971. *The European discovery of America: The northern voyages, A.D. 500–1600*. New York: Oxford University Press.

──────. 1974. *The European discovery of America: The southern voyages, A.D. 1492–1616*. New York: Oxford University Press.

Nebenzahl, Kenneth. 1990. *The atlas of Columbus and the great discoveries*. Chicago: Rand McNally.

Nordenskiöld, Adolf Erik. 1889. *Facsimile-atlas to the early history of cartography with reproductions of the most important maps printed in the XV and XVI centuries*, trans. Johan Adolf Ekelöf and Clements R. Markham. Stockholm. Reprinted with an introduction by J. B. Post. New York: Dover, 1973.

O'Gorman, Edmundo. 1961. *The invention of America: An inquiry into the historical nature of the New World and the meaning of its history*. Bloomington: Indiana University Press.

Pagden, A. R., ed. 1971. *Hernán Cortés: Letters from Mexico*. New York: Grossman.

Parmenter, Ross. 1982. *Four lienzos of the Coixtlahuaca Valley*. Washington: Dumbarton Oaks.

Parry, John H., and Keith, Robert G. 1984. *New Iberian world: A documentary history of the discovery and settlement of Latin America to the early seventeenth century*, vol. 2. New York: Times Books.

Pohl, John M. D., and Byland, Bruce E. 1990. Mixtec landscape perception and archaeological settlement patterns. *Ancient Mesoamerica* 1:113–31.

Prins, Harald E. L. 1992. Ketakamigwa: The homeland of the Wabanaki. In *Exploration, culture and cartography in the land of Norumbega*, ed. Kris Jones, forthcoming. Lincoln: University of Nebraska Press.

Purchas, Samuel. 1965. *Hakluytus Posthumus or Purchas His Pilgrimes*. Reprinted New York: AMS Press.

Quinn, D. B., and Skelton, R. A., eds. 1965. *Richard Hakluyt, Principal Navigations (1589)*. 2 vols. Cambridge: Cambridge University Press for the Hakluyt Society.

Robertson, Donald. 1959. *Mexican manuscript painting of the early Colonial period: The metro-*

politan schools. New Haven, CT: Yale University Press.

———. 1972. The *pinturas* (maps) of the *relaciones geográficas.* In *Guide to ethnohistorical sources,* part 1, ed. Howard F. Cline, 243–78. Handbook of Middle American Indians 12. Austin: University of Texas Press.

Sale, Kirkpatrick. 1990. *The conquest of paradise: Christopher Columbus and the Columbian legacy.* New York: Knopf.

Schwartz, Seymour I., and Ehrenberg, Ralph E. 1980. *The mapping of America.* New York: Harry N. Abrams.

Scott, James C. 1990. *Domination and the arts of resistance: Hidden transcripts.* New Haven, CT: Yale University Press.

Smith, Mary Elizabeth. 1973. *Picture writing from ancient Southern Mexico: Mixtec place signs and maps.* Norman: University of Oklahoma Press.

Stewart, George R. 1982. *Names on the land: A historical account of placenaming in the United States,* 4th ed. San Francisco: Lexikos.

Szegö, Janos. 1987. *Human cartography: Mapping the world of man.* Trans. Tom Miller. Stockholm: Swedish Council for Building Research.

Thrower, Norman J. W. 1976. New geographical horizons: Maps. In *First images of America: The impact of the New World on the Old,* ed. Fredi Chiappelli, vol. 2, 659–74. Berkeley: University of California Press.

Todorov, Tzvetan. 1984. *The conquest of America: The question of the other.* Trans. Richard Howard. New York: Harper Row.

Vargas Llosa, Mario. 1990. Questions of conquest: What Columbus wrought, and what he did not. *Harper's* 282(1687):45–53.

Waldseemüller, Martin. 1507. Cosmographie introductio. Facsimile, trans. Joseph Fischer and Franz von Wieser. Reprint 1966. Ann Arbor, MI: University Microfilms.

Wallis, Helen M., and Robinson, Arthur H., eds. 1987. *Cartographical innovations: An international handbook of mapping terms to 1900.* Tring, Herts., UK: Map Collector Publications and International Cartographic Association.

Waselkov, Gregory A., ed. 1989. *Powhatan's mantle: Indians in the Colonial Southeast.* Lincoln: University of Nebraska Press.

Washburn, Wilcomb E. 1992. Landfall controversy. In *The Christopher Columbus encyclopedia,* ed. Silvio A. Bedini, vol. 2, forthcoming. New York: Simon & Schuster.

Watts, Pauline Moffitt. 1985. Prophecy and discovery: On the spiritual origins of Christopher Columbus's enterprise of the Indies. *American Historical Review* 90:73–102.

Winsor, Justin, ed. 1884–89. *Narrative and critical history of America,* 8 vols. Boston: Houghton Mifflin.

Wood, Denis, and Fels, John. 1986. Designs on signs: Myth and meaning in maps. *Cartographica* 23(3):54–103.

Woodward, David. 1985. Reality, symbolism, time, and space in medieval world maps. *Annals of the Association of American Geographers* 75:510–21.

———. 1987. Medieval *mappaemundi.* In *The history of cartography,* vol. 1: *Cartography in prehistoric, ancient, and medieval Europe and the Mediterranean,* ed. J. B. Harley and David Woodward, pp. 286–370. Chicago: University of Chicago Press.

Addendum: Three Indigenous Maps from New Spain Dated ca. 1580

Karl W. Butzer* and Barbara J. Williams**
*Department of Geography, University of Texas, Austin, TX 78712
**Department of Geography, University of Wisconsin Center, Rock City, Janesville, WI 53545

FAX 608/755-2732

Three indigenous maps were selected from the pictorial maps (*pinturas*) that accompany the official geographical reports (*relaciones geográficas*) prepared in Mexico in 1577–85 (see Robertson 1972; also Butzer, this volume). Of the seventy-five extant *pinturas,* thirty-seven are now at the University of Texas, and they illustrate a wide range of European, mixed, and indigenous cartographic techniques. The three chosen here represent a spectrum, suitable to introduce the reader by stages to the several levels of meaning embodied in Mesoamerican cartographies.

The heuristic advantages of the *pinturas* attached to the *relaciones* are several: (a) They were all drawn at about the same time, and their date is known. (b) Each was commissioned for the same purpose, with explicit instructions to draw a town plan and illustrate the "site" and "situation" of such a town (Robertson 1972, 246). (c) The text of the *relación* provides information on the indigenous officials and elders who were the source of much or most of the information collated in response to the various questions posed, and older indigenous maps were sometimes presented in evidence. (d) The information given by a

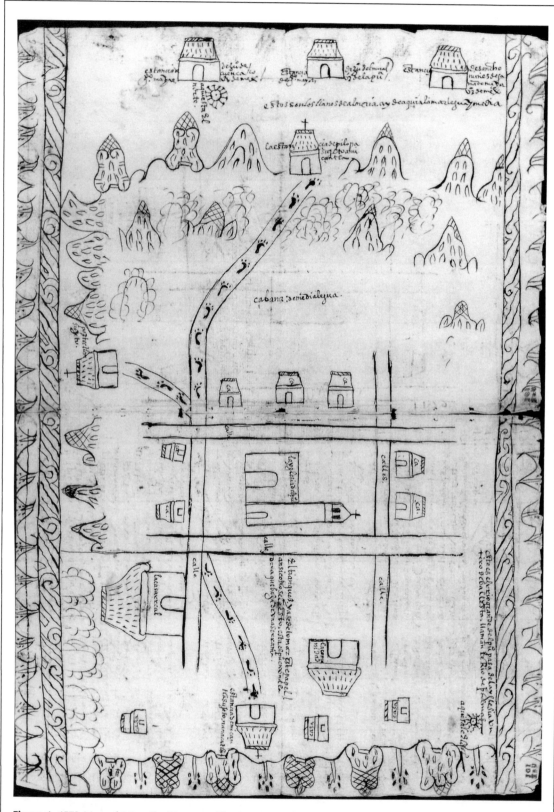

Figure 1. 1579 Map of Misantla, Veracruz. North at top. After Benson Latin-American Collection, University of Texas at Austin, Map JG1-XXIV-13, with permission.

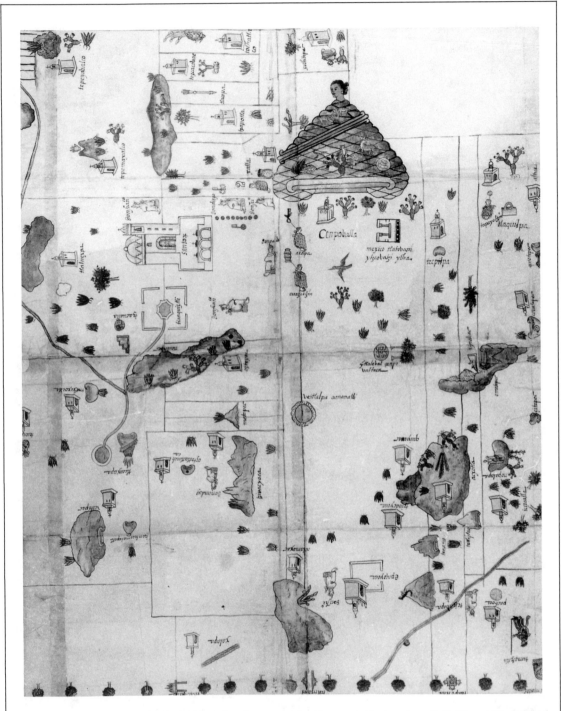

Figure 2. 1580 Map of Zempoala, Hidalgo. South at top. After Benson Latin-American Collection, University of Texas at Austin, Map JG1-XXV-10-4, with permission.

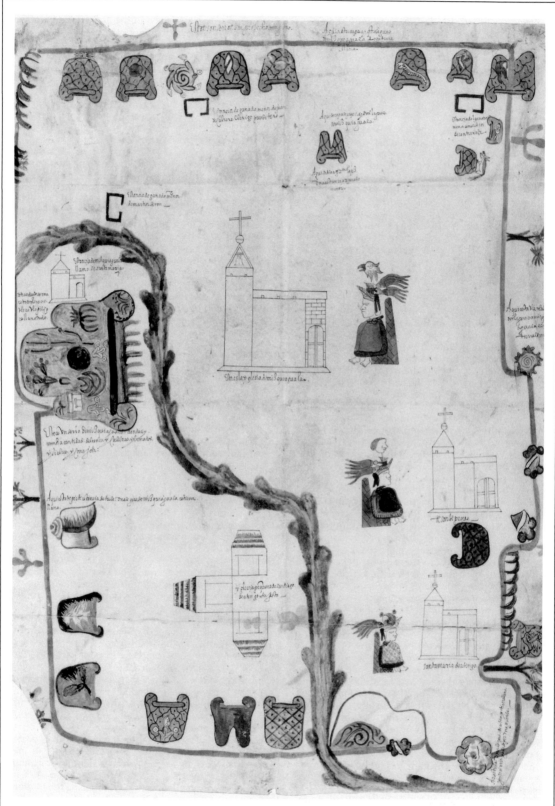

Figure 3. 1579 Map of Atengo and Mixquihuala, Hidalgo. East at top. After Benson Latin-American Collection, University of Texas at Austin, Map JG1-XXIII-12-3, with permission.

relación helps explain the features represented on the corresponding *pintura* (see Acuña 1985a, b). Although drawn in indigenous style, the *pinturas* are not Prehispanic, and they were devised to meet European objectives. But they are ideal as introductions to an unfamiliar cartography, precisely because the context is known, eliminating an excessive number of variables that would otherwise make interpretation unduly difficult.

The three pictorial maps are reproduced and analyzed below. The first appears to be strictly a perceptual map that delineates a visible landscape. The second shows a striking combination of perceptual and conceptual components (see Robertson 1972, 256–57)—an historical, symbolic world, overlain by a contemporaneous cultural landscape. The third is primarily a conceptual map, which seems to express a different idiom. Yet all three are valid and informative cartographic representations of the visible landscape, that have been verified in the field.

Misantla

Misantla is located 112 km north-northwest of Veracruz, in the state of the same name. When the pictorial map (Fig. 1) of this administrative district was drawn, in 1579, the town had an almost exclusively Indian population, speaking the Totonac language. The *relación* was drawn up by the resident Spanish magistrate, with the participation of the parish priest, another Spaniard, and the Indian governor and his officials (see Acuña 1985b, 181–94). The accompanying map is done in black ink on European rag paper. It is inscribed with Spanish glosses, in the same script as the *relación,* but the representational part is replete with indigenous symbols and was drawn by an Indian.

The center of the map is dominated by a schematic, free-hand grid of four streets (*calles*) at right-angles, with the church, the government building *casa real),* and the market (indicated only by the gloss *tianguez*) found in the same relative positions today. The community building ([*casa de*] *communidad*) no longer exists. Footprints mark the roads leading out into the countryside to three dependent villages, symbolized by indigenous thatched roof chapels: Poztectlan (now Poxtitlan), Pilopa, and Nanacatlan, the last two of which are now "lost."

Within its jurisdiction, the town of Misantla is shown adjacent to a series of hills to the west (left side). To the north (top), a broad plain (*çabana*) is indicated, then two rows of hills, and finally three Spanish cattle estates (*estancias*), on the Gulf coastal plain known as the Llanos de Almeria. Two rivers frame the map to the east and west; the river on the right is identified as the Río de Palmas (Río Colipa?), while that on the left is described in the text as the Río de la Torre. The south side is marked by an irregular line and by a row of trees and hills symbolized by a variant of the *tepetl* or hill glyph. At the northern end, the margin of the map coincides with the Gulf coastline. The frame, in other words, corresponds to the natural features demarcating the jurisdiction.

The *tepetl* hill glyphs along the southern margin are similar to those used in the map of Atengo (Fig. 3), and follow strict indigenous conventions. The trees cannot be identified, although the text of the *relación* mentions two tropical genera (*mamey* and *peruétano*) in addition to *cedro* (bald cypress). Most of the hills in the north approximate European conventions, but two are shown by the indigenous hill glyph. The hatched cones atop the "hills" are problematical, but Misantla is surrounded by steep and conical, basalt hills, now crowned by stands of tropical trees. Comparison of the various hills represented on the map shows that some are "decorated" with upside-down U symbols, that are sometimes used to indicate a cultivated field; the cross-hatching may mean uncultivated. The groups of light, elliptical lines between the hills and west of Misantla also are not decorative but symbolic of some environmental characteristic; these areas would probably have been forested. What appears, then, to be an impressionistic topography is in fact rendered by symbols with specific meaning.

The Misantla map differs from that of Zempoala (Fig. 2) or Atengo (Fig. 3) in that it lacks images of indigenous rulers, or toponyms rendered by indigenous glyphs. It appears to be a perceptual map, with no overt reference to the past.

Zempoala

Zempoala lies 22 km south of the mining center of Pachuca, in Hidalgo state. The *relación* was written in 1580 by a scribe for the Spanish magistrate, in the presence of four Aztec governors and many Indian elders, with the aid of a Spanish interpreter (Acuña 1985a, 67–82). The attached pictorial map is rendered in watercolor on heavy European paper. It is a study in cultural contrasts.

Place names are indicated by indigenous glyphs (the "symbols") while the glosses are in Nahuatl, but in European script. The map is subdivided by red lines, drawn with a straight edge, that, following native convention, probably represent noble properties, while dependent communities are indicated by chapels, drawn in three dimensions. At the same time, historical and contemporary local rulers (*teuctli*) are shown: current and historical Aztec lords (distinguished in the text of the *relación*) are shown with name glosses and glyphs depicting their authority—mantle, seated on a backed straw mat (*icpalli*) and wearing a headdress; earlier, Chichimec rulers are shown bare-headed, standing, and dressed in animal skins; and the Spanish magistrate of Pachuca (in the lower right corner) is depicted by the indigenous symbols for Spanish authority—armchair, robes of office, and staff. The map as a whole is dominated by the large symbolic *tepetl* hill glyph, probably representing the foundation of the Aztec settlement; this is hatched and depicts elements of an unsettled landscape or one under Chichimec domination—plants and animals, including the prickly pear, eagle and serpent (foundation symbols also found in the modern Mexican flag), as well as deer, rabbit, and possible pronghorn. Stone glyphs (*tetl*) also appear as well as the glyph for water (symbolizing the Middle American concept of hills as vessels of water). This great hill, surmounted by a female head rendered in a nonindigenous, perspective view, completely dwarfs the finely drawn Franciscan monastery.

This conceptual aspect of the map, as an historical statement, is completed by the "house" of the ruler of Mexico—depicted by a conventional symbol for *tecpan* palace, a flat-facade structure with a framed doorway and supralintel panel with a disk motif, below and to the right of the foundation symbol for Zempoala; this does not refer to an old palace, but to the site of Moctezuma's defeat by Cortés in 1520.

The visible or perceptual landscape is also shown. The terrain conforms with the plain and several hills described by the text, and the many agaves (*maguey*) and prickly pear (*nopal*, shown with red fruits) are also noted in the text. At least eight other kinds of trees are depicted, one a characteristic clump of yucca palms (right margin, at "Iszocalla"). A tree with small, projecting red fruits is a *capulí* cherry tree; another, with large yellow fruits, is a peach tree; and two trees shown with a dense canopy and hidden red fruits suggest apple trees. Other trees mentioned in the text of the *relación* are quince, walnut, and almond, but these cannot be identified among the remaining arboreal types on the map. Many of the hills shown, in part in three-dimensional form, are conspicuous in the field; some have glosses or place glyphs and may have had symbolic significance as well. The famed aqueduct of Zempoala is shown by four arches in the top left corner. It is linked by a blue line to a blue circle and to a blue octagon within an enclosure marked *tianguiz*; the line marks an irrigation canal fed by a spring, leading to the market square and to the aqueduct. Another blue circle, with a border, is located in the center of the map and the gloss identifies it as the spring "in the plain."

The visible topography and cultural landscape of 1580 is quite comprehensive. It includes natural vegetation, water sources, settlements, fields, and irrigation features, as well as indigenous and Spanish fruit trees. Except that most of the dependent villages have disappeared, the landscape looks much the same today, and the vegetation cover has not changed perceptibly. It appears that this visible landscape was intended to serve as a framework for a higher order of representation, namely the conceptual and historical landscape.

The only conspicuous frame to the Zempoala map is the schematic row of trees along the lower margin (north), which suggest the wooded mountains near Pachuca. However, the outermost "property" lines demarcate a jurisdiction identical to that of modern Zempoala.

Atengo and Mixquihuala

The third pictorial map selected here (Fig.3) includes three Indian towns along the Río Tula in Hidalgo state: Atengo, Tezontepec, and Mixquihuala, located 15–20 km north of Tula. The *relación* of 1579 says little about its indigenous informants (Acuña 1985a, 25–38), who were Otomí speakers. The color map on parchment is an Indian work, although the glosses are entered in Spanish.

The jurisdiction is sharply demarcated by a thick and continuous orange line, along which scattered, unidentifiable trees and schematic prickly pear are shown. The text emphasizes agaves (*maguey*) and mesquites; the former remain common but the latter are now replaced by the South American pepper tree (*pirúl*). The Río Tula cuts across the map prominently, its configuration fairly accurate. The cultural landscape of 1579 is highlighted by the monastery churches of the three towns, as well as a small church (representing a dependent village) and a thatched-roof church complex whose three buildings front a courtyard. These symbols of the Spanish presence stand out from the remainder of the map by being drawn in ink, with the aid of a straight-edge. Three partial enclosures near the top show sheep estancias.

Far more prominent is the conceptual map, presumably representing a symbolic interpretation of the Prehispanic past. It is dominated by Mt. Tunittitlan (left center), probably symbolizing settlement foundation, elaborately decorated with glyphs as well as a prickly pear and a branching cactus. The local rulers of the three towns are depicted with their name glyphs and symbols of authority: headdress, mantle, and "throne" (*icpalli*). The *tepetl* hill glyphs that demarcate the margins of the jurisdiction are drawn in bright colors and include glyphs related to toponyms and probably conceptual symbolism. These hills, including one between Atengo and Tezontepec (the two lower towns), approximate the visible topography, but the *relación* mentions temples (*cúes*) on very high hills that were once regularly used for religious offerings (Acuña 1985a, 33).

Although the topography is fairly realistic, the pictorial map of Atengo and Mixquihuala emphasizes a conceptual plan, apparently dominated by sacred points or places. The contemporaneous cultural landscape is shown in a perfunctory fashion, and territorial delimitation was one evident purpose, recalling the map of Misantla.

Towards an Interpretation of the Evidence

The relationships between the *pinturas* of the *relaciones* and traditional, Prehispanic representations are clarified by the 1579 *relación* for Coatepec, an Indian town near Texcoco, east of Mexico City. This detailed report was written by Francisco de Villacastín, "scribe and interpreter" to the royal magistrate (Acuña 1985b, 126–27, 132). His ability in Nahuatl is evident from the complex and sensitive account of indigenous tradition and cosmological symbols that he elicited from the Indian leaders and elders, who were summoned to provide the necessary information. How they presented their ancient charts in evidence can be inferred from the text:

> The explanation [for the name Coatepec] given by the Indian elders and old people . . . and as can be seen by the old *pinturas* they have, which show their ancestors and former elders one on top of the other, so as to remember them . . . And according to the elders and as is apparent from their *pinturas*, there used to be a large white snake . . . above that hill . . . living coiled upon it. And, according to the *pinturas*, that snake disappeared after the founding of the town . . . [The origin of

its founders] is unknown except that the old *pinturas* which the inhabitants of the town have . . . indicate that [the founders] came from distant lands . . . According to these *pinturas,* the town was founded 415 years ago . . . (Acuña 1985b, 132–33).

It appears that the drawings in question combined genealogical histories and symbolic attributions of place with some form of geographical representation. The three maps accompanying the *relación* are primarily perceptual in character, except for one glyph and the symbolic representation of several small (sacred?) hills. The maps that the informants prepared for Villacastín deleted all but the most important conceptual and historical aspects of their landscape, substituting a new iconography of churches and chapels.

The salient importance of the Coatepec report is that it underscores the antiquity of indigenous charts combining spatial, symbolic, and historical information. The maps with the *relación* and those shown in Figures 1, 2, and 3 imply that their traditional counterparts also included a variety of topographical and environmental details, together with a schematic representation of the built environment.

From Columbus to Acosta: Science, Geography, and the New World

Karl W. Butzer

Department of Geography, University of Texas at Austin, Austin, TX 78712,
FAX 512/471-5049

Abstract. What is called the Age of Discovery evokes images of voyages, nautical skills, and maps. Yet the European encounter with the Americas also led to an intellectual confrontation with the natural history and ethnography of a "new" world. Contrary to the prevailing view of intellectual stasis, this confrontation provoked novel methods of empirical description, organization, analysis, and synthesis as Medieval deductivism and Classical ontogenies proved to be inadequate. This essay demonstrates how the agents of that encounter—sailors, soldiers, government officials, and missionaries—made sense of these new lands and peoples; it highlights seven methodological spheres, by examining the work of exemplary individuals who illustrate the diverse backgrounds, abilities, and interests characteristic of the period. These examples include the observational skills of Columbus in 1492, the landscape taxonomy of his son Fernando, the biotic taxonomy of Oviedo, the cultural recording of Sahagún, the regional geography of Cieza, the pervasive role of Velasco in both geographical synthesis and town planning at the government level, and finally, the overarching scientific framework for the natural history and peoples of the New World proposed by Acosta in 1590. The evidence rehabilitates the reputation of Columbus who, like so many others with little or no formal education, had a spontaneous capacity to observe and describe. The origins of Native American stereotypes are identified, but there also were remarkable "insider" studies that, in the case of Sahagún, touched upon the semiotics of culture and landscape. Although Sahagún and Acosta had scholarly training, the confrontation with new environments and unfamiliar peoples probably put observers with rural backgrounds on an equal footing with those steeped in traditional academic curricula. Last but not least, the essay points up the enormity of the primary documentation, compiled by these Spanish contributors during the century after 1492, most of it awaiting geographical reappraisal.

Key Words: Acosta, Columbus, ethnography, geographical planning, gridiron towns, history of science, landforms, López de Velasco, natural history, New World landscapes, Oviedo, *relaciones geográficas*, Renaissance, Sahagún, Spanish geography.

> The world is so vast and beautiful, and contains so many things, each different from the other . . .
>
> —Francisco López de Gómara (1552)

Renaissance Science

THE European encounter with the Americas in 1492 falls within what Western historians call the Age of Discovery. Humanists have long been fascinated with that encounter as a source of myths and images (Green 1968, III, pt. 1; Gerbi 1985; Greenblatt 1991). Historians of science in general and of geography in particular are preoccupied with navigation and cartography (Kimble 1938, chaps. 5, 9–10; Parry 1981; James and Martin 1981, 63–95; Nebenzahl 1990; Harley 1990; Buisseret 1992). The thesis of this essay is that the Spanish encounter with the New World also had a far-ranging impact on environmental and cultural understanding.

The boundless enthusiasm with which the first writers described the landscapes and biota of the New World was integral to the Renais-

Annals of the Association of American Geographers. 82(3), 1992, pp. 543–565
© Copyright 1992 by Association of American Geographers

sance, or reawakening of Western civilization. That Renaissance marked an uneasy transition from the Medieval to the modern world, characterized by many cross-currents of thought and expression. One hallmark of the Renaissance was the rediscovery of Classical writings during the fourteenth and fifteenth centuries and their translation from Greek into Latin, as a new source of information, ideas, and esthetic prototypes. But the resulting humanistic resurgence did not immediately lead to more critical analysis, let alone philosophical reassessment. The deference once given to the Bible or Christian theological authority shifted to that of leading Classical scholars, but empirical contradictions to "new" authorities such as Aristotle were only offered with hesitation. At its worst, the rediscovery of Antiquity led to an unproductive antiquarianism that took precedence over new observations and stifled intellectual progress.

Medieval science had already included a component of empirical, practical observation, but was dominated by scholastic discussions or the excerpting of older texts, seldom introducing materials derived from personal observation. The three realms of natural history, consisting of animals, plants, and minerals, had been studied in a compartmentalized fashion, without a grasp of fundamental interconnections, except as an expression of a divine plan. In many ways it was a period of introverted reflection on the self-sufficient truths provided by theology, and the individual was part of an ahistorical cycle of life and death, of suffering in the present and anticipated reward in the hereafter.

The rediscovery of Antiquity provided a new sense of history, identifying new role models of scholars—not only soldiers or kings—who had made their mark in a secular world of the living. Renaissance scholarship included individuals who were motivated and willing to embark on a new search, with a fresh curiosity. Only a minority of these had both the talent and boldness to emphasize the empirical and the inductive, to reexamine deductive theories critically, and to draw conclusions from direct observation or experiment. Although time-honored religious beliefs set constraints to discussion, the Renaissance was the beginning of a spirit of free enquiry, with renewed interest in verification, accuracy, and systematic understanding.

It can be debated whether Renaissance geography was the revitalization of a Classical tradition or the spontaneous product of a new intellectual climate. Two personalities of the later Middle Ages illustrate the problem. In 1410, the French Cardinal d'Ailly (1948) wrote a world description based almost exclusively on Classical sources; it begins with a series of interesting figures for the astronomical subdivision of the globe, but his regional chapters are a mix of old fables and obsolete toponyms, for which endless fictional or mythological explanations are offered. Quite unaffected by such ballast from Antiquity, the Venetian merchant-traveler Marco Polo (1958) left a remarkable account of his travels in Asia (1271–95) that includes vivid descriptions of landscapes and cultural patterns.[1] Pierre D'Ailly and Marco Polo represent two extremes among precursors of the Renaissance, but the pattern remained.[2] My point is not that intellectual roots are unimportant, but that the prevalent Renaissance paradigm overemphasizes the significance of Classical antiquity, to the degree that it obscures the acuity and originality of Renaissance observational skills and comprehension.

The discoverers, explorers, and observational scientists of the Renaissance were at best familiar with a very limited selection of Classical works, that were frequently cited only for effect, sometimes in the final stages of revision (see Cieza de León 1984, xxxiii, n. 12). Strabo, an available and obvious source, was barely used, and Columbus's consultation appears to have been very selective and from a derivative digest in his possession (see Broc 1980, 18, 200; Harley 1990, 37, 42). More influential was Pliny's *Natural History* (1940–56), the *de facto* encyclopedia of the Renaissance (Broc 1980, 15). For cartography and navigation, the tables of geographical coordinates by Ptolemy (1932), and the maps attributed to him, provided a direct or indirect datum for most large-scale charts from the mid-1300s to the early 1500s.[3]

Geography during this period was a part of what was called *cosmography* (Waldseemüller 1966), which included astronomy and nautical science, particularly as applied to cartography. But between Waldseemüller writing in 1507 and Münster (1968) in 1550, cosmography also began to include what today would be called physical and cultural geography.

The present paper is directed to the origins, rapid growth, and crystallization of physical and cultural geography as a consequence of the Columbian Encounter. My argument is that the European discovery of the New World required new observational and descriptive skills, as well as explicit discussion of environmental and cultural phenomena that could no longer be taken for granted: things were either different or similar on the other side of the ocean. Geomorphology soon received a degree of attention that it had never been accorded in Antiquity, and biogeography was reinvigorated. Ethnographic observations gradually added greater depth to the appreciation of cultural phenomena, and these several geographical strands were integrated into what could be called regional geography. All of this was abetted by the Spanish government's official role in normative urban planning.

The study focuses on Spain and the New World, rather than on research developments in other parts of Europe. Renaissance geography in Italy, Germany, and France has received some attention (e.g., Baker 1963; Beck 1973; Broc 1980), but the originality and quality of Spanish geography during the period has been underappreciated, even by Spanish authors (see Becker 1917; Martínez 1945; Aríja 1972, versus Menéndez Pidal 1944), The emphasis is necessarily selective, and several key authors have been chosen for closer examination. This focus on individuals is not an attempt to create new icons; it is essential to elucidate the interests, abilities, and limitations of the period. The differences among the individuals selected also reveal the degree to which the evolution of sixteenth-century Spanish geography was multilinear, not unilinear. Geography itself was the unifying theme, rather than a by-product of this scientific evolution.

Observation: Christopher Columbus

The discovery of the New World initiated an unprecedented interest in geography and natural history. Somehow, earlier maritime discoveries by Europeans had failed to generate evocative reports of new lands and peoples. Even the exploration of West Africa instigated by Portugal's Prince Henry "the Navigator" (see Fernández Armesto 1987, 185–200) led to such dreary works as the Crónica da Guiné (Beazley and Prestage 1896–98), a leaden saga of seafaring and slave hunting activities from 1434–48, punctuated by incidental comments on indigenous customs; only its commercial prospects stirred interest in Portugal. To the credit of Columbus (Cristóbal Colón), his voyage of 1492 inspired much more than additional coastlines on the portolan charts. Even though he thought he was in East Asia, Columbus recognized the novelty of the landscapes, flora, and people on the other side of the ocean. However observant were other captains or ship's pilots of the period, they lacked his ability to describe the novel in ways that would excite academic and lay curiosity in Europe.[4]

Columbus's credentials as a scientific figure have long seemed unimpressive to his critics. Born 1451 in Genoa under modest circumstances (his father was a weaver), he went to sea as early as age fourteen. During the mid-1470s he sailed the Mediterranean, perhaps on a galley in the service of France; about 1476–84 he was based in Lisbon and the Madeiras, sailing to West Africa, probably with slavers.[5] All we have to attest to his learning are the surviving letters in his handwriting (see facsimiles reproduced in Thacher 1967, III, 84–490; with discussion in Varela 1982, li–lvii); his script was bold and sophisticated, varying in execution according to the formality of the occasion, and comparable to that of educated scribes and notaries of the time.[6] Any doubts about Columbus's ability as a cartographer and geometer are laid to rest by one of his diagrams showing a three-dimensional projection, converted from a sphere to a plane (see Harley 1990, 42, Fig. 36), which is found among his annotated copies of Ptolemy, Marco Polo, and D'Ailly (see Taviani 1985, 446–55; Harley 1990, 34–43). His report on the Third Voyage (1498–1500) also makes numerous references to Classical authors then only available in Latin (see Las Casas 1965, I, 482–96).

Columbus was essentially self-taught, as he admitted in a letter of 1501 to the monarchs of Spain:

> In navigation [God] endowed me generously, of astronomy he gave me what was needed, and the same of geometry and arithmetic, with the talent of mind and hand to draw this globe and upon it the cities, rivers and mountains, islands and ports, all in their proper place (Varela 1982, 251; Las Casas 1965, I, 31) (all translations by author).

Accordingly, he hewed to a pragmatic, cartographic tradition of the period, one concerned with the making of geographically realistic maps intended for the practical world of navigation (see Campbell 1987).[7]

Columbus's insight and intellectual impact deserve more sympathy than has been accorded him by Carl Sauer (1966, chap. 2) and Kirkpatrick Sale (1990, chap. 5), Whatever his motives and however annoying his use of hyperbole, Columbus attempted to inform about the new lands he saw. His descriptions of the people and their lifeways, incidental to his narratives about encounters with the indigenous inhabitants, contain much useful ethnographic information (see Sauer 1966, chap. 3) and novel insights on the physical environments of the New World.

Columbus was untutored in the sciences, and his lack of botanical knowledge frustrated him: "I believe there are many plants and trees (in the Bahamas) worth much in Spain as dyes or medicinals but I do not recognize them, which I greatly regret" (see Spanish transcription of the First Voyage diary, by Dunn and Kelley [1988, folio 15 recto, lines 25–28]). But his lack of formal training did not prevent his from venturing comparisons of the New World palms with those of West Africa or the Mediterranean: "They have a great number of palms of a different kind than those of Guinea or our own, of medium height, with smooth trunks and very large fronds" (Dunn and Kelley 1988, folio 18 recto, 13–16), nor from recognizing six to eight different classes of palms (1493 letter in Varela 1982, 141). He also noted the distinctiveness of the trees, fruits, and plants of Cuba and of Hispaniola (see Varela 1983, 141). And he commented on the unusual association of pines and palms growing in one river valley (vega), whose surface alternated between level hills (montes llanos) and low plains (baxos) (Dunn and Kelley 1988, folio 29 recto, 26–28; see also Humboldt 1845–47, II, 56).

He likewise demonstrated an intuitive grasp of geomorphology. He found it remarkable that the steep slopes of tall mountains were densely vegetated and not rocky (Nov. 14 and 26, 1492), and that broad rivers debouching into the sea lacked sand or gravel bars (Nov. 27), both phenomena that we would now attribute to deep tropical weathering. On another occasion he defined a cala (a local term for drowned valleys of the Balearic Islands and Sardinia; see Butzer 1962) as "a narrow inlet where sea water enters the land" (Dunn and Kelley 1988, folio 24 vuelto 45–25 recto 1). Two sources derived from the lost diary of the Second Voyage (1493–96) offer the first description of a mangrove coast on the southern shores of Cuba; it was replete with ciénegas and swamps for two leagues inland, with almost impenetrable thickets of plants and trees (F. Colón 1984, 189). "According to Columbus this region is completely submerged and covered with water and its coasts are marshy and full of trees" (Martyr 1964, 139).

Finally, there are Columbus's instructive, if debatable, climatological ideas. He explained the great heat of the Bahamas by their low elevation and the prevailing easterly winds (Oct. 29). On the daily tropical showers, he noted that late in every day a cloud bank formed on the western part of Jamaica, resulting in rain for an hour or less; this he attributed to the great forests of the island, with reference to his previous experience on the Canaries, Madeiras, and Azores (July 1494, F. Colón 1984, 193–94). He appended a remarkable ecological note. On those Atlantic islands, "they have cut so much forest and trees that hindered them [from expanding cultivation] that such clouds and rains no longer form as they once used to." The observation is telling because it shows that Columbus was aware of and concerned about environmental degradation on the recently-settled Madeira islands.

Much in the manner of more recent field observers, Columbus repeatedly drew analogies between the Old World and the New: a similar tree but with larger leaves than a counterpart on an Aegean Island (Nov. 12); live oaks and arbutus (madroños) as in Castile (Dec. 7), healthy river waters as compared with pestilential ones of Guinea (Nov. 27), finely cultivated lands recalling the plains of Córdoba (Dec. 14), weather like April in Castile (Dec. 13), or mountains like those of Sicily (Oct. 28).

Some of the comparisons were motivated by natural curiosity, others by economics, and others still by sheer aesthetics. They give point to his verbal paintings of an exuberant tropical vegetation, nourished by an eternally spring-like climate, and inhabited by peaceful and naked innocents. Columbus thus created an image of an Edenic land that was at once primitive yet familiar, and in so doing his rhetorical analogies delineated a powerful theme in European humanistic thought. He demonstrated an ability to observe, compare, and describe, and there are suggestions of partial comprehension.[8] It was his articulation and dissemination of his ideas, his way of putting words together, and his rhetoric that provoked scientific interest in a New World that he himself refused to believe was new. Columbus, though at times a medieval visionary and mystic and given to Biblical metaphors and prophecies, demonstrated tenacity as an explorer and a longing for greatness and discovery that mark him as typically modern and, in thought, action, and results, unlike other of the great personages of the Middle Ages (Gerbi 1985, 13).

Landscape Taxonomy: Fernando Colón

Fernando, born out of wedlock in Córdoba in 1488, was the son of Columbus who had intellectual ambitions, and who had a profound, if little-known, impact on Spanish geography for a century. At the age of five he saw his father off at the docks of Sevilla, and aboard the Fourth Voyage he served as chronicler in 1502–04 (F. Colón 1984, 162, 288). In between, he was a page at the royal court and privately tutored, in part by a key historian of the voyages, the Italian humanist Peter Martyr (c. 1458–1526). At least some of the natural history observations on the Central American coasts were probably made by Fernando, including the first description of pineapples (F. Colón 1984, 317). He was on Hispaniola in 1509, after which he was sent to Castile to study, "because he was inclined to the sciences and had many books" (Las Casas 1965, II, 370). Indeed, he spent much of 1512–16 studying at the Spanish Franciscan monastery in Rome, under the humanist Pedro de Salamanca (De la Rosa 1906; Ponsot and Drain 1966).

Fernando was precocious by any standards. He was captain-general of the fleet sailing back from Hispaniola in 1509; a year later he began the complex lawsuits against the crown, in regard to the titles and New World revenues due to the heirs of Columbus, who had died wealthy but frustrated in 1506; he proposed a circumnavigation of the globe a decade before Magellan; and in 1517 he began what was probably the most ambitious national project yet conceived for Spain, a countrywide geographical survey.

Although this project was designed for and executed in Spain, it later had great impact on physical observation in the Americas. As reconstructed from the surviving materials (F. Colón 1908–15), its purpose was to:

(a) Inventory all settlements, their dependencies or abandoned sites, any castles or monasteries, the distance to the municipal boundaries in different quadrants, and the jurisdiction (royal, aristocratic, monastic) to which they belonged.

(b) Determine the number of resident households (vecinos), presumably as based on local tax rolls and provided by the town councils.

(c) Record the quality of land in each territory (casco); this included location with respect to rivers and mountains, types of land use, and over 15 more-or-less standardized categories of topography and natural or spontaneous vegetations (Table 1). These characteristics were recorded along all roads in all directions, specifying rough distances to each change of land use or landscape, hence the designation of the project as an Itinerario (Itinerary).

This effort was funded by the crown, with salaries paid to a team of assistants who traveled around the country, following explicit but lost guidelines, presumably issued by Fernando.

Close to 10,000 settlements (perhaps 80 percent of those in Spain at the time) were inventoried before the project was terminated by royal decree in 1523, possibly in retaliation for a renewed round of litigation against the government initiated by Fernando in that year (De la Rosa 1906; Ponsot and Drain 1966; Arranz, in F. Colón 1984, 17). Incomplete and lacking official sanction, the results were never collated into the planned, alphabetical gazetteer (Vocabulario), from which a land use and physical map of Spain apparently was to be constructed. The notebooks of raw data were left to gather dust in the remarkable private library of 15,300 volumes and manuscripts that Fernando left behind at his death in 1539. When that library was rescued, at the end of the nineteenth century, only 4,400 of the town inventories and 5,000 of Fernando's books had survived.

Nothing like the Itinerary had ever been conceived before. However abortive or premature it may have been, this sophisticated geographical survey represents the first attempt to develop and implement a comprehensive field approach to the cultural and physical landscape.

Without questioning the pivotal role of Fernando in conceptualizing his geographical survey, the concepts and terminology used (Table 1) do not seem to have been his own. In his biography of Columbus, Fernando Colón (1984) employed a fairly sophisticated geomorphologic vocabulary, including terms such as *montaña, collado* (hill), *peña* (hilltop, cliff), *llanura* (plain), *planicie* (plane), *ciénega* (marsh), *fango* (swamp), *arroyo, espalda* (high slope, mountain crest), *peñascosa* (cliffed), *pedregosa* (rocky) and *quebrada* (broken topography), none of which are used in the Itinerary (Table 1). Only *llano, cerro,* and *aspera* are common to both, while *sierra, loma, cuesta, derribadero,* and *doblado* are exclusively found in the Itinerary. Most important, *monte* in the Itinerary is exclusively used in the traditional Spanish sense of scrub or woodland vegetation, whereas for Fernando it was a hill or low mountain, equivalent to *cerro*. This suggests that the vocabulary and possibly also the systematic approach should be credited to unidentified Spanish collaborators. Certainly the vegetation categories are those of Spaniards with rural backgrounds and, not surprisingly, none of these terms are used by Colón (1984) in his Caribbean accounts.

The only potential consultants of Fernando that can be identified are Pedro de Salamanca, whom he met in Madrid in June 1517, or Antonio de Nebríja, whom he consulted at the University of Alcalá at about the same time, six weeks before he began the Itinerary (De la Rosa 1906).[9] Nebríja (died 1522), is better known for first attempting to standardize Castilian Spanish as a written language (Green 1968, III, 11–18), but he also had geographical interests: he wrote on atmospheric pressure, worked on navigational instrumentation, and assembled an ambitious chart for the longitudes of Spanish cities, based on true time differences between them (Becker 1917, 96, 122; López Piñero 1979, 213–14). He may have stimulated or encouraged Fernando to attempt a national project, but he had no evident background in geomorphology or botany. One must assume that pragmatic Spanish rural experience was critical in developing the bio-

Table 1. Land Use and Landscape Classes Utilized for the Geographical Survey of Spain (1517) by Fernando Colón[a]

Arable land
  Wheat cultivation (*tierra de pan* or *labores, labranza*)
  Olive groves (*olivares*)
  Vineyards (*viñas*)
  Irrigated tracts (*huertas*)
  Minor categories, including almond, fig, citrus, apple, etc. orchards or groves

Grazing land and degraded woodland (*monte bajo*)
  Designated pastures (*dehesa*)
  Rough grass and shrub (*espartinas, monte de atocha*)
  Sclerophyllous scrub (*lentiscales, romerales, matorrales*)
  Thorny scrub (*montes jarales*)
  Scrub oak (*chaparrales, marañales, carrascojas*)
  Palmetto scrub, possibly abandoned farm land (*palmares*)
  Rocky surfaces with shrubs (*berrocales*)

Primary or secondary forest (*monte alto*)
  Deciduous oak (*robledal*)
  Live oak (*encinal, carrascal*)
  Cork oak (*alcornocal*)
  Pine (*pinal, pinar*)

Topography and landforms
  Floodplain (*llano de ribera del rio, vega*)
  Level plain (*llano, tierra llana, campiña*)
  Irregular plain (*tierra doblada*)
  Rough, dissected topography (*tierra aspera* or *derribadera*)
  Flat-topped hill (*loma*)
  Hill or peak (*cerro*)
  Mountain and valley country (*sierras y valles*)
  Escarpment (*cuesta*)

[a]Derived from F. Colón (1908–15); see also De la Rosa (1906); Ponsot and Drain (1966); Butzer (1988).

physical criteria central to Fernando's conception.

Fernando's project, probably conceived within a broader Spanish interest in the basic geography of the New World colonies (see Jiménez 1965, I, 11–37, 267–77), was closely replicated in New Spain in 1547–51 when emissaries were sent out from Mexico City to assemble detailed information on each Indian settlement for taxation purposes. Some 940 such reports, consisting of a paragraph or two of compact data, are preserved and known as the *Suma de Visitas* (Paso y Troncoso 1905a; also Borah and Cook 1960). No dated decree or official explanation is known.

Most of the *Suma* accounts gave the number of taxable households, the dimensions of the lands belonging to the town, and the nature of Indian agriculture and handicrafts (as liable for taxes in kind), together with a description of the topographic setting—*llano, espalda, sierra,* and *fragosa* (rugged) are common terms. Vegetation was characterized by such words as *sabana* (open parkland) or *monte* (woodland); when trees were suitable for timber or firewood, the accounts may specify oak, pine, or key tropical forms. Other features noted include potential pastures for livestock, the presence of wet lowlands (*ciénegas*), and springs or rivers suitable for irrigation. The similarities with Fernando's project are too close to be coincidental, demonstrating that the idea of the geographical survey was by no means forgotten in the deliberations of government at the highest level. Surprising, too, is the implication that lower-placed officials had the competence to make reliable observations of great value for the landscape reconstruction of sixteenth-century Mexico (see Butzer and Butzer forthcoming).

Biotic Taxonomy: Oviedo

Scientific research only began in the New World thirty years after Columbus's fateful voyage, and it was initiated by an unlikely source. Gonzalo Fernández de Oviedo (1478–1557) was a royal official with humanistic credentials who once translated a novel of chivalrous love into Spanish. Raised at the Spanish court, he spent three years as a soldier in Italy, where he became an aficionado of the arts before settling in as a retainer and notary. But at age thirty-five, he was sent to Panama as royal inspector for the gold foundries, and from 1513–47, he spent twenty years in the New World, working in Central America, Hispaniola, and Colombia (Pérez, in Fernández de Oviedo 1959, I, xvi–ccxxxvi). From 1522 onward he devoted a dozen years preoccupied with natural history,[10] for which he lacked any formal training. While in Madrid in 1525, without his records in hand, he wrote a "summary" volume on the natural history of the Indies (Fernández de Oviedo 1950), and in 1535 this was republished in expanded form as the cornerstone of his massive study (410 of 1,900 printed pages, Fernández de Oviedo 1959). Oviedo completed the whole work at age 71. But he clashed repeatedly with

Bishop Las Casas over the character of the New World Indians, whom he had refused to idealize, and Las Casas intervened to effectively stop publication of the remaining volumes (see Hanke, in Las Casas 1965, I, xxii–xxiii), which were not printed until the 1850s.

The bulk of Oviedo's work is devoted to the history of Spanish exploration and conquest, but even his derivative accounts single out important geographic and biotic data, such as the comparison of the cold-temperate biota of Patagonia and Newfoundland (Alvarez 1957). For areas Oviedo knew first hand, his accounts are substantive as well as evocative; they teem with nostalgic, comparative images of townscapes and landscapes in Spain or Italy (Gerbi 1985, 188–94). In an era when academics wrote in restrained Latin, Oviedo deliberately presented his materials in Spanish, salting his text with vignettes of Spanish abuse of the Indians, quips about greedy clerics or armchair historians, and candid personal anecdotes. His enthusiasm for the natural world is illustrated by an incident from his travels between Panama and Nicaragua (August 1527). Spotting what he thought were live oaks, in the mountains above the Gulf of Nicoya, he noted that the trees had no acorns. So he stopped his party and had his companions search the ground around the trees until they found a dozen acorns:

> And I ate them, though they were somewhat dry; and they were no more nor less than in Spain—live oaks in terms of the tree and the leaf, as well as the fruit (Fernández de Oviedo 1959, I, 298).

It is probably fair to say that Oviedo possessed modest abilities for synthetic interpretation, and that his primary contribution in natural history was analytical and systematic. Several broad themes preoccupied him:

(a) Domesticated indigenous plants and their utilization by the Indians (book 7);

(b) Wild food or fiber plants, manipulated and exploited by the Indians (book 8);

(c) Taxonomic comparison of neotropical trees and plants with those of the Mediterranean realm, according to physiognomy, leaf arrangements, leaf morphology, and fruits (books 9 and 11);

(d) Recognition of those genera or families with European counterparts, e.g., cherries, grapes, nut trees, pines, oaks, palms;

(e) Inventories of the neotropical fauna, organized under the categories of quadrupeds (book 12), fishes (book 13), birds (book 14), and insects (book 15), with the recognition that most, but not all, of these diverse animals belonged to families represented in the Old World.

Oviedo was the first to confront the dazzling profusion of unfamiliar plants and animals that made New World biogeography so daunting a subject. Excited but unperturbed, he imposed order through a taxonomy which organized life forms into morphological classes and delineated commonalities and differences with Old World forms. For unfamiliar genera or families, he applied indigenous names that, at the time, were rapidly acquiring an almost universal currency in the tropical colonies of Spain (J. D. Sauer 1976)—the "folk taxonomy" that was generally practiced before the binomial Linnaean classification. His natural history was published promptly, translated into several European languages, and had a profound scientific impact.

Oviedo modeled his taxonomy on Pliny (1940–56), with whom he was familiar, rather than on Theophrastus's more sophisticated conception of plant morphology and ecology, which he did not know. But unlike Pliny, Oviedo's descriptions and organization were based on years of empirical observation, guided by two firm principles: accuracy and inductive approach.[11] By virtue of his lack of formal training, Oviedo broke the mold of Medieval herbalists, who organized their plants alphabetically, not comparatively (Alvarez 1957).[12] In consequence, he offered a bold, biological macro-framework for the New World as well as the first systematic study of natural history since the time of Pliny (first century A.D.).

Although Oviedo seems not to have understood the principles of ecology, his work is filled with suggestions of ecological association that elevate it from taxonomy to biogeography. His is the only document we have that describes the circum-Caribbean region in a relatively unmodified biotic state (Alvarez 1957).

Equally important, Oviedo offered a detailed and focused account of economic botany that remains unique, and that retains its importance for the cultural geography of peoples in the region who have become extinct. In reading these sections, one repeatedly has the impression that Oviedo relied heavily on Native American informants, although he did not admit it. Oviedo's general contributions to understanding the aboriginal inhabitants and their customs also have value. He had no illusions about human nature, and was impartial in his criticisms of Spaniards and Indians and their foibles (see also Gerbi 1985, chap. 19). He heaped sarcastic abuse on Pedrarias, De Soto, and certain other conquistadors noted for their brutality (see also Salas 1954), and he blamed the Indian demographic collapse on Hispaniola squarely on the Spaniards: forced labor and other gross abuses, the resulting suicides, and on smallpox (Fernández de Oviedo 1959, I, 67). His comparative analysis of Spanish exploration or conquest of different parts of the Americas not only convinced him of the common nature of humanity in both world hemispheres, but he was the first to recognize that indigenous peoples of southeastern North America, the Caribbean, and South America had varying forms and levels of human culture (i.e., cultural complexity, a concept later explicated by Acosta [1962, 6.19]). Ballesteros (1957) further detects an implicit recognition of an historical progression of culture.

Like Columbus, Oviedo came to the New World as an amateur and was promptly filled with wonder by what he saw. But unlike Columbus, Oviedo became a dedicated scholar who produced the first great scientific work on the New World. No less an authority than Humboldt (1845–47, II, 298) believed that the foundations of modern physical geography were laid in the studies of Oviedo and Acosta (see below).

Cultural Landscapes: Sahagún

The biggest challenge for the first European observers in the New World was the encounter with new peoples possessed of unfamiliar and puzzling languages, lifeways, beliefs, and values. The problem, then, has been to grasp the indigenous vision of an indigenous world, to move from description to understanding. That vision was elusive because Native American reading of the landscape was set in a different cosmological perspective (see Licate 1980), one which cast the supernatural, the individual, and the community in unaccustomed interrelationships, and lent different meaning to concepts or material phenomena such as property, labor, dwelling, food, or technology.

In the unhappy tradition of European ethnocentrism, while some enlightened individuals sought to understand, many others recklessly destroyed the cultural diversity that they encountered in the "New" World. Not surprisingly, perhaps, some of the most explicit acknowledgments of Native American creative capacity and achievement come from some of the men who knew them best—the conquistadors. Hernán Cortés, in his letter of 1520 to the emperor, expressed wonder at the splendors of Tenochtitlan (later, Mexico City), its markets, and the great temple in a classic description, expanded in 1552 by his biographer, López de Gómara (1966, II 147–58; see the prose of Simpson 1964, 156–67). Indeed, most of the ethnographic materials synthesized by Fernández de Oviedo (1959) came from the chronicles of minor conquistadors or their more articulate rank-and-file. Among the latter is Cieza de León (1985), who assembled the first history of the Inca from oral testimony given by Indian informants.

The most successful students of cultural phenomena are found among the ranks of the missionaries. The first of these came to the Americas with Columbus on the Second Voyage. Although working with little christianizing success on Hispaniola 1493–96, the obscure Jeronymite friar Ramon Pané (Panet) evidently listened with great care. He was able to recount the origin myth, beliefs in the hereafter, and ritual medical practices, as well as observations on ethnic and linguistic distributions of the Taíno people (as in F. Colón 1984, 205–29; see Wilson 1990 on their culture). Even by modern anthropological standards, this account is remarkably objective, and qualifies as a first effort to record the self-perspective of another people. Pané's account is complemented by the descriptive ethnography of the Sevillano physician for the expedition, Diego Alvarez Chanca (Jane 1988, I, 20–73; Gerbi 1985, 23–26). Although Las Casas (1967, II, 178) maliciously described Pané as a Catalan who spoke Castilian poorly and was a bit simple-minded, Las Casas himself fares poorly by comparison.

Las Casas (1967) assembled a massive corpus of information during the 1540s–50s on the rituals and customs of various New World peoples in order "to demonstrate the rational capacity of the Indians." The seemingly strange behaviors can be explained, he argued, by different beliefs and world views, and in this relativist context, the New World peoples did not merit the pejorative connotation of "barbaric." But his ethnographic materials are so highly selected and sanitized that they retain little value.[13] His dogmatic conclusions that human sacrifice and cannibalism once were universal traits and that this demonstrated "a higher concept of God" among "the most religious peoples" (Las Casas 1967, II, chaps. 157, 185) are particularly disturbing.

More solid contributions to understanding New World cultures were advanced by the early Franciscans in Mexico. Diego de Landa controlled missionary activities in the Yucatan 1549–79, and although he was responsible for burning countless Mayan documents (see Lovell 1991), he also assembled an invaluable account of ancient Maya ethnography, history, and religion. Based on his own experiences as well as oral and written information, this account included "the first accurate knowledge of the hieroglyphic writing" (Tozzer, in Landa 1941, vii). Toribio de Benavente Motolinía (1969, 1971), one of the "first twelve" missionaries to arrive in Mexico in 1524, also authored works which include a wealth of ethnographic description on the pre-Contact Aztecs and some of their archaeological sites. Yet unlike Pané, who slips at times into an "insider" presentation, Motolinía's mode remains that of an "outsider."

The main Dominican contribution, completed in 1581 by Diego Durán (1967), reconstructed Aztec historical annals and their ritual calendar, based on indigenous informants and manuscript sources. His writings are interlinked with those of his Jesuit relative, Juan de Tovar. A specialist in three indigenous languages, Tovar was commissioned in 1576 by the Viceroy of New Spain to write the history of the indigenous people he was to govern, "with the assistance of the native historians and their books" (Warren 1973, 80). Although this work was lost, it was used extensively in another Jesuit study (Acosta 1962) of the indigenous civilizations of the New World. These investigations, encouraged by the government, signal a period of genuine and sensitive scholarly activity devoted to Aztec social history, one which presupposes the existence of indigenous documentation which, like many of the missionary writings, has been destroyed or "lost" in private collections.

The finest cultural research of the sixteenth century, the great Florentine Codex, was accomplished by the Franciscan friar Bernadino de Sahagún (1499–1590). Born in a small town of León, Sahagún came in 1529 to Mexico, where he occupied his next forty years with Aztec linguistic and cultural studies, materials that have attracted the attention of a century of international scholarship. Completed in final form in 1579, the thirteen-volume work (Sahagún 1950–69) constitutes an encyclopedia of Aztec culture, recorded in their Nahuatl language with abbreviated Spanish translations. Ranging across cosmology, philosophy, society, natural history, economic botany, and the artifactual realm, the materials stem from decades of in-depth interviewing of indigenous informants in several towns, whose responses to a structured questionnaire were transcribed in Nahuatl and in the cultural style of the informants. Of particular interest to geography are parts 10–12, dealing primarily with crafts and trades, markets and economy, architecture and construction methods, medicinal plants, and the Aztec perception and classification of the environment. These sections contain almost two-thirds of the 1846 indigenous illustrations (see Quiñones 1988) found in the work, but which so far have only been published as simplified sketches (Glass and Robertson 1975, 190–92).

An example best illustrates the complexity of cultural information encoded in what to European perception is merely a material object. In explaining the term *tecpancalli,* a pre-Contact palace, Aztec respondents unraveled multiple levels of meaning as they connected function with physical description:

It means the house of the ruler, or the government house, where the ruler is, where he lives, or where the rulers of the townsmen, the householders, assemble. It is a good place, a fine place, a palace; a place of honor, a place of dignity . . . . It is a fearful place, a place of fear, of glory . . . . There is bragging, there is boasting; there are haughtiness, presumption, pride, arrogance. There is self-praise, there is a state of gaudiness . . . . It is a center of knowledge, of wisdom . . . . It is something embellished, a product of care, made with caution, a product of caution, a deliberated thing made with deliberation; well made, the product of carved stone, of sculptured stone, plastered . . . , It is a red house, an obsidian serpent house . . . , It has a deep footing, a deep foundation . . . . It

has an entrance, vaulted, with cross beams, with a covering . . . (Sahagún 1969, XII, 270–71).

Klor (1988) regards Sahagún as "the father of modern ethnography," and he offers an insightful discussion of Sahagún's methodology and the problems of relating indigenous conceptions to European categories. Entering Aztec culture as a participant observer, Sahagún saw the native cultures as equal and, in some ways, superior to imported European cultures. He grasped what is now called cultural relativism, that each culture is rich in human information, and that the values embraced by the people who share that culture have merit. He "remained convinced that the conquest of the New World brought only one arguable gain: religion" (Nicolau and Cline 1973, 207; Nicolau 1987).

The Florentine Codex marks the close of sensitive research into Native American cultures in Hispanic America. In 1577 the Inquisition and the Council of the Indies barred or suppressed works in native languages by the missionaries. They ordered Sahagún's manuscripts to be turned over, but fortunately they were saved by the Inquisition's censor in Mexico who held different views (Nicolau and Cline 1973). This reversal of policy, directed from Rome, entailed fundamental changes in missionary strategies which the Archbishop of Mexico and the mendicant orders in New Spain strenuously but vainly resisted. From Motolinía in the 1520s to Sahagún in the 1580s, the goal had been conversion, not assimilation. When, in the 1590s, that benevolent Indian policy was set aside, particularly by the Franciscans, a steady erosion of cultural integrity ensued.

The Spanish observers of the sixteenth century had great difficulty in finding a model with which to view and understand the diversity of Native American cultures. Through the widely disseminated elaborations of Martyr (1964), Columbus's account of the Taíno of Hispaniola as generous, guileless, and backward fostered the stereotype of the American Noble Savage. In Mexico, Cortés and his soldiers stumbled upon a great civilization and created a different stereotype, a Clever and Discreet Indian gifted in art and industry (Keen 1971, 60). Las Casas blindly idealized the Indians. Motolinía accented the social inequalities and the poverty of Aztec Mexico, while Durán praised the hierarchical, class-conscious spirit of Aztec society (Keen 1971, 119–20). It remained for Sahagún to recognize the linkages between the world of appearances and the cognitive structures beneath it that influence individual and group actions, a discovery made possible by his linguistic analyses. But Sahagún himself was only rediscovered in the 1880s, and his semiotic conceptualization of culture and landscape should attract postmodern cultural geographers today (see Rowntree, et al. 1989, 213–14).

Regional and Synthetic Geography: Cieza de León

The talent to integrate environmental and cultural information in spatial and logical terms may be inborn rather than learned, at least if Pedro Cieza de León is taken as an example. Cieza (1984) was raised in Llerena, an Extremaduran town of 5000 inhabitants when he and his parents embarked at Seville for Colombia in 1535. At the time he was either thirteen or seventeen years old (his books give two versions), but within a year he was campaigning up and down the Andes as a common soldier. In describing the hardships, he complained of the exorbitant price of a piece of paper, implying that he was taking notes. His terse, informative, and evocative prose indicates an educated man; but that education must have been largely informal, acquired on his own and on-the-go. He died young, in 1554, just as his introductory volume to a four-tomed history of Peru was published. This first book, which relates a district-by-district geography of the Andean world from Panama to Bolivia (Cieza 1984), is of particular interest here.

Again and again he describes the dramatic physical environment, its diversity, and the cultural landscapes and subsistence forms of its various ecozones. In one paragraph he sweeps the reader from the mangrove coasts and rain forests of the Pacific slope into the snow-topped high ranges, describing the semiarid intermontane valleys in between. He directs attention to variations in rainfall and vegetation, windward and lee slopes, habitable and uninhabited regions, and the tortuous roads that bind them together. His superb account of the environs of Quito (Cieza 1984, chap. 40), with its descriptions of planted crops, Indian populations, livestock economy, and the surrounding network of towns, is too long to excerpt. The cogent report on Lake Titicaca is also exemplary and can be reproduced in translation:

> The region of Collao has many snow-capped wastes and mountains, as well as plains covered with good pastures that serve the domestic livestock wandering across them. In the middle is a lake, possibly the largest and widest in [South America], and most of the towns of Collao lie next to it. The cultivated land [and anything of value] is found on large islands within the lake, because these are deemed safer than the towns, which lie along the roads.
>
> This region is so cold that not only does it lack fruit orchards, but maize is not grown because it will not ripen, for the same reason. There are great numbers of birds of many kinds in the reed marshes of this lake, including large ducks and other fowl, and two or three kinds of tasty fish . . . .
>
> The lake is so large that its circumference is 330 km and its depth [according to Captain Juan Ladrillero, going out with his brigs] 25 fathoms or so, more in some parts, less in others. This size, and the waves raised when the wind blows, suggests an embayment of the ocean. It is not known why so much water is held in this lake or where that water comes from: although there are many streams and arroyos flowing into it, this seems inadequate, mainly because the lake is also drained [by a deep river that flows strongly] . . . Possibly the Deluge left this water behind because, as I see it, it should be salty rather than fresh if it had been part of the ocean, and furthermore the sea is 300 km away . . . .
>
> The great lake of Collao is called Titicaca, after the temple built on it . . . (Cieza 1984, chap. 103).

Cieza's account rivals the regional geographies of the nineteenth century, which is all the more remarkable because Cieza was untrained and had no mentors or role models. Although Classical geographers like Strabo provided good regional descriptions, they lacked the ability to shift the scale of vision, to gather so much hard observational data, to analyze interrelationships, or to systematically treat a large region according to a particular set of criteria.

A very different type of regional geography, embracing most of the New World, was attempted 1571–74 by López de Velasco (1971), whose similar lack of formal education is discussed below in relation to government geography. The *Geografía y descripción universal de las Indias* was assembled from reports and maps on the New World and East Indies in the office of the Council of the Indies. Dedicated to the king, and evidently intended to inform the government, Velasco tallied a total of 200 Spanish settlements in the Americas, with 32,000 Spanish households and 4000 other settlers and miners; there also were 8000 Indian towns and 1.7 million Indian "tributaries" liable to tax or work demands as well as 40,000 African slaves, not counting people of partial black ancestry.

Velasco's is a classic regional geography, a coherent work of synthesis. First the coastlines of a region are described, much in the manner of a navigational chart, followed by an outline of the topography, a description of the environment, a summary of the main cultural phenomena, and a systematic account of towns and agricultural activities. Miscellaneous points cover topics such as climatic constraints to settlement or agriculture. Historical digressions or travelers' "tales" are few. Unlike Cieza, who wrote spontaneously on the basis of direct observation, Velasco presented a more "academic" synthesis.

The work's rigor and systematics make it a volume of lasting historical scientific interest, as is shown by Menéndez Pidal's (1944) reconstruction of a New World geography for about 1570, based primarily on Velasco. The modernity of his secular and empirical synthesis, conceived at a global level through its inclusion of oceanic navigation and East Asia (López de Velasco 1971, 29–49, 273–309), contrasts with the continuing use of an obsolete Ptolemaean framework and a theological paradigm to the end of the century for presenting new geographic information in Central Europe (Menéndez Pidal 1944, 4; see also Ptolemy 1966; Münster 1968, Büttner and Burmeister 1979). Unfortunately, Velasco's prototype for synthetic geography remained unpublished until the fourth centenary of Columbus's voyage. Although Velasco's work had no impact on geographical scholarship, it deserves to be considered as a precursor to Carl Ritter and Elisé Reclus.

This first epoch of Spanish geographical inquiry aptly concludes with another compendium of a New World regional geography, that falls a little beyond our period of examination. The Carmelite friar Antonio Vázquez de Espinosa (c. 1570–1630) traveled through most of Hispanic America for fourteen years (1608–22), perhaps to evaluate possibilities for his order to engage in missionary work. Doubtless Vázquez (1969) had important backers because he had full freedom of movement, access to privileged information (such as the salaries of high church officials), and disposition over reams of municipal and economic statistics,

which he put to good use. In the course of his travel and sojourns, he compiled a wealth of papers, maps, reports, and first-hand observations.

Vázquez came from a poor, rural background in the olive-growing country just west of Sevilla. Equipped with a primarily religious education, and lacking the conceptual rigor or analytical skills of Velasco, Vázquez compensated for his shortcomings by a ready appreciation for complex landscapes and a lively interest in the rural economy. He provides, for example, unique quantitative data on wine and olive oil production in Peru; he also remains a key source for demographic data. The Compendium spans the Hispanic dominions, and his regional descriptions brim with quality, systematic information. He was unsparingly critical of what he regarded as short-sighted and abusive administration of the indigenous peoples, by both church and state; yet his own attitude was paternalistic, and unrelieved by sophistication for other cultures. At the time of his sudden death, his manuscript was in press, and like so many others, it remained unpublished.

To the works of Cieza, Velasco, and Vázquez can be added a variety of other travel reports or regional histories, with enlightening geographical introductions. Collectively they show that synthetic as well as analytical geography was an integral part of what would now be described as scientific thinking in sixteenth-century Spain. That normative geography was espoused in government circles should therefore come as no surprise.

Government Geography and Town Planning: López de Velasco

The role of Spanish government policy in urban planning is relatively well known (see Stanislawski 1947), but disagreement continues on the relation of theory and practice and the origin of the Spanish gridiron plan.

The first unambiguous government decree in regard to town location and morphology dates to November 1513 (CDI 1883, vol. 39, 284–85, 295–97); it instructed Pedrarias, the governor of Panama, to choose a town site on the coast or along a river to facilitate transport, making certain that the location was healthy, near woodland (for fuel) and good soil (to cultivate), and not liable to flooding; once the site was selected, the streets, plaza, church, and house lots were to be laid out in an explicitly "regular" (ordenado) manner, from the very beginning. A geometric grid is evidently meant, but no particular arrangements are specified for the various components. Cortés (1963, 589–90) received almost identical instructions in 1523, that added the caveat to avoid locations that were excessively windy, foggy, or steep.

But the details for the gridiron format were only specified in the "laws for settlement," proclaimed in 1573 (Ordenanzas 1973, 112–25). These ordinances called for towns to be organized along four main streets running at right angles to a central plaza and opening to four external gates; eight additional streets should diverge from the cardinal directions at the corners of the plaza. Diagonal alignment of the square and axial streets was thought to avoid direct exposure to unpleasant winds. The town square was to be rectangular, with a ratio of 1:1.5, varying from 60 by 90 m to 240 by 460 m, depending on the initial and expected size of the town. One ordinance specified that, according to Mediterranean custom, the church should be on the highest point and not necessarily on the plaza, with the public buildings located between the two (Ordenanzas 1973, 124). Where possible, location on a river or coast was recommended, with sanitation dictating that craft centers be located near the water.

These ordinances are remarkable in that they dictate norms for urban planning more than two centuries before the rectangular survey began to create checkerboard town plans in the U.S. The approximate grid plan for Santo Domingo (1502) was laid out without instructions to that effect (see CDI 1879, vol. 31, 17). The 1522 foundation document for Nata, Panama specified a traza ("trace"), implying a regular layout, and informs us that the principal streets of Nata converged on the church and public buildings "according to and because of the order and manner that the traza is identified [on the ground]" (Domínguez 1977, 36). Mexico City-Tenochtitlan was first rebuilt in 1523—in a location notorious for flooding and an unhealthy environment; it was then drastically remodeled according to a strict grid plan after 1538, not in response to special instructions, but according to the plan of Viceroy Mendoza (Tovar 1985). The new city of Puebla,

begun in 1531, also conforms to the ideal type of grid layout (Yáñez 1991), and many other examples in various parts of Hispanic America predate 1573.

The ordinances merely articulated and legalized a system already well established and in common use (Hardoy 1978). But the prescribed model was not always followed. Most such grid towns are more or less axially oriented to the cardinal points, not at 45° to them, while the church and public buildings were always on the plaza (or on one of two plazas). Hardoy (1975) examined 292 maps for 134 Spanish Colonial towns, only 22 of which were founded before 1600; he found that only 42 percent had been planned from the outset, another 32 percent were gradually modified to conform to a regular plan, and 26 percent evolved spontaneously. In short, the ordinances were not very effective after 1600.

Some authors argue that the Hispanic American grid plan was influenced by (or even grounded in) the Roman architect Vitruvius or Classical town models, and Mendoza's remodeling of Mexico City was indeed influenced by the Italian architect and planner, Leon Battista Alberti (1404–72), who drew many ideas from Vitruvius (Tovar 1985). But most new towns in Europe founded after about 1200 already had some form of regular layout long before the delayed publication of Alberti's book in 1485 (e.g., Hardoy 1975; Kubler 1978; Benevolo 1980).[14] Considering the inordinate role of leading conquistadors or administrators in determining the actual forms of the first planned towns in the New World, it seems more reasonable to attribute urban evolution to adaptation of already familiar Spanish prototypes to new opportunities and requirements: the availability of abundant space; the need to quickly establish a few dozen initial settlers; the priority of economic over defensive strategies, favoring level terrain and the conjunction of kitchen gardens with dwellings on a single lot; and proximity to vital Colonial institutions: the government buildings, the church, and various shops (see also Hardoy 1978). Instead of an endless and inconclusive search for specific intellectualized antecedents, it seems more productive to explicate particular urban histories (e.g., Butzer 1989), and to explore the function of the city as an instrument of colonization (Hardoy 1978; Morse 1987).

The driving force behind the formulation of

the 1573 ordinances and the role of government in marshalling geographical information was Juan López de Velasco (c. 1530–99). He came from the remote village of Vinuesa (Soria), where his family owned some houses and irrigated fields; checks of student enrollments at various institutions of higher education confirm that he lacked a formal education (Pérez-Rioja 1958). According to his last will, his sister in Vinuesa lived in poverty; some of his money went to her sons that they might go to America—something that he had been unable to do. Despite such impediments, Velasco wrote respectable works on astronomy, a navigation guide to the Atlantic Ocean, and a regional geography of the New World (see above); he also became a national authority on the spelling and pronunciation of the Castilian language. Velasco probably received a rudimentary education from the parish priest in Vinuesa, and then began to work as a young government clerk in Madrid. By 1565 it appears that he was an assistant, possibly responsible for legal work at the Council of the Indies. The proverbial self-made man, Velasco had no rank in his status-conscious society nor the opportunity to travel.

His profound influence on Spanish geographical planning and policy was exerted indirectly, through the authority of his patron, Juan de Ovando y Godoy, the distinguished jurist and statesman. Appointed to revamp the Council of the Indies in 1569–71, Ovando focused his reforms on improving geographical understanding and developing a coherent body of legislation (Cline 1972; González, in López de Velasco 1971, v–xxxvi). Velasco implemented this effort and was appointed cosmographer and chronicler to the Council to that end. After Ovando's death, Velasco was removed from a position of influence in 1577 as the policies of church and state shifted.

Ovando apparently served as a "front" for Velasco's precocious initiatives, which included: (1) reorganization and codification of the legislation applicable to the Americas (by 1571); (2) formulation of the comprehensive "laws of settlement" (in 1573); (3) solicitation of local reports from parishes in the New World, through the various bishops, to provide data on the Indian population, frequently amplified by geographical information (1571) (see Paso y Troncoso 1905b, c, for the Mexican series); (4) compilation of a New World regional geography, based in part on the parish reports; (5) development of a geographic and ethnographic questionnaire dispatched to all district magistrates in the New World (in final form 1577) (Edwards 1969; Cline 1972); (6) the questionnaire produced *relaciones geográficas* for some 500 communities (mainly 1577–86), now available in fourteen published volumes, covering parts of Mexico, the Antilles, and the wider Andean region (Acuña 1984–88; Latorre 1920; Jiménez 1965; Edwards 1980); and (7) a parallel set of questions directed to towns in Spain, which generated *relaciones topográficas* for another 636 communities (Nader 1990). In addition to these diversified and substantial initiatives in government geography and policy, Ovando and Velasco seem to have provided indirect support for the ethnographic research of Durán, Tovar, and Sahagún in Mexico.

The degree to which the Renaissance spirit of rationalization pervaded this effort can be judged by Velasco's thirty-eight questions (with twelve more for coastal locations) (see Cline 1972, 234–37). Question 4, for example, requested information as to whether land was plain or rough, open or forested; with many or few streams or springs, and abundant or deficient waters; fertile or lacking in pastures; abundant or sterile in crops and sustenance. Site and location of each town was to be specified; was the site high or low, level or sloping (question 10)? Other questions asked about distance to the nearest mountains; the nature of adjacent rivers and their sources; lakes or springs serving the town; volcanoes, caves, or other notable natural phenomena in the vicinity; native trees common to the district and their potential economic use; wild animals and birds; information on mineral resources, mines, or quarries; and, for coastal locations, data on shore topography, offshore reefs, tides, and storms. These biophysical questions were complemented by requests for information on crops, soils, livestock, town plans, and the like. Ethnographic questions covered Indian languages, pre-Contact government and religion, native dress, manner of warfare, and past and present means of subsistence.

The *relaciones* therefore solicited a broad corpus of information appropriate to the administrative needs of government policy. The reports submitted by the magistrates or clergy were generally quite good since their accounts were based on interviews of long-term residents in Spanish towns and native elders in Indian towns. In addition, many of the *relaciones* included local pictorial maps, many drawn by Native Americans, that illustrate sixteenth-century cultural or symbolic landscapes, and sometimes include exquisite detail on vegetation. Collectively the *relaciones* provide an inestimable resource of analytical information on landscape change and indigenous cultural geography (see Edwards 1975; Bustos 1988; E. K. Butzer 1989). But that should not let us lose sight of the fundamental fact that the *relaciones*, like other efforts of Velasco as the first government geographer, were designed to facilitate imperial administration and policy at both the meso- and macroscales. In Madrid, by the 1570s, more complex modes of geographical understanding had begun to supersede maps as a tool of government.

Velasco's influence on sixteenth-century scientific observation thus was enormous. Not only did he play a catalytic role in government, but he also challenged others to follow similar norms. Indeed, Antonio de Ciudad Real (1976), a Franciscan friar traveling through Mexico in 1584–89 as secretary to a visiting inspector, seems to have modeled his account on parts of this questionnaire, noting the environments he traversed, land use around each town, and crops grown in the various monasteries. Similarly, requests for land deeds in Mexico increasingly incorporated environmental information, so much so that the land-grant documents can be used to reconstruct the vegetation of the sixteenth century (Butzer and Butzer forthcoming). Yet Velasco was indebted to the earlier efforts of Fernando Colón: in many ways he merely implemented the initiatives of Colón's *Itinerario*, a concept that finally bore rich fruit sixty years later.[15]

A Scientific Framework: Acosta

As the intellectual ferment of the sixteenth century began to diminish with growing religious orthodoxy and censorship (Kamen 1985, chap. 5), it remained for the Jesuit scholar Joseph de Acosta (c. 1540–1600) to place the New World into a new scientific framework. The son of a merchant family in Medina del Campo, a once-prosperous town of Old Castile, Acosta studied philosophy at the university of Alcalá de Henares 1559–67. The fifteen years 1572–87 were spent in the Americas, almost exclusively in Peru, but he had close contacts with Tovar and Durán in Mexico from whom he derived most of his ethnographic information.

In his *Historia natural*, Acosta made significant original observations on physical phenomena, e.g., the latitudinal organization of world climates in which he recognized that the rainy seasons of the tropics were linked to the zenith of the sun (high-sun rains) (Acosta 1962, 2.7), contrary to the opposite argument of Aristotle. He not only reaffirmed Columbus and Gómara to the effect that the torrid zone was quite habitable, but explained that equatorial climates were moderated by relatively short days and abundant rainfall, especially where complemented by coastal breezes (Acosta 1962, 2.10–11). He conceptualized the systematic decrease of temperature with elevation in tropical mountains (Acosta 1962, 2.12) and thus anticipated the montane ecozonation of Humboldt.

But his major contribution rests in his exposition of a scientific and ontological framework for the New World. The first half of his book focuses on the natural world, and there he makes two basic points (O'Gorman, in Acosta 1962, xliii–xlvii): (1) How the Americas form an integral part of the universe, in relation to the global distribution of seas and continents, and the habitable realm; (2) How the Americas are formed of the same four physical elements (earth, water, air, fire) and the same natural orders (mineral, vegetal, animal) as the other continents. The second half of his work, on the human world, is similarly structured according to two arguments (O'Gorman, in Acosta 1962): (1) That the New World peoples are an integral part of the supernatural world as well as of humankind, that is, spiritual, physical, feeling, and rational creatures; (2) That the New World peoples have their own history (in part oral), making them part of a universal history.

This all may seem self-evident today, but Acosta was the first European to explicitly recognize that New World phenomena existed in their own right. Building on ideas already expressed by López de Velasco (1971, 2), he attributed the divergence of the Old and New World peoples to migration, surmising that the

continents were connected or almost connected in unexplored Arctic latitudes:

> the one (world) and the other are joined and are
> continuous or at least approach each other and are
> very close . . . because the Arctic or North Pole
> has not been discovered and the full extent of the
> land is unknown . . . .
> the first settlers travelled to the Indies . . . without
> reflection, progressively shifting locations and ter-
> ritories, some occupying those already found, oth-
> ers looking for new ones, so that in the course of
> time they came to fill the lands of the Indies with
> so many groups, peoples, and languages (Acosta
> 1962, 1.20).

Other, popular fables such as the Lost Tribes
or Atlantis were rejected. As a creationist he
was puzzled by the different degrees of divergence between the Old and New World fau-
nas, and the absence of large mammals on the
Caribbean islands, suggesting that

> through natural instinct and divine providence dif-
> ferent kinds (of animals) went to different regions,
> doing so well in some that they remained, or if
> they moved on, they did not survive or died out
> in time (Acosta 1962, 4.36).

It can be argued that this concept of diverging
migration anticipates biogeography and even
geographical speciation, but without its evolu-
tionary implications.

A more satisfactory solution to the dilemmas
of natural history noted by Acosta was not
forthcoming until Darwin, while the origin of
New World peoples has only been unraveled
during the twentieth century. Although Acosta
remained entrenched in Aristotelian thinking,
his synthetic, ontological framework stands
midway between Medieval attempts to construct a cosmological order and more modern
efforts to lay out a new, scientific counterpart.
Published in 1590, his ideas were disseminated
by twenty-five foreign editions during the next
two centuries (López Piñero 1979, 295).

Retrospect

It is evident that Columbus's encounter with
what came to be called the New World had an
immense intellectual impact on thoughtful
Spaniards in many walks of life, with and without formal education. These included sailors
and soldiers, clerks and clergymen, and a few
men of letters. They were connected less by
academic links or traditions than by a spontaneous capacity to observe and describe, to
compare and classify. The authors and works

singled out here, together with many others,
represent a wealth of original and empirical
observation and analysis of new environments
and unfamiliar peoples, all within a span of
three generations. Separately or in tentative
forms of synthetic integration, they laid out the
components of a scientific, geographical understanding of that "New" World. This was a
veritable Renaissance or rebirth, that easily surpassed any Classical prototypes, and the
challenge to deal with all that was novel put
people with rural backgrounds on an equal
footing with those steeped in academic curricula.

Given the exuberant environmental descriptions of a Columbus, an Oviedo, or a Cieza, or
the love of nature exhibited by Acosta (1962,
1.3), it is difficult to understand how John Elliott
can claim that:

> It is as if the American landscape is seen as no more
> than a back cloth against which the strange and
> perennially fascinating people of the New World
> are dutifully grouped. This apparent deficiency in
> naturalistic observation may reflect a lack of inter-
> est among sixteenth-century Europeans, and espe-
> cially those of the Mediterranean world, in land-
> scape and in nature (1970, 20).

For an influential historian of Spain, the ethnocentric dismissal of South European interest in
the natural world is inexcusable. More important, the inability of such a fine humanist to
grasp the intellectual excitement of geographical observation and perception of that new
world is deeply disturbing.

Unfortunately, the Spanish contributions of
the sixteenth century to geography and related
scientific research had minimal impact on the
German revival of the field during the early
nineteenth century. Humboldt (1845–47, II, 298)
readily acknowledged the importance of
Oviedo and Acosta, but did not know Cieza.
Furthermore, Fernando Colón, Sahagún, López
de Velasco, Vázquez, and the relaciones
geográficas remained unpublished and inac-
cessible, primarily as a result of official xeno-
phobia or religious censorship. The curtain that
began to close in 1577 stifled free inquiry, and
the quality of Spanish research declined long
before the precipitous fall in Spanish scholarly
publication about 1640 (see López Piñero 1979,
377–86). The geography that reemerged in
Spain during the mid-1700s stood in the
shadow of the French Enlightenment (see

Capel 1982), and it did not regain its original vitality until well into the present century.

Acknowledgments

Development of the ideas discussed here was facilitated by free access to the library of Juan F. Mateu (Valencia), discussion with José M. López Piñero (Valencia), and Manual González Jiménez and Fernando Díaz del Olmo (Sevilla), and participation in the symposium "El Nuevo Mundo y los procesos de difusión de la ciencia y la técnica durante el período colonial" at the Universidad Internacional Menéndez Pelayo (Valencia), September 1991. James T. Abbott provided major assistance with the library search. Carville Earle (Baton Rouge), W. George Lovell (Kingston), Geoffrey J. Martin (New Haven), and Carla Rahn Phillips (Minneapolis) offered valuable, constructive criticism. Periodic Saturday breakfasts with Los Amigos de la Frontera in San Antonio and Austin offered a lively forum of discussion, especially with Adán Benavides, Robert Benavides, and Elizabeth John.

Notes

1. Marco Polo (1958) can be cited for descriptions of "Tartar" transhumance and the spring snow melt in Armenia (chap. 22), the landscapes he passed in the Pamir Mountains (chap. 47); moving sands covering tracks in the Lop Nor (chap. 56), the bustle of life and urban layouts of Peking and Hangchow (chaps. 85 and 153), and a series of well-tended Chinese landscapes (chaps. 107–58). Even data he obtained by hearsay for Zanzibar and Madagascar (chaps. 192–93) are remarkably accurate, such as a description of giraffes. The "chapters" refer to the Bennedetto subdivisions, used by some but not all of the many available editions. On the expanding geographical horizons of Medieval Europe, see J. Phillips (1988).

2. For example, the German cartographer Münzer (1952) gave a valuable and remarkably objective eyewitness account in 1494–95 of the Muslim towns and people of recently conquered Granada, without quoting a single Classical author or historical source. By comparison, a more erudite Portuguese traveler, Barreiros (1952), traveled through Spain in 1542, to fashion a self-styled chorography that was little more than a pretext to display his familiarity with Classical literature; observations become little more than incidental.

3. The Ptolemy (1932) edition, in English translation, has been criticized, but it is one of the very few that is accessible and not written in Latin or Greek. The fifteenth-century maps it reproduces presumably go back indirectly to third-century or earlier prototypes, to illustrate the regional information available in Antiquity. By contrast, Ptolemy (1966), in Latin with commentary and maps by Sebastian Münster, is a good example of how these principles were used to redraw the same maps during the early 1500s, using contemporary information. Münster (1968), Waters (1958), Harvey (1987), Campbell (1987), Harley (1990), and Nebenzahl (1990) are recommended for those readers interested in the cartography of the period. The unexpected death of Brian Harley will undoubtedly delay preparation of volume 3 of his and David Woodward's monumental *History of Cartography*, which will treat the Age of Discovery.

4. Questions persist whether the diary of the First Voyage is heavily edited, incomplete, or even a selective summary of Columbus's original by Bishop Las Casas (see Fuson 1983; Henige 1991). These issues do not affect the materials selected here, which clearly do not stem from Las Casas, who later paraphrased the same biophysical data in a singularly lifeless and inept manner (see Las Casas 1965, I).

5. Columbus's background, prior to his appearance at the Spanish court in the late 1480s, has been in hot dispute since 1517. The idealized biographical data for before 1488 all derive from Fernando Colón (1984) and Las Casas (1965), who used the same documentation, almost all of which has disappeared and thus cannot be authenticated. If the lost correspondence with the Florentine cartographer Paolo Toscanelli (1397–1482), as claimed by Colón (1984, 66–71) and Las Casas (1965, I, 62–66), were verifiable, it would date Columbus's interest in circumnavigation and, more important, his scholarly activities, back to before 1481. Las Casas (1965, I) refers to these letters on seven different occasions, implying that he had them in hand. For a lucid but critical analysis of Columbus's career, see Phillips and Phillips 1992; the authoritative biography is by Taviani (1985).

6. Letters securely attributed to Columbus are written in the script known as *humanística cursiva* (see Arribas 1965, I, 166–67 and plate 101), characteristic of the royal court in about 1500.

7. No maps by Columbus have been authenticated, but his younger brother Bartolomé is reputed to have been the author of several nautical charts (F. Colon 1984, 85–86; Las Casas 1965, I, 153–54). "Because Columbus dominates the documentary record, we know less about the other men on the voyage, but his observations . . . can stand as a general description of their experience" (Phillips and Phillips 1992, 157). The geographical competence of contemporary cartographers becomes apparent in the case of Andres de Morales (died 1517), a ship pilot on Columbus's Third Voyage. Morales was commissioned to make a map of Hispaniola in 1508 (see color copy in Milanich and Milbrath 1989, 68), and information from his report is preserved in Martyr (1964, 349–55), subsequently evaluated by Carl Sauer (1966, 41–48). The map is remarkably detailed and accurate, showing the key mountain chains in fifteenth-century, North Italian technique (see Harvey 1987 for examples). Sauer rates highly the information on indigenous territorial organization and land use, but the abbreviated topographic descriptions preserved in Martyr are also intriguing. Morales appears to have had accurate views on the

pattern of ocean currents in the North Atlantic, and later served as Chief Pilot in the Casa de Contratación of Sevilla (Becker 1917, 81, 90–91). That institution in Sevilla was the key European center of navigational science from 1508 onwards (Broc 1980, 194–96). For insights into its curriculum for ship pilots, see Lamb (in Medina 1972).

8. An early appreciation of Columbus's observations is given by Humboldt (1845–47, I, 296–97, 335; II, 55–57, 277, 299–304, 325; IV, 233, 250, 253, 261), who lauds his poetic descriptions, and interprets his observations on botany, wind patterns, and magnetic declination; but at times, I suspect, he reads too much into the statements of Columbus. For a humanistic evaluation, see Gerbi (1985, chap. 2), who also emphasizes the Genoan navigator's feeling for nature, as well as his focus on differences or affinities between the biota of the Indies and the Old World. It is surprising to read in Sale (1990, 102) that Columbus's language is "opaque and lifeless"; I can only infer that Sale did not sample the evocative original language, in favor of a "flat" English translation. Sale (1990, 101) laments the absence of an exultant description of "old-growth tropical forest" from the Bahamas, a curious gaffe for a professed ecologist, both in view of the subclimax woodlands of these low, hurricane-lashed islands and of their considerable indigenous population in 1492. When Sale (1990, 101) further faults Columbus for not writing about melodious bird songs with due excitement, I can only conclude that Sale did not read the journal carefully after the entry for October 28 (a scant ten of his forty references are subsequent to that date). Only a superficial reader or an ideologue could conclude that Columbus "cares little about the features of nature" (Sale 1990, 102).

9. There is some ambiguity in Fernando Colón (1908–15, 1) about the initial entry that the Itinerary was "begun" August 3, 1517, as to whether this meant the project or the writing (see De la Rosa 1906 vs. Ponsot and Drain 1966). Since Fernando had only returned from Rome in October 1516 and was in Spain without interruption until late in 1519 (when he began his peregrinations throughout western Europe in search of books [see Arranz, in F. Colón 1984, 31–37]), his major role in this effort appears to date from 1517–19.

10. O'Gorman (1946) believes that Oviedo's conversion to science began with his trip to the court of Charles V in Brussels (1516–17), where he delivered a formal complaint against the injustices of Pedrarias Dávila, Panama's notorious governor. In Belgium, Oviedo was exposed to Erasmian thought, if not seminars by Erasmus (c. 1466–1536) himself, who taught at Louvain from 1517–21. This Renaissance philosopher, a close friend of Thomas More, emphasized a humanistic rather than a dogmatic Christianity, based on the New rather than Old Testament. According to O'Gorman (1946), Oviedo began to see the European enterprise in the New World as a providential mission that it was his vocation to describe. I have trouble discerning a utopian thread in Oviedo's history, and the only obvious trait he

shares with Erasmus is his frequent use of satire to criticize Spaniards in general and churchmen in particular. The Spanish Erasmian movement, especially as represented by Juan Luís Vives (1492–1540), may, however, be pertinent, with its emphasis on inductive argument.

11. Ideal scientific procedure, according to Humboldt (1845–47, I, 65–70) proceeds from accurate observation and description to understanding, via analogy and induction, a view worth remembering in a time when empirical and inductive research are denigrated by some social scientists. In praising Oviedo's "incredible virtuosity in botany," J. D. Sauer (1976, n. 16) states that he "was far ahead of his only model, Pliny, in accuracy and originality." Also in regard to accuracy, Ferrando (1957) emphasizes that Oviedo's data on the Pacific Ocean were extracted with great care from trustworthy sources, providing a realistic picture of exactly what was known to Europeans about its coastlines and islands c. 1550. There were no imaginary islands on Oviedo's mental map.

12. That Oviedo did not know the work of Aristotle, Theophrastus, or Dioscorides on plants (Butzer forthcoming [b]), nor the late Medieval herbal literature, is readily explained by the fact that these were only used in the medical curriculum of the time (Alvarez 1957). He was also unaware of the agricultural treatise of Gabriel Alonso de Herrera (1970), published in 1513. Far more orthodox as a botanist was Francisco Hernández, Philip II's personal physician, who was sent to the New World to collect medicinal plants (Goodman 1988, 234–37). He spent six years (1571–77) collecting, drawing, and describing thousands of species on Hispaniola and Cuba, and especially in Mexico (Somolinos 1960–84), but died shortly after his return. López Piñero (1991) shows that Fernández's illustrations were probably drawn by indigenous artists.

13. To make his case, Las Casas (1967) gleaned an endless litany of bestial customs from the Classical authors and early church fathers, to show that Old World peoples were more depraved than those of the New World. But all too many of his Old World comparative "data" are no more than ethnocentric hearsay about foreign peoples or practitioners of other religions. For a more sympathetic presentation of this complex personality, see Friede and Keen (1971). In regard to ritual cannibalism in the New World, it is appropriate to cite Phillips and Phillips (1992, 295, n. 22): "To deny that cannibalism existed, one needs to assume that a wide range of European commentators simply made up the stories, an interpretation that defies reason, logic, and the available evidence."

14. There is an extensive literature on urban planning in Colonial Latin America, and several of the above references help identify larger collections of papers, mostly in English. A wealth of translated documents related to the Spanish colonial enterprise, including many of the ordinances or decrees cited here, can be found in Parry and Keith (1984), a treasure trove for students inter-

ested in exploring the possibilities of historical geographical research in the region.

15. The link between Velasco and Colón appears to be the noted cartographer Alonso de Santa Cruz (1505–67), who was appointed cosmographer to the Casa de Contratación in Sevilla 1536 (see Carriazo 1951). He worked in Sevilla until 1564, when he moved to Madrid at the king's request. Although there is no documentation to prove the point, Ovando's reliance on Velasco after 1569 offers a plausible scenario that Velasco had already acquired astronomic and geographic experience while working for Santa Cruz in Madrid. In 1572, Santa Cruz's great map collection was transferred from his old residence in Sevilla into the possession of Velasco, as the new royal cosmographer. In his *Libro de las longitudes* (completed ca. 1557), Santa Cruz notes that he planned to write a geography, while in his *Islario general* (completed ca. 1560), he implies that he was working on a *General geografía e historia* (Carriazo 1951, clxv). Velasco would have been aware of these plans and have had access to whatever notes that had been compiled, although no such materials are separately inventoried for Santa Cruz's estate (see Carriazo 1951). Although Velasco's geography would not have been possible without Santa Cruz's maps, there is no reason to doubt that his scientific organization was his own. In 1556 or 1557 Santa Cruz prepared a set of instructions for explorers in the New World, consisting of seventeen points (Jiménez 1965, 272–77; Carriazo 1951, clxix–clxxiii), evidently a direct antecedent to the questionnaire of Ovando and Velasco, in terms of inventorying environmental features and ethnographic data. Item three instructs the responsible officials to clarify the situation of new lands, "if they are mountainous or level, or if they are swampy or full of lakes, or if they are unhealthy for the natives or for foreigners" (Jiménez 1965, 274). Items twelve and sixteen inquire whether the native peoples have learned men and books, suggesting that indigenous histories be obtained in order to translate them into Spanish (Jiménez 1965, 276)—a remarkable perspective not found in Velasco's questionnaire. These instructions of Santa Cruz, much like the *ordenanzas* for town planning, form part of a chain of ideas, as can be seen from the instruction of Viceroy Mendoza, given in Mexico City in 1538 to Fray Marcos for his exploration of Cibola; he was instructed to make observations on the people as well as of "the climate of the land; the trees and plants and domesticated and wild animals they have; the nature of the land, if it is rough (*aspera*) or flat (*llana*); the rivers, if they are large or small . . . " (Jiménez 1965, 20). Perhaps Mendoza even influenced the scope of the Suma de Visitas in 1547 (see above). It is interesting that Santa Cruz uses *monte* and *montuosa* not for woodland/wooded, as in prevailing Spanish usage, but like F. Colón, for mountain/mountainous—a tantalizing hint for a possible connection with Colón, who would have known Santa Cruz, as a fellow Sevillano with shared interests.

References

Square brackets give dates of original publication or manuscript termination.

Acosta, Joseph de. 1962 [1590]. *Historia natural y moral de las Indias.* Ed., with commentary by Edmundo O'Gorman. Mexico City: Fondo de Cultura Económica. Facsimile ed. with English commentary and anthology by Barbara G. Beddal. Valencia: Hispaniae Scientia, Albatros Ediciones, 1977.

Acuña, René de, ed. 1984–88. *Relaciones geográficas del Siglo XVI,* 10 vol. Mexico City: Instituto de Investigaciones Antropológicas, Universidad Nacional Autónoma de México.

Ailly, Pierre d'. 1948 [1410]. *Imago Mundi by Petrus Ailliacus.* Trans. Edwin F. Keever. Wilmington, NC: Linprint.

Alvarez López, Enrique. 1957. La historia natural en Fernández de Oviedo. *Revista de Indias* 17:541–601.

Aríja Rivarés, Emilio. 1972. *Geografía de España II: Historia de la geografía española.* Madrid: Espasa-Calpe.

Arribas Arranz, Filemón. 1965. *Paleografía documental hispánica.* 2 vol. Valladolid: Universidad de Valladolid.

Baker, J. N. L. 1963. *The history of geography.* Oxford: Oxford University Press.

Ballesteros Gaibrois, Manuel. 1957. Fernández de Oviedo, etnólogo. *Revista de Indias* 17:445–67.

Barreiros, Gaspar. 1952 [1542]. Corografía de algunos lugares. In *Viajes de extranjeros por España y Portugal,* ed. J. García Mercadal, vol. 1, pp. 945–1046.

Beazley, Charles R., and Prestage, Edgar. 1896–98. *The chronicle of the discovery and conquest of Guinea.* London: Hakluyt Society, reprinted New York: B. Franklin, n.d.

Beck, Hanno. 1973. *Geographie: Europäische Entwicklung in Texten und Erläuterungen.* Freiburg: Karl Alber.

Becker, Jerónimo. 1917. *Los estudios geográficos en España.* Madrid: Real Sociedad de Geografía.

Benevolo, Leonardo. 1980. *The history of the city.* Cambridge, MA: MIT Press.

Borah, Woodrow, and Cook, Sherburne F. 1960. *The population of Central Mexico in 1548: An analysis of the Suma de Visitas de Pueblos.* Ibero-Americana 43. Berkeley: University of California Press.

Broc, Numa. 1980. *La géographie de la Renaissance (1420–1620).* Paris: Bibliothéque Nationale, Comité des travaux historiques et scientifiques (Section Géographie, 9).

Buisseret, David. 1992. Spain maps her "New World." *Encounters: A Quincentenary Review* 8: 14–19.

Bustos, Gerardo. 1988. *Libro de las descripciones:*

Sobre la visión geográfica de la peninsula de Yucatán en textos españoles del siglo XVI. Mexico City: Universidad Nacional Autónoma de México, Instituto de Investigaciones Filológicas.

Büttner, Manfred, and Burmeister, Karl H. 1979. Sebastian Münster 1488–1552. In *Geographers: Bibliographical studies,* ed. T. W. Freeman and P. Pinchemel, vol. 3, pp. 99–106. New York: Mansell.

Butzer, Elisabeth K. 1989. Changing patterns of domestic architecture in early Colonial Mexico, 1520–1620. *Abstracts, 1989 Conference of Latin Americanist Geographers,* Queretaro, Mexico, p. 40.

Butzer, Karl W. 1962. Coastal geomorphology of Majorca. *Annals, Association of American Geographers* 52:191–212.

———. 1988. Cattle and sheep from Old to New Spain: Historical antecedents. *Annals, Association of American Geographers* 78:29–56.

———. 1989. Historical Querétaro: Interpretation of a Colonial city. In *Field Trip Guide, 1989 Conference of Latin Americanist Geographers,* Querétaro, Mexico, pp. 3–27. Austin: University of Texas, Department of Geography.

———. Forthcoming (a). Ethno-agriculture and cultural ecology in Mexico: Historical vistas and modern implications. In *Geographers' research on Latin America 1990,* ed. Tom L. Martinson.

———. Forthcoming (b). The Classical and Islamic agronomic traditions. In *Science during the early Middle Ages,* ed. P. L. Butzer and D. Lohrmann. Basel: Birkhaeuser.

——— **and Butzer, Elisabeth K.** Forthcoming. The sixteenth-century environment of the Central Mexican Bajío: Archival reconstruction from Spanish land grants. In *Culture, form, and place,* ed. Kent Matthewson. Baton Rouge, LA: Geoscience and Man.

Campbell, Tony. 1987. Portolan charts from the late thirteenth century to 1500. In *The history of cartography,* ed. J. Brian Harley and David Woodward, vol. 1, pp. 371–463. Chicago: University of Chicago Press.

Capel, Horacio. 1982. *Geografía y matematicas en la España del siglo XVIII.* Barcelona: Oikos-Tau.

Carriazo, Juan de Mata, ed. 1951. *Alonso de Santa Cruz: Crónica de los reyes católicos.* Sevilla: Escuela de Estudios Hispano-Americanos, 49.

Casas, Bartolomé de las. 1965 [1566]. *Historia de las Indias.* 3 vol. Transcribed by Agustín Millares, commentary by Lewis Hanke. Mexico City: Fondo de Cultura Económica.

———. 1967 [1556]. *Historia apologética sumaria,* 2 vol. Transcribed, with commentary by Edmundo O'Gorman. Mexico City: Instituto de Investigaciones Historicas, Universidad Nacional Autónoma de México.

Cieza de León, Pedro. 1984 [1553]. *Crónica del Peru,* vol. 1. Ed., with introduction by Franklin Pease. Lima: Academia Nacional de la Historia.

———. 1985 [1550]. *Crónica del Peru,* vol. 2.: *El señorío de los Incas.* Ed., with commentary by Francesca Cantú. Lima: Academia Nacional de la Historia.

Ciudad Real, Antonio de. 1976 [1590]. *Tratado curioso y docto de las grandezas de la Nueva España.* 2 vol. Ed., with commentary by Josefina García Quintana and Victor Castillo Farreras. Mexico City: Universidad Nacional Autónoma de México, Instituto de Investigaciones Historicas.

Cline, Howard F. 1972. The *relaciones geográficas* of the Spanish Indies, 1577–1648. In *Guide to ethnohistorical sources,* ed. H. F. Cline, vol. 1, pp. 183–242. Handbook of Middle American Indians 12. Austin: University of Texas Press.

Colección de documentos inéditos relativos al descubrimiento, conquista y organización de las antiguas posesiones españolas de América y Oceania. (CDI) 1864–84. 42 vol. Madrid: M. G. Hernández.

Colón, Fernando. 1908–15 [1523]. *Descripción y cosmografía de España por Fernando Colón,* 3 vol. Ed. by Antonio Blázquez. Madrid: Patronato de Huerfanos de Administración Militar.

———. 1984 [1538]. *Historia del Almirante.* Retrans. into Spanish from the Italian publication of 1571, with commentary by Luís Arranz. Madrid: Historia 16. English ed.: *The life of the Admiral Christopher Columbus by his son, Ferdinand.* Trans. Benjamin Keen. New Brunswick, NJ: Rutgers University Press, 1959.

Cortés, Hernán. 1963. *Cartas y documentos.* Ed., with commentary by M. Hernández Sanchez-Barba. Mexico City: Porrúa.

Domínguez Compañy, Francisco. 1977. Actas de fundación de ciudades hispanoamericanas. *Revista de Historia de América* 83:19–51.

Dunn, Oliver, and Kelley, Jr., James E. 1988. *The Diario of Christopher Columbus's first voyage to America, 1492–1493.* Norman: University of Oklahoma Press.

Durán, Diego. 1967 [1581]. *Historia de las Indias de Nueva España e islas de la Tierra Firma.* Ed. Angel M. Garibay. Mexico City: Instituto de Investigaciones Antropológicas, Universidad Nacional Autónoma de México. English ed.: *Book of the gods and rites and the ancient calendar.* Trans. and ed. Fernando Horcasitas and Doris Heyden. Norman, OK: University of Oklahoma Press, 1971.

Edwards, Clinton R. 1969. Mapping by questionnaire: An early Spanish attempt to determine New World geographical positions. *Imago Mundi* 23:17–28.

———. 1975 The *relaciones de Yucatán* as sources for historical geography. *Journal of Historical Geography* 1:245–58.

———. 1980 Geographical coverage of the sixteenth-century *relaciones de Indias* from South America. *Geoscience and Man* 21:75–82.

Elliott, John H. 1970. *The Old World and the New 1492–1650.* Cambridge: Cambridge University Press.

Fernández Armesto, Felipe. 1987. *Before Columbus: Exploration and colonization from the Mediterranean to the Atlantic, 1229–1492.* Philadelphia: Macmillan.

Fernández de Oviedo, Gonzalo. 1950 [1526]. *Sumario de la natural historia de las Indias.* Ed., with commentary by José Miranda. Mexico City: Fondo de Cultura Económica. English ed.: *Natural History of the West Indies.* Trans. Sterling A. Stoudemire. Studies in the Romance Languages and Literatures 32. Chapel Hill: University of North Carolina. 1959.

———. 1959 [1535–57]. *Historia general y natural de las Indias,* 5 vol. Ed., with commentary by Juan Pérez de Tudela. Madrid: Biblioteca de Autores Españoles.

Ferrando, Roberto. 1957. Fernández de Oviedo y el conocimiento del Mar del Sur. *Revista de Indias* 17:469–82.

Friede, Juan, and Keen, Benjamin, eds. 1971. *Bartolomé de las Casas in history: Toward an understanding of the man and his work.* DeKalb, IL: Northern Illinois University Press.

Fuson, Robert H. 1983. The *Diario de Colón*: A legacy of poor transcription, translation, and interpretation. *Terrae Incognitae* 15:59–75.

Gerbi, Antonello. 1985. *Nature in the New World: From Christopher Columbus to Gonzalo Fernández de Oviedo.* Pittsburgh: University of Pittsburgh Press.

Glass, John B., and Robertson, Donald. 1975. A census of Native Middle American pictorial manuscripts. In *Guide to ethnohistorical sources,* ed. Howard F. Cline, vol. 3, pp. 81–252. Handbook of Middle American Indians 14. Austin: University of Texas Press.

Goodman, David C. 1988. *Power and penury: Government, technology and science in Philip II's Spain.* Cambridge: Cambridge University Press.

Green, Otis H. 1968 *Spain and the western tradition.* 4 vol. Madison: University of Wisconsin Press.

Greenblatt, Stephen. 1991. *Marvellous possessions: The wonder of the New World.* Chicago: University of Chicago Press.

Hardoy, Jorge E. 1975. La forma de las ciudades coloniales en la America española. In *Estudios sobre la ciudad iberoamericana,* ed. Francisco de Solano, pp. 315–344. Madrid: Consejo Superior de Investigaciones Científicas.

———. 1978. European urban forms in the fifteenth to seventeenth centuries and their utilization in Latin America. In *Urbanization in the Americas from its beginnings to the present,* ed. Richard P. Schaedel, Jorge E. Hardoy, Nora S. Kinzer, pp. 215–48. The Hague: Mouton.

Harley, J. Brian. 1990. *Maps and the Columbian encounter.* Milwaukee: University of Wisconsin, Golda Meir Library.

Harvey, P. D. A. 1987. Local and regional cartography in medieval Europe. In *The history of cartography,* ed. J. Brian Harley and David Woodward, vol. 1, pp. 464–501. Chicago: University of Chicago Press.

Henige, David. 1991. *In search of Columbus: The sources for the First Voyage.* Tucson: University of Arizona Press.

Herrera, Gabriel Alonso de. 1970 [1513]. *Obra de agricultura.* Ed., with commentary by José Urbano Martínez Carreras. Madrid: Biblioteca de Autores Españoles.

Humboldt, Alexander von. 1845–47. *Kosmos: Entwurf einer physichen Weltbeschreibung.* 2 vol. Stuttgart: Cotta.

James, Preston E., and Martin, Geoffrey J. 1981. *All possible worlds: A history of geographical ideas,* 2nd ed. New York: Wiley.

Jane, Cecil. 1988 [1930–33]. *The four voyages of Columbus.* New York: Dover Publications.

Jiménez de la Espada, Marcos, ed. 1965 [1881–97]. *Relaciones geográficas de Indias: Peru.* 3 vol. Commentary by José Martínez Carreras. Madrid: Biblioteca de Autores Españoles.

Kamen, Henry. 1985. *Inquisition and society in Spain in the sixteen and seventeenth centuries.* London: Weidenfeld and Nicolson.

Keen, Benjamin. 1971. *The Aztec image in Western thought.* New Brunswick, NJ: Rutgers University Press.

Kimble, George H. T. 1938. *Geography in the Middle Ages.* London: Methuen.

Klor de Alva, J. Jorge. 1988. Sahagún and the birth of modern ethnography: Representing, confessing, and inscribing the native other. In *The work of Bernadino de Sahagún: Pioneer ethnographer of sixteenth-century Aztec Mexico,* ed. J. J. Klor de Alva, H. B. Nicholson, and E. Quiñones Keber, pp. 31–52. Austin: University of Texas Press.

Kubler, George. 1978. Open-grid town plans in Europe and America. In *Urbanization in the Americas from its beginnings to the present,* ed. Richard P. Schaedel, Jorge E. Hardoy, Nora S. Kinzer, pp. 327–342. The Hague: Mouton.

Landa, Diego de. 1941 [1566]. *Relación de las Cosas de Yucatán.* Trans., with commentary by Alfred M. Tozzer. Peabody Museum Paper 18. Cambridge, MA: Harvard University.

Latorre, German, ed. 1920. *Relaciones geográficas de Indias.* Sevilla: Biblioteca Colonial Americana, 4.

Licate, Jack A. 1980. The forms of Aztec territorial organization. *Geoscience and Man* 21:26–45.

López de Gómara, Francisco. 1966 [1552]. *Historia general de los Indias*, ed. Pilar Guibelalde. Barcelona: Obras Maestras.

López de Velasco, Juan. 1971 [1574]. *Geografía y descripción universal de las Indias*, ed. Marcos Jiménez de Espada, commentary by M. Carmen González Muñoz. Madrid: Biblioteca de Autores Españoles, 248.

López Piñero, José M. 1979. *Ciencia y técnica en la sociedad española de los siglos XVI y XVII*. Barcelona: Labor Universitaria.

———. 1991. *El códice Pomar (ca. 1590): El interés de Felipe II por la historia natural y la Expedición Hernández a América*, vol. A37. Valencia: Cuadernos Valencianos de Historia de la Medicina y de la Ciencia.

Lovell, W. George. 1991. Meddling with the Maya. *Queen's Quarterly* 97(4):566–79.

Martínez Val, José M. 1945. El paisaje geográfico en los historiadores de Indias. *Revista de Indias* 6:289–322.

Martyr d'Anghiera, Peter. 1964 [1524]. *Décadas del Nuevo Mundo*. Trans. from Latin into Spanish, with commentary by Edmundo O'Gorman. Mexico City: Porrúa.

Medina, Pedro de. 1972 [1538]. *A navigator's universe: The libro de cosmographía of 1538*. Facsimile, with trans. and commentary by Ursula Lamb. Chicago: University of Chicago Press.

Menéndez Pidal, Gonzalo. 1944. *Imagen del mundo hacia 1570: Según noticias del Consejo de Indias y de los tratadistas españoles*. Madrid: Consejo de La Hispanidad.

Milanich, Jerald T., and Milbrath, Susan, eds. 1989. *First encounters: Spanish explorations in the Caribbean and the United States, 1492–1570*. Gainesville: University of Florida Press.

Morse, Richard M. 1987. Urban development. In *Colonial Spanish America*, Leslie Bethell, ed., pp. 165–202. Cambridge: Cambridge University Press.

Motolinía, Toribio de. 1969 [1541]. *Historia de los indios de la Nueva España*. Ed., with commentary by Edmundo O'Gorman. Mexico City: Porrúa. *Motolinia's History of the Indians of New Spain*, trans., with notes by Francis B. Steck. Washington: Academy of American Franciscan History, 1951.

———. 1971 [c. 1541]. *Memoriales o libro de las cosas de Nueva España y de los naturales de ella*. Ed., with commentary by Edmundo O'Gorman. Mexico City: Instituto de Investigaciones Historicas, Universidad Nacional Autónoma de México.

Münster, Sebastian. 1968 [1550]. *Cosmographia: Beschreibung aller Länder, Herrschafftenn und fürnemesten Stetten des gantzen Erdbodens.*

Facsimile, with commentary by Ruthardt Oehme. Amsterdam: Theatrum Orbis Terrarum, 2nd, expanded ed., amplified in successive posthumous editions to 1599.

Münzer, Hieronymus. 1952 [1495]. Jerónimo Münzer: Relación del viaje. In *Viajes de extranjeros por España y Portugal*, J. García Mercadal, ed., vol. 1, pp. 327–418. Madrid: Aguilar.

Nader, Helen. 1990. *Liberty in absolutist Spain: The Habsburg sale of towns 1516–1700*. Baltimore: Johns Hopkins University Press.

Nebenzahl, Kenneth. 1990. *Atlas of Columbus and "The Great Discoveries."* Chicago: Rand McNally.

Nicolau d'Olwer, Luís. 1987 [1952]. *Fray Bernadino de Sahagún (1499–1590)*. Trans. Mauricio J. Mixco, introduction by Miguel León-Portilla. Salt Lake City: University of Utah Press.

——— and Cline, Howard F. 1973. Sahagún and his works. In *Guide to ethnohistorical sources*, H. F. Cline and J. B. Glass, eds., vol. 2, pp. 186–207. Handbook of Middle American Indians 13. Austin: University of Texas Press.

O'Gorman, Edmundo, ed. 1946. *Sucesos y diálogo de la Nueva España*. Mexico City: Biblioteca del Estudiante Universitario.

Ordenanzas. 1973 [1573]. *Ordenanzas de descubrimiento, nueva población y pacificación de las Indias, dadas por Felipe II en 1573*. Madrid: Ministerio de la Vivienda (facsimile).

Parry, John H. 1981. *The discovery of the sea*. Berkeley: University of California Press.

———, and Keith, Robert G., eds. 1984. *New Iberian World: A documentary history of the discovery and settlement of Latin America to the early seventeenth century*. 5 vols. New York: Times Books, Hector & Rose.

Paso y Troncoso, Francisco del, ed. 1905a. *Suma de visitas de pueblos por órden alfabético*, Madrid: Papeles de Nueva España, serie II, vol. 1.

———. 1905b. *Descripción del Arzobispado de Mexico*, serie II, vol. 3. Madrid: Papeles de Nueva España.

———. 1905c. *Relaciones geográficas de la Diócesis de Tlaxcala*, serie II, vol. 5, pp. 183–286. Madrid: Papeles de Nueva España.

Pérez-Rioja, José A. 1958. Un insigne visontino del siglo XVI: Juan López de Velasco. *Celtiberia: Centro de Estudios Sorianos* 8:7–38.

Phillips, J. R. S. 1988. *The Medieval expansion of Europe*. New York: Oxford University Press.

Phillips, William D., Jr., and Phillips, Carla Rahn. 1992. *The worlds of Christopher Columbus*. New York: Cambridge University Press.

Pliny. 1940–56 [c. 75 A.D.]. *Natural history*. Trans. H. Rackham and W. H. S. Jones. 10 vol. London: Heinemann.

Polo, Marco. 1958 [1299]. *The travels of Marco*

Polo. Trans., with commentary by Ronald Latham. Harmondsworth, U.K.: Penguin.

Ponsot, Pierre, and Drain, Michel. 1966. Hernando Colón et son "Itinerario": Commentaire géographique. *Mélanges de la Casa de Velázquez* 2:73–95.

Ptolemy. 1932 [c. 150 A.D.]. *Geography of Claudius Ptolemy* (with maps from Ebner MS of c. 1460). Trans. Edward L. Stevenson, with introduction by Joseph Fischer. New York: New York Public Library.

——. 1966 [c. 150 A.D.]. *Claudius Ptolomaeus geographia.* Ed. and maps redrawn by Sebastian Münster 1540, introduction by R. A. Skelton. Amsterdam: Theatrum Orbis Terrarum.

Quiñones Keber, Eloise. 1988. Reading images: The making and meaning of the Sahaguntine illustrations. In *The work of Bernadino Sahagún,* ed. J. J. Klor de Alva, H. B. Nicholson, and E. Quiñones Keber, pp. 199–210. Austin: University of Texas Press.

Rosa y López, Simon de la. 1906. El Itinerario de Don Hernando Colón y su vocabulario topográfico de España. *Revista de Archivos, Bibliotecas y Museos* 15:106–18, 260–74.

Rowntree, L. B.; Foote, Kenneth E.; and Domosh, Mona. 1989. Cultural geography. In *Geography in America,* ed. Gary L. Gaile and Cort J. Willmott, pp. 209–17. Columbus, OH: Merrill.

Sahagún, Bernadino de. 1950–69 [1579]. *Florentine Codex: General history of the things of New Spain.* Ed., and trans. from the Nahuatl, Arthur J. O. Anderson and Charles E. Dibble. Monographs of the School of American Research and the Museum of New Mexico, 13 vol. (revised or reprinted 1974–82). Santa Fe, NM.

Salas, Alberto. 1954. Fernández de Oviedo, crítico de la Conquista y de los conquistadores. *Cuadernos Americanos* (Mexico City) 74:160–70.

Sale, Kirkpatrick. 1990. *The conquest of Paradise: Christopher Columbus and the Columbian legacy.* New York: Knopf.

Sauer, Carl O. 1966. *The early Spanish Main.* Berkeley: University of California Press.

Sauer, Jonathan D. 1976. Changing perception and exploitation of New World plants in Europe, 1492–1800. In *First images of America,* ed. F. Chiappelli, vol. 2, pp. 813–32. Berkeley: University of California Press.

Simpson, Lesley Byrd. 1964. *Cortés: The life of the conqueror by his secretary Francisco López de Gómara.* Berkeley: University of California Press.

Somolinos de Ardois, German, ed. 1960–84. *Obras completas de Francisco Hernández.* 7 vol. Mexico City: Porrúa.

Stanislawski, Dan. 1947. Early Spanish town planning in the New World. *Geographical Review* 37:94–105.

Taviani, Pablo Emilio. 1985. *Christopher Columbus: The grand design.* London: Orbis.

Thacher, John B., ed. 1967 [1903–04]. *Christopher Columbus: His life, his work, his remains.* 3 vol. New York: Kraus Reprint.

Tovar de Teresa, Guillermo. 1985. Antonio de Mendoza y el urbanismo en México. *Cuadernos de Arquitectura Virreinal* 2:2–19.

Varela, Consuelo, ed. 1983. *Cristobal Colón: Textos y documentos completos.* Madrid: Alianza Universidad.

Vázquez de Espinosa, Antonio. 1969 [1629]. *Compendio y descripción de las Indias occidentales.* Ed., with commentary by B. Velasco Bayón. Madrid: Biblioteca de Autores Españoles, 231. (*Compendium and description of the West Indies.* Trans. Charles U. Clark. Washington: Smithsonian Miscellaneous Collection 102, 1942)

Waldseemüller, Martin. 1966 [1507]. *Cosmographiae introductio* (with the four voyages of Amerigo Vespucci). English trans. Joseph Fischer and Franz von Wieser. Ann Arbor, MI: University Microfilms.

Warren, J. Benedict. 1973. An introductory survey of secular writings in the European tradition on Colonial Middle America, 1503–1818. In *Guide to ethnohistorical sources,* ed. Howard F. Cline, vol. 2, pp. 42–137. Handbook of Middle American Indians 13. Austin: University of Texas Press.

Waters, David W. 1958. *The art of navigation in England in Elizabethan and early Stuart times.* New Haven: Yale University Press.

Wilson, Samuel M. 1990. *Hispaniola: Caribbean chiefdoms in the Age of Columbus.* University, AL: University of Alabama Press.

Yáñes Días, Gonzalo. 1991. *Espacios urbanos del la siglo XVI en región Puebla-Tlaxcala.* Puebla: Universidad Autónoma de Puebla.

Museum Exhibit and Book Review

Seeds of Change: 500 Years of Encounter and Exchange.

An exhibit of the National Museum of Natural History, Smithsonian Institution, Washington, DC, October 1991–April 1993.

Seeds of Change: A Quincentennial Commemoration. *Herman J. Viola and Carolyn Margolis, eds.*

Washington and London: Smithsonian Institution Press, 1991. 278 pp., index and biblio, $39.95 cloth (ISBN 1-5 6098-035-4); $24.95 paper (ISBN 1-56098-036-2).

Reviewed by Stephen C. Jett, Department of Geography, University of California, Davis, CA 95616, and *Joseph S. Wood*, Department of Geography, George Mason University, Fairfax, VA 22030-4444.

Seeds of Change is the National Museum of Natural History's contribution to the Columbian quincentennial. Its focus, and that of the accompanying collection of essays, is the global biological and cultural transformation initiated by Columbus's voyages, the shaping of a new world out of several old worlds. Sugarcane, maize, the potato, the horse, and infectious disease are used as epitomes of exchange, but the visually captivating exhibit and text also touch upon a host of other biological and cultural consequences of 1492 and its aftermath.

Organizations from the National Endowment for the Humanities to Xerox to the National Corn Growers Association to the Potato Museum sponsored the exhibit. An exemplary academic board lent advice, and the exhibit has spawned collaborative shows elsewhere around the U.S. as well as several supporting publications. One cultural geographer, Lydia Pulsipher, contributed to both exhibit and text, as did historians, anthropologists, natural scientists, and ethnic-studies specialists.

To Washington's museum-going throngs, the exhibit offers an intelligent showing of cultural ecologies and cultural geographies. Several galleries successively highlight Tenochtitlan in 1519, Cortés's conquest by invasion of men and disease, discovered archaeological and biological treasures, the enduring global impacts of plant and animal exchanges, and past and contemporary environmental consequences of it all. Much is predictable, as with introduction of the horse to the grasslands of North America. Disease is treated ineffectively. Sugarcane, intertwined with slavery, offers the most dramatic story, played out on Pulsipher's Galways Plantation on Montserrat. Potatoes and maize are dealt with in popular-culture terms, as with a Spanish-style gallery portal reminiscent of the Corn Palace at Mitchell, South Dakota. Art, serious and whimsical, and cartography, historical and thematic, are important parts of the storyline. Roark Gourley's playful three-dimensional montage "Spaghetti Meets Tomato" and a fiber-optic diffusion map of disease within the Americas exemplify such instructional devices.

The Smithsonian's commemorative volume is a mixture of cultural and biological history, and like the exhibit, it attempts to be relevant to contemporary issues. Book coeditor Herman J. Viola provides the introduction. The first and longest substantive chapter, by anthropologists Jean Walsh and Yoko Sugiura, details the rise and fall of indigenous cultures in the Americas. Historian William McNeill's look at the diffusion of American food crops worldwide and Henry Hobhouse's (from whose original work the exhibit and book title is taken) delightful discussion of viticulture in the Americas lead into Alfred Crosby's too brief assessment of the metamorphosis of the Americas. Museum staff members Deb Bennett and Robert Hoffman look at ranching in the Americas while anthropologist Sidney Mintz and historian David Gaspar provide thoughtful cultural histories of sugar and of slaves, followed by Pulsipher's reconstruction of life at Galways Plantation. Then follow successively Robert Hall's look at African foodways in the Americas, Joseph P. Sánchez's reflection on our rich Hispanic heritage, and George P. Horse Capture's powerful American Indian response. Anthropologists John Verano and Douglas Ubelaker assess health and disease in the pre-Columbian world, followed by botanist Stanwyn Shetler's ecotopian view of the past. Botanist Steven King and sustainable development specialist Liliana Campos Dudley conclude the text with a call for the protection of those remaining seeds of an ecotopian future.

Interconnections, and with them historical irony, abound in exhibit and text alike. Slavers' introduction of productive American crops, for instance, allowed dramatic population growth in the African forests, which permitted the slave trade to continue without population depletion. Likewise, American crops sustained population growth in Europe, which fostered substantial migration that ultimately spelled the demise of the introduced horse-based cultural ecology of North America's interior grasslands. Although the tone becomes preachy and even stridently editorial in places, the book's overall approach fosters a sense of shared history among diverse contributing ethnicities in the context of imminent environmental tragedy, an approach not necessarily inappropriate for a national museum and its publications.

Inappropriate is the perpetuation of false "ecotopian" images of the past, as in the disconcerting chapter, "Three Faces of Eden." Here, the museum's acting deputy director, botanist Shetler, imposes his view that pre-Columbian America was "a world of barely perceptible human disturbance" (p. 226). Other authors partially correct that impression but still ignore significant pre-Columbian landscape alterations. The effect is unconscious ethnocentrism overlain by conscious sensitiv-

ity, as confirmed by King and Dudley's statement that "Many seeds of change in [read, 'Western'] agriculture and medicine . . . were gifts [sic] from the people who inhabited the New World before the European arrival. What have we [read, 'Europeans'] given them in return? Destruction of their bodies, souls, culture" (p. 258). One may ask how many Native Americans today would elect to give up introduced crops and livestock, steel tools, religion, and so forth, and would choose to return to ritual warfare and human sacrifice?

Avoidance of the question of pre-Columbian interhemispheric contacts (except by Native American George Horse Capture) furthers ethnocentrism. Columbus's voyages were indeed pivotal in world history for inaugurating permanent links between Europe and the Americas (and Africa) and for initiating unprecedentedly massive interinfluences. However, pre-Columbian exchanges, mainly trans-Pacific and therefore non-Western, certainly occurred and were not unimportant. Historian McNeill baldly asserts that "All of them [maize, potatos, sweet potatoes, tomatoes, peanuts, manioc, cacao, chilipeppers, beans, and squashes] were totally unknown outside the Americas before the time of Columbus" (p. 43). In fact, there is at least some evidence of the pre-Columbian presence of many of these and other crops in Asia and Oceania, as well as of plantains in the New World (contrary to p. 166). Such wider geographical distribution is particularly likely for the sweet potato and for maize (Johannessen 1988), although debate continues. While the pre-Columbian presence of tuberculosis and Old World parasites is at least recognized (p. 214), Verano and Ubelaker draw no inferences about pre-Columbian voyages and their possible impacts, such as episodes of depopulation and collapses of cultures recorded archaeologically. Traits seen as independently invented—e.g., the zero (p. 28) and trephining (pp. 216–17)—might thus be considered in different light.

Notably missing is a critical assessment of the role of religion in competing cultural ecologies, and even more as motive and means for encounter. Despite public tolerance for privately funded critiques, this government and corporate-sponsored project fails to tackle adequately religious assaults on others' ways of life (except, and again, in George Horse Capture's [North] American Indian perspective). We learn more about indigenous reli-gions and their "exotic" tenets, rituals, cere-monies, material forms, and spaces than we learn of European evangelical frenzy. Monte-zuma mistakes Cortés for Quetzalcoatl, but Christianity's take on Montezuma is ignored. Otherwise, missionaries are protectors of na-tive populations and importers of certain im-portant domesticates, including asses and viti-culture. Discussion of *la Leyenda Negra*, the anti-Catholic Black Legend of evil Hispanics, is informative, but no discussion of the perpetu-ation and evolution of Catholicism in the Americas follows.

There is some sense that the book was as-sembled under deadline pressure, resulting in overlaps and differences in writing quality be-tween articles, gaps in coverage, and a variety of internal contradictions and errors. On the other hand, the picture-research team did an outstanding job in assembling hundreds of rel-evant illustrations beyond what is in the ex-hibit. These, combined with excellence of the (all-American) production, make for a very at-tractive book.

Despite our reservations, the emphasis of ex-hibit and book on the enormous positive and negative consequences of the post-Columbian exchange is laudable and usually successful. Scholars will be somewhat underwhelmed. The apparent compromise with potentially inflam-mable matters of religion and the overindul-gence in ecotopian notions challenge scholarly integrity. Yet the exhibit is appealing and nicely orchestrated, and the text will serve as an im-portant resource for reflective Americans wish-ing to understand the making of our world.

Reference

Johannessen, C. L. 1988. Maize ears sculptured in 12th and 13th century A.D. India as indicators of pre-Columbian diffusion. *Economic Botany* 42:164–80.

In Search of Columbus

The Sources for the First Voyage
David Henige

"A scholarly, fascinating exercise in literary-historical detection, which subjects the *diario* to fresh, ruthless, yet as nearly as possible unprejudiced investigation.... The copiously annotated text of Dr. Henige's book provides not only a meticulous study of the *diario*, but also opens up new areas of geographical, maritime, and biographical research."
—Alexander Maitland, *Geographical Journal*

"Henige's vigorously argued and provocatively written textual analysis of the *diario* ... will discomfit all who have used the text as a historical source." —M.A. Burkholder, *Choice*

"A virtuoso performance, showing how hard if not impossible it is to extract the original of Columbus's log from the later paraphrase." —Gary Wills, *New York Review of Books*

$29.95 cloth

Chilies to Chocolate

Food the Americas Gave the World
Nelson Foster & Linda S. Cordell, eds.

Traces the biological and cultural history of New World crops, focusing on their domestication and use by native peoples and their dispersion into the fields and kitchens of the Old World.

Contents:

Europeans' Wary Encounter with Tomatoes, Potatoes, and Other New Word Foods/*Alan Davidson*

The Renaissance of Amaranth/*Daniel K. Early*

Vanilla: Nectar of the Gods/*Patricia Rain*

Maize: Gift from America's First Peoples/*Walton C. Galinat*

Beans of the Americas/*Lawrence Kaplan & Lucille N. Kaplan*

The Peripatetic Chili Pepper: Diffusion of the Domesticated Capsicums Since Columbus/*Jean Andrews*

Forgotten Roots of the Incas/*Noel Vietmeyer*

A Brief History and Botany of Cacao/*John A. West*

Quinoa's Roundabout Journey to World Use/*John F. McCamant*

Epilogue: Native Crops of the Americas: Passing Novelties or Lasting Contributions to Diversity?/*Gary Paul Nabhan*

$13.95 paper/$24.95 cloth

The University of Arizona Press
1230 N. Park Avenue, Tucson AZ 85719 / 1-800-426-3797

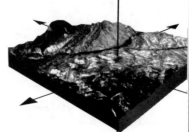

THE HISTORY OF CARTOGRAPHY,
VOLUME 2, BOOK 1
Cartography in the Traditional Islamic and South Asian Societies

Edited by
J. B. Harley
and
David Woodward

This comprehensive history of Islamic and South Asian cartography offers a fascinating picture of maps used not only as practical tools but also as images symbolic of religion and culture.

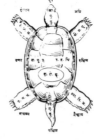

Cloth $125.00 644 pages
40 color plates, 358 halftones

THE UNIVERSITY OF CHICAGO PRESS
5801 S. ELLIS AVE., CHICAGO, IL 60637